# THE 18TH DIVISION

## In the Great War

LIEUT.-GENERAL SIR IVOR MAXSE, K.C.B., C.V.O., D.S.O.

TRAINED THE 18TH DIVISION AND COMMANDED IT IN THE FIELD UNTIL
JANUARY 1917.

*From a Painting exhibited at the Royal Academy in 1915
by Captain OSWALD BIRLEY, who was an officer in
the 18th when it was at Colchester.*

# THE 18TH DIVISION

## In the Great War

BY

CAPTAIN G. H. F. NICHOLS
(QUEX)
AUTHOR OF 'PUSHED AND THE RETURN PUSH'

William Blackwood and Sons
Edinburgh and London
1922

# To Our Undying Dead

THE INSCRIPTION ON THE 18TH DIVISION MEMORIAL IN TRONES WOOD.

When he was at
ft Fusian and things were looking very
black the old 18 Div were confident and
full of heart — Of all the Div's I had
in the IV army the 18 had I think the
longest and most trying time fr in
addition to the March & april fighting
they were one of the only Div' that went
through the whole of the 100 Days battle
from Aug 6 to Nov 11 with merely a
few short rests out of the line

H Rawlinson

[Extract from a letter written by Lord Rawlinson on 18th February 1919. The period to which Lord Rawlinson refers was from March 1918 to November 1918.]

# CONTENTS.

## CHAPTER I.

### IN ENGLAND.

## CHAPTER II.

### FIRST EXPERIENCES IN FRANCE.

## CHAPTER III.

### BATTLE OF 1ST JULY 1916.

## CHAPTER IV.

### THE CAPTURE OF TRONES WOOD.

## CHAPTER V.

### DELVILLE WOOD.

## CHAPTER VI.

### THE TAKING OF THIÉPVAL, 26TH SEPTEMBER 1916.

## CHAPTER VII.

### SCHWABEN REDOUBT.

## CHAPTER VIII.

### WEARING DOWN THE ENEMY ON THE ANCRE—THE
### CAPTURE OF REGINA TRENCH AND DESIRE TRENCH.

## CHAPTER IX.

### THE BATTLE OF BOOM RAVINE.

## CHAPTER X.

### THE CAPTURE OF IRLES, AND THE PURSUIT TO THE HINDENBURG LINE.

## CHAPTER XI.

### CHERISY, 3RD MAY 1917.

## CHAPTER XII.

### A CRICKET MATCH, 1917,

## CHAPTER XIII.

### ZILLEBEKE AND 31ST JULY 1917.

## CHAPTER XVIII.

### 22ND MARCH—THE FIGHT FOR THE CROZAT CANAL.

## CHAPTER XIX.

### TWO VICTORIA CROSSES WON IN THE WITHDRAWAL.

## CHAPTER XX.

### 24TH AND 25TH MARCH—THE BATTLE OF BABŒUF.

## CHAPTER XXI.

### THE DEFENCE OF AMIENS.

CHAPTER XXV.

THE TAKING OF USNA AND TARA HILLS.

CHAPTER XXVI.

TO AND THROUGH TRONES WOOD, AUGUST 1918.

CHAPTER XXVII.

THE CAPTURE OF COMBLES.

## CHAPTER XXVIII.

### THE FIGHTING AROUND RONSSOY.

## CHAPTER XXIX.

### DUNCAN, DOLEFUL, AND EGG POSTS.

## CHAPTER XXX.

### THE BREAKING OF THE HINDENBURG LINE.

# CONTENTS.

# LIST OF ILLUSTRATIONS.

## OPERATION MAPS.

# History of the 18th Division.

## CHAPTER I.

### IN ENGLAND.

*The Division born in the autumn of 1914—Men of the Home Counties
—8th East Surreys first lesson in discipline—The 10th Essex
band — Major-General Maxse assumes command on 1st October
1914—The week's "trek" through Suffolk—From Colchester to
Salisbury Plain—General Maxse's memory for officers' names—
Lieut.-Colonel Lambert in the Artillery Riding School—To France
on 25th July 1915.*

WHEN on 25th July 1915 the 18th Division crossed
to France, the most unthinking optimists were at last
assenting to the belief that beating the Boche would
mean long tireless effort, suffering, bereavement, and
disappointment.

Four weeks before, German generalship had made
short work of Russian numbers and won back Lem-
berg; the torpedoing of the *Lusitania* on 7th May
had revealed the cold brutality of Germany's determination to proceed to any lengths, physical and moral,
in order to handicap and to distress her enemies; the
British had thus far carried out only two set attacks
of importance, the not very fruitful assaults at Neuve
Chapelle and Festubert. Comfortable patriots who
had glowed over the 1914 exploits of our tiny
Regular Army, much as they joyed at the doings of
their favourite professional football teams, had begun

A

dimly to realise that the active-service call might come
even to them; the enthusiasts who honestly believed
that the conscript German Army would crumple up
when the Kitchener volunteers faced them in full
strength had become more tempered in thought. A
slump in sham was indeed setting in : a desire to
look ugly facts in the face. It was a period in the
war that fitted well with the spirit and faith of the
New Army men who composed the 18th Division.

Of the memories that hark back to that sun-scorched
late summer of 1914 the best remembered are assuredly
those that convey the difficulties and the bewilderments of the swift switch from civilian to military life.
As an example, picture the birth of the 8th East
Surreys. On the evening of 10th September Captain
A. P. B. Irwin, at that time the only regular officer
posted to the battalion, waited at the Government
siding at Purfleet to meet the recruits who were to
form it. They arrived, a thousand strong, with no
officers, no non-commissioned officers—rather like a
football excursion crowd—three hundred of them men
of Suffolk, who hoped to join the Suffolks; another
couple of hundred Norfolk men, who had enlisted for
the Norfolk Regiment; a few were Welsh miners.
They knew no words of command. All that Captain
Irwin could do was to tell them to follow him. He
led them to a desolate colony of tents on the marshes.
It was getting dark, and the night was certain to be
cold. In even, contained fashion Captain Irwin gave
this wondering, willing mob its first lesson in discipline.
He halted the men alongside a bank near the tin hut
cook-house. Those who sat down on the bank—and
remained there—would get tea, he said; those who
wandered about "looking for Alf and Bert" wouldn't.
Afterwards he arranged them twenty-four in a tent.
"If you leave your tents," he told them, "it will be
useless coming to ask me which tent I put you in.
. . . And, once more, don't come asking me which
tent Alf or Bill is in, because I shan't know." There

were not enough blankets to go round ; the food was coarse ; there were no recreation huts, no dining halls, no canteens such as the regular recruit found in barrack life.  But the men's mood was to make the best of things.  It was long before they became sufficiently good soldiers to develop the finer points of " grousing."

The remaining units of the 55th Infantry Brigade—the 7th Queens, the 7th Buffs, and the 7th Royal West Kents—encamped, like the East Surreys, at Purfleet.  The other infantry brigades of the Division—the 53rd (6th Royal Berks, 10th Essex, 8th Norfolks, and 8th Suffolks), and the 54th (6th North-ants, 10th Royal Fusiliers, 11th Royal Fusiliers, and 12th Middlesex)—began their training at Colchester, to which centre the 55th Brigade did not move until April 1915.  The four brigades of Divisional Artillery, the 82nd, 83rd, 84th, and 85th Field Artillery Brigades, also gathered at Colchester, as did the 8th Royal Sussex, who became the Division's pioneer battalion.  Later the 7th Bedfords replaced the 10th Fusiliers in the 54th Brigade.

In the main the battalions were representative of their counties.  The 8th Norfolks and the 8th Suffolks were especially strong, territorially, and a large over-flow of volunteers from these counties found its way into other battalions in the Division.  The spontaneity of the recruiting in Norfolk and Suffolk on the out-break of war was indeed a cause of the breaking-up of the 8th Norfolks and the 8th Suffolks at the beginning of 1918.  Recruiting in East Anglia had dried up then, and there were not enough men to feed all the county battalions.  On the other hand, a small county like Northampton kept its battalion up to strength be-cause earlier in the war the boot trade claimed many exemptions : in the culminating stages these previ-ously spared men could be drafted into the county regiment.

The 7th Queens were practically all Surrey men.  A good proportion of the 7th West Kents hailed from the

Erith district. At least twenty-five per cent of the 6th Royal Berkshires were Berkshire ploughmen, a fine type of infantry soldier, patient and brave. Later, Birmingham artisans seemed naturally to find their way to the Royal Berks. Wiry, intelligent fighters they showed themselves too. The 10th Essex, who included one company of Norfolks and a sprinkling from Suffolk, were mostly Stratford and Walthamstow men. The Essex band came practically in one body from Wivenhoe. There is a story of an exuberant Saturday night in that loyal village where the best yachtsmen come from; an eloquent and forceful cornet player—and within the next few days a more or less tuneful battalion band in being.

Those eager, hearty, humorous, sometimes tedious early days! There was the difficulty about uniforms. It is not true that sergeant-majors wore bowler hats to symbolise their rank, but the 84th Brigade R.F.A. did possess one battery quartermaster-sergeant who appeared in a bowler, with a pencil behind his ear; and for a long time some of the officers thought he was a local tradesman who came up daily to arrange food supplies. For the first few weeks the men drilled and marched in the civilian suits and boots that they wore when they enlisted. Rough wear that meant. That was why route-marches began with the order : " Men without boots to the right; men with worn-out trousers to the left " ; why men with soleless boots were set to do slow marching on the grass ; why route-marches through Colchester became impossible. Even 2nd Lieutenant A. S. Tween, the second officer to join the 10th Essex, made his first appearance in mufti. Very well-cut mufti, as became a subaltern whom the Essex always declared to be the best turned-out officer in the battalion. Poor Tween! He proved a real leader of men and earned his majority. He was fatally wounded in front of Frières Wood on 23rd March 1918, when the Germans were swarming across the Crozat Canal.

After those first few weeks, when the men's own civilian clothes had been worn threadbare, the melancholy-looking blue uniforms and forage caps that were served out came as something gay and resplendent. And the excitement when the first khaki uniforms arrived! Enough to provide about one per platoon! Every man going on week-end leave begged and bargained for the loan of that khaki from the individuals to whom the uniforms had been allotted.

There was the selecting of the N.C.O.'s, and it has to be remembered that the Division contained few old soldiers, or Boer War veterans. Captain Irwin, for the East Surreys, adopted a method which served as well as any other. He asked those men to step forward who felt that they could take charge of half a dozen of their fellows. It was, at any rate, a test of their belief in themselves. About twenty men offered themselves; and white tape was tied round their arms as a mark of their new rank. Nearly all these men made good; the N.C.O. who was battalion sergeant-major at the end of the war first got a stripe in this way. Character showed itself in unorthodox ways at that period. There was one platoon commander, Heppel, of the Essex, some of whose men complained that their rations had not arrived. One man was particularly insistent in demanding whether such treatment should be tolerated. No really telling reply suggested itself to the harried subaltern, so he pulled off his coat and announced that he would tackle all grumblers individually, beginning with the chief malcontent. "We'll wait, sir," said the talkative ringleader quickly. And from that moment the 10th Essex believed steadfastly in its officers.

Happy is the Division that has had few changes of Divisional commanders. Such a Division is almost certain to be accustomed to success in the field, and to have developed qualities and characteristics upon which the Higher Command can calculate. The 18th Division can count itself especially fortunate. It

had but two Divisional Commanders, Lieut.-General
Sir Ivor Maxse, from 1st October 1914 until 15th
January 1917, and Major-General Sir Richard Lee,
who commanded from that date until the war
had been won. The Division, moreover, was doubly
favoured. Each of these two supremely able, outstanding men held the command at a period of the
war when his own particular and immediate gifts could
best be exercised. General Maxse afterwards became
Inspector-General of Training for the British Armies,
and ultimately, following the Armistice, succeeded
to the Northern Command. It was General Maxse
who trained the 18th Division, at Colchester, on Salisbury Plain, and on the Somme. He saw his glowing,
markedly personal system, inculcated into civilian
soldiers of the finest New Army type, come to splendid
fruition in the attack of 1st July 1916, at Trones
Wood and Delville Wood, at Thiepval and Schwaben.
General Lee found a Division proud of its record.
And it could keep growing prouder to the very end.
The cruel losses and the awful conditions of Flanders
1917 left few survivors from among the original
officers and men. But the spirit of the Division lived
on. And in the dark anxious days of March 1918,
and in the hundred days of continuous deciding
victory, General Lee achieved very notable results
with young, untried, and frequently exhausted troops.
His dispositions for the moving battles that concluded
the campaign were masterly. The turning movements
by which over seven hundred prisoners were captured
near Combles on 1st September, and the Forêt de
Mormal was cleared on 4th November, are likely to
secure a place in military text-books.

The training before the Division went to France
was largely open-order training : the seeking of cover,
the use of dummy targets for deceiving the enemy,
and the development of the men's powers of endurance.
Seldom did they march less than ten miles a day ;
and their physical fitness was shown in the week's

MAJOR-GENERAL SIR RICHARD PHILIPPS LEE, K.C.B., C.M.G.

COMMANDED THE 18TH DIVISION FROM JANUARY 1917 UNTIL THE END OF THE WAR.

" trek " through Suffolk in April 1915, when sixty-two
miles were covered in the last forty-eight hours, every
officer and man carrying full marching order. This
was the first experience of active service conditions ;
the men slept in barns and billets, and were up
and away each morning. The 55th Brigade, returning
tired and spent from Woodbridge at 10 P.M., were
turned out again at midnight and set to march to
Colchester. There was no irritated surprise, no
grumbling ; every man felt that he was being tested,
and was proud of the fact. The drums met them two
miles out of Colchester and played them in. No one
fell out on that stamina-searching march ; but after
the "dismiss" at 5 A.M. in the square at Colchester,
a hundred men dropped in sheer exhaustion and slept
where they fell. The dominant note of the training
was to strike the topmost standard. Each battalion
was told that it would never be so good as the regular
battalions of the regiment—but it mustn't give up
trying to be.

General Maxse's chief influence was to be exerted
when the Division got to France. But even at Colchester and on Salisbury Plain in May and June 1915
he began making the junior officers feel that they
were the keystone of the Division. At all conferences
his explanations, his advice, his exhortations were
principally for them—delivered in the characteristic,
sometimes unconventional, always compelling manner
that the 18th Division will never forget. His "Good
morning, young officer!" of the earliest days, so
overpoweringly impersonal, changed in France to
"Good morning, So and So!" and the General's
apparently uncanny memory for names threatened to
become legendary. Maybe Captain F. J. O. Montagu,
General Maxse's A.D.C., one of whose tasks it was
to learn the officers' names—and to prompt the General
at the psychological moment—could supply an inner
explanation of the General's gift. But, here again,
this was one of General Maxse's properly thought-out

methods of infusing his personality into the Division. The young officer felt that the General was directly interested in him and his work, and went away persuaded that he was the finest fellow in the world— and the General a good second. As befitted the General who commanded the 1st Guards Brigade in the first days of the war, General Maxse possessed a philosophic understanding of the value of smartness, and the outward and visible evidences of discipline. " Good morning, gentlemen ! " he said on one occasion to a large gathering of officers, who stood to attention when he arrived to give a lecture. " And good morning, that gentleman there," he added abruptly, looking directly at an Essex subaltern who had forgotten to remove his hands from his trench-coat pockets. The officer never made a similar omission in the presence of an officer of high rank.

Doubtless the Divisional Artillery underwent the confusions and harassments of a strange new life to a greater extent than the infantry. If it was weeks before the companies got rifles, it was months before the batteries had their own guns. The detachments had to be trained on one wooden gun per battery, and once a week were allowed to drill with a real 18-pdr. There were no dial sights, and they practised "laying" over sights made of wood, with the degrees marked roughly upon them. The difficulty, at first, when the "fall in" was sounded, was to get the men to fall in with their proper batteries, let alone their right subsections. Men used to be missing for days, and were then found in other batteries. By November 1914 no battery had more than two dozen horses to its two hundred men, and any battery going out in drill order had first to scout round and borrow animals from other batteries. A great number of Scotsmen found themselves in the 18th Divisional Artillery, a large proportion of them Clydeside shipbuilding and engineering men. They were the right material, clear-headed and intelligent, though not great lovers of military eye-wash. As a Regular Major of the 82nd Brigade remarked when the Division had been two years in France, "They are better gunners than our old Regulars, but they will never be soldiers." In the days when some of the officers and N.C.O.'s were not such good horsemen as they hoped to become, the open country outside Colchester witnessed unforgettable exhibitions. Do the survivors of C/83 recollect the battery staff training with the hard-mouthed horses that invariably bolted for home as soon as they got on the grass? And the fat sergeant-major who played sheep-dog, galloping hard and trying to head them off? And the Territorial officer, not a gifted horseman, who rode an old black horse and intended to show the other officers how to draw swords on horseback? He told them to take the time from him, but before drawing his own sword he quickly had to devote all his efforts to sticking in the saddle. And still trying to pull his sword from its scabbard, he began gradually to disappear under his horse, to the great delight of all the onlookers.

The 82nd and 83rd Brigades enjoyed the very real advantage of being trained by Lieut.-Colonel R. P. Lambert and Lieut.-Colonel S. F. Metcalfe respectively. Colonel Lambert became C.R.A. of the 31st Divisional Artillery in December 1915, while Colonel Metcalfe succeeded Brigadier-General C. C. van Straubenzee as C.R.A. of the 18th Division, when General Straubenzee became Inspector of Artillery Training at home. General Metcalfe was made C.R.A. of the XI. Corps in July 1917, and by the spring of 1918 General Straubenzee held the important post of C.R.A. to the Fifth Army.

General Lambert remains one of the best-remembered figures of the Divisional Artillery. His methods were extremely direct. A subaltern, who joined at Colchester, tells of his first experience of Colonel Lambert. It was in the riding-school. Riding was not one of his accomplishments, and he was being badly bucketed about. Colonel Lambert stared at the spectacle for a full minute, and then roared out : "What were you in civil life, sir ?" "A solicitor, sir," panted the new officer, continuing his uneasy career. "Then the sooner you leave off being a solicitor and become an officer of the Royal Artillery the better," was the Colonel's "stuffy" reply. At dinner that night the officer took his place at the bottom of the table. The Adjutant very obviously pointed him out to the Colonel as the latest-joined officer. The Colonel looked his way, and in his never-anything-but-resonant tones remarked : "Yes, a solicitor, I believe!" But when the final Review had been held on Salisbury Plain and the Artillery had been congratulated on the excellence of the march past, the 82nd Brigade knew what they owed to Colonel Lambert's stern forcefulness, and gave credit where it was due.

The Division was on Salisbury Plain on 18th June, 1915, the day of the Waterloo centenary. There was a section commander in the 82nd Brigade who prided himself upon never losing an opportunity to educate his men. That day the artillery were engaged in a long march. One of the ordinary ten-minute halts had been called and the drivers had dismounted. Like a good section commander, the officer had walked along his section, inspecting the harness fittings and looking for galls, when suddenly he remembered what day it was. Obviously it was right and proper that his men should have the glories and the historical purport of Waterloo emphasised to them. He called them to attention and in ringing tones began : "A hundred years ago to-day, on the rain-sodden fields of Flanders——" But the address started and ended there. From the front of the column came the sharp, high-pitched order of Major Cornes, the battery commander : "Mount, please, Mr ——." The men leapt to their horses and Waterloo was forgotten.

There were two further incidents of those days

before the Division left England. The 55th Brigade claim to be the first Brigade of the Division to come under fire. The Boche aeroplane that tried to get to London on Christmas Day 1914 passed over Purfleet Camp, and at 1 P.M. dropped a bomb just as Lieut.-Colonel W. Glasgow of the 7th Queens was wishing the men a Merry Christmas. And the East Surreys believe that the first casualty and the first military funeral was theirs. One dark night in October 1914 a man came out of his tent and tripped over the guy-ropes. His chest was pierced by a tent-peg, and he died of his wound.

# CHAPTER II.

## FIRST EXPERIENCES IN FRANCE.

*France first seen under drizzling rain—Division posted to X. Corps in the 3rd Army—Attached at first to 5th and 51st Divisions for instruction in trenches — Opposite Carnoy and Fricourt — The Division's first casualty on 8th August 1915 — A/83 fires the Divisional Artillery's first shell—The French welcome at Meaulte —1,247 casualties by end of 1915—Lieutenant Maasdorp's exploit with an 18-pdr.—Inspection by the King and President Poincaré— The Boche raid on the 6th Northants—Captain Podmore's D.S.O. —Lieutenant Driver's raid for the Bedfords—How Meaulte petitioned the King.*

THE Division crossed the Channel on 25th and 26th July, and first saw France under a drizzling rain. Divisional Headquarters stayed the night of the 25th at the Louvre Hotel, Boulogne. The transport went by way of Southampton-Havre. The Division had been posted to the X. Corps in the newly-formed Third Army, of which General Sir Charles Monro, G.C.M.G., K.C.B., had the command; and first concentrated in the Fleselles area, about fifteen miles from the line.

Just before coming out certain of the officers had gone to the extent of having their heads shaved—they felt it was the proper soldierly thing to do. Some of the men had blacked their buttons and had had private parades to test visibility. But if officers and men had been keen in England they were doubly so now. Men slept with their arms through their rifle-slings, though they were miles from the enemy; the roads were picqueted for spies; and any practice

"Stand to" in the middle of the night was regarded with deadly earnestness. When on 2nd August the 6th Berks and the 10th Essex moved to Bouzincourt to be attached to the 51st Division for instruction in the trenches and made their first night march up to the front line, the men, imbued with the idea of concealing themselves from the enemy, marched a long way bent almost double, each man keeping touch by grasping the bayonet of the man behind him. Cigarettes were ordered to be put out miles from the front, although, as was afterwards discovered, pipes were smoked in the front line. By 6th August all three Brigades had begun their period of instruction under the 5th and 51st Divisions in the trenches opposite Carnoy and Fricourt, while by 8th August Divisional Headquarters settled at Montigny Chateau, with Divisional Artillery Headquarters at Ébart Farm. On 8th August the Germans exploded a mine at La Boisselle, killing one man and wounding eight. One of the wounded men belonged to The Queens; he was the Division's first casualty in France. The first officer casualty occurred on 10th August, when Lieutenant B. C. Haggard of the 7th Queens was hit.

The Artillery were first of the Divisional troops to come into action, however. They entrained and moved up the line immediately they landed in France. There was tremendous secrecy as to their destination. Captain Farmer, O.C. Train for the 83rd Brigade, was waked at Longeau, near Amiens, by a peremptory R.T.O., who said: "This is your destination. I'll give you half an hour to get off the train." In the latter stages of the war such an injunction might not have been so placidly received, but in those days any betabbed officer was regarded as an extremely wonderful person. The 83rd Brigade thought the war might be lost unless they detrained their guns and horses in half an hour. So in spite of inexperience they achieved the task, and were regarded by the R.T.O. as very clever people indeed. From

Longeau the four Brigades, without maps, marched through Heilly towards Mericourt, and pitched camp in the fields by the river. Next day the Colonels and the Battery Commanders went up to inspect the French O.P., to study the line and to register single guns.

Artillery fire was on such a small scale in those days that both Boche and French knew pretty well where the opposing gun positions were situated. Round the gun-pits which the French handed over to the 18th Division Artillery, so much earth had been thrown up that no one could miss seeing it. The guns were covered with branches, and green turf was used to disguise the turned-up soil, but there was no camouflaging as it is understood nowadays. There was no attempt to conceal the shadows thrown by the mounds, nor the cross tracks that led to the gun positions. On 31st July, A/83, who were attached to the 51st Division, fired the first shell, hitting a machine-gun emplacement ; and by 1st August all four Brigades had relieved the French. The guns were taken by night through Meaulte, with all sorts of precautions regarding the showing of lights and the rattling of gun-shields—although, of course, the enemy was still a long way off. It came as a shock when Meaulte was entered : French soldiers and civilians rushed out brandishing electric torches and giving welcoming shouts. The French pulled their own guns out of the pits that night, but stayed with our gunners until well into the next day. It was the first night in dug-outs—very old dug-outs —and officers and men lay on the chalk floor with rats scampering about.

By 6 P.M. the next night we took over the duty at the O.P.'s. Major A. A. A. Paterson, D.S.O., at that time a subaltern in B/83, describes his first twenty-four hours in an O.P. The enemy artillery strafed the front line that night, and the Black Watch of the 51st Division called to him for retaliation. Now

ammunition was so short—seventy rounds a week was
the allowance for the supporting batteries and thirty
for the reinforcing batteries—that in registering no
rounds could be spared for ascertaining the corrector.
When Lieutenant Paterson received the call from
the Black Watch, he informed Brigade, and Colonel
Metcalfe, who spoke to him, said, " You will want a
corrector." A corrector is obtained ordinarily by
observed shooting, and Paterson wondered how
observation was to be made in the dark. Colonel
Metcalfe told him to keep on the telephone, to order
his battery to fire, and to watch for the shell-burst.
The first shell came over, and Paterson reported its
arrival. " Did you see a flare or sparks ? " asked
Colonel Metcalfe. " Sparks, sir," replied Paterson.
" Then that must be graze," said the Colonel, " so
you must shorten your corrector." Paterson profited
by the Colonel's knowledge, and continued to shorten
his corrector until the shell burst at the proper point.
He exploded about forty rounds that night—and
satisfied the infantry.

During those first days up the line Colonel Metcalfe
spent a lot of time at the O.P.'s training the officers,
particularly in observation of country. " Isn't there
more earth over there than we saw yesterday ? " he
would say, or " What is that black speck opposite
—is it an old boot or a periscope ? "

On 19th August Divisional Headquarters moved
to Heilly, and next day the 53rd Brigade and the
82nd Brigade, R.F.A., were visited by the Army and
the Corps Commanders, and by distinguished French
visitors in M. Pichon and M. Barthou. The period of
instruction with the 5th and 51st Divisions had now
terminated. The 18th Division was going to be in
full possession of a portion of the front. Lieut.-
Colonel Shoubridge, the G.S.O. 1, issued the following historic orders :—

(1) The 18th Division will take over that portion
     of the line held by the 5th Division from the

Carnoy-Mametz road (exclusive) to trench in 104 (inclusive).

(2) Allotment of troops :—

    (*a*) Carnoy-Mametz road (exclusive) to small quarry just east of point 110 (exclusive). Troops : 53rd Infantry Brigade, 79th Field Company, R.E. ; 1 Company Royal Sussex Pioneers.

    (*b*) Small quarry (inclusive) to trench 104, due east of Bécourt (inclusive). Troops : 55th Infantry Brigade ; 80th Field Company, R.E. ; 1 Company Royal Sussex Pioneers.

    (*c*) Divisional Reserve : 1 battalion, 53rd Infantry Brigade.

    (*d*) Corps Reserve : 54th Infantry Brigade.

The taking over of the line commenced on 22nd August.

Though by the end of 1915 the Division had suffered 1,247 casualties, these four months proved to be the quietest and not the least pleasant in its history. Except for the winding ribbon of bare land that marked the opposing trench lines, the Somme country remained green and eye-pleasing. Pozières and Ovillers, in Boche territory, had not yet become crumbled brick-heaps ; it was possible through the glasses to pick out the church clock in Pozières, while Ovillers still hid itself in a bower of trees. The outline of Contalmaison showed graceful and inviting, and though Thiépval, high and forbidding, had its chateau in ruins, the village had not yet been shelled into an abomination of desolation. No large attack had taken place for some time. Shells rarely descended beyond the rival trench systems. If occasional Boche shells flew into Meaulte, it was most likely as a protest against our gunners' disturbing Mametz. It was possible at one part of the Divisional front to bathe in the Ancre river, within 600 yards of the enemy, and battalions doing duty in the line in turn took over a cow that thrived in a dug-out. The waggon lines and back areas were havens of rest, and neither side shelled transport.

The trenches were well made and legibly labelled, so that reliefs were simple. Food was plentiful, and the men looked models of health. Three Brigades were in the line at a time, and on each Brigade front two battalions occupied the forward trenches with two companies. The remaining battalions were in show billets in Ville-sur-Ancre, Dernancourt, Meaulte, and similar villages—with canteens and libraries, and a bed and a seat at table for each man. Eight days was the average tour of duty in the lines. Every morning at stand-to a few muscle-loosening bombs were thrown by both sides. Then the men settled down to watch and to wait. On many an evening a covey of partridges flew down and settled in the barbed wire, and the West Kents got some very good potatoes from a patch of No Man's Land. Fires that gave off heavy smoke would, of course, have drawn enemy fire, but the men soon learnt the art of cooking food on fires made of very thin strips of wood which produced little or no smoke.

During the Division's first week in the line the Buffs had a platoon blown up, and the continued uncertainty as to whether one's trench was undermined proved a strain on the nerves. In the parts where the enemy was closest—at places he was only twenty yards away —the Boche on most days could be heard walking along his own duck-boards. Sometimes he would call, "Good morning, Tommy," through the trench walls. False alarms became normal. On the Bedfords' first patrol a Boche subterranean passage was reported—it proved to be the top of a beer barrel; the Berks were perturbed by a mysterious fall of chalk, and careful investigation was made—a weasel was found to be shifting its quarters. One day a dull tapping was heard in a trench held by the Buffs. A sergeant with his ear to the ground said, "That's mining." The first officer

called corroborated, and the news went from company
to battalion. Lieut.-Colonel W. F. Elmsley arrived. A
whole company of officers and men stood round, solemn
and expectant. The tapping ceased, then started again.
The sergeant-major moved away, and descended a dug-
out. Once more the tapping ceased, then started, then
ceased again. The sergeant-major reappeared. " Did
the noise stop and start again, sir?" he asked. "Yes,"
replied the Colonel. " I've got it then, sir," said the
sergeant-major with an eager smile. " It's a man in
the dug-out chopping wood."

The other outstanding features of the daily fighting
up to the close of 1915 were the guarding against
Boche raids, the patrolling to find ways through the
mine - craters for our own raiding parties, and the
sniping. Here are a couple of E. Surrey patrolling
stories that reveal the temper and the confident,
aggressive spirit of the officers and men who first went
out with the Division.

2nd Lieutenant A. E. A. Jacobs, seeking to gain
knowledge of a path through the 120 yards of crater-
land, went out one night accompanied by Sergeant
R. C. Ruffles and a private. Below the German
parapet they came to a big crater, which silently
they clambered up. They lay a while looking down
into a German trench ; then Lieutenant Jacobs slid
down into the crater, expecting the others to follow
him. He waited, but they did not come ; so he climbed
up again. There was no sign at all of Sergeant Ruffles
and the private. Greatly puzzled, Jacobs still waited
in the expectation that his men would find him again.
Then suddenly the sound of revolver shooting and the
swift flare of Boche lights! Jacobs was now in an
exposed position, so he slid down into the crater
again and crawled back to his own lines. A little
later the private also returned, and told a curious
story to the company commander. "When Mr Jacobs
dropped into the crater," he said, "Ruffles caught
my arm, and said, 'We'll go on.' So we got

into the German trench. When the lights went up,
Ruffles told me to clear off as quick as I could—and I
missed him." Eight hours later Sergeant Ruffles
returned. His thigh had been broken by rifle-fire,
but he had dragged himself through the crater in
No Man's Land, lying on his back and propelling
himself by his elbows and his sound leg. Lieutenant
Jacobs was killed in a Boche raid at Bois Grenier,
near Armentières, in August 1916.

Another night, a very dark night, Captain C. G. M.
Place, complaining that there was nothing to do, went
for a walk in No Man's Land, and took two orderlies
with him. They walked about for some time. Then
Captain Place said, "We'll get back home." The
party climbed over two belts of wire, and dropped
into the trench. "Go to Company Headquarters and
say we're back," the captain instructed one of the
orderlies. At that moment an unarmed man walked
round the corner of the trench. He was a man with a
beard. Captain Place flattened himself and his orderlies
against the trench side. The man with the beard
said, "Gute Nacht." Captain Place replied, "Gute
Nacht." The man with the beard looked at them
and walked on, round another corner. Immediately
Captain Place whispered to his men, "Off like hell!
We're in the Boche trenches." But the Boche knew.
As soon as he rounded the corner he alarmed a sentry,
who shot down one of the two orderlies. The whole
trench was now alive with shouts. Captain Place
made certain that the shot orderly was dead. Then
he and the second orderly shinned up over the parapet.
Shots rang out and flares went up. Captain Place
got through the wire, but the orderly, losing his
sense of direction, ran three hundred yards level with
the German wire, shot at all the way. Eventually he
also reached safety.

Boche snipers remained daring and unsettling, and
seemed to be unceasingly successful. With the
trenches so close it was impossible to bring gun-fire

to bear on them at ordinary ranges. So General
Maxse, Brigadier - General Straubenzee, and Colonel
Lambert decided upon the experiment of an 18-
pdr. fired from just behind the front line. The
undertaking was carried out by Lieutenant W. Maasdorp of C Battery, 82nd Brigade, and he gained the
M.C. by it. The object of this particular operation
was to destroy strong sniper posts established on the
lip of a crater so near to us that they commanded part
of our line, and caused casualties in the front and communication trenches.

On 7th September Lieutenant Maasdorp, with his
battery commander, Captain P. G. M. Elles, marked
out a gun-pit in one of our communication trenches.
On the following nights the height of the parapet
was gradually raised by sandbags so as to screen the
gun : and in order that the outline of the parapet
should not be interrupted an embrasure was cut
beneath the sandbags. The embrasure was then
covered by bushes until the time came for the gun
to be fired. At 11 P.M. on 12th September horses
took the gun to within 250 yards of the position ;
from which point ten men hauled it with drag-ropes
across a route that was uphill and pitted with shell-
holes. In the last 80 yards, a Boche flare went up
and the party had to lie prostrate, but the gun was
not observed, and was brought to its pit and covered
over with wire netting and grass and earth.

The embrasure was watered to prevent dust from
rising, and at 5.45 P.M. on the 13th the gun did six
minutes rapid fire on the sniper post ; after which the
embrasure was blocked up again, and the gun detachment took refuge in a dug-out fifty yards away to
wait for the enemy's reply. But the Boche was completely deceived, and the gun was got comfortably
away by 7.45 P.M., only four revenging shells coming
anywhere near it and Lieutenant Maasdorp's party.

General Maxse in his report upon the experiment
wrote : "In this instance German sniping had gained

the upper hand during the previous three weeks, and
a high sniping post was inflicting losses at 100 yards'
range.   Our gun demolished the post.   It was rebuilt
by the Germans during the night, but German sniping decreased throughout the sector."

In Colonel Lambert's note to the Divisional Artillery recording that in his opinion Captain Elles and
Lieutenant Maasdorp had done their work very thoroughly, there appears a quaint illustration of the
niggardly allowance of shells during that period:
"Sanction is requested," he wrote, "for the expendi-
ture of these 35 H.E. rounds over and above usual
allotments—it being for a special object."

One might add the following entry from the Divisional Diary for another day in September.   "The
Germans sent over 50 shells.   We retaliated with
*about* 19 shells."   Up to the end of 1915 it used to
be the joke that the one round per week per battery
might as well be sent up in the mess cart.   As a
matter of plain fact, it did only require one team per
week to take the ammunition to the batteries.   It
was a sort of state journey.   The officer from the
waggon lines who superintended the undertaking
had his belt and his field boots specially polished—
even the shell cases used to be polished—and at the
gun position every one turned out to welcome the
weekly quota of ammunition with due ceremony.

If there was a shortage of shells there was no stint
of rifle ammunition.   The sentries on both sides fired
all through the night, and in October when two
platoons of the Essex went over the top for the first
time—it was in the " D-français " sector—so many
rounds were fired that the rifles became too hot
to hold.

There were many ruses by which Boche and British
sought to discover each other's strength.   On 21st
September arrangements were made with the 51st
Division to set up a mighty shout at 5.30 A.M. to see
if the Germans would move in their trenches, and to

discover what volume of fire they would loose off. The plan failed, however, probably because the same scheme had been tried by the 51st Division the previous day.

On 21st September Lord Kitchener inspected the 8th East Surreys and the 10th Essex, south of the Albert-Amiens road near Ribecourt. Major Arthur Lee, the liaison officer from G.H.Q., and Major J. Norton Griffiths, Inspector of Tunnelling, also visited Divisional H.Q., while on 25th October battalions from the 5th, 51st, and 18th Divisions paraded under command of General Maxse, one mile north of Ribecourt, and were inspected by the King and President Poincaré. The Prince of Wales was present, as was General Allenby, who had been newly appointed to the command of the Third Army.

In due course the 18th Division received troops for instruction in the trenches from Divisions newly arrived in France. The men will never forget the highly unconventional ways of certain Lancashire men. "How much farther is it to the blinkin' battlefield?" said one of them when he had completed a long tramp up the communication trenches, and was in the front line opposite La Boisselle. There was also the case of the Fusilier officer who was approached by an Oldham man who was doing sentry. "I've been here six hours," he said, "and no one has relieved me." It was a rainy night, and the trenches were at their slimiest. "There must be a mistake," replied the officer, and he sought the man's sergeant, who was sitting dry and snug in a dug-out. "You've a man out there who's been on sentry for six hours. You were to change the sentry every hour."

"I didn't think it's worth while getting more than one man wet," was the sergeant's explanation.

Gradually the shelling on this Carnoy - Fricourt sector increased, and the enemy—who possessed more machine-guns, more bombs, more devices than we did, and was still the master soldier of the war—began to

raid.  On 10th December Brigadier-General Heneker,
who commanded the 54th Brigade—subsequently he
became G.O.C. of the 8th Division—was wounded in
the left thigh by an enemy machine-gun bullet while
walking in the open near Canterbury Avenue.     On
21st December 19 men were killed and 22 wounded
by a mine that exploded in "Tambour."   On 27th
December the 55th Brigade had its first experience
of a lachrymatory shell bombardment.

Two days later there followed a heavy bombardment of "D 2" sub-section, lachrymatory and gas
shells being used, and eighty yards of the parapet were
obliterated.    Goggles and gas-helmets were put on ;
but several men were gassed, and were sent down
vomiting and bleeding at the nose.   Then at dusk a
German bombing party came over and captured nineteen men of the 6th Northants, who were surprised
in a cellar north of Fricourt.    Two other men of the
Northants were killed and three wounded, and one
Boche was afterwards found dead in our trenches.
The Germans remained on the spot twelve minutes,
and had disappeared when our counter - attack
started.

On the afternoon of 31st January 1916 a shell
killed Lieut.-Colonel J. F. Radcliffe, D.S.O., of the
10th Essex, while he was sitting in the telephone
dug-out talking to 2nd Lieutenant Byerley and the
Regimental M.O.    At lunch that day the colonel
had been the third to light his cigarette from one
match.    In March, Colonel Ripley and the adjutant
of the 6th Northants, going to reconnoitre a sector
in Carnoy, were both wounded by a stray shell while
walking between Bronfay Farm and Billon Wood.
Colonel Ripley, who was vastly popular in his battalion,
rejoined in June, but received fatal wounds in the great
attack on Thiépval.

On 31st January the enemy tried a new means
of unsettling us.   Wearing British gas-masks, a party
of them suddenly appeared in front of the Essex

trenches brandishing a red, yellow, and black flag, at the same time shouting in English, "Move down to the West Kents!" They got shot at for their pains, and left the flag. On it was worked the propaganda message: "Brave British boys! Why do you fight for bloated capitalists and captains of industry who sit at home in safety?"

In February, Captain R. U. E. Knox of the 8th Suffolks won the D.S.O.—the first D.S.O. gained in the Division—for daring work in a trench raid.

Spring arrived, and with it the Boche hammer assault upon Verdun. The Division, which on 1st March had been transferred from the X. to the XIII. Corps, knew that it was destined to take part in a big attack, and a new seriousness entered into the desire to learn soldiering quickly and well. Pride of Division was asserting itself; the inner meaning of General Maxse's insistent demand for efficiency had sunk in. The shell supply had steadily increased, and by April the enemy began making determined attempts to secure prisoners and to learn something of our plans. On 13th April he attempted his biggest raid on the sector. At 2 A.M. be began a furious ten minutes' bombardment of Bronfay Farm and on the trenches held by the 6th Northants in front of Carnoy. The Northants had never forgotten what befell them on 29th December, and, in spite of the shelling, they stood to their posts and refused to seek cover. When, under the barrage, the Germans surged to the attack, they were met with admirable steadiness. Two parties of the enemy were driven off by rifle and machine-gun fire. A third party of twenty - five men got into the trench and captured three of our wounded, one of whom escaped later; but they had two killed, and lost one man taken prisoner. To a very large extent the Boche was beaten back by the fine control exercised by Captain Hubert Podmore, who commanded D Company of the Northants. When the Boche barrage started, a

wiring party belonging to Captain Podmore's company were in No Man's Land, and as they came
back to their trench the right company of the
Northants took them to be Boche and fired on
them. As also our S.O.S. barrage came down only
in front of the right company, the enemy was
enabled to come across on the flank of Captain
Podmore's company, in the centre of the line. Simultaneously a raiding party rushed a trench held by the
12th Middlesex, and the Middlesex lost 13 N.C.O.'s
and men. In all, the Northants suffered 46 casualties,
D Company's total being 27.

Corporal Morris of the Northants, hearing that
a sentry had been killed during the bombardment,
hurried up to the post and was pounced upon by a
big Boche, who dragged him across No Man's Land
and then handed him over to two slightly-wounded
Germans. As they neared the German lines one of
the Boche escort dropped from weakness. As quick
as thought Morris knocked down the other man and
scrambled back to his own lines.

Captain Podmore, who received the D.S.O. after
the success in beating off this raid, represented the
best type of officer produced by the 18th Division. A
house-master at Rugby, he was a cultivated man with
a gift for interesting his fellows, and he possessed a
certain nobility of character that inspired them to better
things. He neglected no detail of duty, and believed
in all the outward manifestations of discipline; but
it was the human side of him, the intimate and personal touches in the rough and tumble of the trenches,
and in the cheerful doings behind the line, that gave
him his extraordinary influence over his company.
When going round the lines at night he always produced some unusual comforts for the men, such as
throat pastilles or cow-heel jelly. On a route-march
he would talk to young privates and train their powers
of observation with questions like—"Which way is
the wind blowing?" or "How many cows were there

in that field we've just passed?" He was very tall,
good at games, stuttered, and had a curious habit of
swallowing before he spoke—particularly when angered.
He possessed a whimsical sense of humour. One early
morning he found a man of his company in "D" sector
up to his waist in liquid mud, with difficulty holding
a "dixie" above his head. The dixie contained hot
fried bacon—the men had been bringing up the breakfast. "Do you want some one to give you a hand?"
asked Podmore impassively, "because I don't intend
to help you." The man, who had grinned at first,
looked bewildered as Captain Podmore walked slowly
away; but he still kept the dixie out of the mud. A
few minutes later Podmore returned, drinking a cup
of steaming tea. He stared stonily at the helpless
man for half a minute, and then left him, remarking,
"I think I'll turn in now and have breakfast." When
he got back to Company Headquarters he laughed,
said he had just been playing the part of Levite, and
hurried off a party of servants to the unfortunate
dixie-carrier, whom afterwards he plied well with rum.
Podmore was a poor singer, but, *pour encourager
les autres*, he always offered to sing at company
concerts. His favourite song was "Oh my darling,
Clementine"; and he did his best with "A Police-
man's Lot," "The Sentry's Song" in "Iolanthe," and
"The Silver Churn."

After the Boche raid on the Northants, General
Maxse decided that a retaliatory raid would be good
for moral. The combative spirit of the men needed
an outlet. The raid, admirably planned by Lieut.-
Colonel G. D. Price, was carried out by 2nd Lieutenant Harry Driver, 2 N.C.O.'s, and 30 men of the
7th Bedfords. It provided half an hour of very successful hand-to-hand fighting in the enemy trenches,
and gave the Bedfords good reason to think highly
of themselves.

Previous to the raid Lieutenant Driver took each
of the selected men in front of our wire to show

him the exact position he was to occupy at the
opening of the artillery bombardment, and the spot
he was to make for.   The raiding party blacked
their faces to assist in concealing their movements,
carried bombs and knobkerries, and wore white
bands on their arms for identification among themselves.   At 1.20 A.M. on 27th April Lieutenant
Driver and his men formed up fifty yards outside
our wire.   At half-past one our artillery bombarded
several points on the enemy front.   After fifteen
minutes the barrage lifted and also spread out to
the flanks.   It was then that Lieutenant Driver and
his men moved silently forward, dropping a trail of
chloride of lime as a guide for the return journey.
A 10-foot ladder was lowered into the enemy trench
and the Bedfords climbed down it.   A Boche
machine-gun from a support trench opened a withering fire, and enemy bombers hurried up ; but they
could not prevent the Bedfords adhering to their
plan ; Lieutenant Driver and one party turned to
the left in the trench ; Sergeant Mills and another
party moved to the right.   It was all vivid
personal fighting.   Lieutenant Driver came to a
large dug-out, and, descending it, perceived a lighted
candle.   He shouted to the Germans below to come
out and surrender ; they hesitated, and he threw
down a couple of bombs.   Driver shot a German
who came towards the dug-out, and was himself
wounded in the face and in the foot.

Sergeant Mills's party were at first held up by
bombs thrown from an enemy dug-out.   But this
was a game at which the Bedfords soon showed
superiority, and they passed on to bomb and kill
six Boches who had hid in a sap.   After which
they proceeded farther up the fire trench, bayoneted
two Germans who had tried to defend another dug-
out, and shot a couple more who climbed on top of
the parapet and hurled bombs.   A brainy device
was also introduced by Lance-Sergeant Hope, who

ran along the top of the parapet sprinkling
lachrymatory fluid in advance of the raiders.  As
the wind was favourable, the fumes provided a
miniature invisible barrage which greatly affected
six Huns who tried to stand their ground.  Good
shooting through this disconcerting barrage was
done from the parapet top.  Sergeant Mills's party
were so full of fight that they went 400 yards
beyond their objective.  As Brigadier - General
Shoubridge, who was now commanding the 54th
Brigade, wrote in his report : " Our men's tempers
were roused and they forgot the desirability of
taking prisoners.  The success of the raid greatly
improved the general moral."

In all, 366 Mills bombs were used.  The party
remained half an hour in the German lines, and
though wounded in three places Lieutenant Driver
waited at the appointed rendezvous and refused to
return until his men reported themselves.  Eight of
the Bedfords were wounded, but they were all
brought back.  One man was missing, and it was at
first reported that he had wandered back into
another portion of our lines.  Afterwards, however,
it was learnt that he had been hit and had died in
a shell-hole.  General Shoubridge, who came up to
hear the earlier reports of the raid, met one of the
men, as he returned, in the Bedfords' support trench.
" Did you kill any Boche ? " asked the General.  For
answer the man thrust out a pair of blood-stained
arms and grinned.  Lieutenant Driver, who by sheer
personality made certain of the success of the exploit,
was awarded the D.S.O., and Sergeant Mills the D.C.M.

There can be no doubt that the desire to hood-
wink and worst the Boche was exceedingly keen.
The 8th East Surreys possessed a Sergeant
named Edwards—" Wiggy " Edwards he was known
to his intimates.  He came from Diss, in Norfolk,
and was a very real example of the born athlete.
He won all the flat races at the Battalion Sports'

gatherings, from 100 yards to 5 miles, played half-back in the Battalion Football Team, which was a very strong one, and though a boxing novice when he went to France, won both the Welter Weight and Middle Weight Championships of the Division. There was a piece of ground in front of Fricourt that needed to be reconnoitred. It lay between the mine craters and the enemy front line, and was unknown to us because the Boche watched it incessantly and had snipers posted to protect it. Edwards said that if he were allowed to wear shorts and shoes he could sprint round the craters and be back in fifteen seconds; and he did not think the enemy would have time to hit him. He was quite serious, but his proposition was regarded as too unorthodox and too risky.

There was also the proposal made with all solemnity by Lieutenant Vint, a Canadian rancher, who belonged to the 82nd Brigade's 4·5 battery. Great efforts were being made to capture a prisoner for identification purposes. In Fricourt Trench was a small tunnel under which Germans used regularly to pass. Vint was very keen to go out at night and lasso a German emerging from the tunnel. With the help of a few sturdy Garrison gunners, he said, it would be easy to haul in the trapped man. Colonel Lambert listened to Vint's plan, but refused to put it into effect. Vint will always be remembered by a certain celebrated use of gunnery terms unknown to the text-books. He was on duty at the O.P. opposite Fricourt one day when General Straubenzee and Colonel Lambert arrived, accompanied by a concourse of Corps and Army staff officers. They wanted to see some shooting, and Colonel Lambert told Vint to fire on a particular house on the outskirts of Fricourt. Vint had long desired to make a target of this house, and for weeks past had registered all round it. Accordingly he telephoned pre-arranged orders to his battery. But a gunner who was ignorant of these instructions happened to be on duty at the guns, and the first shell was woefully out of range. Vint did not consult a map and send down a range and angle of sight correction in the manner of F.A.T. He persisted in trying to make the "layer" understand his specially arranged orders. Finally, the distinguished visitors heard the fierce entreaty in strong Canadian accents : " Cock her up, Bill, and loose her off again."

Dennis Neilson Terry, the actor, was a subaltern in the 7th Queens up to the spring of 1916. One night he entered a Boche sap by mistake and took the German sentry to be one of ours. When the sentry challenged him, he repeated " I'm Mr Terry " several times. Then suddenly he realised where he was. The sentry shouted to wake the guard, and Terry had an exciting scramble back to his own lines with bullets pinging about him.

The Division never occupied a trench system so overrun by rats as this one. The Bedfords christened two veteran and elusive rats Tom the Tunneller and Simon the Man-eater—the latter, a grey-faced monster that was very fast on the duck-boards, always offered good sport, and was never scotched. It became an unofficial duty for the orderly officer of the day to kill rats. The best drive, 70, was claimed by Captain, afterwards Lieut.-Colonel, A. E. Percival.

Lieut.-Colonel Wallace Wright, V.C., who succeeded General Shoubridge as G.S.O. 1. of the Division, was actually making out a defence scheme for the Cameroons when the war broke out ; and he acted as Chief Staff Officer to General Dobell until that campaign was brought to a successful termination. Then he came to France. He remained G.S.O. 1. of the 18th Division until July 1918, when he was appointed B.-G.G.S. XVII. Corps. He possessed the balance of mind requisite in a first-class staff officer, and his operation orders were models of lucidity and compression. He was the man of action as well.

This quality sometimes showed itself in odd, vivid ways. Once, when he was a Brigade-Major at Bordon Camp, he went to a boxing exhibition. Some of the men were not fighting in a sporting manner. Wallace Wright got up, and invited any officer to assist him in showing the men how they ought to box. An R.F.A. Captain accepted the challenge. Both he and Wallace Wright had just come from dining in mess, but off came collars and ties and mess jackets, and the spectators were soon cheering and applauding one of the most spirited, most gory fights ever seen at Bordon.

The little village of Meaulte, hard by Albert, and two and a half miles from Fricourt, will always have memories for the original members of the Division. For six months various units were billeted there when in reserve. Of the 1,000 inhabitants, over 700 remained until the retreat of March 1918. In Feb. 1916 plans for the Franco-British offensive that ultimately took place on 1st July were nearing completion, and the villagers learned that they would be evacuated. They petitioned the French authorities, but were told that the sector was under British command ; so they decided upon the unusual and boldly ingenious plan of appealing to the King of England. One is inclined to believe that M. Phené, a popular interpreter attached to the 18th Divisional Artillery, had something to do with the forming of the decision.

Here is a copy of the original letter that was despatched to His Majesty :—

To His Gracious Majesty King George.

Threatened with evacuation, we, the responsible heads of all the families of this village, appeal to your Gracious Majesty for help.

We are all engaged in farming, directly or indirectly, and are now sowing for the crop of 1916.

Taken unawares by the invasion we were unable to save the 1914 crop, which was not gathered. Notwithstanding the shortness of labour, mobilisation of horses, and cattle requisitioned, we ploughed and furrowed as near as possible to the trenches, confident that the Allied troops would withstand the enemy.

The 1915 crop was a failure. But we have anchored our hopes on 1916.

For a year and a half we have given up our homes and our barns for the billeting of officers and men, retaining but one living and one bedroom for our own use. All our chattels, implements, carts, harnesses, horses were utilised by the army for defence purposes, and in the bad days we personally drove the wounded from the trenches to the base hospitals.

The hundred thousand soldiers or more who sojourned in our midst can testify to our willingness, our eagerness to accept the necessary military servitudes.

We are fighting for our homes, which will be wrecked if we abandon them.

We are fighting against ruin inevitable after two disastrous years which would be complete because we would not be able to take away our cattle, feathered stock, implements, and our wheat, which military necessity prevented us from threshing.

We ask not for money but for liberty.

Taking our lives into our own hands, we cannot conceive of any strategical or tactical reasons warranting our evacuation, otherwise we would bow our heads and accept this last sacrifice for the good of the cause.

We have won the title of soldiers; we claim the honour, the right of remaining soldiers, and we humbly beg your Gracious Majesty, for the sake of our sons, all at the front, and for our old age, to prevent that an administrative decision may succeed where 17 months of German shelling failed.

We are of your Majesty,
the Loyal Allies.


Signed by the acting Mayor and Curé, with stamps of office, and by all the male heads of the family.

MEAULTE.    February 1916.


The letter caused some uneasiness at the 18th Division Army Post Office. No officer was anxious to frank it with the Censor stamp, being uncertain of

Army post office customs with regard to petitions. Eventually the letter was accepted, although on the suggestion of a brigade-major a second copy was written out and signed, and posted in an ordinary French post office letter-box.

To their unrestrained delight the villagers received a reply. One of the King's secretaries wrote to the Mayor informing him that the request had been forwarded to Sir Douglas Haig. Later the inhabitants were told that they would not be evacuated; but they were warned that for three days, from 1st July, they would not be allowed to leave their houses.

When the first steel hats arrived in Nov. 1915 they were issued as trench stores, six per company. It was not until June 1916 that each man received his own hat. It was in January that M. Clemenceau paid his first visit to the Division. Sir Douglas Haig, Sir William Robertson, Lord Cavan, and General Mangin, at that time commanding the French 5th Division, were of the party which was taken by General Maxse to view the line from Bontay Redoubt. While they were at Bécordel the enemy sent a few shells over, and General Maxse told M. Clemenceau that he must seek cover. "But remember I am a soldier," objected the tough old veteran. "All the more reason why you should obey," countered General Maxse with a bow and a smile. And M. Clemenceau obeyed.

There was much unofficial friendly liaison between the 18th Division and the officers of the neighbouring French Division about this time; and many guest nights. The British were somewhat disquieted when first they came to return the toothsome hospitality of the French, who did not need to worry about the quality of their mess cooking. But the French artillery officers were so taken with the first dinner given them by Captain W. F. Armstrong of D/82— with the plain roast beef, the sardines on toast as savoury, and the whisky and soda—that some of them wrote long enthusiastic letters to their wives

C

about it; and were grievously disappointed when the next time they came to dine Captain Armstrong's cook essayed a *dîner français*. The 7th Bedfords' savoury—bacon and prunes—and Lieut.-Colonel G. D. Price's curries, also soared into popularity. In Eclusier, a destroyed village on the Somme, whose narrow bridge was regularly shelled by the enemy, lived a white-haired old lady, whose son was rector of a University in the south of France. Though slightly wounded once, she refused to leave her home, and provided coffee for many a French and many a British soldier. A French captain censored her mail both ingoing and outgoing, and our men took her many little presents of food. Captain Hartgill, of the 55th Field Ambulance—the New Zealand "Rugger" player, who played in England for the United Hospitals—brought more than one French child into the world while German shells were coming over.

The difficulty of getting change for use in the canteens led to an unusual experiment by the 11th Royal Fusiliers. The Fusiliers had a sort of godfather in the city of London, Mr S. C. Turner, a well-known business man. Mr Turner devised a special paper currency. The men were paid partly in these "Fusilier one-franc" notes, which were good for their face value in the canteens. Moreover, these special notes won such a reputation among the French people that local shops accepted them, knowing they would be honoured.

On Easter Sunday 1916 a truly impressive Church of England service was held in the quarry near Dragon's Wood, hard by the East Surreys' Headquarters. The Boche was so near that there could be no singing, and the prayers had to be said in low whispering tones.

# CHAPTER III.

## BATTLE OF 1ST JULY 1916.

*A triumph of preparation — 18th Division's capture of Pommiers Redoubt and Montauban Ridge—Rehearsals over model trenches —8th East Surreys and the football incident—Sergeant who killed ten Germans in the crater fighting—Gallant work by the Queens —The Fusilier signaller on the parapet top—54th Brigade's assault on Pommiers Redoubt—Berkshires' heavy losses—Congratulatory message from XIII. Corps—695 prisoners taken—Division's 3,707 casualties.*

ON 1st July 1916, when for the first time the now immense forces of Sir Douglas Haig attacked on the grand scale, and Britain's civilian soldiers made their 'prentice effort to oust the Germans from the labyrinthine strongholds which they had been strengthening for two years, the 18th was one of the few British Divisions to attain all its objectives. This opening battle of the Somme was, for the 18th, a typical Maxse success — a triumph first of preparation and construction and then of grit and determination. The Division never possessed men more magnificent physically than those who fought on 1st July 1916.

The Division, still in the XIII. Corps, but now part of the 4th Army under Sir Henry Rawlinson, advanced 3,000 yards from its original trenches, on a front of 2,500 yards, seized the Montauban Ridge and the west end of Montauban village, and captured Pommiers Redoubt, Caterpillar Wood, and Marlborough Wood. The 30th Division on the right, and nearest the French, also captured their final objective — the main portion of Montauban village.

But further north there was not such complete success.

Every move in the fight made by the 18th had been rehearsed to the minutest detail upon ground in the Picquigny area that was a replica of the actual battlefield. Sir Douglas Haig himself witnessed the full - dress rehearsal over the model trenches, when aeroplanes and flares were used. On the day of the battle each man knew the exact spot he was to make for, and what to do when he got there.

Map-reading skill was indeed scarcely necessary on that famous 1st of July. The artillery bombardment which preceded the advance was in magnitude and terribleness beyond the previous experience of mankind. For a week, guns of all calibres lashed and hammered the deep shelters in which the Boche waited for the assault, harried his communication trenches, churned and tore the fair lands behind the trenches, and seared their greenness into tawny desolation. Then an hour before the infantry moved forward the guns all along the line burst forth into a culminating hurricane that dwarfed their previous fury into nothingness.

Things were very different from Ypres in April and May 1915. Everywhere on our front field-guns, innumerable now, ranged themselves; heavies up to 15 - inch, and, in the trenches, quantities of trench mortars. And the ammunition was plentiful enough to put us on terms with the enemy. Sir Douglas Haig has stated that on 1st July nearly 13,000 tons of artillery ammunition were fired by us on the Western front.

When one considers, too, the careful preparations made for the Somme offensive, one must not forget the miles of new railways and trench tramways and telephone systems that had to be constructed. And armies cannot be moved forward unless there is water supply for thousands of men and horses. Sir

Douglas Haig says in his official report : " Wells and
borings were sunk, and over 100 pumping plants were
installed.   More than 120 miles of water mains were
laid."

The German gunners were naturally not idle during
this preliminary bombardment.   A Fusilier officer has
the following entry in his diary :—

One morning about 1 A.M. I had a party of sixteen men
working in Hyde Road when the Huns suddenly directed
their fire on Park Lane.  As it was impossible for the men
to continue their work I withdrew them towards Piccadilly
(Park Lane and Piccadilly are of course the names of trenches),
and as we moved so did the shells, for they followed us, and
it was with great difficulty that my men got under cover.
Being under cover does not always mean safety.  Five of my
party who were taking shelter in a dug-out in Piccadilly
Circus were wounded, the dug-out being blown in.

It was near the same spot that the Bedfordshire
Regiment had all the officers of "C" Company killed
or wounded on 26th June.   Captain R. L. V. Doake,
one of the survivors, gives the following account :—

The officers' mess in a dug-out in Piccadilly got a direct hit
while all the officers were having supper about 9 P.M.  All
became casualties, as well as some eight servants and other
ranks who took refuge.   A 4·2 howitzer shell struck the
entrance and burst inside.   The doorway was filled up and
the smoke and fumes almost suffocated the survivors.
Luckily a passing man saw my arm which I had pushed
through a hole, and Major (then Captain) Clegg and myself
were got out, but Lieutenants Baden and Hasler were killed,
and Lieutenant Johnson died of wounds.

The rescue of the buried officers was carried out by
Private H. W. Fish.  Although the air was thick
with gas, he refused to be relieved from digging till
the task was finished.  This same man did gallant
work before Pommiers Redoubt on 1st July, crawling
up and bombing a machine-gun that held up the
advance.  He was awarded the D.C.M.

By 2 A.M. on 1st July 1916 all the 18th Division battalions were in position. Now and again a Very light illumined the sky and then died away. Occasionally a gun fired, but the night was quiet, and most of the men sought sleep.

The dawn broke fair, though at first a slight mist —relic of the rains of the past week—shrouded the Boche lines. The sun rose higher, and birds chirped and fed in the charlock that garnished some of the trenches. It was the Division's first battle, and the solemnity of the occasion affected every one—every one except, perhaps, a laughing youngster in the Fusiliers who twitted a grizzled N.C.O. with "Was it like this in South Africa, sergeant?" and munched his double-ration breakfast with the appetite of untroubled youth. The officers were wearing men's uniforms, to prevent them from being singled out by Boche sharpshooters; most of the men wore their tin hats with the chin-strap behind—a custom since it had been noticed that steel helmets struck by flying pieces of shell had a habit of spinning sharply upwards, giving a violent jerk to the chin confined in a chin-strap.

The air warmed under the early morning sun. "I found myself sweating before zero hour," says Lieut.-Colonel E. C. T. Minet, who at that time was machine-gun officer of the Fusiliers, "but that, I suppose, was nervous excitement." Nerves were indeed strung to the highest pitch in that time of waiting. Then at 6.30 A.M. our guns burst forth into their Niagara-like overture. At 7.22 A.M. the trench mortars added to the tumult, and a long line of balloons stretching out of sight soared majestically a couple of miles behind our lines.

At 7.30 A.M. our infantry leapt from their trenches and went to seek the Boche, and the devilish rattle of machine-guns broke out.

The Division attacked with the 55th Brigade on the right, the 53rd in the centre, and the 54th on the left. The Field Artillery programme included

thirty - five "lifts," and it has to be noted that
1st July saw the introduction of the "offensive
barrage" into British artillery shooting.

The 55th Brigade's objective was a trench line
about 200 yards north of the Montauban - Mametz
road, and also the western end of Montauban.  The
7th Queens attacked on the left, the East Surreys
on the right, with the 7th Buffs who supported
them apportioned the task of clearing the Carnoy
craters.  The 7th Royal West Kents were in reserve.

The men never fought more determinedly, or with
cooler understanding of the task to be accomplished, than they did on this day.  And they were
never better led.  Lieutenant D. R. Heaton, who
commanded the right leading company of the Queens,
found their advance checked at the Boche second line,
because from the Boche third line came an unchecked
hail of machine-gun fire.  The Queens had already
suffered heavy casualties ; the company at this period
was unsupported, and there was no communication
with the Norfolks on the left.  The situation was
critical.  Lieutenant Heaton showed what a leader
with initiative and confidence in himself can do.
He organised a bombing party and led them up the
communication trench, and the attack was carried
through with such thrust that the German third
line was cleared, and 163 of the enemy surrendered.
Heaton collected his forces, and two platoons of D
Company, the Buffs, coming to his aid, a dash along
the Montauban-Mametz road was made, and the first
objective was carried.  Captain Neame, O.C. D Company, the Buffs, was killed in this operation.

Five minutes after " going over the top," Lieutenant
C. R. Haggard, who commanded C Company of the
Queens, was wounded in the head.  He lay unconscious for an hour, but afterwards took command
of the remnants of his company, and by 1.45 P.M.
had led them as far as the Montauban-Mametz road
trench.  Then his condition became serious, and he

had to be taken to the rear. There was also 2nd
Lieutenant, now Major, H. J. Tortise, who, on reaching Blind Alley, which he knew to be occupied by the
enemy, took forward a bombing party. So many
bombs had been thrown during the morning that
only one bomb per man could be given out. But
the party captured the trench and twelve Germans
with it. In Montauban itself was a post held by
three machine-guns. For five hours it had held out.
Lieutenant Tortise, who had the Maxse dictum, "Kill
Germans," ingrained in him, made a dash at the position. He and his dozen men got right among the
enemy, bayoneted several of them, and ended in
possession of the post.

The 8th East Surreys were the right assaulting
battalion of the 55th Brigade. It was the East
Surreys who began the battle by kicking a football
as they advanced. As far back as the previous April
this highly unusual, almost bizarre, accompaniment to
an attack was thought of. It sprang from the mind
—always fertile in ideas—of Captain W. P. Neville, a
'Varsity undergraduate who commanded B Company
of the East Surreys. Talk in the mess centred upon
the probable comportment of the men when first they
took part in a big battle. Captain Neville, who held
as vastly important the study of his men's mental and
temperamental characteristics—from the start of the
life in the trenches he had written a sprightly Trench
Gazette and passed it round among his company—exclaimed that he had thought of one way of occupying
his men's minds as they moved over the open to the
enemy lines : he would present each platoon with a
football, and offer a prize to the platoon that first
dribbled its ball into the German trenches. And at
7.30 A.M. on 1st July Captain Neville was himself first
to leave the trench in which his company had assembled,
and first to kick a football in the direction of the enemy.
He was shot before he had gone twenty yards. His
second Captain, Lieutenant R. G. Soames, and the

Company Sergeant-Major, C.S.M. C. Wills, were also killed just outside the German wire. But the quaint whimsical idea had proved to be of real value: the men went on.

Lieut.-Colonel Irwin, Captain C. Janion, then 2nd Lieutenant, and Captain E. C. Gimson, the East Surreys' medical officer, all won the D.S.O. during this attack. On reaching the German lines Janion was the only officer of his company not killed or wounded. His own platoon had been wiped out. He took command of the remnants of the company, led bombing parties down the German trenches, and carried the assault up to the final objective. Captain Gimson worked like one inspired that day. He was a sort of unofficial second in command of the East Surreys. If a junior officer were worried about matters with which he did not want to trouble the Colonel, he would consult " Jimmy." If the Colonel happened to be not quite satisfied with some particular officer, but did not want to interfere officially, he would tell Gimson to have a word with him. On that 1st July Captain Gimson remained three hours in the front-line trenches dressing the wounded. During the afternoon and the whole of the night the trenches occupied by the battalion were shelled incessantly by heavy howitzers. There were very many casualties; but Captain Gimson was tireless, fearless, superb in his devotion. The junction of Mill Trench and Mine Alley proved to be such a death-trap that every occupant of it was killed or wounded. But Captain Gimson went there alone, and remained until he had dressed all the wounded. The East Surreys have never forgotten his heroism during that appalling time.

Here is an instance of good artillery liaison in the early stages of the attack. An F.O.O. reported that the Germans were retiring from Back Trench and falling back upon Montauban Mill. The mill was a formidable position. If the enemy could secure themselves there with machine-guns they would cause

many casualties.   But 2nd Lieutenant Carver, 83rd
Brigade R.F.A., who was liaison officer with the East
Surreys, got a 4·5 battery on to the mill so quickly,
and the shooting was so accurate, that the Germans
had to come out and run, and their machine-guns
were taken.   A party of the Sussex Pioneers did
bombing for the Queens.   Going through the barrage
they did not lose a man, but on occupying a trench
from which the Queens had just moved forward they
lost fourteen men out of thirty-eight.   They were
content, however, because soon afterwards they discovered a Boche post which had escaped capture, and
they took it and brought in seventy prisoners.   The
two small men who escorted the prisoners went down
smoking Boche cigars as big almost as themselves.

And here are two stories that illustrate the splendid
spirit of the men that day.   As Company Sergeant-
Major C. W. Hanks was leaving the front-line trench
his thigh was broken by a bullet, and he fell into the
bottom of the trench.   He shouted to the men, " Never
mind my leg.   Shove me out of the way somewhere."
And he lay there heedless of his pain and of the shells
falling round him, cheering and encouraging the men
as they passed over him.   Lance-Corporal G. Bilson, a
runner, was sent off to the 55th Brigade H.Q. with
the historic message that the East Surreys were on the
final objective at 12.30 P.M.   The corporal did not
return till next morning.   " I noticed," says Colonel
Irwin, " that his clothes and equipment were in tatters,
and that his eyes were crossed in an extraordinary way.
' Where have you been ? ' I asked.   He said he had
delivered his message, and coming back was blown up.
He had only come to himself half an hour before.
But his first thought, you see, had been to report
himself."

The 7th Buffs, who had been given the task of
clearing the Carnoy craters, did nobly, although the
task was a severe one for 2nd Lieutenant Tatam of
B Company and his two platoons.   The 6th Bavarians,

who defended the craters, fought finely, and it was one
and a half hours before their resistance was broken.
It was the crater that saw most of the bayonet
fighting.    Dead British and Boche, in couples, were
found afterwards, each man transfixed by the other's
bayonet.

There was one man, Sergeant P. G. Upton, whom
eye-witnesses credit with killing ten Germans in this
crater fighting.    During the two hours of intense
conflict he led an attack upon a concrete machine-gun
emplacement, and killed all the detachment.    Sergeant
Upton was a small man, full of confidence in himself.    He took his soldiering very seriously.    Once,
after a wire-cutting expedition, when some one in the
platoon pretended to doubt the completion of the task,
Upton went out again in the dark, by himself, and
returned in two hours' time, bringing a piece of the German wire.    He died in 1917 of wounds received in the
ghastly Poelcappelle fighting.    Captain A. G. Ken-
chington, O.C. B Company, who directed the operation of clearing the craters, was the only officer of the
Division who received a French decoration for this
battle.    Three platoons of A Company, the Buffs,
under 2nd Lieutenant Dyson, co-operated with the
East Surreys, occupied the final objective, and remained there until relieved on the following day.

In the centre of the line the 53rd Brigade went
methodically about their task.    By 7.50 A.M. the 8th
Norfolks had passed through Mine support trench,
while the 6th Berks had captured Bund support.

Meanwhile the 54th Brigade, on the left, had pressed
steadily forward to their main objective, the capture
of the Pommiers Redoubt, an outstanding example of
a Boche Somme strong point—a circle of heavily-
wired trenches, mounted with machine-guns and
manned by two companies of Germans, who, sheltering
in the solid, fifty-foot dug-outs in the centre, had a
right to feel safe from our artillery fire.

The assaulting battalions of the 54th Brigade were

the 7th Bedfords on the right, and the 11th Royal
Fusiliers on the left. They were supported by the 6th
Northants, with the 12th Middlesex in reserve. Two
machine-guns went with each assaulting battalion;
while the 54th Trench Mortar Battery had eight guns
in position for hurricane bombardment. As was found all along the line, the enemy was not
holding his front trenches in great strength, although
his machine-guns immediately behind were very well
placed. But although the opening ten minutes went very
well for the 54th Brigade, the assaulting companies moving collectedly and according to plan, they had suffered
heavily when they reached Emden Trench. All the
officers of one company of the Bedfords were casualties
—it was the same company that in the preliminary
bombardment had lost all officers owing to a shell
hitting their mess ; and of another company, only one
officer reached the enemy second line, the sergeants
also being practically wiped out. Machine-guns still
harassed them from the flanking trench, known
as Austrian support. But the preliminary training
had been so thorough that the men remained cool
and undisturbed. In spite of the noise and of their
unaccustomedness to this deadly type of fighting,
the minds of individual men were so set on their own
immediate job that they carried on methodically.
Austrian Trench was rushed by Lance-Corporal A.
Payne of the Fusiliers, and a check, owing to uncut
wire between Bund Trench and Pommiers Trench, was
turned into solid triumph by a party of twenty Bedfords and twenty Berkshires, of the 53rd Brigade, who
joined them. They completed the cutting of the wire
in a cool workmanlike manner, in spite of heavy fire
from the German field-guns. Also, when the enemy,
alive to the check, sought to break into the left
flank of the Fusiliers from the direction of Mametz,
2nd Lieutenant Parr - Dudley wheeled his platoon
half-left, and by most courageous hand-to-hand fighting broke up the assault. Not one of the enemy

escaped.   Lieutenant Parr-Dudley was unfortunately killed.

Pommiers Trench was captured twenty minutes from the opening of the battle, but the 7th Division was held up before Dantzig Alley, while the enemy was still in possession of Fritz Trench, which led into Black Alley, a long trench which the Fusiliers had now reached.   The forty-minute halt arranged to follow the capture of Pommiers Trench proved, therefore, to be no sort of siesta.   The Fusiliers, who fought with spirit judiciously combined with intelligence, dealt with the threat from Fritz Trench in a most effective manner.   Two Lewis guns were sited to command the approach to Fritz Trench.   Then a couple of three-inch Stokes mortars were brought up, and Fritz Trench was pounded with such goodwill that the enemy had to abandon it.

"The men were cool and collected, and apparently very happy," wrote an officer in his letter home a day or two later.   "Several of them were holding little sing-songs; others were shaking hands and wishing their officers good luck.   Numbers of them were puffing huge cigars, while shoals of soda-water bottles were found in the Boche dug-outs."

On the way to Pommiers Trench Private J. Nicholson of the Fusiliers shot six German snipers.   Then, although wounded, he bombed and knocked out a machine-gun which was holding up our advance. Private W. T. Taverner, also a Fusilier, reached a machine-gun in Pommiers Trench, and, unable to get at the German gunner who was barricaded in, stood on top of the emplacement, and braving the Boche snipers, shouted to his companions to scatter right and left—and thus he prevented a number of casualties. A Fusilier signaller, Private J. W. Hughes, had to send an urgent message.   He picked out a white flag, stood on top of the parapet, and although wounded, continued signalling until a shell knocked him unconscious.   There was also the dramatic quickness

in thought and action of Private V. C. Taylor of the
Bedfords. In Pommiers Trench he saw one of our
men going round a traverse. A German was waiting
for him with fixed bayonet. Twelve more Germans
waited behind. Taylor seized the British infantryman
by his equipment and pulled him bodily out of the
trench. Then he bombed the surprised Germans, killing six of them. The others were made prisoners.

The way was now clear for the 54th Brigade's *chef-
d'œuvre*, the taking of Pommiers Redoubt, which rose
up about 400 yards in front of Pommiers Trench. The
Bedfords and the Fusiliers knew that the severity of
the previous fighting would be nothing compared to
what they now would go through. But again the
thoroughness of the behind-the-line rehearsals showed
itself justified. In spite of withering rifle and
machine-gun fire they pressed on. Captain Johnston,
an exceedingly stout fighter who came from railway building in the East to play his part in the war,
carried the assault to within sixty yards of the end of
Black Alley ; but a machine-gun commanded the whole
of the straight piece of trench, and when he rallied his
men and tried to work round behind the redoubt they
suffered casualties from snipers who had them in
full view from Beetle Alley. But again courage and
knowledge of what to do saved the situation. 2nd
Lieutenant Savage headed a party that rushed the
Boche snipers, and the Fusiliers then closed up to the
redoubt. It was, however, 9.30 A.M. before the redoubt
was completely in the hands of the Bedfords and the
Fusiliers, the Germans in the dug-outs being little
disposed to surrender.

The wave of battle passed onwards. Our artillery
barrage lifted off Beetle Alley, which was beyond the
redoubt, and reinforced by the 6th Northants the
Fusiliers and Bedfords seized Beetle Alley. So beaten
was the Boche at this stage that parties of the Bedfords and Fusiliers reached White Trench, a winding
trench that lay nearly 1,000 yards beyond the redoubt,

and within easy distance of Mametz Wood. By 10.20
A.M. the Loop, a trench system running from Pommiers Trench, had been captured by the Norfolks;
while by 11 A.M. the left parties of the 53rd Brigade
were in touch with the 54th Brigade at the north-east
corner of Pommiers Redoubt.

Before noon, however, the Berks found themselves
held up within 75 yards of Montauban Alley, while
the Norfolks had also to fight hard at the junction of
Loop Trench and the Montauban-Mametz road. When
Captain N. B. Hudson, now Lieut.-Colonel Hudson,
came up with a reserve company of the Berks, one of
the two officers with him was killed immediately ; and
Colonel Clay told him that eight other officers of the
battalion had been killed, and that he was to take
charge of the operations on the left flank. The Essex
had also come up to reinforce the Berks and to support
them in their advance towards Montauban Alley. As
they got out of the trenches a small mongrel dog ran
towards Captain Banks. " I patted him," said Captain
Banks afterwards, "and a Boche machine-gun opened
fire, hitting the dog in the leg. We bound the little
fellow up, left him in the trench, and went on."

Steadily the advance of the three brigades continued.
By 1.30 P.M. the 55th Brigade were on their final
objective, and aided by three companies of the 8th
Suffolks were working west along Montauban Alley
towards Loop Trench. The 8th Norfolks had bombed
their way up Loop Trench, and the Berks were in
Montauban Alley. The 54th Brigade held Pommiers
Redoubt and parts of Beetle Alley firmly, but had to
keep in mind that the enemy had not been dislodged
from Fritz Trench on their left flank.

During the afternoon our patrols and detachments
of machine-gunners searched and probed the Boche
support lines towards Caterpillar Wood Valley,
whither the Boche, now soundly beaten, had retired.
By 5 P.M. most of our wounded had been cleared from
the battlefield, and Germans could be seen pulling

guns out of Bazentin towards Longueval, and trickling
reinforcements towards Thiépval and La Boisselle.

By 8 P.M. the Division had received a congratulatory
message from General Congreve, commanding the XIII.
Corps; and in sending out this communication to his
brigades, General Maxse added : " Well done. It's
what I expected. Now hold on to what you have
gained so splendidly."

The Boche prisoners captured that day were nearly
all men of fine physique, well trained, stout of heart,
and unwilling to believe that the British attack could
make much headway. There was evidence that they
did not expect quarter. One young Bavarian, taken
by the 10th Essex, perceived the remains of Carnoy
Church as he was marched from the front trenches ;
and he asked, " Is that where you are going to
bury us ? "

The 18th Division had taken 695 prisoners by nightfall. The Division had suffered 3,707 casualties, including 45 officers killed and 871 other ranks. The
wounded numbered 103 officers and 2,692 other
ranks. But deep satisfaction ruled. The Division
had done well, and knew it. The Boche had been
met and outfought. The hope and trust of Britain
in her New Army had been splendidly vindicated.
The men understood that, and were proud to be able
to assert that the 18th could have taken still more
ground had it not been for the check received by other
Divisions farther north.

The enemy was too occupied during the next three
days to make a serious effort to dislodge the Division
from the ground won. On 3rd July Lieut.-Colonel
F. A. Maxwell, V.C., who in the latter days of June
had come to command the 12th Middlesex—and later
was to show inspiring leadership in Trones Wood and
at Thiépval—reconnoitred nearly two miles in front
of the new line, taking with him a Vickers gun and
its gun team for emergencies. On the night of 4th
July, Captain S. Le F. Shepherd, of the Northants,

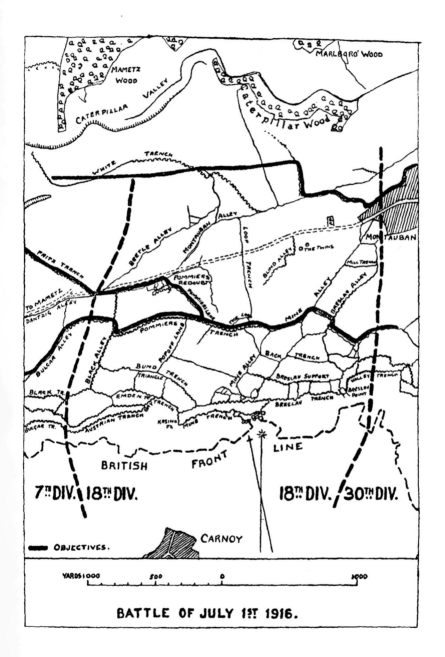

BATTLE OF JULY 1ST 1916.

D

brought in two German field-guns that had been
abandoned 400 yards from White Trench, while the
same morning two companies of the Essex, creeping
stealthily down the hill from Montauban Alley to
Caterpillar Wood, found that the enemy had stolen
away. They learned how comfortable the Germans had
made themselves during their two years' stay. There
were dug-outs with tapestried walls, and easy-chairs,
and grand pianos. And the men helped themselves
with alacrity to silk shirts and well-conditioned cigars
abandoned by the fleeing Boche.

By 8th July the 3rd Division had taken over the
18th Divisional front. The 53rd Brigade settled at
Grove Town, the 54th in Bois de Tailles, and the 55th
at Bronfay Farm.

# CHAPTER IV.

## THE CAPTURE OF TRONES WOOD.

*The newspaper notice at Cox's—The 18th Division Memorial in Trones Wood — Why the capture of the wood was so important — Battalions swallowed up among fallen trees and dense undergrowth —The isolated West Kents—Queens fail to link up—54th Brigade ordered to the attack at 12.25 a.m.—Colonel F. A. Maxwell, V.C., in command—Northamptons and Middlesex sweep through the wood—Sergeant Boulter's V.C.—The West Kents and the "4 to 8" hours' telegram.*

IN D Branch at the Head Establishment of Messrs Cox's Bank at Charing Cross, behind the counter where officers of the Queens, Royal Fusiliers, Oxford and Bucks Light Infantry, West Kents, Scottish Rifles, West Yorks, and some other infantry regiments were wont during the war to conduct their over-the-counter transactions, is a pillar on which up to April 1919 was pasted a strip of paper containing the newspaper headlines, "Forty-eight Hours in Trones Wood: Gallant Stand by the West Kents." The strip had been there since July 1916.

These headlines, as is known now, were not in accord with the ascertained facts—though the newspapers had acted on official information wired from General Headquarters; but they do remain as a reminder of one of the 18th Division's most glowing achievements. On the confines of the battered straggly remnants of Trones Wood stands a granite obelisk. The inscription upon it reads, "To the glory of God and in imperishable memory of the Officers, N.C.O.'s, and Men of the Eighteenth Division

who fell fighting for the sacred cause of liberty in the
Somme Battles of 1916 and 1918." The site of the
monument was well chosen, for upon two cruelly
bloody occasions, once in July 1916, once again in
August 1918, did the 18th Division successfully
strive and endure for possession of the tangled shell-
stricken grove that stands between Caterpillar Valley
and the confusion of shell-holes and broken bricks
that once was Guillemont.

Properly to understand the bitter drama of 13th
and 14th July 1916 and the imperative need for the
capture of Trones Wood, it is well first to read General
Maxse's notes on the Somme situation as it presented
itself on 11th July :—

"Trones Wood had already changed hands several times
during the preceding day. On the 11th the 30th Division
reported that they had taken Trones Wood and were holding
it, but that all three Brigades of the Division had been fighting
desperately during several days, and one was nearly exhausted.
Every one knows that sheer exhaustion is common to all
troops after hours of intense wood fighting, and the 18th
Division was accordingly ordered to send one infantry Brigade
to act as Divisional reserve to the 30th Division in place of
an exhausted Brigade which was withdrawn. The 18th Division had already lost 3300 in casualties on 1st July, but had
had a rest since the 7th of July.

"As Trones Wood was supposed to be securely in our hands,
it was not thought that the Reserve Brigade would be called
upon immediately, and the 55th Infantry Brigade, which had
been longest out of a fight, was moved to Maricourt and
Trigger Wood valley on the morning of the 11th July and
attached to the 30th Division. The task of the 30th Division
was one of great importance in view of contemplated operations—namely, to safeguard the right flank of an attack
northwards by two Army Corps—the XIII. and the XV.—
against the German second-line system of trenches between
Delville Wood and a point north of Contalmaison Villa. This
attack was timed for 3.20 A.M. on 14th July, and it was of vital
necessity that Trones Wood should be securely held on the
flank of the attack. Indeed the success of the battle of the
Somme may be said to have depended upon the retention of
Trones Wood and the trenches between it and Maltzhorn Farm

at that particular moment. With Trones Wood in German
hands the main attack northwards might be seriously delayed.

"It was therefore somewhat disconcerting to the higher
command to learn from the 30th Division on 12th July that
the Germans had retaken all Trones Wood, with the exception
of a small portion of the southern end of it. The result was
that on the evening of the 12th July the 18th Division was
ordered to relieve the 30th Division. The relief was completed by 10 A.M. on the 13th.

"*The 13th Corps Commander's orders were that the 18th
Division must recapture Trones Wood by midnight 13/14th
at all costs.*

"The 55th Infantry Brigade had already relieved the 89th
Brigade of the 30th Division on the line Maltzhorn Farm—
south end of Trones Wood—on the 12th July; it was accordingly detailed to recapture the whole of Trones Wood.

"Also the 12th Battalion Middlesex Regiment and 6th
Battalion Northamptonshire Regiment, both of the 54th
Brigade, were placed at the disposal of the Brigadier 55th
Infantry Brigade in case he should require them. They were
quartered in Maricourt and north of it. At the time the 55th
Brigade were ordered to capture Trones Wood they were
disposed as follows:—

The 7th Buffs, holding a line of trenches from the junction
with the French (just south of Maltzhorn Farm) to near the
southern corner of Trones Wood. The 7th Royal West Kents
occupied the southern end of Trones Wood with two companies, one company (for counter-attack) was in the sunken
road south of the wood, and the fourth company (in battalion
reserve) holding the southern part of Bernafay Wood. The
7th Queens were in support in and about Dublin Trench.
The 8th East Surreys were in Brigade Reserve in Silesia
Trench in the original German system.

"It will be noticed that the above distribution made it
difficult for any Brigadier to collect his C.O.'s and give them
attack orders at short notice. Moreover, owing to heavy
barrages placed on the open ground within the area Briqueterie,
Trones Wood, Maltzhorn Farm, Maricourt, communications
by telephone were constantly cut and visual signalling could
not be rapidly organised. Consequently officers commanding
battalions were unable to make that personal reconnaissance
which every one knew was most desirable. The military
situation demanded instant action without time for forethought
or elaborate preparation.

"Sir Thomas Jackson, the Brigade Commander 55th Infantry Brigade, accordingly issued the following instructions after a conference with the Divisional Commander at 10 A.M. :—

(a) The West Kents to attack from the south and capture the southern half of Trones Wood.

(b) The Queens to relieve a South African battalion in Longueval Alley and attack the northern half of Trones Wood from that place. The dividing line between the Queens and the West Kents in the wood to be the railway running east and west through it.

(c) The Buffs were told to hold the line Maltzhorn Farm, Trones Wood, and to capture strong point A (S.E. end of Trones Wood, see sketch attached). They were also directed to hand over one company to the Queens in Longueval Alley. The Queens were only 280 strong since their fight on 1st July.

(d) The East Surreys (in Brigade Reserve in Silesia Trench) were detailed to carry R.E. Stores to forward dumps, and were subsequently scattered in small parties all over the area of ground occupied by the 55th Infantry Brigade. Their total strength was little more than that of the Queens.

"The time for both attacks to start was 7 P.M., at which hour a bombardment by heavy artillery and field-guns was to lift off Trones Wood. This bombardment was directed specially on the German trench running north and south through the centre of the wood and upon the trench facing Longueval Alley, on the western side of the northern half of Trones Wood.

"In the event of success the West Kents were to consolidate the eastern edge of the southern half of Trones Wood with strong points and machine-guns every hundred yards. The Queens were to consolidate the eastern side of the northern half of the wood with similar strong points and machine-guns.

"The information received from the 30th Division was meagre concerning the local circumstances in Trones Wood. We were given to understand that a line of trenches ran more or less straight from near strong point A through the wood to its western edge. As a matter of fact only a shallow trench with a low parapet was held in patches. It was in this trench that the West Kents relieved a battalion of the 30th Division. The trench was anything but straight. Owing to its irregular trace, troops forming up behind it and marching thence to their front could never reach the north end of the wood. They would inevitably meet one another instead. This was one reason for the many failures to take the wood. Also the German strong-point marked X in the sketch-map broke up formations to such an extent that they probably lost cohesion from the very start. The idea that the Germans had tunnels from Guillemont to Trones Wood, or deep dug-outs holding companies and battalions, is an exploded myth. A much simpler solution is probably the correct one, namely, that stubborn Boches held with great tenacity strong-point A on the east, strong-point X in the centre, and strong-point S on the western edge of the wood. Those of our infantry which came up against these strong-points in the dark were shot at, but those of our troops which passed between them wandered about in a dense jungle of fallen trees and thick brushwood, and lost all notion of their whereabouts. This," continues General Maxse, "is how I account for the fact that Trones Wood swallowed up battalions, that these battalions disappeared and failed to report, and that consequently we were continually capturing and losing the place.

"So much for the southern portion of the wood. The northern portion presented other aspects. Its main defence depended upon Longueval Alley south of the apex and the deep trench in the centre of the wood. When it is realised," concludes the General, "that barrages of fire, both British and German, had been directed upon all parts of the wood for many hours during several days and by all calibres of British and German artillery, some notion may be formed of the difficulties encountered by any battalion which had to attack it, unreconnoitred, in the night."

A tremendous barrage was put up by the Germans, and the general attack launched by the 55th Infantry Brigade at 7 P.M. on the 13th July fared no better than previous attacks by other Brigades. Wave after wave of men came under intense shelling as they moved over the open from the sunken road ; but they kept on. The two attacking companies of the West Kents reached the railway in the centre of the wood, although every yard of the advance had meant casualties.

Being July, the trees were in full leaf. The big trees knocked down by shell fire gave cover to the Boche snipers. The ground was full of slits and holes mostly filled with dead. The situation was indeed such that the very best of troops must have wandered. And, as the men advanced, their formation was further broken up by the Boche strong points previously referred to. Sergeant Roffey, who found himself commanding D Company of the West Kents, came upon Sergeant "Nobby" Clark, A Company, crouching with a few men in a shell-hole. Both Clark's officers had been killed. An excited sergeant rushed up and said warningly, "You've got too many in that hole. One shell will kill the lot."

Even at that nerve-racking moment Sergeant Clark sustained his reputation as humourist. "If you know of a better hole, you had better go to it," was his quick reply.

Sergeant Roffey advancing, found that the left flank of his company was in the air—the Queens had not joined up on the left. On the right, however, he got into touch with Captain Holland, whose company, C Company, was digging in. Captain Holland told him to hold on ; so he posted two Lewis guns to fire along the cutting in the wood made by the railway. In the misty distance Germans could be seen going to and fro across the railway carrying ammunition.

Scattered in small parties in other quarters of the wood, holding on to a long scattered line without communication with the 55th Brigade Headquarters, was a further 130 men of the 7th Royal West Kents, under the Adjutant, Captain Anstruther. "Coats undone is the order of the day, boys," Captain Anstruther had told those with him. And with his own jacket unfastened, a rifle over his shoulder, and a revolver in his hand, he had set the example. In the pleasant days before 1st July Captain Anstruther had been a welcome figure at all West Kent concerts. He was a really talented pianist, and Sir Thomas Jackson and even General Maxse had more than once called at the West Kent's Headquarters to hear him sing. Captain Anstruther's high spirits meant much to his men during that grim night of 13th July in Trones Wood, when the Germans had cut them off from Battalion Headquarters.

Meantime the attack of the Queens on the northern half of the wood had been begun under a concentrated barrage along the whole of the trench between Trones Wood and Bernafay Wood. The losses from machine-guns and rifle fire, as well as from tremendous shell fire, as the men made short dashes across the open ground that led towards the wood, were appalling; and with the exception of a few brave desperate men under Lieutenant B. C. Haggard, who bombed up to the apex of the wood, and remained there for some time with a machine-gun in action, none of the Queens penetrated the western edge of Trones Wood.

The 7th Buffs, who had been ordered to capture the concrete strong point at the south-eastern corner of the wood, had had a hard spell of intensive digging prior to the attack, and some of the men were so worn out when they assembled for the assault that they fell asleep in the trenches within twenty yards of the enemy. But when the order came they forged ahead, and, by the aid of two trench mortars, Lieutenant Hayfield and Sergeant Ashwell worked along the trench that led from the end of the wood to Guillemont, and so on towards the strong-point A. Like the West Kents, they learned that the trees and the undergrowth contained German snipers, and Lance-Corporal Harrison brought down one Boche, who had installed himself in a tree-top, by a very fine piece of shooting. In the waning light men of A and D companies of the Buffs got into the strong-point; but the Boche possessed a good store of reinforcements, and, after hand-to-hand fighting, forced them out again.

By midnight a drizzling rain descended. The Boche gunners continued to shell the wood heavily, not caring apparently if they killed their own men as well

as ours.  Sniping went on all night, and at 12.15 A.M.
the West Kents along the railway were made aware
by a sudden stick-bomb attack that the enemy had
worked round behind them.  "We reversed every
other man, and put in rapid fire," says Sergeant
Roffey, "but creeping up under cover of the fallen
trees Germans got to within ten yards of us.  They
killed Sergeant Batchelor and three men.  Then they
organised attacks in relays, and came at us every
quarter of an hour."

During these confused desperate hours both Divisional and Brigade Headquarters remained without
exact information as to what was happening.  All
telephone wires had been cut; the officer commanding the West Kents, and the 55th Brigade Commander, only knew that a battalion had disappeared
into the wood; that, after their disappearance, strong
German attacks had been launched against our weak
entrenchment at the southern end of the wood; and
that the 55th Brigade could only hold the ground
which it had originally taken over from the 30th
Division.  By midnight the question, what was to be
done in view of the main attack to be undertaken
by the XIII. and XV. Corps at 3.30 A.M., became an
exceedingly serious one.  The XIII. Corps Commander
asked General Maxse on the telephone what he meant
to do.  General Maxse replied that he would relieve
the 55th Infantry Brigade by the 54th Infantry
Brigade; and that he still hoped to get possession
of Trones Wood by the time that the main attack
began.  At 12.25 A.M. on 14th July Brigadier-
General T. H. Shoubridge, C.M.G., D.S.O. (afterwards G.O.C. 7th Division), was told by telephone
that the 54th Brigade would have to capture Trones
Wood.

The situation, therefore, in the dark melancholy
early hours of 14th July, was that the attempt of the
55th Brigade to take Trones Wood had failed; that
General Maxse had guaranteed the capture of the

Wood, which was of such importance for the successful carrying out of the main attack on the German
second lines between Longueval and Bazentin-le-Petit;
and that there could be no question of a postponement
of this larger operation.

On receiving General Maxse's message that the
54th Brigade was to attempt what the 55th Brigade
had failed to achieve, Brigadier-General Shoubridge at
once ordered the 11th Royal Fusiliers and the 7th
Bedfords, who lay in Trigger Valley, to march to
Dublin Trench and Maricourt.  As these two battalions
reached their assembly point, the sky was lit up and
the ground was shaken by an intense German barrage
that descended upon Trones Wood.  The 12th Middlesex
and the 6th Northants, who had been warned that
they would be the attacking troops, were already
gathering in the Sunken Road.

It was still dark, and there was no time for a reconnaissance of the ground over which the men would
advance, so General Shoubridge decided upon the
simplest and most straightforward method of attack.
He resolved to move upon Trones Wood from the
south, from the Sunken Road, and to sweep through
it to the north, and then to establish a defensive flank
east along the eastern edge of the wood.  The attack
would be carried out by the Middlesex, supported by
the Northamptons, who were to "mop-up" and to
establish the defensive flank.  The Fusiliers and Bedfords would be held in readiness to follow up.  As it
was calculated that the assaulting troops could not
reach the railway in Trones Wood before 4.30 A.M.,
it was arranged that the supporting artillery barrage
should not begin before that hour; the barrage was to
start along the railway and move slowly northwards
in front of tho advancing Middlesex.

General Shoubridge made another decision that had
much to do with the ultimate success of an extraordinarily difficult operation.  As had been found by
the 55th Brigade, shell fire made such havoc with the

telephone lines that reliable communication, particularly with Brigade Headquarters, was next to impossible. General Shoubridge accordingly placed Lieut.-Colonel F. A. Maxwell, V.C., C.S.I., D.S.O., in full command of the 6th Northants as well as of his own battalion, the 12th Middlesex. Colonel Maxwell was the Frank Maxwell who won the Victoria Cross at Sanna's Post in the South African War by helping to save the guns of "Q" Battery, R.H.A. In 1900 he became A.D.C. to Lord Kitchener, and afterwards was Military Secretary to Lord Hardinge in India.

In temperament and in every other attribute, physical and mental, Colonel Maxwell was fitted for the task assigned him. In the few weeks that he had had command of the 12th Middlesex, his personality had exerted a tonic effect upon the moral and fighting qualities of the battalion. There was a steely quality in his personal bravery that seemed accentuated by the almost studied tranquillity of his speech and general manner. One story told of him when he was in India before the war strikes those who knew him in France as thoroughly characteristic. A young and not popular officer became noisy and abusive in mess. Maxwell listened in silence for some time, and then saying suddenly "I am tired of this," seized the young man and threw him through the window. Next morning he mentioned casually to the mess steward, "I damaged the window last night. Charge the repairs to me," and made no further reference to the incident. Of not more than middle height, he was, however, well built, and was unmistakably the Regular soldier. He spoke very little at conferences, and probably relied upon personal influence and inspiration in actual battle for the success of his own particular unit. General Maxse, in one of his memorable phrases, described Colonel Maxwell as "my best platoon commander"; and, indeed, at Trones Wood, and later in the triumphant turmoil of Thiépval, Maxwell ran the 12th Middlesex and other battalions

BRIGADIER-GENERAL F. A. MAXWELL, V.C., C.S.I., D.S.O.

that came under him with a direct personal touch
that was peculiar to the man. On that morning of
14th July he went forward about 2.30 A.M. to the
Sunken Road with his revolver in his right hand and
his British Warm over his left arm. " I am going this
night to instil the spirit of savagery into my battalion,"
he told a padre during that walk.

In the Sunken Road he found the Northamptons
ready to move, but only one company of the Middlesex
in position. Of the remaining companies one was
already in Trones Wood, one was on its way from
Dublin Trench, and one was in Bernafay Wood, out of
all touch. Dawn was breaking. The assault could
not be delayed longer. Colonel Maxwell decided,
therefore, to alter the rôles of the two battalions : the
Northamptons were to attack, and the Middlesex, as
they arrived, were to " mop-up " and form the defensive flank.

Major Charrington, who was in command of the 6th
Northants, had gone to the 54th Brigade Headquarters
for final instructions, so when at 4 A.M. the Northants advanced from the Sunken Road across an open
space of a thousand yards or so and entered the south-
west corner of Trones Wood, they were led by Major
Clark. They moved on through a heavy Boche barrage of 5·9's and larger shells, and the shelling was so
severe that it was only by good leading that they
reached the wood. Appreciating the difficulty of
keeping touch amid the bewildering mass of fallen
trees and undergrowth, Major Clark went on ahead of
his company. He did not go many yards before he
was shot down ; and the two leading companies, coming under heavy rifle and machine-gun fire, dashed
forward to the attack on their own initiative.

There were still isolated bodies of the 7th West
Kents in the wood. At first they knew nothing of
the arrival of the Northamptons, and as they were
certain that parties of the enemy had worked round
behind them, it is possible that shots were fired at the

advancing Northamptons in the belief that they
were Germans. "We got our first real intimation at
4.30 A.M.," says Sergeant Roffey of D Company,
"thirty to forty Germans came running towards us
from our rear. I saw one Boche bayoneted by a West
Kent, and we shot most of them after they had dashed
past us. The Northants were behind them then."

By 5 A.M. Major Charrington, who had now come
forward and was commanding the 6th Northants, found
one company bombing its way up a trench which ran
north-east from the south-west corner of the wood
and ended in a strong point about 350 yards inside
the wood. This strong point was holding up the
Northants advance, chiefly by machine-gun fire. Two
other companies of the Northamptons were pushing
through the undergrowth to attack the strong point,
and Captain S. Le Fleming Shepherd, though wounded
in the shoulder, was standing up cheering on his men.

By 6 A.M. determined bombing brought about the
fall of the strong point, and the enemy retreated leaving about fifty dead.

Parties of the Northamptons then advanced farther
into the wood and worked up towards the northern
end of it and down again on the eastern side. They
subsequently lined the southern half of the eastern
edge of the wood.

Meanwhile Colonel Maxwell at his headquarters
near the south-west end of the wood had received no
information as to the progress of the Northamptons,
other than two verbal messages asking for bombs.
Single men, couples of men, and small individual
parties were creeping about firing their rifles, not
really knowing whether they were coming upon
friends or foes. One person who came upon
Colonel Maxwell, lying in the open with shells falling
around him, was Captain Lister of the 55th Field
Ambulance, another of the distinctive figures of the
Division. Lister was consumptive, a frail man,
but possessed of extraordinary vitality and of the

very great gift in a medical officer of being able to decide on the spot the best and safest way of removing the wounded. He stumbled over Colonel Maxwell, who snapped out, "Who are you? What the hell are you doing?" "I'm looking for the Middlesex Headquarters," said Captain Lister. "I am the Middlesex Headquarters," replied Colonel Maxwell. That was practically their first meeting, but when Trones Wood was finally in our hands Colonel Maxwell could report to the Divisional Commander upon the magnificent work done by Lister.

As at 8 A.M. Colonel Maxwell was still ill informed as to the position and especially as to the progress of the Northamptonshire Regiment, he went deeper into the wood himself. At point "D" he found a conglomeration of units, principally West Kents, with some Middlesex and some Northamptons. At point "E" he discovered a group of Northamptons, but he could neither see nor hear anything of the remainder of the battalion. Meanwhile the wood was still being heavily shelled, and from many points, north and east, came the continuous crackle of machine-guns. Colonel Maxwell came to the conclusion that with the exception of the parties he had first seen and the two Middlesex companies he had left at his Headquarters in the south-west corner of the wood, there were no organised units visible, and certainly no units in being strong enough to sweep the wood and push home the attack. He decided therefore to start afresh; to form a line right across the wood, composed chiefly of groups of Middlesex and Northamptons from points "D" and "E"; and then to sweep northwards.

This line moved steadily northwards, beating the woods as it went. Little opposition was met until the railway line was reached, when a Boche machine-gun in strong-point "S," which had not hitherto been noted, opened fire. The strong point was attacked and taken by 70 men; all the Boche defenders were killed and the machine-gun was captured. Colonel Maxwell's line then resumed its advance. Hardly a German was seen among the trees, and no serious opposition was encountered until the second railway line was crossed; then a number of the enemy ran out of the wood on the east side and made for the village of Guillemont. As the enemy broke away they were fired at in the open by Lewis guns of the Northamptons and of the Middlesex, who were now in possession of strong-point "A," which had been captured about 9 A.M. by two platoons of the 7th Buffs and part of a company of the 12th Middlesex. Still moving forward, firing as they advanced, Colonel Maxwell's party reached the apex of the wood; and soon after 9 A.M. Captain Podmore reported that all Trones Wood had been secured. Captain Podmore said afterwards that he counted 600 dead Germans in the north end of the wood.

In a letter to his wife, Colonel Maxwell, describing the drive through the wood, said :—

" I had meant only to organise and start the line, and then get back to my loathsome ditch, back near the edge of the wood, so as to be in communication by runners with the brigade and world outside. But . . . I immediately found that without my being there the thing would collapse in a few minutes. Sounds vain, perhaps, but there is nothing of vanity about it, really. So off I went with the line, leading it, *pulling* it on, keeping its direction, keeping it from its hopeless (and humanly natural) desire to get into a single file behind me, instead of a long line either side.

"Soon I made them advance with fixed bayonets, and ordered them, by way of encouraging themselves, to fire ahead of them into the tangle all the way. This was a good move, and gave them confidence. . . . The Germans couldn't face a long line offering no scattered groups to be killed, and they began to bolt, first back, then, as the wood became narrow, they bolted out to the sides, and with rifle and automatic guns we slew them.

" Right up to the very top this went on, and I could have

TRONES WOOD.

had a much bigger bag, except that I did not want to show my people out of the wood, or too much out, for fear of letting the German artillery know how we had progressed, and so enable them to plaster the wood *pari passu* with our advance. . . .

"And finally the job was done, and I was thankful, for I thought we should never, never get through with it."

It was during the sweep towards the apex of the wood that Sergeant Wm. E. Boulter of the 6th Northants won the V.C. The official account of his action reads :—

During the capture of Trones Wood one company and a portion of another company was held up by a machine-gun which was causing heavy casualties. Sergeant Boulter, realising the situation, with complete disregard of his personal safety and in spite of being severely wounded in the shoulder, advanced alone across the open in front of the gun under heavy fire and bombed the team from their position, thereby saving the lives of many of his comrades and materially assisting the advance which eventually cleared Trones Wood.

Sergeant Boulter, afterwards Lieutenant Boulter, was before the war in the haberdashery department of the Co-Operative Stores at Kettering. It was always difficult to persuade him to describe his exploit. As a rule, all he would say was that he had with him that morning a revolver that kept going off, and so he killed Germans.

One of the N.C.O.'s, Corporal E. Radley, while out reconnoitring, ran into a party of four Germans; he went for them with his bare fists, knocked one out, returned and reported to his officer, and then took out a party of bombers and dealt very satisfactorily with the remaining Germans.

Another man, Private J. F. Norris, came across two Germans with a machine-gun; he ordered them out of their shell-hole, shot them when they refused, and though fired on heavily brought in the machine-gun. But the confused fighting in Trones Wood was full of such personal incidents. It was an operation that tested the resource and the personal courage of every one engaged in it.

The enemy made no attempt to retake the wood, but he subjected the whole of it to an incessant and heavy shelling by guns of large calibre. In another letter, quoted in the volume 'Frank Maxwell : a Memoir and some Letters,' published by Mr Murray, Colonel Maxwell describes the three days and nights during which the 54th Brigade held the wood under murderous and ceaseless shell-fire.

"Having cleared the shambles of live Germans, or practically so, I had then to think of keeping what we had got with the utterly tired men. Poor things, they thought, as one always does, that having done one job, somebody else would pop up and do the next, but there was nobody else; every man in the wood was now needed to cram on to the edge facing the Germans to hold it against them—in fact, far more than were available.

"Having roughly placed them in position, I then made for my starting-point, attempting to pass through the wood in doing so. And in that I learnt a lesson, which was valuable for the rest of the period we were in it. For I completely lost my way, adjutant and orderly with me. It was a black, clouded day, and smoke of shells hung over the shattered tree-tops—those that had tops! And we simply seemed to walk in circles round and round incredibly horrible débris, amongst which were sights to make one weep; men were wounded and lying there, some for days, unbandaged and with every sort of shattered limb. One could only do what one could for the moment—bandage till they ran out, water till that ran out, and tell them we should send for them, but all the time knowing that if we were losing our way in Hell, we should never be able to lead or direct anybody else to bring them in, even if there were any available to send. . . . I met the Northants doctor coming in, but he was killed a few yards after passing. . . . The Middlesex doctor told me he had found a man wounded five days previously, and still alive, and thought he might live.

" . . . Very shortly after I got back, I suppose at about 7 P.M., the Germans learnt of our presence all over the wood, and then came their artillery. And didn't it come! And

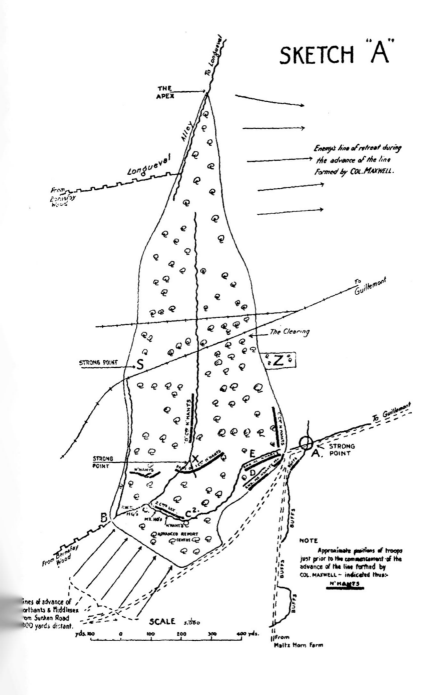

SKETCH "A"

Enemy's line of retreat during
the advance of the line
Formed by COL. MAXWELL.

NOTE

Approximate positions of troops
just prior to the commencement of the
advance of the line formed by
COL. MAXWELL ~ indicated thus:-

N'HANTS

SCALE 1/5.000

yds. 100    0    100    200    300    400 yds.

lines of advance of
Northants & Middlesex
from Sunken Road
300 yards distant.

what an inferno from then to midnight, when it shut down
dead after knocking everything to pieces, and laying out a
number of my people.

"A dead German's greatcoat outside and a tin of bully
beef from one of our poor dead fellows inside, made amends
for an otherwise poor night.

"Next day, 15th, we endured intermittently violent hates
from 6 A.M. onwards, with an occasional terrific onslaught,
winding up with a snorter from 9 P.M. till midnight.

"Next day, 16th, much the same, except that heavy rain was
added to the bright surroundings, and a real winner of a bombardment from 9.15 to 12.30, which fairly made things hum,
and necessitated my making the men "stand to" (absolute
readiness to attack) in case it prefaced a big attack to turn
us out.   At 6 P.M., told we should be pulled out of the line,
and relieved by a bantam battalion, Cheshires, and not long
after their colonel arrived during a rain and shell storm. . . .
I got in at 6 A.M., unwashed and unshaven since morning of
13th, and my exterior marvellously filthy with mud and
grime.   Just very soon I shall go and sleep and make up the
shortage of the last four nights, during which I had somewhat less than three hours' sleep as a grand and poor total."

On 14th July the 53rd Infantry Brigade moved up
in support, while the wood was held by the 54th
Infantry Brigade, till relieved by troops of the 30th
Division at 3.30 A.M. on 17th July.   General Maxse
in his report gives great credit to Brigadier-General
Shoubridge for the manner in which he set about and
carried out a task which had already absorbed the
efforts of four Brigades without complete success.
"No praise," continues General Maxse, "is too high
for the gallantry and determination shown by the 6th
Battalion Northamptonshire Regiment and the 12th
Battalion Middlesex Regiment, who finally wrested
the wood from the Germans.   The Northamptons lost
15 officers and about 300 other ranks, and the Middlesex 7 officers and about 300 other ranks.   It will in
no way detract from the merits of this operation, so
successfully carried out by the 54th Infantry Brigade,
to give also a word of praise to the brave men of the
7th Battalion Royal West Kent Regiment, who

through the night of 13th-14th July maintained their
position in isolated parties in the wood in which also
were a large number of Germans."

In the official report to Corps it was mentioned that
these men of the West Kents had been in the wood
from four to eight hours.    By the time that that
official report reached London the telegraph had transformed " four to eight hours " into " forty-eight hours."
Hence the splendid but mistaken publicity given at
the time to the West Kents, at the expense of the
other battalions who made history for the 18th Division on that unforgettable night.

The total casualties of the 54th and 55th Brigades
were—officers killed, 21 ; wounded, 55 ; other ranks
killed, 206 ; wounded, 1,245.

# CHAPTER V.

## DELVILLE WOOD.

*A glorious page in the 53rd Brigade's history—Two days and nights against Boche counter-attacks—" Not a single man faltered "— Death of Major Markes—The Padre to the 10th Essex—Captain Ackroyd, Medical Officer of the Berks, a heroic figure.*

TRONES WOOD has imperishable memories of 1916 for the 54th and 55th Brigades; Delville Wood, a spot of similar strategic value half a mile north of Trones, and chiefly associated by the ordinary public with the South African Brigade, fills a glorious and mournful page in the records of the 53rd Brigade. Five days after Trones had been retaken by the 54th Brigade, the 53rd Brigade were sent to recapture the southern half of Delville Wood, when the South African Brigade had been forced out of it. On the morning of 19th July Brigadier - General Higginson's Brigade fought their way into Delville, and for two days and two nights remained dug in and held the ground they had gained against furious and continuous counter-attacks and under appalling shell-fire. Delville Wood was the grave of the 53rd Brigade as it was constituted when it landed in France : the casualties amounted to 12 officers killed and 39 wounded, and 181 other ranks killed and 773 wounded. Like Trones Wood, Delville Wood was a triumph of individual bravery and resource — particularly on the part of the non-commissioned officers.

The Division, after the hard fighting since 1st

July, had calculated upon a lengthy period out of the line, and was indeed preparing for it, when at 7 P.M. on 18th July a telephone message from the XIII. Corps demanded the immediate despatch of a brigade to assist the 9th Division. The 53rd Brigade, which had been relieved from the task of guarding Trones by the 105th Infantry Brigade of the 35th Division, at once marched to Talus Boisé, and, coming under the orders of the 9th Division, learned that the northern part of the battered village of Longueval and all Delville Wood, with the exception of the south-west corner, had been lost by the South African Brigade. The 53rd Infantry Brigade was to recapture these positions at dawn next day. General Higginson pointed out that it would be impossible to get the Brigade up in time, and ultimately it was decided that the attack should take place as soon as the Brigade was ready, and that the artillery barrage should be put on by the 9th Division.

The general scheme for the recapture of the wood was as follows : The 8th Battalion Norfolk Regiment were to clear the wood south of Princes Street—a drive that ran east to west through the wood—and, as soon as this was done, the other three battalions of the 53rd Brigade were to attack northward—the 10th Essex on the right and the 6th Royal Berks in the centre. The 8th Suffolks were to clear Longueval village on the left.

It was arranged that the O.C. of the Norfolks should inform Brigade Headquarters of the hour at which he would be ready for the artillery barrage to be put on. The hour was provisionally settled for 6.15 A.M. on 19th July; but subsequently this hour had to be altered, and it was not until 7.15 A.M. that the attack could be launched. A message to this effect was sent to Brigade Headquarters, but it was not received until 7.51 A.M.; consequently no artillery support was arranged for, and the attack proceeded without it.

There was only one entrance into the wood on the south side, and the way from Longueval to this entrance was under direct machine-gun fire, which became so intense that the Norfolks, who were in front, could not at first get into the wood, although subsequently they managed slowly to clear the ground south of Princes Street and work as far eastwards as Buchanan Street. The holding up of the Norfolks delayed the 10th Essex, who were behind them. Colonel Scott, commanding the 10th Essex, pushed on through the Norfolks with his battalion head-quarters party and got into the wood. His signalling officer, Lieutenant L. Bird, was shortly afterwards instructed to join him in the wood with six runners. There was such a galling fire to be passed through at the cross-roads at Longueval, that Lieutenant Bird arrived with only one runner; two had been killed and three wounded.

The other battalions followed the Norfolks and the Essex into the wood, and the men had to run in singly under withering machine-gun fire and shelling, which increased in severity once the attack had been launched. "I did not, however, see a single man falter," says Colonel N. B. Hudson, who at that time was a company commander in the Berkshires. The tremendous shell-fire having cut off the battalions from communication with Brigade Headquarters, General Higginson sent Major J. C. Markes, his Brigade Major, and Lieutenant Neild, the Brigade Intelligence Officer, to investigate the situation. Major Markes was, how-ever, hit in the chest and killed soon after passing through Longueval.

The fighting was of the confused and individual nature that had characterised the struggle in Trones Wood. The Norfolks pushed on east of Buchanan Street, and a considerable number of the enemy were killed by Lewis guns and grenades, the remainder retiring to the south-east corner of the wood. By

1.30 P.M. the Norfolks had cleared the whole of the
wood south of Princes Street, and the Essex, Berkshire, and Suffolks started to attack northwards.
Little progress was made with this advance owing to
exceedingly heavy machine-gun fire, and at 5 P.M. all
four battalions were ordered to halt where they were
and dig themselves in. In Longueval the Suffolks
had not been able to progress farther than the cross-
roads in the middle of the village. So the battalions
dug themselves in, and for two nights held on to what
they had gained. It was two days and two nights of
the grimmest kind of warfare, for the Boche shelling
did not cease, and the enemy poured in reinforcements
in desperate attempt to recapture the stretch of
tangled undergrowth and shell-smitten trees that he
had lost. The wood was littered with wounded and
dying men, hundreds of them—men of the South
African Brigade as well as 53rd Brigade men, and
Germans too. There was great difficulty with regard
to water. There was only one well in the wood, and
that was close to where the enemy was strongest;
while the Berkshires received no food supplies the
whole of the time they were in the wood. The hand-
to-hand fighting between small parties of men was of
so desperate a nature, and the German attacks were so
persistent, that non-combatant David Randell, padre
to the 10th Essex, who was with Colonel Scott and
the battalion headquarters party, armed himself with
a rifle to be ready for all emergencies. Colonel Scott
was hit in the head by a piece of shell and was caught
by his Adjutant, Captain R. A. Chell, as he fell down
the steps of a dug-out; Lieut. J. D. Archibald of
the Essex was mortally wounded; and Lieutenants
Byerley, Bird, and Pinder-Davis were hit. The 10th
Essex lost 200 other ranks in this engagement, and
the other battalions of the brigade lost as heavily.
Captain Hudson of the Berks, in private's uniform, was
talking to the Regimental Sergeant-Major; a Boche

sniper saw them and killed the Sergeant - Major. Captain Hudson had a second escape when a bullet passed through his tin hat. One of the South African Brigade, a Scot, who was picked up by the Essex, had been lying out for five days with a broken leg, a smashed arm, and a hole in his back. While he was being carried down to the dressing-station another piece of shell struck him in the head; but in the long-run he was removed safely to the rear.

When Colonel Scott had been taken away, Captain A. S. Tween took command of the Essex, and his work during those two days stamped him as a leader of men. "His character rose to wonderfulness," says Padre David Randell. Chell, the Adjutant, and that man of tranquil temperament, "Willie" Hunt, also showed up nobly. The 6th Berks had one of their battalion taken prisoner for the first time in the war in Delville Wood. They claim that they only lost nine men in that way during the whole war—before the 6th was disbanded.

Captain Ackroyd, the medical officer of the Berks, was a heroic figure during those two days. The fighting was so confused and the wood so hard to search that the difficulties of evacuating the wounded seemed unconquerable. But Captain Ackroyd, be-spectacled and stooping, a Cambridge don before he joined the forces, was so cool, purposeful, and method-ical, that he cleared the whole wood of wounded, British and Boche as well. Later, he was to do more magnificent work, to win the Victoria Cross, and to sacrifice his life while tending the dying on a Flanders battlefield.

It was a shattered 53rd Brigade that was relieved on the night of the 21st-22nd July by the 4th Royal Fusiliers and other battalions. The whole of Delville Wood was not yet in British hands; almost a month passed before it was completely cleared of Germans. But the 53rd Brigade had hung on to the ground it had gained.

August was spent in a quiet part of the line in front of Armentières, and there was intensive training. Then, early in September, the Division returned to the Somme, to carry out a very big undertaking indeed, the assault and capture of Thiépval and Schwaben Redoubt.

# CHAPTER VI.

## THE TAKING OF THIÉPVAL, 26TH SEPTEMBER 1916.

"The capture of Thiépval village and Schwaben Redoubt were distinct and important episodes even in a great European war. They involved in each case a deliberate assault and the capture of a considerable depth of intricate trenches defended by stubborn regiments who had held the ground against many previous attacks. After visiting the ground at leisure and in peace, I am to this day lost in admiration at the grit shown by the British battalions which fought continuously from 26th September to 5th October, and conquered such strongholds as Thiépval and Schwaben."—Lieut.-General Sir IVOR MAXSE.

*A memorable exploit at one time ascribed to the Canadians—Unsuccessful attempts on 1st July 1916 and afterwards—Wurtembergers pledged to hold Thiépval to the death—General Maxse's battle message—18th Division attack launched at midday—Colonel Frizell arrives to command the 10th Essex—General Higginson's ruse to dodge the German barrage—Fine advance of the 8th Suffolks: "Glued to our barrage"—53rd Brigade's 1,000 yards' advance—Colonel F. A. Maxwell, V.C., and the 12th Middlesex reach Thiépval Chateau—A tank's timely arrival—Colonel Ripley of the 6th Northamptonshires mortally wounded—Two Victoria Crosses won by the 12th Middlesex, one by the Bedfordshires—Fusiliers fire a dug-out to get Germans out—53rd and 54th Brigades consolidate for the night—Outpost fighting in the dark—The night relief by the 7th Bedfords, and an attack next morning—Second Lieutenant Adlam's V.C.—His whirlwind bombing attack—Thiépval completely captured—Germans' 3,000 casualties—Haig's congratulations.*

BEFORE the war Thiépval was an ancient sleepy village, perched on a plateau 500 feet up, with a church and a chateau, roomy barns, and snug, red-tiled cottages. In the summer the people of Albert made it a place for Sunday afternoon pilgrimages.

When on 26th September 1916 the 18th Division took it, the shelling had pounded this pleasant, peace-

ful place into a waste of churned-up earth, tree-stumps,
shell-holes filled with green stagnant water. A brick
left standing upon another brick was something to
be noted. The winding trenches wrested from the
Germans were knee-deep with oozy, greasy mud.

To this day Thiépval remains shapeless and desolate, overrun by grass and weeds ; here and there
traces of the defence works that the German invader
built ; here and there the graves of British and
German soldiers. Bloody and desperate were the
struggles that took place on this spot of tragic,
affrighting memories.

The Thiépval position was undoubtedly one of the
main pivots of the whole northern section of the
German defence on the Western front, and with it
should be included Schwaben Redoubt, which lay on
the ridge about a thousand yards to the north and to
the rear of Thiépval. French military opinion adjudged
the capture of Thiépval to be one of the chief exploits
of 1916. In England the kudos for a long time went
to the Canadians, not to the English troops of the
18th Division. Sir Ivor Maxse tells how, soon after
Thiépval had fallen, he called upon a neighbouring
Canadian Division. The Canadian General was out,
but to a young staff officer General Maxse mentioned
that the Canadians were being credited with the
taking of Thiépval. The young officer's face lighted
up, and he said quickly : " Oh ! but you don't understand, sir. That's propaganda. We are Colonials.
We have to be credited with everything."

The gallant Ulster troops had attempted the
Thiépval position on 1st July, attacking from the
western face, in vain ; for in spite of all their eagerness
and dash, in spite of the fact that they actually got to
Schwaben Redoubt, it was impossible for them to
maintain themselves there, and on the second day of
the battle they were perforce compelled to relinquish
what they had won at so great cost, and the advance
posts were withdrawn. The progress of the fighting

during the following weeks made it possible for the
18th Division, when their time came, to launch the
attack from the south instead of from the west, which
made by far the more practicable operation.

The three weeks' battle training in the Third Army
area came to an end on the 8th of September, from
which date the division formed part of the Second
Corps under the command of Lieut.-General C. W.
Jacob, C.B. To the II. Corps and the Canadian
Corps was assigned the task of capturing the whole
ridge running from the north-west of Courcelette to
the Schwaben Redoubt, a ridge which provided the
enemy with his last remaining observation points over
the Albert area. No sooner had the 18th Division
arrived than the work of preparation for the attack
was begun. Arrangements were made by which all
company, battalion, and brigade commanders might
become familiar with the ground over which operations
were likely to be carried out. By the help of motor-
cars and motor-buses parties of officers were carried
everywhere, and came to know the ground and all
approaches and peculiarities most thoroughly. At
the request of General Maxse, a lecture was given
to brigade and battalion commanders by Brigadier-
General P. Howell, General Staff, at Corps Headquarters, on the local situation and on recent fighting
experiences on this front. "To a division arriving
fresh from Flanders such a lecture," declares General
Maxse, " was of inestimable value, and several battalion
commanders told me afterwards that it made them
put life and intelligence into the work of preparation.
They felt they were being trusted, and liked being
placed in direct touch with the Corps Commander's
Chief Staff Officer on reaching new ground. At any
rate the result was excellent, for when orders did
come out every battalion and each company realised
the importance of Thiépval and the high ground about
Schwaben, and was determined to take both. Moreover, Brigadier-General Howell possessed in a special

degree the art of imparting his thought, and his subsequent loss was deeply felt in the Division."

On the 25th September the Headquarters of the 18th Division were moved to Hedauville, where they remained until 6th October. The field artillery of two divisions, the 25th and the 49th, were allotted to the 18th Division for the attack, as its own artillery had previously been attached to the 1st Canadian Corps (Tara Hill). One battery of 6-inch howitzers was placed by the II. Corps at the direct disposal of General Maxse, and the Corps artillery devoted special attention to the demoralisation and isolation of the main strongholds, Zollern Redoubt, Stuff Redoubt, Thiépval, and Schwaben Redoubt. Certain German trenches marked down for our own occupation, and certain communication trenches in the enemy lines, were carefully exempted, as far as possible, from destruction. Four tanks were allotted to the Division, one of which was to do yeoman service at a critical point in the attack on the Chateau.

On 21st September the trenches for the attack were taken over from the C.R.E., 49th Division, and Colonel Lotbinière at once set to work to organise them. He found the front-line trenches in very bad order, and only one communication trench—Prince Street—which was barely passable by day. The 79th, 80th, and 92nd Field Companies of the Engineers, and the 8th Royal Sussex Pioneers, were employed on the job, and with them the 7th Queens and the 8th East Surreys belonging to the 55th Brigade, which was to stay in reserve at Crucifix Corner east of the Ancre. They dug two assembly trenches for the 53rd Brigade and three for the 54th Brigade, in all about 2500 yards, making all possible use of existing trenches, as well as the communication trenches, Pip Street, running from Wood Post to the assembly trenches for the 53rd Brigade, and Fifth Avenue for the 54th Brigade, which had to be improved and connected with Prince Street. The Germans' old front line was also dug out and turned into a communication trench from the Quarry to our front. Dumps were laid down, and a great deal of necessary work was carried out by way of improving existing trenches, deepening them, and putting down grids, &c., &c. All this was done in the four nights previous to the assault, and required highly intensive digging on the part of the men, who rose magnificently to the occasion, knowing that the success of the attack depended greatly on their efforts. They were very tired on the morning of the attack, but did splendid work during its progress, consolidating various points after capture and improving and making communications. The road from Authuille to Thiépval was cleared, and a brushwood screen put up along its whole length. This road was at once taken into use and proved absolutely invaluable for bringing up rations and stores and for taking back wounded. Thanks to the screen, it was very little shelled, though always crowded and within easy observation by the enemy.

With the usual Maxse thoroughness the attack was prepared, and the men trained and practised with the utmost care and precision. It was General Maxse's firm doctrine that "without proper preparation the bravest troops fail and their heroism is wasted. With sufficient time to prepare an assault on a definite and limited objective I believe a well-trained division can capture almost any 'impregnable' stronghold." Impregnable the Germans considered Thiépval, and for two years it had proved so in the face of several stout assaults. From the very beginning it had been held by the 180th Regiment of Wurtembergers, who were so much identified with the place that they were given it in permanent charge; instead of being relieved and sent to other parts of the front they were allowed to arrange their own reliefs company by company, using Bapaume as their rest camp. The men actually in Thiépval were survivors of the original first-line troops of the German army, high in spirit, intensely proud of their record and their regiment, of splendid physique, and pledged to hold Thiépval to the death.

Under the heavy bombardments hurled upon it the village had been sadly battered, but the apple orchard still formed an advance work before it, and at the southern point there was still the pile of bricks that marked the chateau, which had been in the possession of a German tenant, and under which it was said huge cellars had been made before the war. From these cellars as a centre there radiated an enormous and complicated system of tunnels used as storehouses and shelters. From the middle of the village there ran a sunken road—lined with dug-outs—up to the cemetery, and all round the chateau there lay immensely deep and strong dug-outs, while along the original enemy front line facing to the west there were no fewer than 144 deep dug-outs marked on a German map that we captured. The whole made a most formidable system of defences, and in the keeping of a tough and determined enemy such as the Wurtembergers it promised to be an exceedingly hard nut to crack. Still General Maxse's message went round on the evening of 25th September : " *The* 180*th Regiment of Wurtembergers have withstood attacks on Thiépval for two years, but the* 18*th Division will take it to-morrow.*"

Zero hour on the 26th was fixed for 12.35 P.M., a very notable point, as the usual practice was to attack at dawn. In General Maxse's view the proper plan was to make zero hour four hours after dawn *at earliest*, much later whenever possible, and as a general rule to calculate it backwards from sunset. Roughly speaking, he wanted to have troops allowed not more than two or three hours daylight in their final objective to start their work of consolidation ; then they should work all night in the dark, in this way avoiding exposure to "observed" barrages. In the three days before zero hour a tremendous bombardment was directed against the whole position—

F

the artillery of the II. Corps firing 60,000 rounds of field artillery, and 45,000 rounds of heavy, ammunition; also on the night of the 24th Thiépval was heavily gassed.

The 53rd Brigade was in touch with the 11th Division on the right of the assault, and the 54th Brigade was on the left of the 53rd. The assaulting battalions of the 53rd were the 8th Suffolks (Lieut.-Colonel G. V. W. Hill, D.S.O.) on the right and the 10th Essex Regiment (Lieut.-Colonel C. W. Frizell, M.C.) on the left. Colonel Frizell, who for over two years was to be the heart and soul of the 10th Essex, had only come to the battalion on 18th September. He went to the war with the 1st Royal Berkshires in the original Expeditionary Force as battalion machine-gun officer. At Loos he was in command of his battalion. Prior to coming to the 10th Essex he had been a few weeks in command of a battalion of the Wiltshire Regiment. He had had the proper fighting training to fit him to command a battalion in the 18th Division. He was young, likeable, and forceful. After September 1918 he became a Brigadier in the 25th Division.

The 8th Norfolks (Lieut.-Colonel H. G. de L. Ferguson, D.S.O.) supported the two leading battalions, and found the necessary parties for clearing up German dug-outs, for organising forward dumps, and for furnishing escorts for two tanks that started on the right flank of the brigade. The 6th Royal Berks (Lieut.-Colonel B. G. Clay, D.S.O.) were in brigade reserve dug-outs near Crucifix Corner ready to move forward at zero hour. Where "Pip" Street crossed the old German front line, General Higginson stood to say a word to every man of his brigade that passed. The General was on his way back from his last reconnaissance before battle.

Precisely at 12.35 the barrage started — heavy shrapnel firing so deafening that no one could even hear himself speaking, and the first waves of the assault moved out and forward across No Man's Land at a slow walk.  The distance to the German trenches was about 250 yards, and the barrage "lifts" were to move at the rate of 100 yards in three minutes to begin with, speeding up to 100 yards in two minutes when the shelled area was passed.

By a clever ruse General Higginson's men dodged the German barrage that was expected in our trenches after the zero hour.  Instead of filling up his assembly and Hindenburg trenches automatically as our front waves rolled forward, General Higginson deliberately left these trenches empty.  Soon after zero they were heavily shelled, but without causing any casualties to the reserve battalion, while the assaulting battalions got well away into No Man's Land, and their waves adjusted distances according to previous instructions.  When the enemy barrage ceased the reserve battalion moved rapidly forward over the open in small columns.  By this well-thought-out method General Higginson undoubtedly saved the brigade what might well have been serious losses.

On the extreme right of the Division the Suffolks pushed forward steadily, and from Joseph Trench there emerged a number of Germans running towards them through our barrage, half-dressed, unarmed, hands well up, yelling and shouting, far gone in sheer terror, with only one idea—to surrender as quickly as possible.  The Suffolks took no notice of them, and ultimately they became prisoners.  Others of the enemy came out of the trenches, presumably with the same intention, started, hesitated, and then ran back to their own trenches, though most of them were shot on the way.  But they were by no means typical, and the Suffolks, as they went on, "glued to the barrage," found a very stiff resistance in Schwaben Trench, Zollern Trench, and Bulgar Trench.  For all that they went straight on to their objective without flinching, until a cross fire from rifles and machine-guns in Medway Trench, which was

within the area assigned to the 33rd Brigade (11th
Division), brought their progress to a standstill at
2.30 P.M. Many prisoners were now being sent down
to the rear, and General Maxse pays a special tribute
to the "discipline, steadiness, and fighting qualities
öf the Suffolks. They moved and fought with a precision which greatly impressed artillery and other
close observers."

A small party under 2nd Lieutenant S. H. Mason
even reached a point well in advance of the battalion,
and started to dig themselves in under heavy fire
from Medway and Bulgar Trenches. They hung on
till 6.30 P.M., though Mason was killed and several of
his men were killed and wounded.

It is worth noting that the reserve company of the
Suffolks reached No Man's Land in good time without
a single casualty, thanks to judicious leading and care
with regard to the enemy barrage.

On the left of the Suffolks the 10th Essex had
also reached their objective, just beyond Thiépval
village, well up to time and without serious losses,
though not without a good deal of miscellaneous
fighting in all the trenches. The enemy machine-
guns on their side of the village appeared, however,
to have been dominated or destroyed by our artillery.
During the hour's halt on this objective the reserve company of the Essex arrived, having given
substantial help on the way to the company of the
Norfolks that was engaged in clearing dug-outs of
fighting Germans in the rear of the assault.

The padre of the 10th Essex, David Randell, went
over the top with the second wave. The Boche
machine-gun fire was now at its hottest. The padre
and his party dropped flat, crawled into a shell-hole,
and then worked their way to another shell-hole.
Soon after, the padre, working forward, startled three
young Germans who had a machine-gun in a shell-
hole.

"I said 'pastor,'" says Randell, "and they looked

at my badge and black tabs.   One of them who spoke
English a bit told me he had been to London.   Then
more men of the 10th Essex came along, and the
three were taken prisoners.   I got a saw-bayonet as
a trophy."

A brave N.C.O., Sergeant Seeley of the 10th Essex,
dealt with one German bomb-stop, and then tried to
take another.   He was knocked down and bayoneted
three times in the legs, but got away with the help
of his men, and assisted in holding the bomb-stop first
captured.

So far so good : the 53rd Brigade had reached its
objective and made good everything to a depth
of about 1,000 yards, and had done it by sticking close
behind its barrage.   On its left it was in touch with
the Middlesex right, but when the arranged hour's
halt ended and the brigade pushed forward towards
Schwaben Redoubt, its final objective, it was found
practically impossible to go on, as the north-west corner
of Thiépval had not yet been cleared by the 54th
Brigade, and the Essex were held up by every kind
of fire from this area.   A heavy fire was poured into
the assaulting companies from Martin and Bulgar
Trenches, and they were also enfiladed by machine-
guns, so that although they actually advanced 150
yards, the battalion came to a standstill after suffering
numerous casualties.   Gallant efforts throughout the
afternoon to bomb a way forward were unsuccessful, and at 8.30 P.M. the Essex were ordered to consolidate the positions already gained and await further
instructions for attacking Schwaben Redoubt.

In the meantime the 54th Brigade had moved out
at zero to assault the Thiépval position.   Their task
was one of enormous difficulty, and the frontage of
their attack was accordingly restricted to 300 yards.
Their final objective was 1,800 yards away, and
included the capture of the whole of the enemy
original front-line system of trenches and dug-outs
covering Thiépval from attack from the west.   As

the various strong points in this system were practically immune from shell-fire, it was plain that unless the left flank were effectually cleared the attack of the 18th Division must fail.

In these circumstances General Shoubridge assigned to the 12th Middlesex, under Lieut.-Colonel Maxwell, V.C., the task of capturing Thiépval village, and to the 11th Royal Fusiliers, under Lieut.-Colonel C. C. Carr, the task of capturing and clearing the German network of trenches and dug-outs on the left flank (as well as clearing the dug-outs behind the Middlesex, for which job " C " company was detailed). The 6th Northants, under Lieut.-Colonel G. E. Ripley, were to move up in close support of both Middlesex and Fusiliers. The 7th Bedfords, under Lieut.-Colonel G. D. Price, were posted in dug-outs in Thiépval Wood and its neighbourhood so as to be close up and available.

Both battalions got away well close to the barrage. Five minutes later the German barrage fell on our forming-up trenches, but these were empty, as it had been arranged to correct distances in No Man's Land, and only the left of the line (chiefly " A " and " B " Companies of the Fusiliers) was affected. First of all the Fusiliers struck the enemy, coming on a strong point where Brawn Trench joined the old German front line. Here " D " Company was held up as well as the left flank of the Middlesex, and the place was only captured after a most desperate resistance and hand-to-hand fighting, in which Captain Thompson and Lieutenant Maill-Smith were killed and Lieutenant Cornaby wounded. Here many Germans were killed and twenty-five sent back as prisoners, and " D " Company pushed on along the trenches up to a point abreast of the chateau, fighting and overcoming parties of Germans coming up out of their dug-outs by the help of the two Lewis guns that had been brought along. This hard fighting had delayed progress, so that the barrage could not be followed

up closely, but meanwhile the 12th Middlesex
had carried line after line of trenches until they
reached the chateau, where one company was
checked by deadly machine-gun fire. Just at this
critical moment the leading tank came up, having
crossed over from Thiépval Wood, and its arrival
was most opportune, as it dealt with the enemy
machine-guns; and the leading companies of the
Middlesex passed determinedly round both flanks of
the chateau. Two tanks had been assigned to the
brigade, and were intended to lead the infantry into
Thiépval and then on to Schwaben Redoubt. Unfortunately, having done excellent service, this tank
subsided into the mud and remained there, while its
fellow arrived a little later and suffered the same
fate. That was the end of the " Crême de Menthe "
and " Cordon Bleu " as active combatants on this
great day.

At 1 P.M. then the right wing of the Middlesex
was moving satisfactorily towards its objective north
of the village, in close touch with the Essex, having
taken many Germans and killed many more. The
left of the battalion was not making such good progress, for besides holding their old front very strongly
the Germans had large numbers of men in the western
part of Thiépval well supplied with machine-guns.
The left company of the Fusiliers was still held up
in a stationary fight which went on till next morning.
The dug-out clearing party of the Fusiliers, " C " Company, was with the Middlesex near the chateau, and
Major Hudson of " A " Company, seeing the Middlesex
in difficulties, pushed his men forward. After passing
the chateau our line inclined to the right, and the
Fusiliers seem to have got into the 53rd Brigade's
country, getting mixed up with the Essex. Captain
Johnston of " B " Company, Fusiliers, saw this, and
fearing a gap in the attack, put in his men and attacked
to the north, with the result that the first objective
was secured.

A Fusilier officer's diary may be quoted here :—

"On the left 'D' Company had very hard fighting along the old Boche front line. They were eventually held up on that line about level with the chateau, having got on well, but with very heavy losses. Captain Thomson was hit in the head, but continued fighting until hit again and killed. Of the three platoon commanders, one was killed, one wounded, and one (Hawkins) stunned by the explosion of a trench-mortar shell, but kept on with the company.

"'C' Company killed a great many Boches in a trench about 250 yards west of the chateau, and running north and south. Along this same trench Major Hudson of 'A' Company was hit through the shoulder, but continued until the final line was taken and consolidated. On his way down he got a bullet through the thigh, breaking the bone, and died a few days later.

"Battalion headquarters in the Leipzig salient had no news of the fight, so about 1.15 Colonel Carr took headquarters forward. There was still an intense barrage, and a number of men were hit going up. On getting to the chateau ruins, which were merely a heap of broken bricks, we found that Colonel Maxwell, commanding 12th Middlesex, had just arrived there. As there was doubt as to what was happening on the left ('D' Company's sector), Colonel Carr and Captain Cumberledge, the adjutant, proceeded in that direction. A machine-gun immediately opened on us from very short range, and Colonel Carr got three bullets through various parts of him—fortunately none of them serious,—and Cumberledge was also hit.

"Major Hudson had been hit just previously, so Captain Johnston was now in command of the Fusiliers until the evening, when Major Meyricke, the second in command, who had been left out, came up and took over. But Colonel Maxwell virtually commanded both battalions, and also two companies of Northamptonshires who had come up, Colonel Ripley of the Northamptonshires having also been wounded (he afterwards died).

"The line eventually held was about 300 yards in front of the chateau. The Boche shelled the whole area, and particularly the trench from which the attack started, until dark, but slacked off during the night."

After the first objective had been reached progress became slower. Every yard of the ground had to be

searched by fire, for in addition to the usual organised
defence there were snipers lying up in shell-holes and
they were exceedingly busy.

During this pause innumerable acts of bravery were
performed, only a few of which were ever recorded.
Two men, both belonging to the 12th Middlesex—
Private F. J. Edwards and Private R. Ryder—won
the Victoria Cross.

According to the official account of Private
Edwards' gallant feat, " his part of the line was held
up by a machine-gun. The officers had all become
casualties. There was confusion and even suggestion
of retirement. Private Edwards grasped the situation at once. Alone and on his own initiative he
dashed towards the gun, which he bombed until he
succeeded in knocking it out. By this gallant act,
performed with great presence of mind, and with
complete disregard for his personal safety, this man
made possible the continuance of the advance, and
solved a dangerous situation. His was probably one
of those decisive actions which determine the success
or failure of an operation."

In the case of Private Ryder, " his company was
held up by heavy fire from the trench in front of
them, and all his officers had become casualties. The
attack was flagging for want of leadership. Private
Ryder, realising the situation, without a moment's
thought for his own safety dashed absolutely alone
at the enemy's trench, and by skilful manipulation of
his Lewis gun succeeded in clearing the trench. By
this brilliant act he not only made possible, but also
inspired, the advance of his comrades. It seems possible that this single heroic action made all the
difference between success and failure in this part
of the attacking line."

Many other acts of courage and decision distinguished this rather confused and bitter fighting.
For instance, when a machine-gun suddenly appeared
and began to fire on our line, Lance-Corporal L.

Tovey of the Fusiliers hurled himself upon it and bayoneted both the gunners. Later on, when nearly all the senior officers and N.C.O.'s had become casualties, he led his comrades in the stiff rough-and-tumble in the heart of the village until he was shot through the head and killed.

Clearing the dug-outs was tough work, and by the time the first objective was reached "D" Company of the Fusiliers had dealt with twenty-five belonging to the front line of the German system, finding in many of them a very resolute resistance. One in particular contained a large garrison with two machine-guns, and as the Germans refused to come out it was set on fire. Many perished inside, eleven were killed as they bolted, and fourteen were wounded and taken prisoner.

As the dug-outs were cleared the Germans would bolt to the north, dodging about among the shell-holes and little broken heaps of earth left by the high explosives; and, knowing the ground, they were "as hard to hit as snipe"—in the phrase of an officer on the spot. But Lieutenant Sulman of "C" Company, which had been specially told off for this work of clearing up, got two Lewis guns in position to enfilade a trench, and managed to bring down some fifty of them as they ran. So well, by the way, did Lieutenant Sulman carry out his job of "mopping-up" behind the 12th Middlesex, that there was no case of any attack on the assaulting battalion from behind. Another excellent piece of work by this officer resulted in the capture of the German Telephone Headquarters, which he discovered on a captured German map given him half an hour before zero. This he showed to his men, explaining just where it should be. Lance-Corporal F. Rudy, with four men, cast around like hounds till they found it—a palatial dug-out with a magnificent installation in direct communication with the enemy artillery, and containing twenty operators and others, whom they took prisoner. Rudy cut all the wires and held the place without relief or support for twelve hours, during which he was heavily shelled.

By 2.30 P.M. Colonel Maxwell reported that on the right his objective north of Thiépval had been reached, but that his left was held up and his casualties were heavy. Meanwhile as Colonel Carr and his adjutant, Captain Cumberledge, and Major Hudson had all been wounded, the command of the Fusiliers had devolved upon Captain Johnston, who did admirably. But the Germans were still active and determined, and directed a galling machine-gun fire from the high ground to which they stuck like leeches.

It was soon clear that the 12th Middlesex had edged off on the right into the 53rd Brigade area, and that there was a gap between the Middlesex and the 11th Royal Fusiliers, who, with both flanks in the air, had asked the Middlesex for reinforcements on their right. Two platoons—or what was left of them, about fifty men—were sent out, but only six men managed to get to the Fusiliers. The rest were killed or wounded on the way.

So many officers had become casualties that it was by no means easy to discover with certainty the exact position of the various units. The messages mostly came from N.C.O.'s, of whom many had no maps, and though the news seemed to point to a considerable success, aeroplane reports were less favourable. The enemy had laid down a heavy barrage on the southern fringe of the village, and was carrying out very lively bombing against our left flank.

However, soon after half-past three a message got through from Colonel Maxwell, sent from the chateau by pigeon at 3.20 P.M. This made it clear that a great success had been obtained by the Middlesex and the Fusiliers, but that both battalions had been practically expended in the effort. The companies and platoons were greatly split up and intermingled, and were still engaged in hard fighting. Accordingly it became abundantly apparent that the advance on the final objective, still a thousand yards away, would have to be made by fresh troops, and a defensive barrage was therefore arranged in front of the line we were holding at 4.5 P.M.

The position then was that the 54th Brigade had gained its objective on the right, where it joined the 53rd Brigade, but was well behind its objective on the left. Much mixed up, the Fusiliers and the Middlesex were holding a connected line through the north-eastern corner of the village, and fighting was still going on hammer and tongs on the extreme left, where the Germans were both active and enterprising. Our men rushed one particular strong point, but were flung back. When we endeavoured to establish a strong point of our own close by, we were several times beaten back by an intense cross-fire from machine-guns and bombs. "It was not unusual," says an eye-witness, "to see from twelve to twenty German stick-bombs in the air at the same time, and the whole area looked like a firework display owing to the number of egg-bombs the enemy showered on us." While these did not give rise to many casualties, their long range kept our people at arm's length.

Meanwhile the 6th Northants, moving up in support, had been having a fairly stiff time. Their leading company left their trenches at 1 P.M. and went forward under an exceedingly heavy barrage, which the Germans had by that time put down on our communication trenches. The battalion headquarters at Campbell Post were completely wrecked. The leading company had by 1.40 P.M. arrived well within the German lines south of the chateau, but had lost its captain, Captain Evans, and another officer. At 3.30 P.M. battalion headquarters were transferred to the dug-outs in our lines that had been vacated by the Middlesex, but unhappily Colonel Ripley, the Northants commanding officer, was severely wounded on his way up, and later died of his wounds. His adjutant also was wounded. Major Charrington

took command of the battalion, establishing headquarters at a point in the German lines where a
brigade signal section had been fixed.  As all the
telephone wires were cut by shell-fire, it was impossible
to maintain communication except by means of
runners and pigeons.  When at four o'clock the
remainder of the Northants got forward there were
only two unwounded company officers in the battalion.
"A" Company had 2nd Lieutenant Gotch, "D"
Company 2nd Lieutenant Bates.  "B" Company was
in charge of Sergeant Partridge, and "C" was commanded by Sergeant Pullen, who was noted by
General Maxse as having "carried out his duties
during the remainder of the action with courage,
coolness, and success."

Major Charrington in these circumstances decided
to take his headquarters on to the chateau and join
Colonel Maxwell at the Middlesex headquarters there.
He accordingly joined Colonel Maxwell at 5.15 P.M.,
and got his staff into deep ex-German dug-outs where
they were at least safe from shell-fire.

By 6 P.M. then the 54th Brigade had three battalions pretty well used up, and it was extremely
lucky that the fourth battalion was still in its dug-
outs in Thiépval Wood, instead of having followed
the Northants through that shattering barrage.
In the 53rd Brigade the Essex battalion also was
used up, although its units were still trying to get
forward to Schwaben Redoubt according to original
orders.

On that evening the 53rd Brigade was in position,
with the Suffolks and the Essex consolidating the
Zollern line, a third battalion, the 8th Norfolks, in
support in the Schwaben Trench, and the fourth
battalion, the 6th Berks, broken up into carrying
parties which struggled throughout the night to
bring food, water, ammunition, &c., up to the exhausted troops in front.  What really made any
further advance impossible was the fact that in the

peculiar local fighting the three battalions of the 54th Brigade had become mixed up and incapable of cohesive action. All that could be expected of them was for each unit to hold fast to whatever it had gained, and this they did.

Colonel Maxwell took command of every one of the 54th Brigade on the spot, and with the assistance of Captain Johnston, commanding the Fusiliers, and Major Charrington, commanding the Northants, formed the scattered units of three battalions into two defensive lines with about fifty yards between the two lines. The front line was composed of groups of six men at intervals of about fifteen yards, each finding a double sentry, and these men dug towards each other in order to form a continuous line. The second or support line was not continuous, but composed of groups with a sentry over each. The whole formed a system of defence for the chateau, which became the keep, and a strong point was made round one of the stranded tanks lying north of the chateau by taking out its machine-guns and giving it a garrison of twenty men. On the right and centre the task of organising the line was assigned to Major Charrington of the Northants, assisted by 2nd Lieutenant Odgers of the Middlesex and 2nd Lieutenants Bates and Gotch, the only company officers of the Northants left to the battalion.

In view of the information available soon after 5 P.M. in Divisional Headquarters with regard to the whole situation, orders were issued that it was not proposed to advance any farther that night, that the 53rd and 54th Brigades were to consolidate what they had won, that any troops beyond the consolidated line were to hold on to what they had won, and that further orders would be issued as soon as a proper artillery programme could be arranged for an attack on the following day. Also one battalion, the 7th Queens (Lieut.-Colonel M. Kemp-Welch, D.S.O., M.C.), of the 55th Brigade, was placed at

the disposal of the 53rd Brigade, and one battalion,
namely, the 1/5th West Yorkshires (Lieut.-Colonel
H. D. Bousfield, D.S.O.), of the 146th Brigade, was
placed at the disposal of the 54th Brigade. The
G.O.C. 146th Brigade (Brigadier-General Goring
Jones) was asked to push out standing patrols to
get in touch with the enemy and keep contact with
him throughout the night between Thiépval Wood
and the German lines as far west as the Ancre. This
they did with excellent effect, and even in some places
found it possible to raid the German trenches. Meanwhile a defensive barrage was arranged along the
front, and steps were taken to block certain specific
localities with continuous howitzer fire. These barrages were kept up throughout the night, and gave
great confidence to the infantry.

Not till 11 P.M. was the line held by the 54th
Brigade finally organised and partially consolidated,
and up to that hour there was continual fighting at
particular spots, especially at the block in the trench
where our line on the second objective ran into the
north-west corner of the village which was still in the
enemy's hands. In all, thirty-six men were sent up to
this block, and of these no fewer than twenty-eight
became casualties. All the bombing raids made by
the Germans to test our lines were repulsed, and at
11 P.M. they gave up the struggle, and judging by
their Very lights they vacated two of their strong
points.

During the night the 53rd Brigade outposts fought
German bombing parties in Bulgar and Martin
trenches, but no serious counter-attack was attempted
by the enemy, though he shelled the village and the
back areas viciously. It is possible, as General Maxse
drily observes, "that the German higher command
found even greater difficulty than we experienced in
locating the exact whereabouts of the new front."

As for the 54th Brigade, General Shoubridge at
midnight reported the exact position of his front by

telephone to Divisional Headquarters, pointing out that it was quite impossible to make any further attack until the rectangular section of Thiépval that was still in possession of the enemy should have been cleared. It was decided that this should be done by the 7th Bedfords, still in reserve in Thiépval Wood, and that a fifth battalion, the 7th Royal West Kents, under Lieut.-Colonel Fiennes of the 55th Brigade, should take the Bedfords' place as reserve to the 54th Brigade. General Shoubridge had already arranged for the relief of his three exhausted battalions, and General Maxse thoroughly approved.

"The story of this night relief," wrote General Maxse in December 1916, "deserves to be told at length because it was, in my opinion, the finest example of efficiency and battle-discipline which has been seen in the 18th Division during the course of the Somme and Ancre operations of the past five months.

"There is not space in this report to describe the incident in full, but the following points are of interest. The problem was to extract three tired battalions from their battle positions and to put one battalion in their place. This had to be done in pitch darkness by troops who had never seen the locality, but had to get to it through a hostile barrage. The relief could not be started until a decision had been come to regarding the further prosecution of the attack. Under these circumstances, General Shoubridge, at about 10 P.M., ordered reconnaissances to be made to facilitate the relief, but directed that it should not occur until he gave further instructions. Thereupon Lieut.-Colonel Price, commanding the Bedfords, made such excellent arrangements, and these arrangements were so well carried out by his company officers, that before daylight the fresh Bedfords faced the Boche in the place of the three spent battalions which were almost in touch with him.

"My reason for praising this relief in high terms is that it disclosed a system of training in the 54th Brigade which reflected the highest credit upon General Shoubridge and his commanding officers. They had the pluck to attempt an operation which might have led to a disaster, and they had sufficient confidence in the capacity of their subordinates to warrant them in the risk they took. These remarks apply especially to Lieut.-Colonel Price of the Bedfordshires and to Captain Johnston of the Fusiliers, who arranged matters on the spot.

"The company officers made previous reconnaissances which were not discovered by the enemy. They worked out all details among themselves, they controlled their units throughout the night over devastated ground, and they carried out the whole movement with precision and dash directly they got their definite orders by telephone at midnight.

"Lieut.-Colonel Price was at a conference at Brigade Headquarters until 12.20 A.M., when he proceeded to Thiépval Chateau to confer with Lieut.-Colonel Maxwell. He then concerted a plan for clearing the rectangle held by the enemy, and thus, by the time the companies of the Bedfordshires had completed the relief, their officers were in possession of Colonel Price's definite orders for the next attack. Only a well-trained and high-spirited battalion such as the 7th Bedfordshire can accomplish such a feat and be ready for a day's fighting the same morning."

The plan for clearing the rectangle still held by the Germans was a very straightforward and simple one. The Bedfords were to be brought into position during the night, and in the morning at six o'clock two companies were to storm the position and clear it with the bayonet in one rush.

The Bedfords got their orders about midnight, and in the profound darkness, lighted up only by the bursting of shells, with no guides to meet them, following a line that had been run across to the chateau in daylight by the signallers, they went up in "sneak formation," and arrived in position about half-past three.

Colonel Maxwell was as wonderful in this Thiépval struggle as he had been in the Trones Wood drama. His extraordinary personality—a burning forcefulness beneath an ice-cool exterior—whipped into courage and efficiency many a waverer. By now Maxwell had become the complete hero to the men of his battalion. Wounded men in the dressing-stations could be heard arguing about what Maxwell was

G

doing when they saw him. "Did you hear what he said to Bill?"—"Did you see him standing there near the chateau?"—"You never see him duck to a shell"—"I tell you I saw him eating a ration biscuit, that's what he was doing," were some of the things said—commonplaces, but indicative of the hero-worship aroused by this unforgettable leader of men.

Maxwell stayed at the chateau, which was merely an arch with a few steps leading below, until the Bedfords attacked in the morning. In the midst of the shelling with which the Germans pounded Thiépval that night, he wrote an eight-page letter to his wife.

In the memoir of Frank Maxwell, published by Mr John Murray, appears this letter that Colonel Maxwell wrote describing the taking of Thiépval:—

"We pushed off over the most awful country that human being ever saw or dreamt of. July 1st was a playground compared to it, and the resistance small. I knew it would be, and I confess I hated the job from the first—which was only three days before we began it. So many attempts had been made, and so many failures, that one knew it could only be a tough thing to take on, and I hadn't personally any particular hopes of accomplishing it, more especially as the distance to be covered—nearly one mile—was enormous for these attacks under any circumstances, and under the special one, of country absolutely torn with shell for three months, it was, I considered, an impossibility. Added to these pleasant anticipations, I was a sick man for the three days, one of which had to be spent looking over the ground, so far as one could see it; the second we marched most of the day; the third we took over trenches from 8 A.M. till about 10 P.M.; fourth day start over the parapet at an unknown hour, but happily the tonic of battle seized my rotten carcase and I slept the few hours available and woke up fit.

"This is much about the task and its difficulties—not diminished (I add to its burden) by the fact that the Prussians and Wurtembergers, who had held up this line for a year, and were supposed to have been relieved, were found at the last moment to be still there! An enormous advantage to the enemy, who thus knew every inch of the ground they had themselves prepared for our annihilation, when we should attempt to attack it.

"We accomplished three-quarters of it, and were extraordinarily lucky at that, and it seems to have surprised the Higher Command, which at least is something. But the price has been heavy—how heavy I don't know as regards men, but as regards officers I have, of the twenty who went over, nine killed, seven wounded, and four, including myself, untouched. Two other regiments, who came most of the way with us, lost heavily in officers, and a third engaged later suffered fairly heavily. I lost all my regimental staff—viz., three officers and regimental sergeant-major killed.

"It was an extraordinarily difficult battle to fight, owing to every landmark, such as a map shows, being obliterated—absolutely and totally. The ground was, of course, the limit itself, and progress over it like nothing imaginable, the enemy quite determined to keep us out, as they had so many before. And I must say that they fought most stubbornly and bravely, and probably not more than 300 to 500 put their hands up. They took it out of us badly, but we did ditto; and I have no shame in saying so, as every German should, in my opinion, be exterminated, I don't know that we took one. I have not seen a man or officer yet who did, anyway. I will not describe the details of the battle—they would be very difficult to understand. Briefly, we worked up and up our long journey, but left untaken, on our left, a very strong place filled with machine-guns and a determined garrison. This was a thorn in our side, indeed, and it defied all our efforts to take it till this morning, but not till it had done us in for a large number of casualties from first to last.

"All the regiment spent its night out, of course, either in shell-holes or (a very few) in dug-outs, either bombing or engaged with the enemy at close quarters. I had a safe place in a pile of ruins, which managed to ward off shells and all the other unpleasant things of modern battle. It was a busy night for me, though, and not unmixed with anxiety—in fact, very much to the contrary. Perhaps the most trying business is to keep your generals informed of how things are going. It is extraordinarily difficult, for on a field like that of Thiépval telephone wires don't remain uncut by shells for more than five minutes. And yet they must know things, of course, and must get their information by lamp or runner. By lamp it is laborious, for no answer to say that the message, or each word, is received, is possible, in case enemy should see the replying lamp, and put artillery on to its position, which always happens to be in the middle of a nest of artillery observation posts (places where gunner officers sit all day with telescopes, watching the effect of their gun-fire), and must therefore be kept absolutely hidden. If message is sent by runner, it means long distances on foot, over country already described, and at night as well as by day. By day the runner is usually killed or wounded ; by night he gets lost.

"This morning I had orders to clear out on relief by another regiment, but, much to the C.O.'s delight, I disobeyed the order and stayed on to see him through the attack on the stronghold that had beat us till then. I was in no mind to lose what we had so hardly won by going before he had done his job. And he only did it after three hours' attempt. But I have paid the penalty of a dressing-down by the general, who is furious. And more furious because I don't mind, and he knows I would do it again if even the King had given me the order."

Maxwell's reference to the general was to his brigadier, Brigadier-General Shoubridge, who "told him off" for remaining to expose himself when he had received his relief orders. Maxwell's cheerful reply to General Shoubridge was popularly supposed to have been, "What are you grousing about? I've got you another medal." Major M. C. Scarborough, Colonel Maxwell's second in command, had had a bullet through the head. When the Bedfords came up his body was still in a sitting position, near the chateau arch, as though he slept. One story told of Maxwell that night concerned a runner whose nerve had gone ; he whimpered every time a shell came near. Suddenly Maxwell got up from his writing, saying, "Send that man here!" He then told every one round to stand in a line, and added, "Give him a kick, and pass him along!" The runner whimpered no more.

"I cannot but wonder at the behaviour of the battalion," wrote Maxwell later. "If there were ever an occasion when things might have gone wrong, and the attack died or fizzled out, that one occurred on the 26th. The ground was made for skulking, and every yard of it afforded opportunity for men to drop down unseen and stay there without being seen. . . .

If I saw evil and wicked sights in Trones, I saw more
and varied ones at Thiépval." He himself came out
unscathed, with only the glass of his wrist - watch
broken by a shell splinter.  He was awarded a bar
to his D.S.O. for what he did on those two days, but
he often said he would rather it had been for Trones
Wood.

In a tender letter to Mrs Maxwell, written on
October 13th, he said :—

". . . I like to hear of the children learning rural and
garden things.  There is so much more joy in Nature if you
know something about it.  And it's Nature on which one
falls back so often in times of stress.  The mere reading of
your pruning ramblers, walking through fields and the like,
obliterates some of the vile bloodiness of this War from one's
mind as one reads your letters, just as getting into that
wood after Thiépval did, and as that evening I found myself
trudging in ankle-deep mud to get out into the fields at dusk,
and the joy of it."

On 23rd October Maxwell was appointed to the
command of the 27th Infantry Brigade of the 9th
Division.  On September 21st 1917 he was killed by
a sniper while out reconnoitring in No Man's Land.
He was a mighty fighter, a man among men, and the
18th Division was proud to have its name associated
with his.

What had to be done on 27th September had to be
done quickly, and before daylight.  "C" and "D"
Companies of the Bedfords went forward under Captain L. H. Keep, and, thanks to Captain Johnston and
Lieutenant Sulman, both of the Fusiliers, who knew
the ground and gave invaluable assistance, both companies were got into position by 5.45 A.M.

There was no chance of any help from artillery.
The business was one for the plain fighting man on
his own.  From the very start a most determined
resistance was encountered, and although the left
company managed to make steady progress, the right

ran up against a machine-gun, snipers, and standing patrols established in shell-holes, all of which they dealt with, though they were delayed in doing so.

A little later, about seven o'clock, the right-hand platoon of the right-hand company was held up by heavy rifle and machine-gun fire from several strong points. The moment was a very critical one, and 2nd Lieutenant Tom Edwin Adlam, who commanded the platoon, displayed the conspicuous bravery and gallant leadership that amply deserved the Victoria Cross awarded to him. Adlam was twenty-two years old, had only been two months in the trenches, and in civil life had been a schoolmaster and a sergeant in the Territorials.

Seeing that time was the most important element in the success of the attack, he dashed out across the open under all the fire that had checked his platoon, and gathered up his men from the shell-holes for a combined rush. One of his personal gifts stood him in good stead—he could throw a cricket-ball about a hundred yards. So he got together as many German bombs as possible and started a whirlwind attack on the enemy with these. Thanks to his powers, he could fling a stick-bomb farther than an ordinary Mills, and he pulled off all his equipment to throw the better, and bombarded the Germans furiously. Wounded in the leg, like Widdrington he kneeled and "fought on upon his stumps," and even in that posture managed to out-throw the Germans. Finally he snatched an opportunity to lead in his platoon, killed or captured everybody who stood up to them, made his objective by 8.30, and exploiting his success went on and gained a further 300 yards. Wounded as he was, he continued at the head of his men all day and the next, when he was wounded again.

"There is no doubt," says General Maxse, "that 2nd Lieutenant Adlam by his bravery and example, as also by his prompt and skilful handling of his unit, was chiefly responsible for the success of the two companies of the Bedfordshire Regiment who cleared and made good the last bit of the Thiépval objective."

By 11 A.M. the affair was over, and the whole of Thiépval was in our hands. The two Bedford companies had taken about 70 prisoners in the dug-outs, and 81 dead Germans were counted. The casualties among the attacking troops were fewer than among the enemy. In short, it had been a remarkably successful minor operation of the utmost value. With the north-west corner of the village in German hands it would have been impossible to continue the attack on Schwaben, also it would have been difficult to withdraw the remnants of the Middlesex, Northants, and Fusiliers without heavy casualties. As it was, they went down in broad daylight almost unscathed.

The 53rd Brigade was in position along the Zollern line, in touch with the 11th Division on the right, and the 54th had now made good its first objective at all points. Schwaben Redoubt was the next objective for the 18th Division. During the 27th the Essex tried to rush a block and strong point in Bulgar Trench under cover of a Stokes mortar barrage. After they had gone fifty yards they came under very heavy artillery fire from two directions.

Captain H. J. Impson, commanding the 53rd Trench Mortar Battery, made a very daring reconnaissance, crawling from shell-hole to shell-hole until he could see a strong party of Germans in another strong point, and others holding Hessian Trench in force.

It was clear that it would be impossible to take Hessian, Martin, and Bulgar trenches without a deliberately planned attack on these and the high ground on Midway line. Opposite the left brigade of the 11th Division there was high ground, well provided with machine-guns and dominating the whole valley in which the 18th Division was operating. General Maxse, therefore, was of the opinion that it would be futile to prosecute the attack on

Schwaben without another bombardment on our front and a simultaneous attack by the 11th Division on the right.

A conference on the situation was held on the afternoon of the 27th, and when it ended at 4.20 orders were actually given for the attack at 5 P.M., which gave exceedingly little time to effect company relief and get orders out. However, the attack was cancelled at the last minute, and most of the night of the 27th was spent by the search-parties hunting for wounded, who were found in every shell-hole.

So far the taking of Thiépval had gone well enough. In casualties it had cost us 64 officers and 1392 other ranks, a total of 1,456. The heaviest losses fell upon the 12th Middlesex, with 10 officers (including Major Scarborough and Major Whinney) and 60 men killed, and 8 officers and 233 men wounded. The Fusiliers lost 3 officers and 49 men killed, 7 officers and 171 men wounded. The Northants' loss was 4 officers and 24 men killed, 10 officers and 109 men wounded. The Essex lost 3 officers and 23 men killed, 5 officers and 134 men wounded; while the Suffolks lost 1 officer and 18 men killed, and 2 officers and 86 men wounded. The Bedfords lost 1 officer and 43 men killed, 4 officers and 50 men wounded, and the Norfolks 2 men killed and 1 officer and 36 men wounded. The Berks had 1 man killed and 11 wounded.

The enemy's losses were severe. Four officers and 606 other ranks were counted prisoners in the cages, belonging to four different regiments. Although the German killed were numerous, it was not possible to ascertain accurate figures, as so many were hit by shell-fire on the days before the infantry assault. General Maxse had a rough estimate made by areas on the 29th, which resulted in over 900 bodies being counted on the ground in and around Thiépval, and this does not take into account those killed in dug-outs or buried by shell-fire. Nor is it possible to reckon up the wounded except by taking an average proportion of wounded to killed. But taking the figures given as a basis for a rough calculation, the enemy casualties would seem to have been somewhere round three times the number of our own, and General Maxse does not consider it an exaggeration "to assert that well over 3000 Germans were incapacitated at the Battle of Thiépval."

Immense quantities of ammunition and stores were left buried in the ground, but certain trophies were recovered, including 2 heavy and 2 small trench mortars, 10 German machine-guns and 1 English machine-gun that had been converted, 9 automatic rifles, 5 gas cylinders, 2 enormous flammenwerfers or gas engines, besides 8 boxes of aerial torpedoes, &c.

Thiépval was another battle by which Captain William Howard Lister, "little Lister," of the 55th Field Ambulance, will be remembered. He did wonders in getting away the wounded. His devotion knew no bounds. His reliant temperament spread confidence around him. As General Maxse has said, "Lister's eager temperament and immovable standard of duty made him indispensable to the troops whenever fighting was on, and we all recognised his value, from the last recruit to the Divisional commander." Lister gave himself with such zest to organising the relief of our wounded in the involved fighting at Thiépval and Schwaben that he broke down afterwards, but his courage and tenacity of purpose during an action, his example and influence over his subordinates, had by now become known in wider fields, and later he was promoted to a bigger command. When he died in action in Italy nearer the end of the war there were many who sorrowed in the 18th Division.

Another 18th Division figure, the Fusiliers' medical officer, Captain J. C. Sale, R.A.M.C., was awarded the M.C. for his work at Thiépval. When owing to shortage of stretcher-bearers it became difficult to convey the wounded to dug-outs, he repeatedly carried them in on his back under very heavy shell, rifle, and machine-gun fire. In the course of his work he was twice flung down and half stunned by the concussion of heavy shells bursting close to him, but he continued his magnificent work undeterred, affording the finest possible example to all concerned, even remaining in Thiépval for some hours after his battalion had been relieved.

Other Fusiliers awarded the M.C. were Captain W. H. H. Johnston, upon whom the command of the battalion devolved, and Lieutenant A. E. Sulman, whose good work and whose coolness and capacity were very conspicuous both during the fighting and in the very arduous tasks of the night of the 26th.

While the fighting was still actually going on an official message arrived from General Jacob, the Corps commander, and was delivered in the trenches.

"To 18TH DIVISION.

*G* 1881.  *Corps Commander wishes to thank you and all ranks of your Division for their admirable work to-day. Thiépval has withstood all attacks upon it for exactly two years, and it is a great honour to your Division to have captured the whole of this strongly-fortified village at their first attempt. Hearty congratulations to you all.*

FROM II. CORPS."

26th *September* 1916.
9.10 P.M.

The effect of this appreciative message was very inspiriting to the Division, and next day the personal congratulations of Sir Douglas Haig were added, and conveyed to the 53rd, 54th, and 55th Brigades in the following message :—

"*G* 221.

*The Commander - in - Chief personally called to-day on General Maxse to congratulate the Division on its success at Thiépval.*

FROM 18TH DIVISION."

27th *September* 1916.
4.30 P.M.

The Division had certainly done well, and had every reason to be satisfied with itself so far. But the task allotted to it had not yet been fully accomplished. Schwaben Redoubt and the intricate network of trenches surrounding it were still a thousand yards away across a slope of broken ground held in great strength by the enemy.

## ORDER OF BATTLE AT THIÉPVAL.

| | |
|---|---|
| Commander . . . . . | Major-General F. I. Maxse, C.B., C.V.O., D.S.O. |
| A.D.C. . . . . . . . | Captain F. J. O. Montagu, Coldstream Guards. |
| A.D.C. . . . . . . . | Captain M. M. H. Nevile, Yorkshire Regt. |
| General Staff Officer, 1st Grade | Brevet Lieut.-Colonel W. D. Wright, V.C., C.M.G., Royal West Surrey Regt. |
| General Staff Officer, 2nd Grade | Major F. H. Harvey, East Yorkshire Regt. |
| General Staff Officer, 3rd Grade | Captain P. R. Meautys, North Staffordshire Regt. |
| Assistant Adjutant and Quartermaster-General | Brevet Lieut.-Colonel E. V. D. Riddell, D.S.O., R.A. |
| Deputy Assistant Adjutant-General | Captain J. A. Churchill, M.C., Durham Light Infantry. |
| Deputy Assistant Quartermaster-General | Major R. H. L. Cutbill, A.S.C. |
| Assistant Director of Medical Services | Colonel J. Poe, D.S.O., R.A.M.C. |
| Deputy Assistant Director of Medical Services | Captain A. J. Clark, R.A.M.C. |
| Deputy Assistant Director of Veterinary Services | Major L. M. Verney, F.R.C.V.S., A.V.C. |
| Deputy Assistant Director of Ordnance Services | Captain J. H. Vernall, A.O.D. |
| Commander, Royal Artillery | Brigadier-General S. F. Metcalfe, D.S.O., R.A. |
| Brigade-Major, Royal Artillery | Major A. F. Brooke, R.A. |
| Staff Captain, Royal Artillery | Captain A. H. Edwards, R.A. |
| A.D.C. to Commander, Royal Artillery | Lieut. H. H. Gardiner, R.A. |
| Commander, Royal Engineers | Colonel H. J. Joly de Lotbinière, D.S.O., R.E. |
| Adjutant, Royal Engineers | Captain B. I. Chambers, R.E. |
| Assistant Provost-Marshal | Captain H. C. Stockwell, Highland Light Infantry. |
| Commander, Divisional Train | Lieut.-Colonel D. C. E. Grose, A.S.C. |
| Commander, Divisional Signal Company | Captain M. T. Porter, R.E. |

## 53rd INFANTRY BRIGADE.

| | |
|---|---|
| Commander . . . . . | Brigadier-General H. W. Higginson, D.S.O., Royal Dublin Fusiliers. |
| Brigade-Major . . . . | Captain C. H. Hoare, West Kent Yeomanry. |
| Staff Captain . . . . . | Captain H. Ramsbotham, Bedfordshire Regt. |
| 79th Field Co., R.E. . . | Captain T. B. Harris, R.E. |
| No. 2 Section, Signal Co. . | Lieut. G. E. Pelham-Clinton, R.E. |
| 8th Bn., Norfolk Regt. . | Lieut.-Colonel H. G. de L. Ferguson, D.S.O., Norfolk Regt. |
| 8th Bn., Suffolk Regt. . . | Lieut.-Colonel G. V. W. Hill, D.S.O., Royal Fusiliers. |
| 10th Bn., Essex Regt. . . | Lieut.-Colonel C. W. Frizell, M.C., Royal Berkshire Regt. |
| 6th Bn., Royal Berkshire Regt. | Lieut.-Colonel B. G. Clay, D.S.O., 7th Dragoon Guards. |
| 53rd Machine Gun Co. . | Major J. K. Dunlop, London Regt. |
| 53rd Trench Mortar Battery | Captain H. J. Impson. |
| 150th Co., A.S.C. . . . | Major H. G. Peachy, A.S.C. |
| 56th Field Ambulance . . | Lieut.-Colonel K. D. Murchison, R.A.M.C. |

## 54th INFANTRY BRIGADE.

| | |
|---|---|
| Commander . . . . . | Brigadier-General T. H. Shoubridge, C.M.B., D.S.O., Northumberland Fusiliers. |
| Brigade-Major . . . . | Captain E. G. Miles, M.C., King's Own Scottish Borderers. |
| Staff Captain . . . . . | Captain C. H. S. Runge, Middlesex Regt. |
| 80th Field Co., R.E. . . | Captain A. A. Chase, D.S.O., R.E. |
| 11th Bn., Royal Fusiliers . | Lieut.-Colonel C. C. Carr, D.S.O. |
| 7th Bn., Bedfordshire Regt. | Lieut.-Colonel G. D. Price, West Yorkshire Regt. |
| 6th Bn., Northampton Regt. | Lieut.-Colonel G. E. Ripley, Northampton Regt. |
| 12th Bn., Middlesex Regt. | Brevet Lieut.-Colonel F. A. Maxwell, V.C., C.S.I., D.S.O., 18th Lancers. |
| 54th Machine Gun Co. . . | Captain The Earl of Caledon, 1st Life Guards. |
| 54th Trench Mortar Battery | 2nd Lieut. J. D. Unwin. |
| 151st Co., A.S.C. . . . . | Captain H. H. Hewson, A.S.C. |
| 55th Field Ambulance . . | Lieut.-Colonel M. G. Winder, R.A.M.C. |

## 55th INFANTRY BRIGADE.

| | |
|---|---|
| Commander . . . . . | Brigadier-General Sir T. D. Jackson, Bart., M.V.O., D.S.O., King's Own Royal Lancaster Regt. |
| Brigade-Major . . . . | Captain G. Flemming, M.C., Gordon Highlanders. |
| Staff Captain . . . . . | Captain J. M. Mitchell. |
| 92nd Field Co., R.E. . . | Captain O. W. Tyler, R.E. |

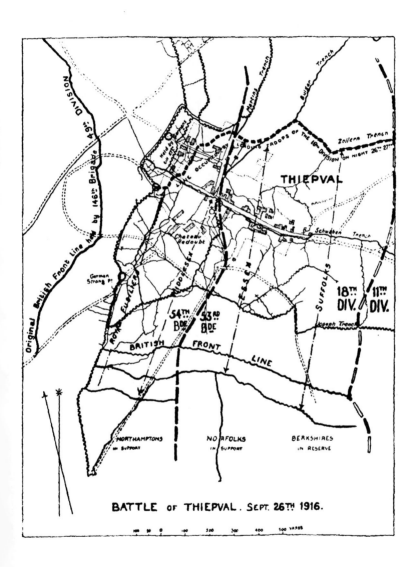

BATTLE of THIEPVAL. SEPT. 26TH 1916.

| | |
|---|---|
| No. 4 Section, Signal Co. . | Lieut. T. E. B. Young, R.E. |
| 7th Bn., Royal West Surrey Regt. | Lieut.-Colonel M. Kemp Welch, D.S.O., M.C., Royal West Surrey Regt. |
| 7th Bn., East Kent Regt. . | Lieut.-Colonel A. L. Ransome, M.C., Dorsetshire Regt. |
| 8th Bn., East Surrey Regt. | Lieut.-Colonel A. P. B. Irwin, D.S.O., East Surrey Regt. |
| 7th Bn., Royal West Kent Regt. | Lieut.-Colonel J. T. T. W. Fiennes, Royal West Kent Regt. |
| 55th Machine Gun Co.. . | Captain H. Heyland. |
| 55th Trench Mortar Battery | Captain K. M. M'Iver. |
| 152nd Co., A.S.C. . . . | Captain E. M. West, A.S.C. |
| 54th Field Ambulance. . | Lieut.-Colonel D. C. Barron, R.A.M.C. |

## ROYAL ARTILLERY.

| | | |
|---|---|---|
| Divisional Trench Mortar Officer | | Captain D. G. Butler, Leinster Regt. |
| 82nd Field | Artillery Brigade | Lieut.-Colonel A. Thorp, R.A. |
| 83rd Field | Artillery Brigade | Lieut.-Colonel T. O. Seagram, R.A. |
| 84th Field | Artillery Brigade | Lieut.-Colonel H. Cornes, D.S.O., R.A. |
| 85th Field | Artillery Brigade | Brevet-Colonel H. Johnstone, R.A. |
| Divisional | Ammunition Column | Lieut.-Colonel F. C. Johnston, R.A. |
| No. 1 Section, Signal Co. . | | 2nd Lieut. E. V. Riley, R.E. |
| 153rd Co. R.E. . . . . | | Captain A. W. Chichester, A.S.C. |

## (Attached) ROYAL ARTILLERY.

| | |
|---|---|
| Commander, 25th Divisional Artillery | Brigadier-General B. R. Kirwan, C.M.G. |
| Commander, 49th Divisional Artillery | Brigadier-General W. H. Kay, D.S.O. |

# CHAPTER VII.

## SCHWABEN REDOUBT.

*On from Thiépval—General Maxse's six hours' minimum for prepara-*
*tion—Zero hour 1 P.M.—Suffolks and Queens meet obstinate*
*resistance— Captain H. R. Longbourne's fine exploit enables*
*Queens to enter the Redoubt—Bedfords on their final objective by*
*2 P.M.—Methodical "mopping-up"—The sergeant-major with the*
*tremendous voice—Enemy's powerful counter-attacks during next*
*five days—Fine work by Lieutenant Wightman of the East Surreys*
*—The terrible conditions—German estimate of the importance of*
*Schwaben.*

THE position on the 27th of September, as far as the
18th Division was concerned, was that the 53rd and
54th Brigades were lying in a continuous line running
north of Thiépval and along the Zollern Trench to
the point where the 53rd were in touch with the
11th Division on the right.

Originally it had been intended that the 53rd and
54th Brigades should go straight on from their first
objective, now attained, and take the Schwaben Redoubt. But in the fighting for Thiépval the 54th
had had three of its battalions used up, and the fourth
battalion, the 7th Bedfords, had been partly used up
in the morning attack that finally completed the
capture of the village. Fusiliers, Northants, and
Middesex had sustained so many casualties and lost
so many officers, that for the moment they could not
be of much service for an organised attack. In the
53rd Brigade the Norfolks and the Essex were to
some degree spent, but the Suffolks and the Berks
were still strong and available for an attack.

There were therefore three possible plans for consideration. The 54th Brigade could be taken out, relieved by the 55th, and the action continued with two brigades, the 53rd and the 55th. Or both 53rd and 54th Brigades could be withdrawn, and the task of capturing the redoubt given to General Jackson and the 55th Brigade. Or, finally, the 53rd and 54th Brigades could be reinforced by the fresh battalions from the 55th Brigade, and Generals Higginson and Shoubridge would then continue to direct the assault according to the original plan. Besides the 55th Brigade, another fresh battalion, the 1/5th West Yorkshire Regiment of the 49th Division, had been placed at General Maxse's disposal by the Corps commander for this fighting.

The problem stated itself clearly on the afternoon of the 26th, when the nature and effect of the broken desperate fighting in Thiépval was known. The determining factor was simply which method promised best for ensuring the capture of Schwaben, and accordingly the third plan was adopted on the 26th and adhered to after Thiépval was finally in our hands. Among other advantages, it was the one that could be put in operation with the greatest rapidity—a very important factor if the enemy was to be overthrown before he could recover from the first defeat.

A conference has been referred to as taking place on the afternoon of the 27th. Although at one point orders were given to proceed with the attack at 5 P.M., and preparations for this were at once begun, the attack was cancelled and postponed until the 28th.

General Maxse held the view that so long as Stuff Redoubt had not been taken and held by the 11th Division on the right, and the high ground commanding the 18th Division area definitely cleared, it would be impossible to attack with reasonable hope of success. Furthermore, to form up and attack at 5 P.M. would have been most hazardous, a mere gamble, whereas on the 28th success could be made practically certain, and overwhelming artillery preparation and co-operation could be arranged. In his opinion, "to form up infantry for such an assault takes six hours *as a minimum* from the time the order is issued at Divisional Headquarters, and, if less time is given under stress of circumstances, the attack is likely to fail because the platoons do not know where they are or where they should go."

There were no forming-up trenches here for the assault, and as there was no time to dig them, the ground had to be taped out under fire so that the companies might start properly and be directly opposite their objectives. This work was begun on the 27th, otherwise it could never have been finished in time for zero hour on the 28th.

Zero hour was fixed at 1 P.M. on the 28th September, and the difficult job of forming-up in daylight was carried through creditably and with few casualties.

The 53rd Brigade deployed on a front of 500 yards. The Suffolks and the Queens from the 55th Brigade were to be the assaulting battalions; the Essex, who had been badly mauled on the 26th, were detailed to garrison the Zollern Trench; and the Norfolks were called on to provide "mopping-up" companies to attend the assaulting battalions. The Berkshires, who were almost entirely recently-joined recruits, were in brigade reserve in Authuille Wood.

The dividing line between the 53rd and the 54th Brigades was changed slightly so as to diminish the width of the final objective laid down for the 54th. As in the Thiépval attack, the 54th Brigade once more had to deal with the tremendously fortified and difficult German trench - system on the left of the advance. For the assault the two fresh companies of the Bedfords were to be deployed, and of the two companies who under Captain L. H. Keep had so gallantly completed the capture of Thiépval, one was to move in close support of the assaulting companies and the other was to take over the job of "mopping-

H

up" dug-outs behind the attacking wave. One company of the West Yorkshire Regiment was given to Lieut.-Colonel Price of the Bedfords as his battalion reserve, the other three companies were in support. The West Kents (from the 55th Brigade) were held in reserve, two companies being disposed in dug-outs around the Thiépval Chateau and the rest in Thiépval Wood and North Bluff.

Two battalions of the 55th Brigade, the Buffs and the East Surreys, were therefore left in divisional reserve under Brigadier-General Sir Thomas Jackson.

Precisely at 1 P.M. the barrage came down and the front waves of the assault dashed off.

On the right the Suffolks and the Queens carried the Bulgar Trench and Martin Trench by assault, and took a number of prisoners. Certain strong points in Bulgar, Hessian, and Martin Trenches held out most obstinately, and the leading waves came under heavy rifle and machine-gun fire from the southern fringe of Schwaben Redoubt. In spite of this check and the delays due to the hard fighting over these strong points, by 2.30 P.M. the Queens and the Suffolks had established themselves along the line running through Point 92, Point 64, Point 45, Point 72, and Market Trench, thus gaining a footing in Schwaben Redoubt itself.

But the Germans were still holding Points 45, 27, and 65 in great force, and we sustained many casualties in front of these. Swerving too much to the left the Queens made a gap between themselves and the Suffolks, but Captain J. S. Walter of the Queens seeing this, brought in his company into the gap and at once attacked and captured Point 15. Then pressing westward towards Point 65 he captured more than 50 prisoners in the trenches and dug-outs between the two points, but could not get to close quarters with Point 65.

This same Point 65 also was holding up the left assaulting company of the Queens under Captain H.

R. Longbourne. They reached it about 2 P.M., but
could not press home in face of its two machine-guns,
that kept up a continuous and well-directed fire.

Captain Longbourne took the matter into his own
capable hands, got hold of a bag of hand-grenades,
and ran or dodged from one shell-hole to another
until he finally reached a hole some five-and-twenty
yards away from the strong point. With delicate
accuracy he lobbed his grenades into the strong point,
and succeeded in knocking out one of the machine-
guns, but he expended all his bombs in the process.
There was still the other machine-gun to be dealt
with, and Captain Longbourne signed to Private
Waldron to bring up a further stock of bombs. Then
the contest was resumed, with Captain Longbourne
placing his bombs and Private Waldron covering him
by sniping at any German who showed over the
parapet. The Germans were also exchanging bombs
with Captain Longbourne, but failed to hit him
ensconced in his shell-hole.

This ding-dong struggle went on for 45 minutes,
and then Sergeant Punter managed to get up to the
other two and joined in the sniping, until Captain
Longbourne had expended all his bombs but two.
Hurling these into the enemy, he charged on them
with Sergeant Punter and Private Waldron. They
found the crew of the gun had all been killed—
15 dead Germans were strewn around the two
machine-guns. Thus the strong point was captured,
and presently they received the surrender of 46
unwounded Germans, who had been hiding in dug-
outs at hand.

"In this gallant manner," says General Maxse,
"Captain Longbourne led his company into Schwaben
Redoubt, and assisted his battalion in capturing its
southern face with the minimum of loss to themselves." For this service he was awarded the D.S.O.

Much the same sort of incident was being enacted
at all the strong points where the German resistance

was naturally concentrated and strongest, thanks to
the complete system of deep dug-outs with which they
were furnished.  While his company was collecting
the 46 prisoners referred to, Sergeant Punter led a
bombing party of the Queens up towards Point 39 ;
and as the Germans were now on the run, other men
of the Queens dashed at Point 45 and seized it.  The
sergeant then established a block half-way between
Points 45 and 39, and in this area a considerable
number of dug-outs were cleared.

Among the intricate network of trenches that filled
all this quarter, it was by no means easy for any one
to know exactly what the position was ; but as it
began to grow dusk after 5 P.M., the situation on the
53rd Brigade front appears to have been that on the
right the Suffolks had made good their final objective
and were established at Point 10, in touch with
the 11th Division ; that they held Points 92, 64,
and 45, and were in touch with the Queens at Point
15.  Point 27, however, had baffled every effort
made by both Queens and Suffolks to take it, even
with the help of Stokes mortars.  The Queens were
holding Points 15, 65, 45, and 37, at Point 45 were
in contact with the West Yorkshires, and probably
at Point 37 also.

On the western face of the redoubt there were
still Germans in the dug-outs, and these were being
" mopped up " little by little.  On the 29th September
two brave fellows were found in a dug-out near
Point 65 still operating a field telephone that once
had been British, and paid the penalty of their
stubborn courage.

As, of course, the various units had suffered the
usual amount of disorder and entanglement one with
another, inevitable after a hard confused piece of
fighting, no attempt was made to organise an attack
on the northern trench of the dug-out that night.
The positions won were consolidated, and any further
fighting was confined to bombing between the

outposts, which went on steadily throughout the night.

The 54th Brigade shared in the forward movement at the opening of the excellent barrage, and the 7th Bedfords went out in perfect order, keeping close up to it. The West Yorkshires also pushed forward from their forming-up trenches behind. About 11 A.M. a German map that had been captured the previous day in Thiépval reached brigade headquarters. It showed the position of several German machine-guns, and the information was at once sent off, both to the artillery and to the assaulting battalions, proving of the greatest interest and value to both.

The assault went steadily on until it reached Market Trench, which was a little less than half-way to the objective. Here the right platoon of the Bedfords came under heavy machine-gun fire, and was completely knocked out. Although they also suffered from machine-guns, the leading waves of the Bedfords rushed a number of strong points, and established themselves on a line fronting the west side of the redoubt and some 250 yards away. A machine-gun at Point 45 gave them a good deal of trouble from the left, but luckily the telephone to brigade headquarters was open, and a battery supporting the 54th Brigade got to work and completely silenced the machine-gun complained of.

As the right of the Bedfords was now under shell-fire, and as also their front was becoming extended as they pushed on, the West Yorks were put in between the Bedfords and the Queens to make good the western face of the redoubt. Unfortunately, in spite of every effort to direct fresh troops straight on to the redoubt, the reserves of the Bedfords and the West Yorkshires lost direction and edged off to the left, becoming involved in the fighting there. The Bedfords, however, before the barrage lifted, had actually seized Points 13, 95, and 86, and Sergeant Shepherd from this vantage-ground could see the

Germans streaming back away to St Pierre Divion along the Strassburg communication trench. All this area was well under the direct observation of our artillery from their post on high ground near Hamel, and the guns took heavy toll of the retiring enemy.

At 1.42 P.M. Lieut.-Colonel Price reported by telephone that the Bedfords were in possession of Points 13, 91, 84, 95, and that they were close up to their barrage and on the final objective. Part of the Bedfords were at the same time seen moving on towards Point 19, but the ground between this and Point 22 was pitted with shell-holes, and the shell-holes were full of Germans, and contained a few machine-guns as well, so that the whole area had to be gone through and "mopped up" carefully and systematically, while the machine-guns had to be dealt with and silenced by the slow methodical process of bombing.

By 2 P.M. Captain L. H. Keep sent down a message by visual to say that he had reached the final objective. The Bedfords had behaved magnificently, and followed and fought close on the heels of the barrage from start to finish. The 5th West Yorkshires in support had also done well, except that, as already said, they unfortunately failed to keep direction, and some of their platoons even edged off to the left of the Bedfords instead of going in on the right.

All through the afternoon there was a continuous series of disjointed fights going on, good hard hand-to-hand fighting and bombing attacks, especially on the right of the brigade where the line touched the redoubt. Much of this bombing was organised by Captain D. S. H. Keep, and many conspicuous feats of courage and skill were performed. Sergeant Wyatt was awarded the D.C.M. According to the official account of his action, " volunteering to carry out a bombing raid, he pushed his way along two enemy trenches in face of heavy opposition, and established blocks in both. He then went forward with two men and

cleared the trench, bringing back thirty-four prisoners
from the dug-outs. Later, after his officer had become
a casualty, he organised the defence of the position,
and beat off repeated bombing attacks."

A D.C.M. also fell to Private G. Goldhawk, who
"volunteered as observer during a bombing attack,
and ran along the parapet directing the throws of
the bombers. When the attack was held up by
a machine-gun, he rushed the gun and put the whole
team out of action with bombs."

By 5 p.m. the 54th Brigade was holding Points 39,
19, 86, and 45. A unit from the 146th Brigade (49th
Division) had seized the Pope's Nose, at the point
where the old German front crossed the Thiépval
road. Points 47 and 16 were still in the hands of
the Germans, and very strongly held, while in and
around Points 19 and 39, and the trenches connecting
them, continuous bitter fighting was going on with
bombs, rifles, and Lewis guns. In fact, in this area
our hold was very far from secure, in spite of every
effort to strengthen the small posts in possession.
The whole of the Bedfords were deep in the actual
fighting, so were three companies of the West Yorks,
and consolidation parties were sent up from the rear.
This absorbed the last company of the West Yorks.
Only two officers were now left in the Bedfords,
Captain L. H. Keep and his brother, Captain D. S. H.
Keep. Two company sergeant-majors also survived,
C. Hall and R. M. Brand, and a line was taken up a
little in the rear of the line that had actually been
won, and with the help of some sappers who had come
up under Lieutenant Knight, strong posts were formed
and the line made good.

Both the company sergeant-majors spoken of above
were awarded the D.C.M. Hall was endowed with a
tremendous voice, and used it with immense effect to
encourage and direct the supporting troops who were
missing direction, and lift them on to their objective. That voice was heard above all the din of

bombs and shells and clattering rifles and machine-guns. When all his officers had become casualties, Hall took command of his company and carried out the relief with the greatest skill. Brand also commanded his company on this eventful day, and was awarded the D.C.M. "for conspicuous courage, initiative, and powers of leadership."

Second-Lieutenant Adlam, who won his V.C. at Thiépval, did yeoman service at Schwaben. "Though again wounded, this time in the right arm, so that he could no longer throw bombs himself, he continued to lead his men with utter contempt of danger till he was ordered to the rear. There is no doubt that this officer, not only by his personal bravery and magnificent example, but also by his prompt and skilful handling of the tactical situation, was largely responsible for the success of the very important minor operation on the morning of the 27th, and materially assisted in the capture of Schwaben Redoubt."

On the south-western face of the redoubt there was, not unnaturally, a slight confusion between the brigades. Both the 53rd and the 54th thought they were in possession, and as a matter of fact each was right, for the 53rd were in the support line with its clusters of dug-outs, while the 54th were in the front firing line more to the west. Both brigades therefore were in their proper places, but the ground was so confused and the trench-system so complicated that neither brigadier could discover with any degree of certainty just what the other brigade was doing on the western face of the redoubt. General Maxse points out that "owing to its magnificent deep dug-outs the support line was the harder nut to crack, and therefore the Queens had the more difficult task." Their losses were heavy—11 officers and 391 other ranks, comparing with those of the 12th Middlesex at Thiépval—17 officers (of whom 10 were killed) and 413 other ranks.

Schwaben that day was indeed a "soldier's" battle.

There was the case of Sergeant H. J. A'Bear of the
Queens. The crew of one of the Lewis guns had
been put out of action, so Sergeant A'Bear worked
the gun himself, and at one decisive stage kept out
a party of thirty Germans who attacked down a
trench towards him. Also there was the example of
another N.C.O. of the Queens, Corporal W. Hatten.
His platoon was held up by some enemy snipers, and
his officer became a casualty. Corporal Hatten crept
forward to a shell-hole close up to the enemy, and
sniped so successfully that he accounted for ten Germans in quick succession ; and his platoon was able to
advance.

All night long bomb fighting went on without
respite in the outpost line, which the Germans tested
over and over at many different points, seeking a
weak spot where they might manage to smash
through. All attacks failed, and the line held while
reliefs were carried out, but about 7.30 A.M. on
29th September the enemy flung forward a powerful
counter-attack and wrested Points 39 and 19 from
our hold.

The Suffolks were relieved by the Berkshires ; the
West Yorks were withdrawn from the battle and
sent to join their own Division in another army.
The Bedfords had lost, at Thiépval and in the day's
fighting west of Schwaben, 15 officers and 250 men,
and were spent. It was necessary that they also
should be relieved, and by the night of the 28th
General Maxse had taken his decisions and issued
preliminary instructions to the 53rd, 54th, and 146th
Brigades that their relief would be carried out on the
night of the 29th-30th September.

The West Kents were on the spot, and began on
the morning of the 29th to take over the 54th
Brigade front, and on the following night they also
relieved the 146th Brigade in the Thiépval Wood
trenches, thus extending themselves along a very
wide front of 1,500 yards from Schwaben Redoubt to

the Ancre. The Queens remained on the southern face of the redoubt, and the Berks stayed on the front they had taken over from the Suffolks, coming under the orders of Brigadier-General Sir Thomas Jackson, 55th Brigade, when he took over the command from Brigadier-Generals Higginson and Shoubridge at 10.30 P.M. on 29th September.

The effect of these dispositions was to give General Jackson the four battalions belonging to his own brigade with one fresh battalion of the 53rd Brigade (the Berkshires). In this way every battalion in the division would in its turn pull its last ounce of weight, being relieved only when it was fully expended. Thirteen battalions were thus entered in the fighting up to 5th October, the twelve battalions of the division and the 5th West Yorkshires.

It should not be forgotten, however, that in such a piece of work as the Thiépval and Schwaben fighting, a "fresh" battalion meant merely a battalion that had not actually been involved in the assault, whose effectives were more or less numerically intact. They had been fully used in the arduous and exhausting labour of carrying up rations, water, ammunition, and stores every night to their comrades in contact with the enemy, and were by no means fresh in the matter of physical fatigue.

The business before the 55th Brigade then was to complete the capture of the Schwaben Redoubt and occupy all the high ground north of it. For this task General Jackson had two "fresh" battalions, the Buffs and the East Surreys, while his flanks were held by the Berks and the West Kents. The Queens were also in position, but had had one heavy day's fighting with severe losses.

Brigadier-General Jackson and his staff had been in the closest and most constant communication with General Higginson and General Shoubridge, and kept themselves fully in touch with the tactical situation as it developed from hour to hour. Before 26th

September all were warned that the 55th Brigade might be called upon at any moment to take part in the fighting. Definite orders were given on 28th September for the relief of the 53rd and the 54th Brigades and for the pressing of the attack by the 55th Brigade. The East Surreys relieved the Queens on the night of the 29th September and prepared to attack on the afternoon of the 30th.

At dawn on the 30th the East Surreys were ferociously attacked, after ten minutes' intense bombardment, by three bombing parties of the enemy, but beat them off successfully.

"D" Company of the East Surreys only having taken over the line during the night, had had small opportunity for reconnaissance, while the heavy shelling from both sides had obliterated most of the trenches. So "D" Company were at first forced 200 yards back and suffered 40 casualties. But 2nd Lieutenant J. Wightman, who was to prove one of the finest regimental officers the Division possessed, organised a model little counter-attack. One platoon, led by himself, bombed back up the main trench, one platoon under 2nd Lieutenant G. Milner counterattacked over the open on the right, and one platoon under 2nd Lieutenant W. N. Barfoot went over the open on the left.

The enemy knew the ground. Also they were armed with "egg" bombs, with which they ought to have been able to out-throw our bombers. But Lieutenant Wightman was an extremely powerful thrower and actually out-bombed the Germans with the Mills bomb. This, combined with the spirited attacks led by Barfoot and Milner, drove the enemy out of the occupied trench and even gained another 50 yards of ground for the East Surreys. The men fought with a deadly purposefulness that was irresistible. And they kept their heads. Sergeant C. Palmer, who brought up a Lewis gun, fired his first shots from it with the muzzle close up against the breast of a German. And he mowed down others at close range. "I was so close," he said afterwards with explanatory gesture, "that I could see their tunics shaking like *that* as the bullets went through them." His companions were equally collected and resolute. When the supply of bombs ran out and Lieutenant Wightman sent back Privates James and Newman to battalion headquarters with an urgent message for bombs, at the same time saying, "If he comes again we shall use the bayonet, and no man goes out a prisoner," his men took off their coats and stood ready. The enemy did not attack again for the moment, and with cool rapidity a bomb - stop was built. The reinforcing party arrived before the Germans, and the ground so gallantly won was held.

It was ascertained from reports and from the observations of patrols that the Germans had been strongly reinforced, and that they were repairing and consolidating the northern part of the redoubt on the line running through Points 27, 99, 69, 49, 39, and 19.

At 4.30 P.M. on 30th September a heavy barrage was laid down, under cover of which two companies of the East Surreys and two platoons of the 7th Buffs attacked and captured the whole of this line, but were at once heavily counter-attacked by the Germans and driven back. They managed, however, to retain Point 27, which was of great importance, and made good their possession permanently.

Greatly stimulated by this success, the Germans organised powerful bombing assaults and reoccupied Point 37; they even took Point 45 and held it for some time, but were finally flung out of it with some loss, including 22 unwounded prisoners, one of whom proved to have been a waiter at the Trocadero Restaurant in London.

On the 1st October the 7th Buffs relieved the East Surreys, and while two local attacks from Point 27 failed to capture Point 99, in the afternoon the Buffs seized Point 37 once more, and finally held it.

For the next few days, until 5th October, it is practically impossible to describe what took place in the disputed area. Heavy bombing attacks were delivered on both sides, fierce hand-to-hand fighting with varying fortune, at least ten attacks and counter-attacks on a considerable scale ; and the Germans made great use both of gas and flammenwerfer. The trenches, knee - deep in slimy mud, were thick with British and German dead; the ground was so torn and shattered that every landmark almost had disappeared, and it was practically impossible to derive assistance from maps. Tremendous shelling went on day and night, and there was persistent rain. Schwaben Redoubt may have had dry days, but the 18th Division saw it only in the autumn and the winter. It took 10 hours to get the rations up from 3,000 yards away. Many of the severely wounded, Boche as well as British, lay in the deep dug-outs for days : the shelling was so heavy and the going so muddy and treacherous it was impossible to shift them. As the fighting went on and our casualties increased, there were even cases where, in order to make room for our own wounded, dying Germans had to be lifted out of dug-outs and laid in the open while German shells were falling all around. The Berkshires had one wounded Boche who became a sort of mascot, being handed over to each relieving platoon until eventually he was got away by the stretcher-bearers.

On the 2nd October some of the points in the fateful northern corner of the redoubt changed hands three and four times. The Germans heavily shelled one bomb-stop defended by 2nd Lieutenant A. L. L. Chamberlain of the 7th Buffs. They shelled for three and a half hours, and then began a furious bombing attack. But a combination of picked bombers and snipers and a Lewis gun skilfully placed drove them back, and half of the attackers were killed. Sergeant G. J. Steel and five other men threw 250 bombs during the hour and a half that the assault lasted. The German artillery put in another half-hour's burst of shelling, and again their infantry surged to the attack. But when a dozen of them had been killed they gave up, and Lieutenant Chamberlain and his men remained in unmolested possession of the bomb-stop.

On 3rd October the Germans made a swift flammenwerfer attack and took 200 yards of trench on the north-east face of the redoubt; but 2nd Lieutenant A. S. Hayfield of the 7th Buffs, leading a bombing party that was supported by Stokes mortars and Lewis guns, got back all the lost ground, and in addition captured 100 yards more. But at dawn on the 4th, using gas and flammenwerfer, the Boche made a still more desperate assault. Their bombers got into our trenches and fought their way forward with fierce determination. One glorious instance of self-sacrifice was that of Private Lake of the 55th Trench Mortar Battery. Two trench mortars were behind a bomb-stop held by our infantry, and the attacking Germans drove in this post. Shouting to his companions, "Get back with the guns—I will stay here," Private Lake held off the enemy, single-handed, for nearly ten minutes. He was killed outright by a bomb, but he had made it possible for the trench mortars to be got away. When the 55th Brigade moved out to rest in the Candas area Sir Douglas Haig personally thanked the 55th Machine-Gun Company, and the 55th Trench Mortar gunners, for the fine work they had done in Schwaben Redoubt. Later on the 4th, the 55th Brigade got back all the yielded ground, but there was never any rest in Schwaben, and next day the bitter, costly efforts were renewed. Lieutenant A. S. Hayfield was wounded on the 4th, and, owing to the conditions, could not be moved. He died, suffering intense pain, while the 7th Buffs were engaged in repelling an attack made on 5th October. All his thoughts

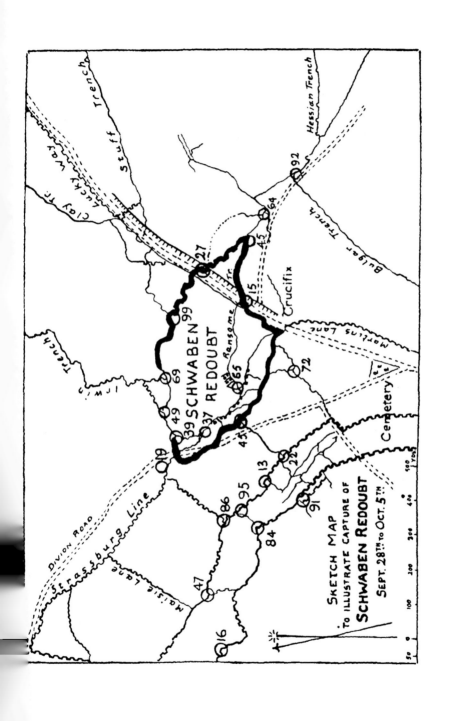

SKETCH MAP
TO ILLUSTRATE CAPTURE OF
**SCHWABEN REDOUBT**
SEPT. 28TH TO OCT. 5TH

during the last moments were for his brother, Lieutenant C. D. Hayfield, who was taking part in the action. C. D. Hayfield, as intelligence officer to the 55th Brigade, became later one of the best-known officers in the Division. At the Armistice the distinctions he had won included the D.S.O. and the Military Cross with two bars.

In the end, by the 5th October we had captured and made our own the whole of Schwaben Redoubt except a small strip along the north-west corner, including Points 19, 39, 49, and 69; and on that day, 5th October, the 18th Division was relieved by the 39th Division. While no little regret was felt that our troops had not remained to complete the clearing of the redoubt, it was beyond question that they needed a rest.

The capture of Schwaben Redoubt had cost the Division 1,990 casualties—80 officers, 1,910 other ranks —in the eight days' fighting. The 7th Queens lost 11 officers and 391 other ranks, the 7th Buffs 11 officers and 158 other ranks, the 8th East Surreys 9 officers and 284 other ranks, and the 7th West Kents 16 officers and 324 other ranks. The Norfolks lost 4 officers and 176 other ranks, the 6th Royal Berkshires 6 officers and 176 other ranks, and the 7th Bedfords 10 officers and 138 other ranks.

The German killed were very numerous, though no exact figure can be given. An estimate made on the spot placed the dead at 600. No estimate can be framed as to the wounded; but General Maxse declares that in his opinion it would not be an exaggeration "to say that in and around Schwaben Redoubt we incapacitated 2,500 Germans from first to last." Four German officers and 233 other ranks surrendered to the 18th Division in and around Schwaben Redoubt, and, of course, the Germans lost also the stronghold itself, on whose retention they set the highest possible value.

Its loss was a very heavy blow to their whole

position, as is shown by the terms of a captured German Regimental Order of 20th October, which proclaimed the necessity of recovering the Schwaben Redoubt. "Men are to be informed by their immediate superiors that this attack is not merely a matter of retaking a trench because it was formerly in German possession, but that the recapture of an extremely important point is involved. If the enemy remains on the ridge he can blow our artillery in the Ancre valley to pieces, and the protection of the infantry will then be destroyed."

I

# CHAPTER VIII.

### WEARING DOWN THE ENEMY ON THE ANCRE—THE CAPTURE OF REGINA TRENCH AND DESIRE TRENCH.

*Lieut.-Colonel Price succeeds to the command of the 55th Brigade— 250 Germans killed in Regina Trench fight—10th Essex Padre's story—Desire Trench attacked in a snowstorm—Two companies of 7th Queens missing—The death of Captain Dyson of the 7th Buffs.*

OCTOBER and November 1916 were months in which the Staff proposed and the weather disposed. Plans for the forcing further eastward of the German masses included one operation in which 10 tanks were to assist the 18th Division; there was even talk of an attempt to cross the Ancre. But as the persistent rains and the steady virulence of the shelling had turned the whole region into a morass, trenches becoming ditches of liquid mud, or being blotted out altogether, and with the river in flood—300 yards wide at this time—it was wisdom for our aims to be limited. Actual achievements in these two months were the consolidation of Schwaben Redoubt, the capture of Regina Trench in mid-October, and of part of Desire Trench, 500 yards farther on, after a hard, somewhat disappointing struggle on 18th November.

Small as these results appeared at the time, they were significant of the beginning of the end of the long spell of trench warfare. They formed a very definite part of the slow disintegrating process to which Sir Douglas Haig was subjecting the German defensive system. They helped to loosen the Boche's grip upon the Somme area; they weakened his moral;

they were among the primary causes that led to
March's swift retreat to the Hindenburg line. Also
they were operations that served very practically to
stiffen and to fit into the Division the reinforcements
that flowed steadily across the Channel.

It was about this time that Lieut.-Colonel G. D.
Price, who had commanded the 7th Bedfords, succeeded Brigadier-General Sir Thomas Jackson in the
command of the 55th Brigade. Lieut.-Colonel G. P.
Mills, D.S.O., now commanded the Bedfords.

Regina Trench was taken by the 53rd Brigade on
21st October. The assaulting battalions were the
10th Essex and the 8th Norfolks. It was a well-
planned and effectively executed piece of work. 250
Germans were killed; 6 Boche officers and 309 men
were taken prisoners, and 5 machine-guns fell into our
possession. The 53rd Brigade's total casualties from
21st October to 23rd October inclusive were 48 killed,
including one officer, and 8 officers and 189 other
ranks wounded. 32 men were reported missing.

General Maxse and General Higginson were particularly pleased with this success, not alone for its
strategical value. It proved that the infantry recruits
who had replaced the many men lost on 1st July, and
at Thiépval and in Schwaben, were up to standard.
The 10th Essex in particular had become practically
a new battalion; and in this connection the Rev.
David Randell, who was Padre to the Essex from
February 1916 to the end of the war, quotes a queer
illustration of how doubt was turned into confidence.
Just before the attack he and Major A. S. Tween,
the second in command, who had gained his D.S.O.
in Delville Wood, were walking together during the
march up the communication trench.

"We both had a feeling," says the Padre, "that
the old 10th Essex had gone, and Tween confided to
me that he was a little anxious as to how the new
men would bear themselves. But, just afterwards,
along Rifle Trench we came upon a half-buried dead

German. One leg stuck out of the mud ; it displayed
a sock of vivid and wonderful hue. 'My Gawd,
warn't he a knut,' exclaimed one of the men up in
a front-line trench for the first time. It sounds
trivial, but that remark removed Tween's apprehen-
sion. He felt after that that things would go well
with the battalion. And he was right." It was one
of those partly seasoned men of the 10th Essex who
found himself disarmed in the struggle in Regina
Trench. He went for the German who was threatening him with a bayonet, seized him by the neck with
his bare hands, and throttled him.

The attack was carried through with such vigorous
swiftness that in the main the German defenders did
not resist long. A party of Landwehr put up a good
fight, however, against the company of 8th Norfolks
that was led by Captain Morgan, D.S.O. Only most
aggressive bombing caused them to give in. Afterwards Captain Morgan took 16 prisoners in very easy
fashion. He was superintending the cleaning up of
the trench, when he noticed a waterproof - sheet
hanging from the parapet. Lifting it, he found
that it screened the entrance to a dug-out, eight
steps deep. On each step sat a couple of Germans,
their backs to the entrance. When Captain Morgan
called to them to come out they came, unarmed.
When the Norfolk and Essex were in full possession
of Regina, a dozen Germans who had lost themselves
descended into the trench, not knowing it had changed
hands. They did not seem unduly depressed when
they found themselves prisoners.

During the remainder of October and the early
part of November it rained nearly every day, and
most parts of Regina Trench were more than knee-
deep in oozy clinging mud. Once the 10th Essex
went up to carry out a relief by daylight, and the
enemy started shelling. The men had been walking
along the top where the ground was less holding,
and some of them dived into the trench to avoid the

shells. Next morning Lieut.-Colonel Frizell and the
Padre found two men buried in mud to their shoulders. They had fallen in the previous day, could not
release themselves, and had gradually sunk. And
no one had passed near enough to hear their shouts.
It was not until ropes were tied round them that
they could be pulled out.

The wastage in men during those weeks when it was
only a matter of guarding the line may be gathered
by a study of the Division's weekly records :—

*Nov.* 3. No active operations during the week.
     Killed, 67 ; wounded, 266; missing, 25.

*Nov.* 10. No active operations during the week.
     Killed, 45 ; wounded, 121 ; missing, 4.

*Nov.* 17. No active operations during the week.
     Killed, 29 ; wounded, 158; missing, 1.

Enemy aircraft were particularly active at this
time, and there was much shelling of Pozières Cemetery, Courcelette, Mouquet Farm and Kay dumps.

The attack on Desire Trench at dawn on 18th
November was part of a more ambitious undertaking
made in conjunction with the Canadians on the right
and the 19th Division on the left. It happened to
coincide with the first snowfall of the winter of 1916-
17. The Canadians gained their objective and advanced beyond it. The 55th Brigade, who attacked
for the 18th Division, also reached the arranged line,
but in their case touch was never gained with the
assaulting companies of the 19th Division, who in the
mist swerved to their left and descended towards
the Ancre. The German machine - gunners were
hurried up into the gap thus made between the 18th
and 19th Divisional troops, and two companies of
7th Queens vanished entirely, being overwhelmed by
machine-gun fire.

A few days before the attack, when the 10th Essex
were holding Regina Trench, a piece of unofficial
reconnaissance work in the direction of Desire Trench
was carried out by Lieutenant J. A. B. Thompson and

Sergeant J. Culver, who afterwards became an officer of the battalion. They knew that a gully lay in front of Regina Trench and that sniping fire came from that direction, but it was not known whether or not the gully was held in force. Crawling up to the gully, the subaltern and the sergeant noted much uncut wire, they also noted a dead horse; and then, looking into the gully, they perceived a number of dug-outs. While they were debating in whispers whether they should search the dug-outs, a German infantryman popped up his head five yards from Lieutenant Thompson. The Boche gave a yell and Thompson shot him dead with his revolver. Then zigzagging to avoid the burst of German rifle-fire that immediately broke out, the pair scrambled back to Regina. Thompson was taken to tell his story to General Maxse and to General Metcalfe, the C.R.A. As he was able to supply information as to the German wire that had not been cut by our artillery fire the reconnaissance was of value. Sergeant Culver, a man of a robust and impetuous personality, received a commission soon afterwards, and won the M.C. at Irles. He was taken prisoner during the great German onrush of 21st March 1918, and became notable in yet another direction : he was the British officer who was with the American officer when the German sentry shot him for going outside the wire of a prison camp after the Armistice had been signed.

There is direct evidence that the men of the 7th Buffs and the 7th Queens who were cut off on 18th November died game, for Lieut.-Colonel A. L. Ransome, O.C. of the 7th Buffs, went over the same ground months afterwards—after the Boom Ravine victory— and found over fifty dead, the bodies having been preserved during the long intense frost of February 1917. The Buffs had been brought into the attack unexpectedly. Through trench fever and heavy fighting losses they were below strength and sorely in need of rest. But at the eleventh hour the 55th Brigade

were called upon almost to double the length of their
front in order to join up with the 19th Division, so
that the Buffs, instead of being kept in reserve, became
assaulting troops, with no opportunities for preliminary
reconnaissances. The Buffs, when the attack opened,
suffered heavy losses, because in front of Desire Trench
in their sector the Germans had dug narrow slits
through which they crept to shell-holes when the
battle began; and, avoiding our artillery barrage,
sniped our advancing troops from behind. All the
officers of the 7th Buffs were killed, save one who
was severely wounded. Among those who fell was
Captain Dyson, who did valiantly on 1st July 1916.
Captain Dyson was O.C. of "A" Company, and was
one of the first officers to join the 18th Division's
Buffs. He possessed knowledge and judgment, and
was a great personal force. The men placed implicit
trust in him. More pregnant still in misfortune for
the Buffs and Queens was the fact that the troops of the
57th Brigade of the 19th Division, failing to secure
their objective, returned to their original trenches by
10.46 A.M., thus exposing our left wing. Despite their
losses, the Buffs fought their way to their objective
and were holding it, but at daylight next day they
withdrew in obedience to a Divisional order.

On the Division's right everything went well. The
East Surreys, who had the Canadians as neighbours,
forged ahead and took 86 prisoners in two hours.
Major Place won his M.C. for his enterprising work
that day. The 7th Royal West Kents, commanded
on that day by Lieut.-Colonel O. C. Clare, who had
been Adjutant of the 8th East Surreys, also secured
their objective with few casualties. But as no reports
had been received at Divisional Headquarters from
the portion of Desire Trench which should have been
occupied by the Buffs and the Queens and the left
company of the 7th Royal West Kents, and as
seven runners had been killed by rifle-fire in trying
to reach this trench, it was resolved to work along

Desire Trench to the west from the left flank of the West Kents. A bombing assault, and an attack across the open by one company of the West Kents, was carried out with dash and determination. Several German bomb-stops had to be broken down; twenty-five of the enemy were killed; and many of them bolted, some down the trench, and some across the open. Darkness descended, and it was difficult to determine all the ground that had been gained; but next morning strong patrols were again pushed westward along Desire Trench, and by nightfall the whole trench, as far west as Stump Road, was reported to have been evacuated by the enemy.

On the morning of the 19th Lieut.-Colonel Irwin of the East Surreys, while superintending the consolidation of the new position, was wounded by a sniper. Private Dunkley, the Colonel's orderly, was sent off to convey the news to 55th Brigade Headquarters. Dunkley was hit in the stomach while going through Death Valley, but though mortally wounded he crawled 600 yards and delivered his message. He died next day.

One other incident of the struggle for Desire Trench should be recorded. When after the first set-back our left moved forward, some of our wounded were found in a German dug-out carefully bandaged. Food also had been left for them by the enemy.

By the beginning of December the Division had left the line for Christmas rest in the Abbeville area. When it came back to the Somme it was to fight under a new leader. General Maxse, whose name must always be associated with that of the 18th Division, had been promoted to the command of the XVIII. Corps. Major-General Richard P. Lee reigned in his stead. General Lee had come to France from Gibraltar, and served his apprenticeship in the great war as C.R.E. of the famous 7th Division. He shared in General Sir Hubert Gough's promotions, and accompanied Sir Hubert as his C.E. when he rose to

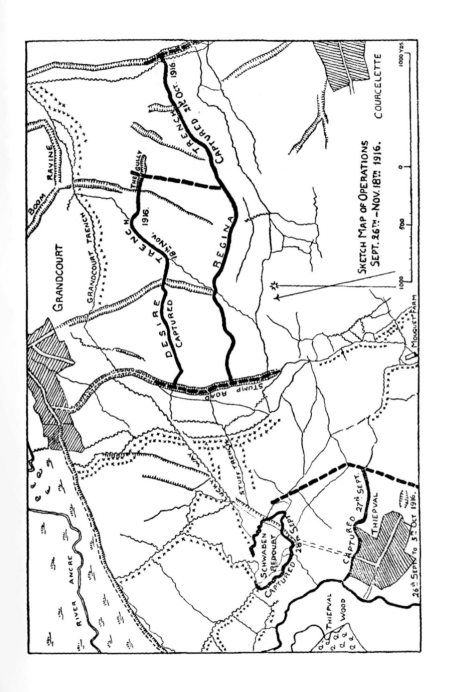

SKETCH MAP OF OPERATIONS
SEPT. 26TH – NOV. 18TH 1916.

command a Corps and then an Army. General Lee
was C.E., 5th Army, when he was given command of
the 18th Division. Curiously enough, he had been
wounded in the arm by shrapnel while reconnoitring
for one of the earlier assaults on Thiépval. The officers
and men of the 18th Division were unfeignedly sorry
that General Maxse, the creator of the Division, should
be taken from them, although they understood per-
fectly well that his promotion was an honour to them
and to their record of successes as well as to the General
himself. But they came also to learn that General
Lee was a great general too. As a Divisional commander he displayed infinite knowledge, quick grip
and decision. His opinion was considered and not
easily changed, as indeed it rarely had need to be. He
had a great gift for map-reading, and consequently
never failed in his battle dispositions to make full
use of ground. As a study of the later history of the
Division shows, he had a settled distaste for frontal
attacks : the large hauls of prisoners and correspond-
ingly small casualties in the successful actions in the
closing stages of the war can be traced to his determination to manœuvre. Under General Lee the
Division experienced triumphs that will become historic ; it also endured much tribulation. But all
through it remained as General Maxse left it, a first-
class Division.

# CHAPTER IX.

## THE BATTLE OF BOOM RAVINE.

*Battle that broke the backbone of German resistance on the Ancre—The intense cold of February 1917—Hour of attack known to the Germans — Their annihilating surprise bombardment — Royal Fusiliers' advance without officers—How Lieutenant T. R. Price of the Northamptons won his D.S.O.*

IT was known to General Lee when the Division returned on 16th January from rest near Abbeville to the same piece of line that had been handed over to the 61st Division in the previous November, that an offensive was in prospect. The Somme fighting of 1916 had given Sir Douglas Haig command of both sides of the Ancre Valley. Owing to the big successes of the 18th at Thiépval, and of the 63rd, the Naval Division, at Beaumont Hamel, the Germans were in a salient projecting westward like a pyramid. Against the southern wall of this triangular bulge the 18th Division was to launch itself; so the Division found itself approaching Grandcourt and Petit Miraumont, the former lying in ruins on the left front and Petit Miraumont 2,000 to 3,000 yards away over the ridge. Simultaneously with the 18th Division's attack another was to be launched in the north from Arras so as to pinch the German divisions in between.

As events proved, the Germans were too wary to allow the squeeze to take full effect. At the earliest sign of pressure they withdrew, fighting a series of rearguard actions to the Hindenburg Line. In the last week of the month, places like Warlencourt, Pys,

Miraumont, and Puisieux came tumbling into Sir
Douglas Haig's lap like ripe apples; from Gomme-
court to Grandcourt on a front of about a dozen
miles the Germans yielded ground to a depth in
some places of three miles. Fought about midway
between those points, the Battle of Boom Ravine
broke the backbone of the German resistance on
the Ancre, and accelerated this satisfactory harvest
gathered in very unseasonable conditions.

To those at home who may have regarded Boom
Ravine as a minor obstacle in an otherwise triumphant walk-over, it will come as a surprise to hear that
the casualties that day to the 18th Division totalled
54 officers and 1,135 other ranks. Mention was made
by the war correspondents at the time of a certain
amount of fighting at the Ravine, but into the cheering picture of progress no darkening suggestions of
costly effort were permitted to intrude. Doubtless
it was part of the Censor's business to see that that
was so. But there has been a smaller toll of life in
many battles writ big on history's page than there
was at Boom Ravine.

Boom Ravine was won by steadfastness and endurance in the most trying circumstances. It was one
of the few proved cases of the war in which there
was British treachery : two men of a neighbouring
Division went over to the enemy and revealed the
hour of the offensive, with the consequence that
our attacking infantry were cut up by shell-fire as
they assembled in the dark, in exposed positions.
Also the battle coincided with the break-up of the
five weeks' biting frost that no one who was on the
Somme in January and February of 1917 will forget.
17th February was the first day of the thaw, and the
hard surface of the ground turned first into one big
slide, and then became a sea of mud, in which rifles
and machine-guns got clogged, and through which
the infantry pressed a slow, floundering, stamina-
testing way.

Let it also be realised that the intense cold which
preceded this attack of 17th February had made the
ground so bone-hard that it was impossible to dig
new trenches, or to improve the battered mud chan-
nels—apologies for trenches—that were in being, and
had become floored with ice.  Consequently the preparatory work had to be carried out in an area practically shelterless.  The deep German dug-outs in the
lines Zollern, Regina, Hessian, and Desire did indeed
afford cover to the men ; but the outposts had nothing better than shell-holes, and they underwent a
consistently miserable time, although there were
days early in February when the blue skies and
the sparkle on the undulating frost-bound ground
revived memories of winter sports in Switzerland.
There were a certain number of cases of frost-bitten
feet — not to be confused with trench feet — until
Colonel Poe and his M.O.'s found that the best protection for feet and legs lay in sandbags stuffed with
straw.  On many nights there were twenty degrees
of frost, and, as has been mentioned, these conditions
lasted until the very day of the battle.

There was another highly important point in the
preparations for the battle, well understood and continually emphasised by General Lee.  The first thaw
might mean a serious shortage of supplies for the
front-line troops.  The total absence of any metalled
road in the Divisional area leading to Petit Miraumont
from the south, and the distance entailed by sending
transport by way of the much-damaged Ancre Valley
road, made the question of supply exceedingly difficult ; and since the arrival of the Division on 16th
January the General had reiterated the imperative
necessity of pushing forward the water supply and
of laying light railways and duckboard paths.  Four
thousand yards of shell-churned wilderness separated
our front from the head of the Nab Valley road.
Forward of this were no signs of a metalled road.
More than once General Lee, a pick over his shoulder,

was to be seen walking with a staff officer, generally Major Guy Blewitt, the G.S.O. II, prospecting for a road which appeared on the map but nowhere else. And had it existed it would have been covered with frozen mud, with on top of that a four-inch layer of snow. But these expeditions never disclosed more than perhaps a track upon which the Boche had laid a sprinkling of chalk and flints leading from the Ancre Valley to some old German gun position behind the Zollern line.

Let us now consider the topography of the battle-field of Boom Ravine. One of those deep sunken roads so typical of the Somme district, Boom Ravine ran south-east from the Ancre Valley for a distance of 500 yards, and then from its junction with The Ravine proper—another sunken road some 30 feet deep that ran due south for 700 yards—extended itself east for another 500 yards until it linked up with the west Miraumont road. The whole lay-out of these sunken roads formed for our purposes a rugged letter "T," of which the stem was The Ravine proper. Troops attacking on the east side of the Ravine proper would have to take Grandcourt Trench, and the eastern arm of Boom Ravine immediately in its rear, and then secure Miraumont Trench at the top of the bluff overlooking Petit Miraumont  This was the task of the 54th Brigade. Troops on the west side of the Ravine proper—the 53rd Brigade—were faced with another stretch of Grandcourt Trench, and beyond that three short lengths of newly-wired trenches known as Rum, Coffee, and Tea Trenches. These were on less elevated ground, for compared to the bluff on the east side of the Ravine the slope westward to the Ancre is gradual.

No precaution that forethought could suggest was omitted. The 54th Brigade were taken out of the line for three days for rehearsals, and General Lee, always a master in the use of ground and machine-guns, had arranged an effective machine-gun pro-

gramme not only for our own guns, but for those
of the 63rd Naval Division on our left.   The 63rd
were able to enfilade, and in some cases to take in
reverse, the enemy positions to be attacked.   Our
own divisional artillery was augmented by that of the
31st Division.

In preparation for the offensive small enterprises
to feel the strength of the enemy were undertaken.
It was in the course of these raids that symptoms
of the German intention to withdraw were perceived.
The first indication came on 6th February, when the
63rd Division reported the evacuation of the German
lines west of Grandcourt.   The Germans left Grandcourt itself—it lay in ruins—next day.   Then two
companies of the 10th Essex, who stole into Folly
Trench to stalk Germans on a moonlit night, with
snow on the ground and the temperature 20 degrees
below freezing-point, found no one there.   The Germans were then doubtless busy strengthening their
wire a few hundred yards farther back.   The incident
of Folly Trench has a bearing upon the story of the
battle, for it marked the jumping-off place of the
53rd Brigade, and in particular of the 6th Berkshires,
being 500 yards ahead of their main line—Regina
Trench.   The 54th, for their part, had a forming-up
place 200 yards in advance of The Gully, a depression
at right angles to the Ravine proper (the stem of
the "T"), and joined to it at a point called Oxford
Circus.

The battle of Boom Ravine was timed for 5.45 A.M.
on 17th February, and the troops were ordered to be
in position an hour earlier.   The 18th attacked in
conjunction with the 2nd Division on the right, the
63rd Division performing a minor operation on the
left.   But the defence was to strike the first blow.
Just as our troops began to assemble, yellow and
green lights illumined the sky over the German
trenches, and the German artillery acknowledged
the signal with an annihilating bombardment of our

lines and assembling points. Shells fell thick and fast in the vicinity of the Gully, at a time when it was crowded with Royal Fusiliers, making for Oxford Circus and the forming-up positions. The regiment sustained in the Gully about half its total casualties that day. At zero hour only two of the fourteen officers about to go over the top remained—Captain Morton, and that most popular officer, Captain Collis Sandes. Collis Sandes fell, shot in the neck before he had gone 200 yards; and before Grandcourt Trench was reached, Captain Morton was killed by a shell that amputated his foot. Consequently, so far as the Royal Fusiliers were concerned, the attack was carried through without an officer, although John Sale, the regimental medical officer, with ever-ready advice and invigorating example, was certainly no non-combatant that day. A platoon of the North-ants was practically wiped out on its way to form up; while to the left of the Ravine the headquarters of the 6th Royal Berks were blown in before zero hour, and Lieut.-Colonel Clay had to transfer to Regina Trench.

And even had there been no German barrage, forming up in the open in the misty darkness was a difficult enough operation. Men had to grope their way in follow-my-leader fashion, more or less by instinct. But in point of fact the attack was launched to the minute, and from the correct form-ing-up line—a circumstance that speaks for the dog-gedness of the men and the discipline that had been instilled into them. General Higginson himself super-intended the assembly of the 53rd Brigade, whose line he had seen marked out in screw pickets and wire. The 53rd Brigade attacked with the 8th Suffolks (with one company of the 8th Norfolks attached) on the right, the 6th Royal Berks in the centre, and one company of the 8th Norfolks on the left. The 54th Brigade had the 11th Fusiliers in and astride the Ravine proper, and the 6th Northants

on the right; and each of these units had a company
of the 12th Middlesex Regiment following in its
wake. The 55th Infantry Brigade were in reserve.
The German surprise barrage had lasted by official
records some 40 minutes. It ceased soon after our
own artillery opened, except for a short-lived burst
of activity in response to the German S.O.S. lights.
The assault was carried forward on the left with fine
impetuosity. The Berkshires took a bit of Grandcourt Trench so far ahead of their fellows that they
were fetched back to keep in line with the others,
and had to retake what they had already gained.
The battalion reached their objective on the railway
line, but their right flank had to fall back slightly.
The Berks captured in the course of the day 160
Germans. During the whole time they were in
France, the battalion of Royal Berkshires originally
attached to the Division lost only nine prisoners, and
the Boom Ravine fight was responsible for eight of
them. They were the men who wandered in the
dark to the right towards the objective of the 2nd
Division. The bodies of two platoons of men belonging to the Berks were found in a trench taken by the
2nd Division, showing that they had fought to the
last. Among the Berkshires wounded near Boom
Ravine was Colonel N. B. Hudson, then Captain, but
this did not prevent "B" Company from reaching
their second objective, a feat marked by the sending
off of a carrier-pigeon with the bald message, "Second
objective reached. — Sergeant - Major Hine." The
pigeon reached the Corps loft safely, and the message was the cause of every battalion in the Corps
receiving immediately afterwards urgent inquiries for
Sergeant-Major Hine.

Like the Berkshires, the 8th Suffolks gave a very
sturdy account of themselves. Lieut.-Colonel G.
V. W. Hill's battalion struck a bad patch in front
of Coffee Trench, where most of its losses occurred.
But though the Suffolks fell behind the barrage, they

K

were in Boom Ravine by 8 A.M., and did all that was required of them. Grandcourt Trench presented no difficulty, save at one point, at the junction of Sixteen Road, which was found to be badly damaged and practically evacuated. The Suffolks were able, therefore, to help the Fusiliers. It was perceived that progress on the right was arrested, and that three enemy machine-guns east of the Ravine were doing much execution. These were put out of action by the promptness of Lieutenant Walker and Sergeant Eaves, who wheeled round the right platoon of "A" Company and brought rapid fire to bear. Sergeant Rose also did effective work with a Lewis gun, and eventually the Suffolks saw Germans holding up their hands, and the 54th Brigade were thus enabled to go forward.

None of the 8th Suffolk companies escaped punishment. Captain Whitehead was wounded when trying with Lieutenant Green to prevent "B" Company losing direction towards the left. "C" Company lost 2nd Lieutenant Walters, wounded fatally, and Lieutenant A. S. Jeffery was wounded as well. This company had only one officer left—2nd Lieutenant Hall. Hall and Lieutenant Green worked together thenceforward, and their intrepidity and dash earned them deserved encomiums from their superior officers. "D" Company of the Suffolks lost Captain J. R. Keats, wounded, and 2nd Lieutenants A. Hubbard and C. E. Bird, killed, and Sergeant Bailey had to take command. Sergeant Bailey was wounded himself later, and had to hand over to Sergeant Sheppard. Opposite the line of advance taken by this company was a bank a little to the north of Coffee Trench. It was a German strong point. It looked impossible to take this stronghold except by a flanking movement; but before the movement developed Lance-Corporal Savage and seven men forced their way with splendid dash through a small gap in the wire, and rushed the position. The Germans were

more than two to one, but they seemed unnerved by
the dash of the Suffolks. Corporal Savage killed the
first four Germans he met. Fourteen others who
were round a machine-gun surrendered. Lance-
Corporal Savage's act, taken on his own initiative,
transformed the situation. The loss of the machine-
gun—the second "D" Company had taken that
morning, a gun had been captured already on the
Sixteen Road—had an immediate effect upon the
Germans, who were holding the ground farther to the
right; from this point the enemy's resistance at the
Ravine was overcome, and two platoons of "C" Company who cleared the dug-outs took 70 prisoners. By
8.30 the Ravine was clear of Germans, and Lewis
guns had been pushed up the slope on the northern
side. Over 100 dead Germans were counted in the
Suffolks' area alone.

The mist from the Miraumont Marshes favoured
the consolidation of the positions gained, and the
evacuation of the wounded. It was one of the 53rd
Brigade's greatest days. All the objectives were
gained, and the highest fighting qualities were displayed by all ranks.

In the area of the 54th Brigade on the right the
fortunes of the struggle were of a more fluctuating
character. Opposite the Northamptons and the Fusiliers the Germans were very numerous, and with
reserves at hand in Petit Miraumont they offered a
fierce resistance. It was in this quarter that the
enemy counter-attack began at 8.30 A.M. As has
been said, the 54th Brigade's battalions had to go
forward with depleted ranks, and with very few
officers left. Much responsibility in gathering up
the Northamptons fell upon 2nd Lieutenants Boulton
and Higham, whose efforts were splendidly seconded
by Company Sergeant-Major Cuthbert. When the
men were lining up the last-named stood at the top of
the bank and acted as a human direction post. Soon
after the assault was launched he was wounded, but

he refused to leave his men until he had handed them
over to the senior sergeant. This sort of incident
became familiar enough on Boom Ravine day, when
so many to whom the men looked for leadership
were knocked out. Sergeants, corporals, and in
some cases privates, carried on and showed resource
and initiative.

At the first obstacle—Grandcourt Trench—the
centre and left companies of the Northampton Regiment were stopped by an unsuspectedly strong fence
of uncut wire. The men had to wander groping for
gaps in the face of German snipers and machine-gunners. To the left the Fusiliers were luckier, finding
their openings immediately, and with the Trench
Mortar Battery and the 54th Machine Gun Company
well up, they pressed forward. The right company
of the Northamptons kept up with them, leaving their
companion companies a good way behind. The delay
on the 54th Brigade's left allowed many of the enemy
to get back to the Ravine, and to the trenches behind
it. An attempted trap by one party of Germans,
who held an isolated machine-gun point near Grandcourt Trench, brought about their own undoing.
They shammed death, hoping to take a handful of
Northamptons in rear. The Germans stretched themselves in the mud, each man with his rifle within
reach. The hidden machine-gun stood near. But
Private J. W. Walsh, of the Northants, was a man
of an inquiring disposition. He considered that the
complexion of one of the prostrate Germans looked
remarkably fresh, and removed the man's cap. In-
stantly the supposed corpse sprang up. But he did
not fire. He held up his hands. So did his comrades.

From Grandcourt Trench one platoon of Northamptons was led forward to Boom Ravine by Private
Charles Cantrell, an officer's servant, who took charge
when no officer or N.C.O. remained. Cantrell cleared
out a number of the enemy, reorganised his little force
in the ravine, and carried on in business-like style.

The Fusiliers surprised many Germans coming out of the dug-outs in Boom Ravine and took 100 prisoners. Captain Sale, bearing in mind the 4,700 yards to the advanced dressing-station, used these prisoners as stretcher-bearers. The cases were carried about two kilometres uphill to Hessian Trench, whence they were pushed along a light railway track for the remainder of the journey. In this way, wounded who otherwise must have lain in the icy slush for hours, were quickly evacuated.

From Boom Ravine, the Fusiliers were led forward by Company Sergeant-Major Fitterer of "B" Company, who was already wounded in the thigh. Sergeant Choate was at the head of "A" Company, Sergeant Berry of "C" Company, and Sergeant Hazell of "D" Company. These four companies with the right company of the Northamptons re-formed north of the Ravine, leaving the Middlesex men to search the dug-outs. It took time to sort out the men—it was barely daylight—and the advance towards the second objective and South Miraumont Trench was not begun until 6.30 A.M. By this time the barrage had gone far ahead, and as the Fusiliers and Northants clambered up the ridge they became targets for Germans who lined the trench behind a thick wire palisade. One of the officers to fall was Lieut.-Colonel R. J. F. Meyricke, the Northants commanding officer, killed by a bullet—a heavy loss indeed. Colonel Meyricke had previously belonged to the Fusiliers, and had only taken over command of the Northants on 3rd February. He was very able and very popular. Dropping into shell-holes and working steadily forward over the mud-clogged ground, both Fusiliers and Northants gained a footing in South Miraumont Trench. The Northants party was under Lieutenant T. R. Price, the Adjutant, who had been with Colonel Meyricke when he was shot, and 2nd Lieutenant Higham. But with a good part of the whole line held up this trench was not

long in our possession. The German reserves were
released for the counter-attack. They poured from
dug-outs in the Bluff against the 54th Brigade, and
at the same time launched an attack from the quarries
against the 2nd Division on the 18th Division's right.

And it was at this crucial stage in the day's operations that Lieutenant Price revealed himself as a young
man of the greatest decision and force of character.
To the end of the war what he did that day was
quoted as one of the notable achievements in the
history of the Division. "Tommy" Price was a
Maxse-trained young officer; and when it was all
over and he was being congratulated upon having
got the Northants out of a most serious situation,
his characteristic reply was that he had based his
line of action upon what his Divisional Commander's
training had taught him ought to be done.

Under this fierce new German pressure our line was
falling back. Many of the Lewis guns were clogged
and useless. There were numbers of rifles that had
become choked with mud and could not be fired.
Not a few of the men were worn out by the terribly
heavy going and had lost their earlier spirit. The
remnants of companies were in confusion. Moving
along the line under ceaseless rifle and machine-gun
fire, Price checked the retirement and then gathered
up a band of survivors to protect his exposed right
flank on the West Miraumont Road. His resolute
handling of the situation extricated the Northamptons
from a most threatening position and brought to Price
a very popular D.S.O. What Price did on the right
for the Northamptons was done for the Fusiliers by
two signalling officers, Lieutenant C. F. Chute, R.E.,
the Brigade signalling officer, and 2nd Lieutenant G.
S. Pearcey, signalling officer of the Fusiliers. These
two officers saw the brave remnants of the Fusiliers
being driven back; they went into the leaderless line
at the crumbling points, steadied the men, secured the
flank, and retrieved the position. Lieutenant Chute,

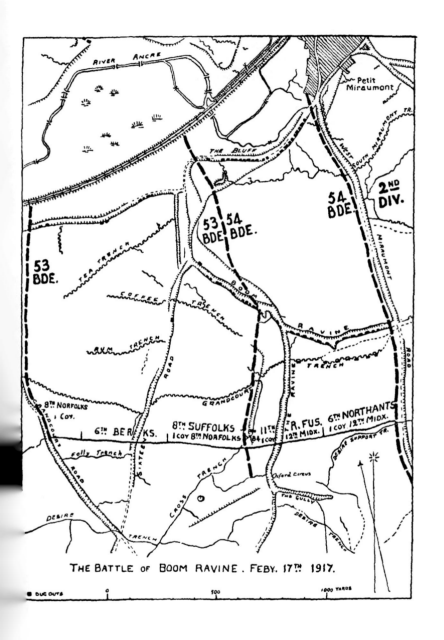

THE BATTLE OF BOOM RAVINE. FEBY. 17TH 1917.

after rallying the men on the ridge, sent a message to headquarters that explained the state of affairs with clearness and precision, with the result that reinforcements from the Middlesex Regiment arrived in time to strengthen our footing on the high ground. Chute was awarded the M.C.

Farther to the left of the line Lieut.-Colonel Carr, D.S.O., and his Adjutant, Captain G. F. J. Cumberlege, D.S.O., also exercised a steadying influence, and put fresh heart into the sorely - tried troops. The reports afterwards showed that some of the positions were only held as by a thread with the scantiest material. One advanced post held by Corporal Hart, who had taken charge of an officerless party, was defended by him against several attacks until the following day. An epic of the wavering struggle on the Spur was the last stand of Lieutenant W. B. Godwin and his handful of men. They lost touch with the line in a thick mist and found themselves surrounded by Germans. Outnumbered, they fought on till every man but one was killed.

One company of Middlesex men was led for two days by Sergeant G. Rowe after all the officers had fallen. A platoon that had not even a sergeant left carried on under Private A. Humphries, and finally dug in successfully. A defensive line along which the Middlesex men fastened themselves on the ridge was marked out by Lieutenant V. D. Corbett and consolidated under heavy shell and rifle fire.

The afternoon found the Division consolidating upon a line some 300 yards from South Miraumont Trench. The Ravine was in our hands and we were almost on the crest of the ridge.

There are two features of the Boom Ravine battle that stand out : the enterprise of the Lewis gunners and the tirelessness of the men who had to maintain communications.

Again and again messengers got through when hope of seeing them had been abandoned. They did not

know fatigue; no mission was too forbidding for
volunteers, none was deemed too impossible for effort,
sometimes competing effort. "The runners never
fail," is a note made by an officer to whose jottings
is owed the preservation of some of the above details.
One man in the Signal Service, Pioneer W. Jones,
R.E., continued laying lines for 48 hours—most of
the time under shell - fire—without rest. One particular message cost the lives of three runners, but
a fourth, a man named Morgan, at once presented
himself. He was blown up on the way, but escaped
serious hurt. Having accomplished his mission he
returned, rallied several scattered men who were
retiring, and kept the position for the rest of the
day. When the relieving East Surreys came up it
fell to one messenger, Corporal Osborne, to search in
the pitch darkness over the shell-churned slime of
the battlefield, country entirely new to him, for the
Suffolk headquarters. The Surreys had been instructed to take over 200 yards more ground on the
left of the Suffolks, but no one knew just where
the Suffolk headquarters were. All that Colonel
Irwin could tell Corporal Osborne was that Colonel
Hill was last reported to be in Grandcourt Trench.
Corporal Osborne undertook to find Colonel Hill, and
did so within an hour and a half.

A few days afterwards the pursuit of the enemy,
as he sought the refuge of his celebrated Hindenburg
Line, had begun. The hard-won victory at Boom
Ravine had quickened his decision to retreat.

# CHAPTER X.

## THE CAPTURE OF IRLES, AND THE PURSUIT TO THE HINDENBURG LINE.

*The silent Boche retirement—A trying time for our artillery horses —8th Suffolks take Resurrection Trench—53rd Brigade's brilliant surprise assault at Irles—An unusual artillery barrage—10th Essex attack in "snow mantles"—Lieut.-Colonels Henderson and Chase killed—54th Brigade take up the pursuit—Private C. A. Cox of the Bedfordshires wins the Victoria Cross.*

WE now come to the swiftly-moving events of March 1917. During this time the German retreat from the Ancre gathered impetus. Silently and methodically the enemy were stealing back towards the Hindenburg line that they had spent the autumn and winter in fortifying, and our troops were confronted suddenly with new problems, foremost being that of pursuing the enemy at his own pace across the intervening wilderness of broken roads and boggy mud. Men who went up as they thought to do battle for the Loupart line in the second week in March, found themselves a week later on a triumphant march to St Leger, about 12 kilometres farther east as the aeroplane flies. Spring had come with radiant days to revive drooping spirits. It was a season of wonderful tidings and high hopes.

At this period we had had no experience of advanceguard actions. Attempts were made to control troops from too far behind, and too much reliance was placed upon field telephones when they should have been abandoned for mounted orderlies and for visual signal-

ling. And the artillery could not be got forward
when it was wanted. The real trouble was not
muddle so much as mud. There were shell-holes large
enough to warrant the Sussex Pioneers and the
Divisional Engineers building quite imposing bridges
as the quickest means of making the way forward
practicable. Guns and waggons sank in the ooze
up to the axles, and fresh teams were always being
called for to drag them out. Vehicles that were in
difficulties had to be relieved of part of their load.
For many of the horses the struggle was altogether
too severe. Following the extraordinarily severe
winter, this was probably the most trying time for
horses the 18th Division experienced in France.
With the Boche so soon out of range the guns
had to be pushed forward. And often the water
problem was so acute that the only water for the gun
teams was shell-hole water. There were horses so
fast in the mud that they had to be shot. And on
some occasions the trails of the 18-pounders sank so
deep that to shift them during firing two detachments
were required for each gun. Fierce snowstorms added
to the miseries of the time. The guns of two batteries and their ammunition supply were carried
to forward positions on Miraumont Hill on the light
Decauville railway ; such roads as had existed on this
hill had been completely obliterated by our bombardments during the battle of the Somme. This piece
of country was quite impassable for either man or
beast, except by the thin iron track and its attendant
duckboard.

The 7th Buffs were perhaps the first to find that
the enemy was falling back. On the night of 23rd
February "D" Company (Captain Wood) found South
Miraumont trench evacuated, and reported this fact
to Colonel Ransome; but the patrols of "C" Company,
directed to search along the West Miraumont Road,
lost their way in the intense darkness.

Early in the morning, however, West Miraumont

Road was occupied, and patrols were pushed on to Petit Miraumont, Miraumont, and East Miraumont Road. Splendid patrol work was done on this day by 2nd Lieutenant Mathias, 2nd Lieutenant Church, and Captain Rowland. By nightfall a line was established running along East Miraumont Road as far as the railway at Miraumont. This line was held by " A " Company (Captain Allen) right, and " C " Company (Captain Clapperton) left.

At midnight, 24th-25th February, Colonel Ransome received orders by telephone that the advance was to be continued at 6 A.M., 25th. At this time the companies of the 7th Buffs were very scattered—one at Miraumont, one at E. Miraumont Road, and two at Boom Ravine. Orders were got out, and the companies, notwithstanding that it was pitch dark, assembled in perfect order by 6 A.M. To show how dark it was, the only way in which Colonel Ransome's headquarters party could find the way from Boom Ravine to East Miraumont Road was by walking along holding on to the telephone wire connecting with Company Headquarters in the East Miraumont Road.

The edge of Irles was the final objective, and the mist when the advance began was so dense—worse than that of 21st March 1918—that compasses had to be used. But in spite of the perplexities the appointed objectives were reached, and touch was gained with the 2nd Division. Captain Wood did excellent work all through, and Captain C. D. Hayfield, the Buffs Reconnaissance officer, earned his first bar to his M.C.

The Germans certainly left Miraumont very hurriedly, for their gun-pits were swept as though they expected to remain. One prisoner was caught asleep in bed with his boots beside him. This man possessed an obstinacy of his own. When told to put on his boots he said he would not obey a British order. He conformed to the order to march off, but he per-

sisted in walking the three miles along duckboards
from Miraumont to Mouquet Farm in his stockinged
feet.

On 6th March the 8th Suffolks took Resurrection
Trench on the outskirts of Irles—quite a spectacular
effort, as they had to go down one steep and slippery
slope and ascend another that had been badly cut up
by shell-fire before getting into the trench. But the
operation was neatly carried out, and four days later
came the 53rd Brigade's brilliant capture of Irles, a
surprise assault that turned the retreating enemy's
dawdle into a scamper. The garrison had received
orders to evacuate the village that evening, but the
53rd Brigade went over in the morning and spoiled
the German plan. It was a converging, not a frontal,
attack, worked out after systematic gathering of information. It was, indeed, a very bold conception
for that period of the campaign. The village itself
was "refused"; but the 10th Essex worked round it
from the north-west and the 8th Norfolks from the
south. The Divisional 18-pounder barrage was confined to the flanks, while the 4·5 howitzers shelled the
already ruined village. Major W. A. Stirling, D.S.O.,
the Divisional Artillery brigade-major, was deservedly
complimented upon the way in which he worked out
and placed on paper the details of the barrage arranged
by General Metcalfe, the C.R.A.

General Higginson impressed upon his officers the
importance of keeping the position of assembly secret,
for there were no proper approach trenches to Resurrection Trench; and, another innovation, the 10th
Essex, when in the early morning they advanced over
open ground that was lightly powdered with snow,
were wearing snow mantles to make them less visible
to the enemy. Very ghostly they looked in the half
light, although it was not long before a rapid thaw
turned them into a white host scrambling across black
mud.

With the exception of one company, the Essex men

had spent the three previous nights in a quarry known
to the enemy and persistently shelled. The dug-outs
were of the most wretched description, and the air in
them was fetid. It was impossible to lie down properly,
even in the officers' quarters; and it was a tired force
that gathered for the attack, which makes the dash
and spirit displayed in the fighting all the more
commendable.

A couple of nights before the attack a sergeant and
his platoon had disappeared when on patrol in the
outskirts of the village. Lieutenant Astington went
off next day with a party of six men to seek them,
but the search party did not return either. Evidently
Lieutenant Astington, in his eagerness and anxiety,
went too far. His body was found lying in the main
street of Irles, and three of his companions had fallen
with him. Other greatly regretted losses at Irles
were those of Lieut.-Colonels H. M. Henderson and
A. A. Chase, both of the Royal Engineers. They were
killed by a shell about 5 P.M. on the 10th, close to Irles,
whilst on their way to see how and where to dig
assembly trenches for the attack on the Loupart line.
Lieut.-Colonel Henderson, a very bold and zealous
officer, had only recently joined the division, having
succeeded Lieut.-Colonel Joly de Lotbiniere as C.R.E.
in January on the latter's appointment to the XVIII.
Corps as General Maxse's chief engineer. Lieut.-
Colonel Chase was one of the finest types of British
officers; he formerly commanded the 80th Field Company, and in December 1916 succeeded Lieut.-Colonel
A. E. Glasgow in command of the 8th Royal Sussex
Pioneers on the latter's promotion to command an
infantry brigade. The Pioneers had been building a
light railway for evacuating the wounded; it was,
indeed, a strange trick of fate that their much-loved
commanding officer should have been almost the first
to be carried along the line he had prepared.

Irles was a very pretty little victory. Sixteen
machine-guns were captured, and the number of

LIEUT.-COLONEL A. A. CHASE, D.S.O., M.C.

prisoners, 68, exceeded the total number of our casualties.

This was the first occasion on which the 18th Division had come across numbers of Boche 8-inch howitzers and the handsome long brass high-velocity cartridge cases. These were stacked ready for withdrawal, but they are now in use in many homes in the south-eastern counties as umbrella stands, palm stands, gongs, &c.

The silent Boche retirement now gathered speed. An Anzac patrol creeping into Loupart Wood at 3 A.M. found that the birds had flown. About the same time venturesome spirits of the Northamptonshires crept into the enemy trench in front of our right centre to find it empty. Away to the left the enemy sniped at the Royal Fusiliers from Achiet-le-Petit. Lieutenant E. L. Jones had three men picked off beside him and only escaped himself by lying full length in a hollow. Lieutenant Little, one of the picked shots of the battalion, fell to a German marksman in the same region. A pen-and-ink artist, Lieutenant Little is remembered as the designer of the 54th Brigade's 1916 Christmas card. It showed the leaning figure of the Madonna on the ruined church at Albert, with the square full of troops.

By 10 A.M. on the 13th, the 54th Brigade had occupied the Loupart line. The Germans remained in Achiet-le-Petit on our flank another day, and they were still in strength in Bihucourt and Achiet-le-Grand. In a short skirmish in that direction the Bedfordshires won two machine-guns and some higher ground, while on the 14th, Germans observed assembling in considerable numbers south-west of Achiet-le-Grand, near the railway junction, formed a rare target upon which our artillery directed a concentrated fire. If the enemy's intentions were aggressive they were soon dissipated. A Middlesex patrol worked through to Bihucourt on the 15th and caught a glimpse of German transport moving east. On the

17th Achiet-le-Grand and Bihucourt were in our possession, the former falling to the Bedfordshires and Bihucourt to the Middlesex.

It was during this period of open skirmishing, with the enemy conducting with very great tenacity rear-guard actions on picked ground, that the fifth Victoria Cross came to the Division. The man who won this further distinction for the 18th was a stretcher-bearer, Private Christopher August Cox, of the Bedfordshires, who in all the engagements since July 1916 had displayed great personal courage and the highest devotion. Cox won his V.C. for splendid gallantry in front of Achiet-le-Grand on 15th March and subsequent days. During the 54th Brigade attacks on the 15th he was an outstanding figure, carrying back wounded men on his shoulders under heavy rifle, machine-gun, and shell fire; and on the 16th and 17th he continued this work without rest and with a complete disregard of his own safety.

Falling back to drier ground, the Germans had all the advantage in the race that now began, for they left us struggling in a slough of mud—the muddy and bloody battlefields of the Somme. But once we had passed the Loupart line we revelled in free un-churned country, good roads only mined at intervals, and fields that could be galloped across.

The advance of the field artillery to Bihucourt was ordered at 6 P.M., and it took all night to get the 18-pounders two miles across the mud. Major E. F. Budden, B/82, provided the advance-guard up to Bihucourt; then C/82, commanded by Major L. I. C. Paul, went on with four guns. That night the horizon was lit by the flames from burning houses and stores —signs that the Boche meant to leave only a stricken blasted countryside behind him.

Our patrols made good another 800 yards, and then allowed an advance-guard to go through in pursuit of the vanished foe. The composition of the advanced guard that set out on the 18th of March from Bihu-

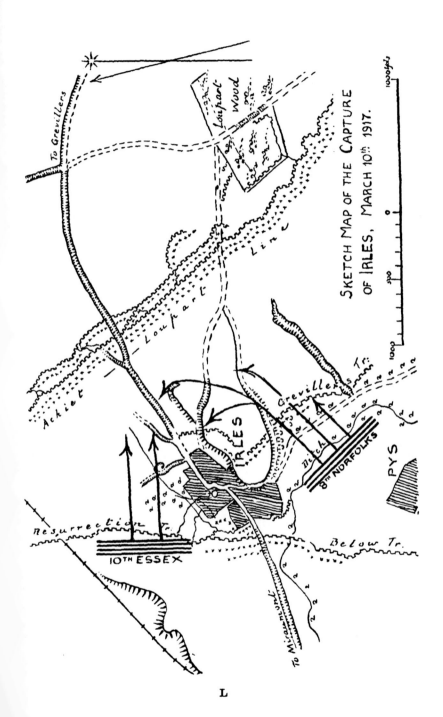

SKETCH MAP OF THE CAPTURE OF IRLES, MARCH 10th 1917.

To Grevillers

Loupart Wood

Loupart Line

Achiet

Grevillers Tr:

Ditch Tr.

IRLES

8th NORFOLKS

PYS

Below Tr.

Resurrection Tr.

10th ESSEX

To Miraumont

L

court must be given. It was commanded by Colonel
R. Turner, D.S.O., of the Northants, and consisted
of—

> 6th Northamptonshire Regiment.
> 1 Squadron Yorkshire Dragoons.
> 1 Section 54th M.G. Company.
> 1 Company 80th Field Company, R.E.
> 2 Sections 82nd Brigade, R.F.A.

The cavalry led the way, and there was an uninter-
rupted progress through Ervilliers. After night on
the line of the Ervilliers-Behagnies road the advanced
guard marched to St Leger, having covered five and
a half miles. The Germans had blown up cross-roads
further to bar our progress and had strewn the main
routes with felled trees. In the dark six horses and
a waggon belonging to "C" Battery 82nd Brigade
toppled into a mine crater the other side of Ervilliers,
and only the fine horsemanship of the three drivers
got them out of the pit. The Boche had destroyed
their poled-telephone cables; they had fouled all the
wells; and it was at this period that they began
destroying fruit-trees, stripping off the bark and saw-
ing through the trunks.

They made their stand at Croisilles, an outpost of
the Hindenburg line, a kilometre or so from St Leger,
with an excellent command of the valley between.
Up this valley the Northamptonshires tried to fight
a way against terrific machine-gun and shell fire. But
Croisilles was clearly more than a one-battalion job.
The little force with cavalry protecting the flanks had
only six 13-pounders supplied by "A" Battery, Royal
Horse Artillery, the "Chestnut" Troop, and four
18-pounders of C/82, to furnish a barrage.

With tanks the advance might have gone further.
As it was, the Northamptons, somewhat battered, fell
back to St Leger, and did creditably in extricating
their left companies, C and D, from an awkward
position. Forty men of the latter had to lie hidden

in a fold of the ground till darkness fell, and at one time looked as if they were going to be outflanked by a party of Germans. But they succeeded in getting back in driblets without casualty.

The Bedfordshires, who arrived at St Leger as reinforcements, were not put into the line, for the enemy was now safe in his Hindenburg line. The British advance against a vanished foe had come to a halt.

The enemy, by shortening his own line of defence, had shortened our front too, and troops were becoming congested on the decreasing front. Consequently orders arrived for the pinching out of the II. Corps, in which we were, by the V. Corps, who were on our left, by 21st March.

General Shoubridge's connection with Croisilles was not to finish with the attack on that place with his 54th Brigade, for oddly enough, in a few days, he returned to the attack with the 7th Division, to the command of which he was appointed, whilst the 18th Division was out of the line.

# CHAPTER XI.

## CHERISY, 3RD MAY 1917.

*The 18th Division's first substantial check—Part of a vast operation —Failure through a start in the darkness—General Allenby's sardonic verdict—Along the Hindenburg Line—54th Brigade's loss of direction—The uncut wire in front of Fontaine Trench—Wandering tank and the fatal word "retire"—The adventure of Captain Batten-Pooll, V.C.—East Surreys on the left reach their objective—A gap between the assaulting brigades—The German counter-attack: again the word "retire"—The story of "Sandy" Turnbull, the professional International footballer—The death of Captain Neate of the 11th Fusiliers.*

THE battle of Cherisy on 3rd May 1917 has sombre memories for survivors of the 18th Division. It was the first set fight in which the Division received a definite and substantial check. Cherisy formed part of a battle on the biggest scale, for a wide sweeping advance was attempted from Bullecourt in the south almost to Lens in the north, and General Allenby, who had charge of the operations, had units belonging to three armies under his command. It is known now that this ambitious and imposing effort, following upon General Allenby's well-planned victory at Arras, was in the nature of a political battle, undertaken to remove the German pressure upon the French. It might even be termed a "rush" operation, at any rate upon the Cherisy front, for the 54th and 55th Brigades, who attacked for the 18th Division, had less than three days in which to become acquainted with the ground over which they were to advance; while immediately before the battle the line held by the Division was altered, a side-step of about 500 yards to the left being made.   In addition, the artillery preparation had not been thorough enough to cut a way through the thick wire in front of Fontaine Trench, about 500 yards from the 54th Brigade's forming-up line.   It was this wire that held up the whole of the 7th Bedfords, and half the 12th Middlesex; Boche enfilading machine-gun fire, from Cherisy and from Fontaine Wood, took a merciless toll of these unlucky troops.   But the main cause of the Cherisy failure, and of the failure along the whole line on 3rd May, was the darkness.   Zero hour, 3.45 A.M.—2.45 A.M. solar time—was too early, and the puzzling start in the dark had an adverse effect upon the operations during the whole of the day.   Good communication was again to seek, and this accentuated all the changing difficulties of attack and counter-attack.

An evening attack was ordered to extricate bodies of the 8th East Surreys, 7th Buffs, and 12th Middlesex, who, according to the information at Divisional Headquarters, were in forward positions east of the village of Cherisy; but it was learnt later that these troops had been withdrawn previously to our original line, although news of this withdrawal had not reached Divisional Headquarters.   The Germans fought well, and were very strong in artillery, but our disappointment over the failure of 3rd May was in proportion to the confidence, born from the success at Arras, with which the Divisions engaged went into the fight.   General Allenby's expressive comment is said to have been, "We aimed at the stars and hit the ceiling."

It was on 26th April that the Division received orders to move to the neighbourhood of Arras, and to be transferred from G.H.Q. Reserve to the VII. Corps.   Following the first experience of open warfare, and of pursuing the Germans to the St Leger

area, there had come a month's rest in the Aire and
Hazebrouck country. Training had been interspersed
with football, boxing tournaments, and cross-country
runs, not forgetting the officers' smoking concerts—
at one of which Brigadier-General Price of the 55th
Brigade contributed a notable and popular performance. And it was during this month's rest that the
Division received news that Brigadier-General Shoubridge had been promoted to command the 7th Division, which had won a particularly fine name in 1914.
The 18th felt a genuine pride in the distinction accorded to General Shoubridge. Brigadier-General C.
Cunliffe-Owen, a gunner, succeeded General Shoubridge in the command of the 54th Brigade on
6th April.

Between 26th and 29th April the 54th and 55th
Brigades had moved by road and rail to Neuville
Vitasse, and relieved the 21st and 89th Brigades of
the 30th Division in the line west of Cherisy. The
18th Divisional Artillery moved into the line next
day, and on 1st May the 53rd Brigade, who were in
reserve, settled in Neuville Vitasse. The attacking
infantry brigades and the Divisional Artillery now lay
on the German side of a section of the famous Hindenburg line, and they knew that their task was to
extend the breach made by Allenby's Arras assault
in that amazing and monumental piece of field engineering, with its concrete pill-boxes and its thirty-foot
wide stretch of wire in front of the first of the dual
trenches; and, 150 yards behind, the magnificent
support trench, spacious and deep and splendidly
fashioned. Thirty feet below this support trench ran
a still more impressive example of Germany's military
forethought and industriousness — the Hindenburg
tunnel, cut out of chalk : walls, ceilings, and floors
boarded, well-made stairs and air-shafts, a plentiful
supply of sleeping berths, and safe shelter for armies
of men. The tunnel was explored for seven kilometres from the point where it entered German

territory during the time that the 18th Division lay opposite Cherisy.   One could not but admire the thoroughness and solidity of the work.

The countryside looking towards the enemy lines—towards the Arras-Cambrai road—was wide and rolling, less battered than the dreary Somme expanse, and excellent for observation.   Spring those days was at its brightest.   Larks sang gaily from clear blue skies, and to sleep on a camp bed beneath a simple tarpaulin shelter in the roomy Hindenburg Support Trench, was to experience a night's rest such as the doctors recommend.

The orders for the attack on 3rd May were issued on 1st May.   The VII. Corps, for whom the 21st Division attacked on the right, the 18th Division in the centre, and the 14th Division on the left, was to advance simultaneously with the VI. Corps on its left, and Fifth Army on its right.   The first objective, as shown on the map, was along a line running through St Michael's Statue, on the north-eastern outskirts of the ruined village of Cherisy, across the Sensee river, and then south-west to where the river flowed east of Fontaine Wood.   The final objective allowed for an average advance of 2,000 yards, and brought the British forces within 750 yards of the village of Vis-en-Artois.   The 18th Division advance, preceded by a rolling barrage, was to be at the rate of 100 yards in two minutes to the western outskirts of Cherisy, a downhill advance; through Cherisy to the line of the first objective at 100 yards in six minutes; thence to the final objective, 100 yards in three minutes.   Sixty-pounder batteries were to search the ground 600 yards beyond the rolling barrage for machine-guns and other likely targets.

The Division attacked with the 54th Brigade on the right, and the 55th Brigade on the left.   The disposal was as follows :—

(a) 54TH BRIGADE.

7th Bedfords on right; 12th Middlesex on left.

11th Royal Fusiliers in support, and 6th Northants in reserve.

One company of the 11th Royal Fusiliers detailed as moppers-up, with two platoons detailed to each assaulting battalion.

Another company of the same battalion was detailed to find carrying parties.

The remaining two companies of the 11th Royal Fusiliers were to occupy the original front line, immediately the first objective was captured.

The 54th Machine-Gun Company was distributed as under :—

Two guns with each assaulting battalion.

Six guns ready to go forward to the strong points " A," " C," " D," " F," " G," and " H," as soon as they were established.

Six guns in Brigade Reserve with the 6th Northants.

The 54th Trench Mortar Battery had one Stokes mortar and sixty rounds with each assaulting battalion, and the remaining six mortars in reserve.

(b) 55TH BRIGADE.

7th Buffs on the right, with three platoons of the 7th R.W. Kents as moppers-up.

8th East Surreys on the left, with one platoon of the 7th R.W. Kents as moppers-up.

The 7th R.W. Kents (less two companies, one employed as moppers-up and one furnishing carrying parties) were in support.

The 7th Queens were in reserve.

The 55th Machine-Gun Company was disposed as follows :—

Two guns with each assaulting battalion.

Four guns to come into action at zero hour, and to cover the advance of the assaulting bat-

talions up to the final objective.  This section
was also expected to take on any enemy
machine-guns and strong points which might
be located during the action, and also to deal
with any enemy movement in the Vis-en-
Artois-Cherisy Valley.

[This section was unable to carry out its instructions, and altogether failed in its object.]
Four guns to move forward at zero hour, plus
forty-five, into the old front-line trenches.
Four guns in Brigade Reserve.
The 55th Trench Mortar Battery had two Stokes
mortars with each assaulting battalion, and four
in reserve.

The moon had set, and there was such darkness
at zero hour, 3.45 A.M., that it was impossible to see
our waiting men until one came within two yards of
them.  It soon became manifest, too, that the enemy
was standing by, expecting our attack, for immediately our barrage opened he replied with heavy fire
from machine-guns and rifles.  Still our assaulting
battalions were clear of our front line before the
Boche reply barrage descended, about four minutes
after ours had opened.  The ground being hard and
chalky, the shelling caused an enormous curtain of
dust to spring up, making it still more difficult
to see.

The 7th Bedfords and the 12th Middlesex went
forward in the dusk with the men in extended order,
about ten yards apart, and at once lost direction.
They had to go about 500 yards up a slope, over
a crest, and down the other side before they came
to the first Boche trench; and reaching the top of
the slope the Bedfordshires found themselves enfiladed from Cherisy on the left and from Fontaine
Wood on the right, by extremely accurate machine-
gun fire.  The loss of direction was due principally
to the darkness; but it was due also to the left

Brigade of the 21st Division, whose battalions, owing to faulty synchronisation of watches, did not start simultaneously with the 18th Division battalions. When they did leave their jumping-off line they ran into the German protective barrage, which by that time was an intense one. A report from an F.O.O. of the 14th Division also stated that this left Brigade of the 21st Division twice left their trenches and twice came back. This no doubt contributed to the loss of direction, as both the 7th Bedfords and the 12th Middlesex inclined to their right, the right company of the 12th Middlesex getting across the front of the left company of the 7th Bedfords.

However, resolutely led by Captain L. H. Keep, the officers of the 7th Bedfords rallied their men, and pushed through the machine-gun fire. The 12th Middlesex also forged ahead. But when they descended into the dip which held Fontaine Trench, a most disconcerting discovery was made. The deep belt of wire in front of the trench had not been properly cut, and in the dark what gaps there were could not be located. Confusion resulted, and though small parties of both battalions fought their way across Fontaine Trench and passed on—never to return—the bulk of the 7th Bedfords, and half of the 12th Middlesex, were held up in the open in front of the wire. The confusion was added to by a tank, which also had lost direction, coming back through the 18th Division lines—a tank allotted to the 21st Division, which had ploughed a way too far to its left.

At this critical moment the word "Retire" was passed along the line. It is not known from where the cry emanated; but the very heavy casualties to officers and N.C.O.'s had knocked the confidence out of the assaulting companies of the Bedfords and the right company of the 12th Middlesex, and they fell back to their original front line. Here they were reorganised and sent forward again, but the barrage had been lost, and all that the Bedfords and Middlesex could do now was to collect in shell-holes and lie out some distance in front of Fontaine Trench—and, as the Divisional report stated, " to all intents and purposes they passed out of the picture, as they took no further part in the action until the evening attack."

Captain A. H. Batten-Pooll, V.C., General Lee's A.D.C., had joined in the advance of the 54th Brigade, being keen, as he said, to see a " going over the top " again, and to gather information for the General. When in the dark things went wrong, and bodies of Bedfords, Fusiliers, and Middlesex started to follow tanks that had circled to the left and were retiring through the advancing companies, Captain Batten-Pooll with Lieutenant Redmile, the Bedfords' signalling officer, turned parties of the men round and led the way forward again. Captain Batten-Pooll and Captain Keep, Lieutenant P. J. Reiss and Lieutenant Driver of the Bedfords, were among those who lay out all day in shell-holes under persistent Boche sniping and machine-gun fire. They sent messages by wrapping message forms round stones and flinging them to one another. When at seven o'clock in the evening the Northamptons attempted to take Fontaine Trench and to clear up our wounded, they got into the Boche trenches but did not meet Batten-Pooll and Reiss, who continued to exchange messages. Reiss, who had been wounded, was got away, and Batten-Pooll also got back in the darkness and reported to Colonel Turner of the Northants at about 11 P.M. As Reiss had already been sent to the dressing-station, he and Batten-Pooll never actually met, although from their respective shell-holes they had hailed each other all day long.

Though his left hand was withered, the legacy of a wound earlier in the war, Batten-Pooll itched to return to regimental duty. Before the end of the year he had rejoined his regiment, the Munsters, and been taken prisoner. Gentle of speech, complacent in manner, he was in effect the natural fighting soldier.

While the 7th Bedfords and the right company of the 12th Middlesex were definitely held up about 200 yards in front of Fontaine Trench, the left assaulting company of the 12th Middlesex had gone forward upon its correct line, had reached the northern end of Fontaine Trench and got into Cherisy. The enemy machine-guns, which checked its advance by firing from the sunken road west of Cherisy, were knocked out by rifle grenades, but reaching the eastern edge of the village the company came under heavy fire; and as by now he realised that his right flank was in the air, Lieutenant Gore, the Company Commander, formed a line along the west bank of the Sensee river and sought to get his left in touch with the 7th Buffs. In rear of Lieutenant Gore's company came the left supporting company of the 12th Middlesex, and they established themselves in the ruins of the houses in the southern part of the village. As it began to get light, Captain H. Perks, who commanded this support company of the Middlesex, a very gallant soldier, perceived that his right flank was uncovered and that German reinforcements were pouring in from Fontaine-les-Croisilles, so he established a strong point at the cross-roads at the southern end of the village and garrisoned it with fifty men; but in doing so he was hit by a sniper in the head, fell, and was afterwards taken prisoner. 2nd Lieutenant Stevens of the same company was killed by a sniper, and shortly afterwards Lieutenant Gore, hurrying with some of his men to render assistance, was also killed.

Lieutenant Pyman, commanding the right support company of the 12th Middlesex, as soon as he noticed that the right assaulting company of his battalion was going too far to its right, diverted his company to the proper line. Some of the men were held up by the wire in front of Fontaine Trench; others got through as far as the " V "-shaped trench in front of the village, but found this point too strongly held by the enemy. 2nd Lieutenant Coleman was killed here, while Lieutenant Pyman and his Company Sergeant-Major, going forward to reconnoitre, were never seen again. The enemy opposition was undoubtedly stiffening, and it was clear that in this part of the Divisional front more men and a sustained effort would be required to push the attack through.

Meanwhile, on the left of the Divisional front, matters had gone more smoothly, and at 6.10 A.M. the 55th Brigade informed the 54th Brigade that their left assaulting battalion, the 8th East Surrey regiment, was on its objective and in touch with battalions of both flanks. Thus the position at about 5.30 A.M. was as follows :—

(a) Left Brigade of 21st Division back in the original front line.

(b) The assaulting companies of the 7th Bedfords and the right assaulting company of the 12th Middlesex held up in shell-holes in front of Fontaine Trench.

(c) Left assaulting company of the 12th Middlesex holding the west bank of the Sensee river, east of the centre portion of the village, with the left supporting company partially among the houses in the southern half of the village, with a posse of fifty men covering the right flank.

(d) The right support company of the 12th Middlesex partially in front of Fontaine Trench and partially above the junction of Cherisy Lane and the sunken road, where they were encountering strong opposition.

(e) The assaulting companies of the 8th East Surreys on their first objective, in touch on their right with the left company of the 7th Buffs, and on their left with the 8th Battalion Rifle Brigade of the 14th Division.

What was certain, however, and of urgent im-

over by the assaulting waves, and also that owing to the existence of the gap and the failure to block Cherisy Lane and the Cable Trench at the north end of Fontaine Trench, the enemy was feeding his old front line with reinforcements.

The situation regarding the gap was obscure for some time, and it was not known at Divisional Headquarters that except for the two companies of the 12th Middlesex, who had got forward round the north end of Fontaine Trench, the 54th Brigade were completely held up in front of Fontaine Trench.

Some time after 10 A.M., however, when the situation had become clear, an order was issued to G.O.C. 55th Brigade—at 10.35 A.M.—to put in an attack from the north, to take Fontaine Trench in reverse and to cut Cherisy Lane. This attack was not carried out, for reasons which will presently be made clear.

It is now necessary to deal with events which had been taking place away on the left of the 18th Division.

It will be remembered that at 5.30 A.M. the East Surreys were on the first objective and in touch with the 7th Buffs and the 8th Battalion Rifle Brigade to right and left of them. At 5.45 A.M. our shrapnel barrage moved forward, and Colonel Irwin sent two waves of men upon the advance to the final objective. The Germans again retreated, and it being now light enough for targets to be recognised, the East Surreys' Lewis guns did plenty of execution. At 6.45 A.M. Colonel Irwin could see his men at intervals along the whole brigade frontage on the final objective.

The East Surreys were in touch with the 8th Rifle Brigade on their left, but their right was completely in the air, and the line was very thin; and Captain Latter, commanding the company of the 7th Royal West Kents attached to the 8th East Surreys as "moppers-up," who earlier had reported to Colonel Irwin that they had cleared the 55th Brigade front in Cherisy village, was ordered by Colonel Irwin to prolong the line on the first objective to the right, and to try and get touch with the 7th Buffs or the 54th Brigade. Captain Latter and his seventy men carried out this undertaking under flanking machine-gun fire with great gallantry, but touch could not be gained on the right. Captain Latter was severely wounded, and died the same day in German hands.

It is clear that at about this time the enemy were beginning to reoccupy Cherisy, as at about 8 A.M. Colonel Irwin saw some forty Germans gathering in the sunken road south of the village. A machine-gun was brought to bear on them from the neighbourhood of St Michael's Statue, and casualties were inflicted. The range, however (1,400 yards), was too long to be effective.

At the same time the enemy began a systematic bombardment of the village, and the method he used to cover his reoccupation with artillery fire was interesting and instructive. Undoubtedly large numbers of the enemy were being pushed up through the gap, by way of Cherisy Lane. On reaching the southern end of the village, at the point where Cherisy Lane cut the sunken road, the leading enemy infantry put up two Very lights. The German artillery then lifted off about 100 yards at the south end of the village, and continued to bombard the remainder. After an interval of twenty minutes two Very lights were again put up, about 100 yards farther north, and again the artillery barrage lifted. This process was continued until two Very lights were put up at the north end of the village, to signal its complete reoccupation. During this operation the enemy, whose observation seemed to be very good, had started to shell our troops wherever he could see them.

At 11 A.M. the 8th East Surreys were still unsupported, and Colonel Irwin's Headquarters at St Michael's Statue were under direct machine-gun fire down the road from the north end of Cherisy village.

M

He decided, therefore, to withdraw, and to take up
a position on the western outskirts of the village.
Colonel Irwin had just given orders for this to be
done, when the enemy counter-attacked the 55th
Brigade on its front and left.

It will now be noted that the gap between the
brigades was very wide indeed. Except for a few
isolated men in Cherisy, which village was now to
all intents and purposes in the hands of the enemy,
there were no British troops between the line of men
of the 54th Brigade holding on in front of Fontaine
Trench and Colonel Irwin's small post. Between
them lay the village now reoccupied by the
enemy. A thin line of the 7th Buffs and the 8th
East Surreys was on the final objective, with their
right flank completely in the air, and their left flank
not much better off.

The order to the 55th Brigade to put in the attack
to take Fontaine Trench in rear, left General Lee's
headquarters at 10.35 A.M. At about 11 A.M., however, and before this order had been put into operation, a general retirement on the left had begun.
The thin line of Buffs and East Surreys on the final
objective had already driven off several small counter
attacks, but seeing that Germans were behind them
in their right rear, and being again counter-attacked
from the front and left flank, they began to withdraw, with the enemy advancing close up to them.
The remaining companies of the 7th Royal West
Kents had been ordered to advance to the support
of the East Surreys, and to take up ammunition and
water, but by the time the stores asked for had been
collected from the dump, the retirement had begun.

When the retirement started, the whole of the
original front lines on the 55th Brigade front, both
ours and the enemy's, were held by our troops. Two
companies of the 7th Queens held our trenches, and
one and a half companies of the West Kents and the
reserve company of the 7th Buffs occupied the Cable,

or old enemy front-line trench. The Germans followed so closely upon our troops as they came back from the valley of the Sensee river, that our men in Cable Trench could not fire for fear of hitting their own comrades. The enemy's observation must have been extremely good, for at this moment his artillery began an intense barrage on No Man's Land, on the original British front and support trenches, and on the valley in rear of them. Those farther in rear, with wider range of observation, could see that the retirement was a general one, and extended right along the line. Some of the enemy as they advanced began to put up their hands, but two Boche officers showed themselves possessed of energy and inspiration; each seized a flag, and getting on the flank they came forward with their men in between them. It is probable that Cable Trench would have been held by us, as there were several officers in the trench, Lewis guns were in position, and the men, who showed no signs of being shaken, had their rifles on the parapet in readiness to shoot. But again in mysterious fashion — how, it could never be ascertained — the word "retire" began to be passed from man to man. The troops withdrawing from Cherisy passed over Cable Trench, and were rallied in the original front and support trenches, and in the valley in rear. And then the men in Cable Trench, waiting until the enemy was within thirty yards of them, also retired to the original front trenches. Men of the 14th Division and of the 54th Brigade, all crowded into the 55th Brigade trenches, and Colonel Hickson of the West Kents, and Colonel Irwin, had a difficult task sorting them out, particularly as the communication trenches were few. A Lewis gunner belonging to the West Kents bore his gun away from Cable Trench, and was then blown up by a shell; the German barrage increased as our men returned to the morning's original starting-point. Lieut.-Colonel W. H. H. Johnston, commanding the 12th Middlesex,

hostile machine-gun fire. One of the enemy machine-guns was silenced by means of bombs and a Stokes mortar; but these guns could not get forward any farther, and, in company with the single gun which had gone ahead on the right, went back to Cable Trench, and eventually withdrew with the reserve company of the 7th Buffs.

Another section of the 55th Machine-Gun Company suffered very heavy casualties in crossing No Man's Land, and also in the old enemy front-line trench. The section commander was killed and the company commander wounded. The guns were all destroyed by shell-fire.

The Stokes mortar which went forward on the left reached its correct destination; then came a message from the right company commander of the 7th Buffs asking for assistance. This mortar came into action at about 7 A.M. and fired fifty - five rounds, silencing several German machine-guns in Cherisy Lane; but at about 9.45 A.M., after the mortar had been moved to the north end of Cherisy, the whole team and the mortar were knocked out by one shell, and only the officer escaped.

Such a battle as Cherisy, with its confusions and its tense demand during a period of about nineteen hours upon individual determination and resource, was bound to produce almost numberless instances of courage and sacrifice. There is the story of " Sandy " Turnbull, the Scottish International professional footballer, who played inside left for the Manchester United team when they were champions of the Football League. Turnbull had become a sergeant in the 8th East Surreys. He was a good soldier, earnest, extremely wide-awake, and a man of good influence. He had gone through towards Cherisy with Captain Lonergan and his company; he was wounded, but went on. Early in the advance he spotted some enemy machine - guns, and turned a Lewis gun on to them. He got hit again when trying to rush an enemy gun; then a third bullet smashed his knee and brought him down. But he waved his companions forward, shouting instructions from the map which he carried. He directed other men who came up, and refused to be taken back. Afterwards he was missed; it was hoped that he had been taken prisoner, with a chance of recovery from his wounds. But nothing has ever been heard of him. He was a gallant man, and met a soldier's end with calm fearlessness. There is the case of Private S. Dye, a stretcher-bearer, belonging to the East Surreys. Looking above the trench parapet he saw an arm waving from a shell-hole; it waved again and again. Boche snipers and machine-gunners lay in wait not many yards from that shell-hole. Bullets pinged at any head that showed above our trenches. The arm waved once more. Dye and another stretcher-bearer got out of the trench and, heedless of the bullets, walked steadily to the shell-hole. There they dressed the wounded man. Dye's companion was killed; but after a while Private Dye, to the proud wonder of his comrades, walked slowly back, smoking a pipe and carrying the wounded man on his back. To the credit of the Germans, let it be known that they did not fire upon this heroic man and his human burden. And there was the fine devotion of Private Gladwish, servant to 2nd Lieutenant Kydd of the Bedfords. This officer was killed near Fontaine Trench. Gladwish tried to carry him back, but lost his way, and in the evening found himself on the wrong side of Fontaine Trench. For three days and three nights he hid in shell-holes by day, and at night tried to get back to our lines. At last, exhausted and looking like a hunted creature, he heard himself challenged by a British sentry. He was in our lines again, and knew that he was safe.

One would like also to tell of Captain Neate, of the Fusiliers, who with his company joined in the left part of the Middlesex attack, got right through, and helped to clear the enemy out of Cherisy. After the German counter-attack, few men and no officer of " B " Company, the Fusiliers, got back to tell the story. Neate met his death firing his revolver at the oncoming German infantry. A Fusilier officer, writing his reminiscences of the fight, says : "Neate was as gallant a boy as ever breathed. He was badly wounded in the head by a trench mortar early in 1916, and was never really fit afterwards. His sight was permanently damaged, but he managed to persuade a medical board to send him out again. He was wounded, and awarded the M.C. at Achiet-le-Petit. While in a casualty clearing station he heard that his battalion was marching through the village, and he got out of hospital and rejoined. He was nearly left out of the Cherisy fight, but in the end Colonel Carr allowed him to go. He was a lad of very high ideals, a most efficient officer, as brave as a lion. He was loved by the whole battalion."

War is war, and there is the quaintly gruesome, accredited account of a Boche killed by a penknife. The German, a big fellow, had been brought into a dug-out as a prisoner. In the dug-out lay a wounded British officer, whose servant was cutting his jacket so as to dress his wounds. As the servant bent over his officer the German leapt upon him, and sought to grasp the knife, not a soldier's jack-knife but a small penknife. The two men rolled on the ground ; the struggle was a fierce one, but the Englishman kept his knife, though he had to kill his assailant by stabbing him in the neck.

As has been shown, it was not known at Divisional Headquarters during the afternoon that the 8th East Surreys, and the elements of the 7th Buffs and 12th Middlesex who had pushed forward to the final objective east of Cherisy, had come back to the original front line. The evening attack made to extricate these troops was, therefore, a purposeless one : another unfortunate chapter in a day of supreme disappointment.

This attack, which was to be made by the 6th Northants and the 7th Queens in conjunction with the 110th Brigade of the 21st Division, was at first fixed for 6.15 P.M. Later the hour was altered to 7.15 P.M. News of the postponement did not reach the 7th Queens until 6.25 P.M., by which time the battalion was formed up ready to go over; but as no barrage opened the troops did not advance.

When at 7.15 the assault began, our advancing troops at once came under heavy rifle and machine-gun fire. One officer of the Queens killed that day was Major Longbourne, who won the D.S.O. at Schwaben. Major Longbourne went in pursuit of a wounded partridge, and was shot through the head by a sniper, near a gap in a trench wall made by a shell; there, earlier in the day, Lieut.-Colonel Hickson of the West Kents had been wounded. Major Longbourne had done fine work during the main attack, rallying the returning troops and reorganising them. The right company of the Queens, reinforced by the support company, reached Cable Trench and got into touch with the 6th Northants; but the left and support companies failed in the attempt to reach Cherisy.

"C" Company of the Northants, under Captain Shepherd, followed our artillery barrage right up to Fontaine Trench, which they got into at 7.25 P.M. There was little hostile shelling on this part of the front, and most of the enemy's machine-gun fire went high overhead. But the right company of the Northants, commanded by Captain Mobbs, had a greater distance to traverse, and as soon as they started down the slope towards Fontaine Trench they met heavy machine-gun fire both from the front and from the right flank. The fire was very low, and many of the men were hit in the legs. The first wave of this company was held up about 50 yards from the Boche wire, and had to remain in shell-holes; they were just in touch with the second wave of Captain Shepherd's company. During this evening attack a

as the 54th Brigade used to say, his sleeve, as it was, looked as if it bore a harp upon it. It became a 54th Field Ambulance jest that a permanent card was kept for Shepherd with name and regiment filled in, and the only space vacant one for the actual wound.

Poor Shepherd would not finish with soldiering even when the Armistice arrived. He and that adventurous fighter, Captain Harry Driver of the Bedfords, volunteered to join Brigadier-General Sadleir-Jackson in his Russian campaign. And both of them were killed—a sad, rather side-ways ending, when one reflects upon the lifetime of hardship and danger they went through in France, and the proud record of gallant achievement that was theirs when the 18th Division completed its task.

On the very day that the Division came out of the line for the rest that was preparatory to their march up to the Salient, the 53rd Brigade lost their Brigade-Major, Captain P. R. Meautys, M.C., killed by a shell while making a last tour of the trenches. Highly intelligent, full of energy and love for his work, Meautys was the perfect "right-hand man" to that Apostle of Duty and Efficiency, General Higginson. His sprightly good-humour made him well-liked by officers and men. General Higginson himself had a narrow escape in this part of the front. A shell burst near him in Foster Avenue, and he was blown down a dug-out shaft with his runner on top of him.

# CHAPTER XII.

## A CRICKET MATCH, 1917.

OUR armies on the Western Front, no matter how much they were overworked, always raised a bit of spare energy for games. On the hottest afternoons the batteries and battalions of the Division, when it was out at rest, played cup-tie football. One could see an outside right displaying amazing nippiness in heavy field-boots; or a half-back, who had raked up a pair of real football boots and what looked like blue bathing-drawers, complete the professional effect by winding puttees with special neatness round his bare calves, in lieu of stockings.

And once, in the neighbourhood of Hazebrouck, was to be observed a spectacle never to be seen on the most luxuriously-appointed football ground in England. " A " battery of the 82nd Brigade R.F.A. were playing the D.A.C. team in the Divisional Cup, and their players were brought to the field in a newly-painted and varnished G.S. waggon, drawn by six grand-moving blacks, the battery's showiest gun-team. Also there were enough chargers, ridden by brigadiers and brigade-majors, and staff-captains and ordinary officers come to see the tie, to make one think it was a point-to-point meeting. It is true the ball burst when the game was twenty minutes old, and the match had to mark time until two other teams had finished; but with the mercury soaring towards the "nineties" no one minded a long "breather."

There is no need to tell of the Old English Sports,

and the wrestling on horseback, and the cricket-nets concocted out of pit-props and trench-revetting wire, and the occasional plunges into polo and tent-pegging.

But there was an impromptu tug-of-war on a sweltering night in June after the Cherisy show. It was at Divisional Headquarters, near Boileau St Marc, and during dinner "C" Mess challenged "B" Mess.

"B" Mess's team of eight contained the Assistant-Adjutant and Quartermaster-General, the D.A.A.G. Major J. A. Churchill, the D.A.Q.M.G. Major Duncan Campbell, and the A.P.M. Captain Percy Cazenove. These were the heavyweights. The other side included the Intelligence Officer Lieutenant Myers, the Assistant Director of Veterinary Services Major L. M. Verney, two padres, Church of England and Presbyterian, the Baths' Officer Captain Simmonds, and D.A.D.O.S. Major C. A. Worssam.

Lieut.-Colonel Wallace Wright, the G.S.O. 1, gave the word to pull, and General Lee himself came out to see the fun. It was a night of glory for the lightweights. They were coached by an officer who took part in a certain international gathering in Albania a few weeks before the Great War broke out; and he described a tug-of-war final there in which a select few of the real old British Army took the strain of the Prussian Guard, and then to the command "About Turn" got the rope over their shoulders and marched off, dragging the ponderous Guardsmen behind them. (But that, of course, is a separate story.)

Well, the pull surprised the spectators and distressed the performers by lasting 4 min. 48 sec. The lightweights, having won by blindly obeying the commands of their coach, collapsed on the grass, "D.A.D.O.S." in particular being "all out."

Another thing to remember was a cricket match, played at Boiry-au-Mont before the Division left the line.

The match was Divisional Headquarters v. The

Sussex Pioneers, and General Lee himself took the
field. The ground was not a long way from enemy
view, and the only boundary was the 20-ft. wide
wire remnants of the old Wancourt line. A ten-line
telegraph system crossed within thirty yards of the
pitch, and an exacting batsman had no opportunity
to demand that the white screen should be moved to
behind the bowler's hand. He had to be careful not
to allow lines of horses going past to water to attract
his attention. A huge wired-in manure-heap was
another feature of the playing-piece, and any one
who lifted the ball direct into it had six added to
his score. There were odd shell-holes in the out-
field, and fielders sprinted warily. A strip of canvas,
in imitation of cocoanut matting, had been pegged
down to lessen the menace of the most nobbly
portions of the pitch.

Headquarters began with Lieut.-Colonel C. B. O.
Symons, who commanded the Divisional Engineers,
and the D.A.A.G. Major J. A. Churchill. The
opposing eleven put on a fast bowler with a
long threatening run, and a heady fellow named
Palin, who bowled left-hand over the wicket and
possessed a gift for length. The C.R.E. shaped like
a cricketer, but the loose ones proved too fast for
him, and the first straight one shot right under his
bat. The first wicket thus fell for None, combined
with the astonishing fact that there had been no
byes off the fast bowler, although the wicket-keeper
was without gloves.

And now, what was that on the skyline, to the
left of our Divisional front — a half-mile bank of
smoke rolling towards us and a sustained rumbling
boom? An enemy barrage!

The match was delayed exactly three minutes,
while every player and every spectator turned a
professional eye in that direction.

" Quite a good barrage," said the incoming batsman,
Colonel Wallace Wright, as he took the bat from

the C.R.E. After which he turned a fast ball from off his legs and broke his duck in confident, upstanding fashion.

The only stand of the innings was made by the G.S.O. 1 and a young staff lieutenant, Lieutenant Nicholson, whose stance reminded one of the late A. O. Jones. He presented the full face of the bat to the ball that wanted watching and opened his shoulders most refreshingly to the overpitched ones. When, twice in one over, the ball kicked up and caught him on the left shoulder, that vastly popular brigadier, General Price, whose sayings were always being quoted, called out, "Another on the same spot and that arm is out of action." Colonel Wright played a strong forward game, and had scored twenty-two, mostly by clean-hit off-drives, when the "heady" bowler got him in two minds and he cocked one up to cover-point. Lieutenant Nicholson had reached nineteen when the Church of England padre ran him out. The rest was disaster. General Lee, in leggings and rolled-up shirt-sleeves, slashed out vigorously, but his bat came down the tiniest fraction of a second too late for each of the first five balls he received ; they just missed his wicket. The sixth didn't. The A.P.M., Percy Cazenove, made one lusty swipe, and the ball skidded off the corner of his bat on to the bails. The Presbyterian padre, Major Fraser, who was acting as scorer, stopped questioning a recent visitor to Albert as to the rumour that the celebrated statue had sunk to a still more hazardous pose, and went out to take his innings. Bowled first ball. The side's full total—fifty-four.

The Pioneers' first pair were a fair-haired captain, with a rolling walk and a rare eye for a long hop on the leg side, Captain Kemp, and a compactly-built sergeant—Sergeant Cæsar. The captain had run up sixteen before his partner scored. But this sergeant with a classical name played with a certain smooth commanding confidence that betokened more than ordinary knowledge of the game.   He never seemed to be trying to make runs, but when he scored odd singles the ball somehow went to where no one was fielding.   Once he hit a six—into the manure-heap, and off one bowler he obtained fourteen from one over; but most of the time he appeared to be playing to keep his wicket up.   When some one asked who he really was, Colonel Walker of the Pioneers smiled, and said he was on the Surrey ground staff, and was grandson, or great-grandson, of a cricketer famous in the days when—according to old prints, at any rate—the players added to the solemnity and intensity of an important match by batting and bowling in extraordinarily high top-hats. Sergeant Cæsar was not out at the finish, with his score sixty something, and looked as if he would have been batting exactly the same when he had topped the double century.

The last thing one noted was the Intelligence Officer running out between overs to make a report and show some fresh information to the G.S.O. 1, who was preparing to bowl.   "Is it important?" asked Colonel Wallace Wright before looking at the papers. He dictated a message, gave swift and fluent instructions, and resumed his cricket.   Slightly akin to the invariable delivery of a telegram at the wicket during a Lord's match, and an improvement, perhaps, on the Drake-Bowls-and-Beat-the-Spanish-Too incident which no history book allows us to forget.

# CHAPTER XIII.

## ZILLEBEKE AND 31ST JULY 1917.

*The worst period of the whole war—Divisional Artillery's heavy casualties—The A.T.N. track—The splendid exploit of "D" Battery, 82nd Brigade—The calm man who had been on the 'Daily Mail'—The attack: 30th Division troops' tragic mistake—Dr Ackroyd, 6th Berks medical officer, wins the Victoria Cross—Lieut.-Colonel Pritchard-Taylor and the German prisoners.*

ONLY those who fought through and survived the Flanders summer and autumn campaign of 1917 probed the war's awfulness to its deepest depths. Nothing in the war—in any war—can compare in fearfulness, foulness, and misery to what was undergone by both British and Germans in that phase of the struggle. The shelling was heaviest; the slippery, water-logged ground could not be dug into deep enough for protection; hard roads disappeared and men were drowned in the shell-holes of the bogged wilderness that night and day was battered and churned afresh by affrighting artillery fire. In four months the British losses totalled 268,000.

Day after day, from July to November, our casualty-ridden Divisions floundered across the slime to meet murderous machine-gun fire from the concrete pill-boxes which the Germans made so potent a feature of their new system of "Defence in Depth." Ground was gained, but at what a cost! The British attempt to oust the Germans from the hill ridges that commanded beleaguered Ypres was made against an enemy more powerful and better sited than in any

period of the war. Our guns were pushed so far into
the Salient that 18-pounders stood almost wheel to
wheel—not protected by solid earth-cover as on the
Somme; and 60-pounders and 9·2's were within voice
hail of them. And they were there just to be shot
at. The German artillery, stronger than ever it had
been before, had all the advantages of position and
observation, and took deadly toll of us in man-power
and guns. Flanders, 1917, was indeed the gunners'
hell.

The 18th Division, rested after the Cherisy fighting,
went up to the neighbourhood of Dickebusch early in
July, happily confident in its strength and quality.
It had come magnificently through the struggle on
the Somme, and the whole world knew that no fighting had been so stubborn, so bitter, so much on the
grand scale as that of the Somme. And up here the
pioneer parties reported that there were trees in leaf
and grassy stretches about Bedford House, and upon
the open land that led across the railway towards
Maple Copse and Sanctuary Wood. We thought of
the blasted wastes around Beaumont Hamel, Grandcourt, and Boom Ravine, of the mud-heap that once
was Thiépval, of the tree-stumps that could just be
picked out along the Albert-Bapaume road, and of
the terrible shelling that had made them so. Those
frightful times were over and done with! The British
Army had grown so; the new munition factories were
turning out guns and shells in such vast numbers;
a turning-point in the war had been reached. True,
there were rumours of disheartenment, of mutiny
even, among the French. But again came the proud
realisation that the British Army was becoming
more and more the perfect fighting force, and now
was out to accomplish a great crowning achievement
—the widening of the Ypres salient and the freeing
of the Belgian coast.

And through every unit of the 18th Division ran
the feeling that we were about to succeed where other

troops had failed. Fond, foolish dream! How soon was there to be agonising disenchantment!

The Divisional Artillery—the 82nd and 83rd Brigades R.F.A.—were first to realise the severity of the task that had been set the Division.

The two brigades were never more splendidly competent than when they came up to the Zillebeke area in the first days of July 1917. Brigadier-General Sydney Metcalfe had not only stamped his own singularly efficient personality upon them. In particular, by patience and discrimination in selection, he had seen to it that they were well officered: it was one of the quiet boasts that seven of the eight battery commanders were regular officers with an average of eight years' sound training, while the remaining battery commander, Major A. A. A. Paterson of C/83, was a born gunner and horse master—in the final stages of the war he acted as Divisional Artillery brigade-major.

Before August was out, only two of the eight, Major Paterson and Major M'Pherson of D/83, had escaped death or wounds.

The 82nd and 83rd N.C.O.'s and men were certainly as capable and as bodily fit as those of any field artillery brigades in France. They were about 1,100 strong at that time.

Before the ghastly effort to capture the Passchendaele Ridge ended, the reinforcements to make up the casualties in the two brigades numbered 1,400.

General Metcalfe was promoted to become G.O.C.R.A. of the XI. Corps while the Division was on the march towards Flanders; his successor in the command of the Divisional Artillery was Brigadier-General W. ("Bill") Evans, who previously had commanded the Guards' Divisional Artillery; and early one misty morning the new C.R.A., with Lieut.-Colonels Austin Thorp and T. O. Seagram, and the battery commanders, met Brigadier-General Stevenson, C.R.A. of the 30th Division at Bedford

House, for a first reconnaissance of the battery positions and O.P.'s near Zillebeke Lake that the 18th were to take over from the 30th Division.

They came back to their waiting men and officers with the report that so far the battery positions on the north side of Zillebeke Lake had not been badly shelled, but that water was reached when the earth was dug into a couple of feet, and the men at the guns would have to rely mainly upon "elephant" iron for cover; that ammunition waggons would have to complete their journey from Shrapnel Corner by a wooden track; that the enemy, from the cover of the woods on the slopes north of the Menin Road, dominated all our positions; and that German aeroplanes were ceaselessly active watching every move made by the British.

The Division was now once again attached to General Jacob's corps—the II. Corps of Sir Hubert Gough's Fifth Army—and on the night of 7th July the 55th Infantry Brigade, relieving the 30th Division Infantry, occupied the section of the front that ran from the northern boundary of Sanctuary Wood to Observatory Ridge Road. The 54th Brigade, in support, went into huts at Dickebusch. The 53rd Brigade, who were destined to lead the attack when the great day arrived, remained in training at Steenvorde, finding billets in farm buildings. Trips were made to a field between Ouderdom and Poperinghe, where a vast model of the area to be attacked had been prepared, and many explanatory lectures were given.

Lieut.-Colonel C. B. O. Symons, the Divisional C.R.E., set about making the famous A.T.N. track, a traffic way, off the map routes, marked by white yard-high posts, that went from Reninghelst along the south side of Zillebeke Lake to Clapham Junction. Elaborate arrangements were also made by Major J. C. Willis, O.C. Divisional Signals, for the big attack to be followed up from Yeomanry Post by a

regular officer, was next to go, and then young
Carver, who was always so keen searching for enemy
targets. Lieutenant Abley of A/82, who could sing
a good tenor song, had an arm blown off; Major
E. F. Budden of B/82 got wounded at the O.P.; and
Sergeant Miller, a most competent No. 1, of C/82, was
killed. Between 13th July and 31st July 7 men
were killed and 40 wounded at C/83's gun position.
In twenty-six days the battery fired 19,219 rounds
out of 22,000 rounds brought up to the guns. Five
guns were knocked out of action and twelve had to
be taken away for repairs.

D/82 had four of its six 4·5 howitzers rendered
useless while completing a special wire-cutting task.
This was the battery to which Sir Douglas Haig
made the following reference in one of his despatches :—

" A howitzer battery had received orders to cut a section of
German wire in the neighbourhood of Hooge, and 400 rounds
had been allotted for the purpose. The battery, situated in
an unavoidably exposed position in the neighbourhood of
Zillebeke Lake, had already been subjected to constant
shelling.

"On the occasion referred to, not more than 50 rounds
had been fired at the German wire, when a hostile 15 cm.
battery opened a steady and accurate fire in enfilade. Each
time the British battery opened, salvoes of 15 cm. shells raked
its position. Four of its six guns were put out of action and
two ammunition dumps were blown up, but the remaining
two guns continued in action until the last of the 400 rounds
had been fired.

" A few days later, when our infantry advanced over the
sector this battery had shelled, the enemy's wire was found
to have been completely cut."

The Canadian tunnellers, hearty gallant fellows,
who, one night when the Boche was expected to
attack, sent a message to the East Surreys, " 2 officers
and 80 men entirely at your disposal," built a
dug-out in Ritz Street Trench, near Dormy House,
for Colonels Seagram and Thorp and their headquarter

staffs. The day the dug-out was reported to be ready,
a German 5·9 descended upon it, cut through the five
feet of soft earth that formed the roof as if it had
been butter, and obliterated four of the six bunks
that had been built for the officers. So the tunnellers
set to work again. Two days after the battle of 31st
July a 5·9 burst through the roof of this dug-out as
Colonel Seagram was reading aloud the 5th Army
Report upon the operation. The very next day
another 5·9 came right through the hole made by the
first shell. Another direct hit killed the 82nd Brigade's staff-sergeant artificer and wounded one of the
servants and one of the signallers.

The bringing up of ammunition and supplies along
the tree-lined road from Dickebusch to Zillebeke
became a nightmare horror for Battery and Divisional
Ammunition Column drivers, and indeed all Transport
men. The road at night was one long procession
of slowly-moving waggons. The Boche knew this and
plastered it with shells. Sometimes the smooth flow
of traffic was held up for hours while killed horses and
men and smashed vehicles were got out of the way.
As one of the padres said, "Many a man learned
Christianity while waiting at Shrapnel Corner."

In the mind of every man in the line dwelt the
thought that he might be the next to be taken.
That was why the coming of the big set attack was
anticipated with relief, with a feeling that the worst
period would then be over, that the German gunners
would no longer have us at their mercy. There was a
three or four days' delay. All our heavies, coming
from Messines, were not yet up; the French also
demanded an extra wait. But finally, 31st July
became the day appointed, and on 28th July the
18th Division Infantry Brigades moved up for the
final concentration.

The 53rd Brigade went into trenches about Dormy
House, Zillebeke Bund, and the railway dug-outs; the
54th were in the Chateau Segard, Canal Reserve,

and Dickebusch areas, and the 55th were split up, two battalions being with the 54th, one detailed for forward work on communications, and the other in reserve at Micmac Camp.

The 79th and 80th Field Companies, R.E., were attached to the 53rd and 54th Brigades for work on strong points. The 92nd Field Company was kept in reserve at Dickebusch.

The rôle of the Division was to leap-frog the 30th Division after that Division had taken what became known as the Black Line—a line which ran east of Shrewsbury Forest at its southern extremity, east of Dumbarton Lakes and Inverness Copse, and bisected Glencorse Wood. Deep into the German territory behind Glencorse Wood was Polygon Wood, which was to be the 18th Division's final objective. The High Command plan was to strike with the Fifth Army between the Zillebeke and Zandvoorde Roads and Boesinghe on a front of seven and a half miles.

The night of 30th July, the eve of the Fifth Army attack, was warm and calm. The sky was clouded. Lines of men moved steadily through the broken brick remnants of the village of Zillebeke up to Ritz Street —the 8th Suffolks and 6th Royal Berks going to their assembly stations. Occasionally some signaller out repairing telephone lines, or some runner who had missed his way over the shell-pitted ground, flashed an electric torch, and there were angry shouts of " Put that light out." Boche shells came over continuously; most of them fell in the usual spots, in Zillebeke, and about Transport Farm and Shrapnel Corner : the enemy seemed to be carrying out ordinary night firing. At 10 p.m. a tank, one of five which had lumbered up and tucked themselves against a stunted hedge near Dormy House, was hit, and burst into flames, and the German Artillery, knowing they were on a target, poured salvo after salvo around Dormy House. One shell burst in Zillebeke just as " C " Company of the 8th Suffolks was passing through, killed five men outright and wounded three others.  The 6th Royal Berks lost two officers and seventeen other ranks while crossing the canal.  The 53rd Machine-Gun Company, moving up to Maple Trench, also had casualties from shell and gas shell fire.

The enemy shelling increased.  When at 10.30 P.M. there was a final testing of the "buries," the underground telephone wires that ran from Yeomanry Post and other forward stations, through Dormy House, the Chief Forward Exchange of the Divisional Signal Company, and thence to Brigade and Battalion Headquarters, over half the wires were found to be broken : six feet of earth cover was not enough to protect them from the tons of metal that lashed and tore up the dismal stretch of land east of Zillebeke Lake.  At that hour Dormy House—the telephone exchange part of it—was "fuggy" with the smell of sweating human bodies, and of the mud-clogged clothes of signallers and linemen who had been out trying to get lines "through."  Crawling about in those trenches did not leave buttons bright, nor puttees clean and tidy.

One calm man in Dormy House was Lieutenant Lepper of the 18th Divisional Signal Company, a plump, rosy-cheeked, soft-voiced officer, who kept his head and responded with optimistic pleasantness to urgent, sometimes angry, demands that smashed wires should be repaired by zero hour—3.50 A.M.  Lepper kept his word in most cases, although tempestuous enemy shelling went on all through the night.

A long time afterwards, when the 18th Division lay in front of Albert getting ready for the historic advance of 8th August 1918, an officer, who on that fateful night in Dormy House had had dealings with Lepper, said, "I believe you were the most unflurried man among that seething crowd."  Lepper replied with his smooth drawl, "Well, I had had a good training for it.  You see, I was once a night sub-editor on the 'Daily Mail.'"

The sun's first pale light was breaking through
the morning mist when zero hour arrived, and our
guns—General Jacob was said to have crowded 1,000
pieces upon his front, with twelve brigades of field
artillery to cover each Division—crashed out an awe-
inspiring tornado of flame and sound.

The troops of the 30th Division, which the 53rd
Brigade were to leap-frog when the first objective was
taken, moved forward with the 8th Division on their
left and the 24th Division on their right. The 8th
Suffolks and the 6th Royal Berks, ready and expectant, waited for the front-line reports that would tell
them the way was clear for their advance. The word
came—by lamp signal, by aeroplane message, and by
runner—but it was the wrong word. By a tragic
mistake the 30th Divisional Infantry wheeled to their
left and assaulted Chateau Wood instead of Glencorse
Wood. The misleading information that Glencorse
Wood was in our hands caused the 53rd Brigade to
plunge into a fatal gap. By 9 A.M. it was definitely
established that the 30th Division was not on the line
of the first objective; and for the rest of the day the
53rd Brigade was fighting against the fully-prepared
enemy for ground which the 30th Division should
have taken. This fateful error caused the offensive
in the Glencorse Wood region to be held up for several
days.

At 5 A.M. Lieutenant J. W. K. Wernham, the
53rd Brigade Intelligence Officer, Lieutenant Waddy,
Intelligence Officer of the 54th Brigade, and Lieutenants H. H. Gardiner and Pinhey, forward Observation Officers for the 82nd and 83rd Brigades,
R.F.A., moved forward with their runners and signallers. At 5.50 A.M. officers' patrols of the 8th
Suffolk Regiment and the 6th Royal Berkshire Regiment started off to get in touch with the 90th
Infantry Brigade of the 30th Division and to ascertain the situation.

One of the Suffolk's scouts met, near the Menin

Road, an officer of the 17th Manchesters, who reported that Glencorse Wood had been captured. Contradiction came from Lieutenant R. C. Bolingbroke, who, before being wounded, penetrated as far as the line of the first objective. Bolingbroke reported that the enemy was still holding ground west of Glencorse Wood.

No such correction reached the Berkshire Regiment, and the Berks went gaily towards Glencorse Wood shouting and cheering, preceded by an officer guide who carried a yellow flag. Suddenly, without warning, the leading companies were met, just short of the Menin Road, by intense machine-gun fire from Clapham Junction and from a number of pill-boxes on the left of that strong point, from positions thought, till then, to be in British hands. Every volley made the situation more starkly clear. With the artillery barrage now a long way ahead, the Berks and Suffolks had to assault strong points that the 30th Division had completely missed. First the sticky, shell-broken slope from Sanctuary Wood to the Menin Road had to be carried; then the road itself taken; then a chain of pill-boxes between the road and Glencorse Wood. To add to the intense drama of the situation, it became certain that our left was no longer in touch with the 8th Division.

Once again the stubborn quality of the 18th Division Infantry revealed itself. The great thing was that the men understood what had happened, and that their spirit would not allow them to accept the check. No personality shone more glowingly than that of Lieut.-Colonel G. V. W. Hill of the Suffolks. He moved to and fro among his men, telling them he was certain they were going to carry out their task, imparting to them some of his own unquenchable fire. The Berks officers, headed by Lieut.-Colonel B. G. Clay, did the same. Already they had lost one popular officer — Captain N. B. Hudson's brother. But to advance was the dominating impulse; and it

was sheer moral—the moral of small parties of men
that carried the two battalions onward, against the
hurricane shelling concentrated upon the approaches
to Glencorse Wood, against the deadly machine-gun
fire that the cool, well-placed German machine-gunners
sustained. The Berks were next to the 8th Division,
and to help them gain touch with the 8th, sappers,
pioneers, and fatigue parties of the 79th Company,
R.E., joined in ; and right nobly they carried out their
unplanned task. Headway was gained dearly, a few
yards at a time. The method was by sharp rushes from
shell-hole to shell-hole, under cover of our Lewis guns.

As they emerged from Sanctuary Wood, the 8th
Suffolks came under hot rifle and machine-gun fire
from the Menin Road and from Stirling Castle. The
companies deployed, and, heedless of losses, pressed
forward. By nine o'clock, after two enemy detachments armed with automatic rifles had been killed,
the Menin Road was gained. There followed a stern
struggle for a ridge south-east of Surbiton Villas.
The ridge bristled with machine-guns ; one in particular was holding up the left company of the
Suffolks. Private F. Read and a handful of men
took it upon themselves to deal with this obstacle.
With splendid dash they rushed the position, killed
the whole of the gun team, and put the gun out of
action. The ridge was won, but the enemy's fire was
too heavy to allow of much progress, and Lieutenant
Wheeler and Lieutenant Chibnall were killed trying
to gain further ground under a hail of fire. Lieutenant Wheeler had been nobly conspicuous in the
work preceding the capture of the ridge.

While the fighting round Surbiton Villas was in
progress, five tanks came up. Their crews made
gallant efforts to push forward, but the tanks got
bogged in the mud, and four of them were knocked
out by shell-fire. The accuracy of the German field-
guns was unpleasantly impressive. It owed something, doubtless, to the daring of German airmen.

No one who saw it will readily forget a reconnaissance made about 11 A.M. by three enemy airmen. They swooped down so low over our lines, that men trying to dig dropped their spades and fired at them with their rifles. As some set-off to the loss of the tanks, the Suffolks' right section captured a German anti-tank gun. What is more, they fired sixty rounds with it, using it to reduce a strong point that was holding up their advance. This strong point lay some hundreds of yards beyond Jap Avenue. At first the Suffolks brought up a Stokes mortar, but they found themselves with only fifteen rounds of ammunition, because of casualties to the carrying party. These were soon exhausted, and it was then that the anti-tank gun was brought into play. Lieutenant Angles and several men finally dashed into the German position and took 20 prisoners. The ground round the machine-gun that they destroyed was strewn with corpses in field-grey. Simultaneously our heavies began to pay attention to the strong point. They were so persistent that the Suffolks' tenure of the position became impossible. However, in withdrawing, the Suffolk companies regained a connection on the right that had been lost beyond Jap Avenue.

Meanwhile, before ten o'clock, the 6th Royal Berks, on the left of the Suffolks, had taken Jargon Switch and the cross-roads north-west of Glencorse Wood; touch had been gained with the 2nd Lincolns; the Surbiton Villas' line had been consolidated, with a support line in shell-holes; and battalion head-quarters were established in the Menin Road tunnel. In the gap between the 53rd Brigade and the 25th Infantry Brigade of the 8th Division, a strong point was dug which was reinforced by a party of the 30th Division's Manchesters. To stiffen the second line of defence at the southern edge of the Menin Road, four Vickers and four Lewis guns were borrowed from the derelict tanks.

The 53rd Brigade's position was still precarious. There were gaps to be filled between the Berks and the 8th Division, the Division commanded by Major-General Heneker who, earlier in the 18th Division's history, commanded the 54th Brigade. The situation had become so involved that companies intended for "mopping-up" were now in the fighting line. Some of the 10th Essex and some of the 8th Norfolks had worked forward seeking to help their hard-pressed comrades of the Berks and Suffolks. Trying to strengthen the junction with the 8th Division, Captain Patten of the Norfolks found himself at 3.30 in charge of a few men of the 10th Essex, a platoon of 8th Division infantry, and the left company of the 6th Berks, now officerless and reduced to 21 men. The Norfolks had drawn stores from the R.E. dump at Zillebeke for consolidating work. When it was learned that the day's objective had not been taken, the men kept under cover and were eventually ordered to withdraw. But Captain Patten and his company had already passed the 53rd Brigade Headquarters, and, under persistent enemy fire, had joined the remaining Berkshires in their shell-holes. All through the afternoon these men of the Norfolks kept feeling for the Lincolns of the 8th Division, but found snipers instead.

The Boche shelling into No Man's Land, and upon the whole battle area right back to Bedford House, was so tremendous that one company alone of the Sussex Pioneers suffered 47 casualties upon the A.T.N. track. The Signal Company's party that set out under Lieutenant C. F. Riley to unroll across the open the five pairs of telephone cable from Yeomanry Post onwards had a man killed in the first hundred yards. They reached Sanctuary Wood and linked up with Captain Welch, who was trying to conduct a Divisional Information Bureau, sitting in a shell-hole. Again and again wires ripped and scattered by shell-fire were repaired. Fourteen separate "breaks" were

mended on the final occasion; it was plain that no
overland cables could "live" under that shelling.
Trench wireless and power buzzers were tried, but were
useless. Only the Lucas lamp, flashing Morse signals,
survived that day's signalling test. The little signalling
party came directly under enemy machine-gun fire. A
Boche aeroplane swooped down and tried to machine-
gun them; after which it dropped bombs upon a heroic
battery of Australian Horse Artillery that had brought
its 18-pounders up to within 200 yards of the original
No Man's Land. There was the odd spectacle of a
horse hit by a shell splinter dashing about madly for
a few seconds and then, heedless of the deafening din
from exploding shells, settling down quietly to graze
upon the patches of gas-drenched grass that here and
there showed up in the vast sea of mud.

And in all that hellish turmoil, there had been
one quiet figure, most heroic, most wonderful of all.
Doctor Ackroyd, the 6th Berks medical officer, a
stooping, grey-haired, bespectacled man, rose to the
supremest heights that day. He seemed to be everywhere; he tended and bandaged scores of men, for to
him fell the rush of cases round Clapham Junction
and towards Hooge. But no wounded man was treated
hurriedly or unskilfully. Ackroyd worked as stoically
as if he were in the quiet of an operating theatre.
Complete absorption in his work was probably his
secret. When it was all over and the reports came
in, it was found that there were twenty-three separate recommendations of his name for the Victoria
Cross. Some of the recommendations came from units
of the 8th Division. Ackroyd's own battalion, the
6th Royal Berks, were accustomed to the bravery
always shown by this middle-aged man of science—
will the 53rd Brigade ever forget his glorious labours
in Delville Wood? — and they did not ask for a
Victoria Cross to be awarded him.

Doctor Ackroyd went to the war from the Downing
College Research Laboratory at Cambridge. He was

# CHAPTER XIV.

*The four days' rain from 31st July to 4th August—Major Farmer, B/83, and three subalterns killed by one shell—The attack of 10th August held up by intense machine-gun fire—54th and 55th Brigades fail to gain touch—The cheering Bedfords in Glencorse Wood—German counter-attack crushed—Captain Harry Driver's adventure—11th Royal Fusiliers' many officer casualties: 5 N.C.O.'s win the D.C.M. — The death of Major Paul, R.F.A.—The case of Lieutenant Compton of the 10th Essex — The unavailing search for Will Thorne's son.*

THE luck was dead against Sir Douglas Haig and his plans. It rained ceaselessly from 31st July to 4th August—real "Haig's weather," as it used to be called. There was no longer hope that the big attack could be carried out as a "surprise assault." The enemy opposite the Fifth Army front still held all the advantages of position. His tremendous artillery and his stoutly-held "pill-boxes" still dominated our infantry, whose lot was to lie in wait night and day in water-logged shell-holes, and, in the attack, to plod heavily, whipped with machine-gun bullets, through the quagmire. Meanwhile 'Punch' continued to amuse with happy cartoons of poor-spirited Germans holding up their hands, bleating "Kamerad" to easy-going individual British privates, while Government myrmidons fed the comfortable public with buoyant accounts of Britain's world triumph in munition-making.

The enemy devoted the breathing-space granted him by the four days' rain to re-strengthening his

defences in front of Glencorse Wood, and to the
further crushing of our exposed artillery.

On 2nd August occurred a cruel tragedy on the
shores of Zillebeke Lake.  "B" Battery of the 83rd
Brigade, R.F.A., Major Cyril Farmer's battery, had
an officers' mess, a hole and a tarpaulin cover, in the
bank by the edge of the lake.  German shells fell
night and day in the lake itself, and on the lake-side
where the Divisional Artillery batteries were.    On
2nd August a 5·9 fell plunk upon B/83's ramshackle
mess.  Four officers were sitting there, Major Farmer
himself,  and  three  young  subalterns,  Lieutenants
K. F. G. Pinhey, E. J. Pearson, and C. Scott.  Major
Farmer succumbed next day.  The others were killed
outright.  A kitten, a pet that had been found near
the lake, was the only occupant of the mess to creep
out when the smoke and flames that followed the
crash of the explosion passed away.  It was the worst
calamity the Divisional Artillery had yet had.

Major Farmer was an exceptionally fine soldier;
like Lieut.-Colonel Austin Thorp of the 82nd Brigade,
a Garrison gunner who made a perfect Field Artillery
officer.  B/83 was always a good battery.  At the
Divisional horse shows it was usually a toss - up
whether B/83 or C/82, Major P. G. M. Elles's battery,
would be adjudged to have turned out the best-kept
horses.  Major Farmer was as cheery and human as
he was competent.  No regular officer understood
better how to turn the civilian acquirements of the
officers  and  men  serving  under  him  to  war-time
account.  Pinhey, a popular young fellow, had done
F.O.O. on 31st July.  Down at the waggon line he
kept a pointer, whose faithfulness was by way of
being proverbial.  Captain Keville of the D.A.C. took
charge of the dog after Pinhey's death.  Lieutenant
Shelley, another officer of the 83rd Brigade, was hit
by a piece of shell in the throat while at the guns.
It was an awful case.  Shelley walked a hundred
yards or so to the dressing-station in Cow Farm,

Zillebeke, blood gushing from him. Then, when he saw Captain Batt, the 83rd Brigade's medical officer, he suddenly croaked, "God! I'm going to die," and dropped dead. "That case affected me more than any other," said Captain Batt a long time later. Another officer of the 83rd Brigade who was hit was Lieutenant Gilbert Ashton, who after the war became captain of the Cambridge cricket eleven, and of the Association football eleven as well. He was so badly wounded that he did not rejoin the brigade. His even more celebrated brother Hubert came out, though, and ended as Reconnaissance Officer of the Divisional Artillery.

Captain R. K. Hewer came up from the waggon lines to take command of Major Farmer's battery. The guns and the new mess were hit again three times, and Hewer obtained permission to shift the battery to near Halfway House. It took from 4.30 A.M. till 11 A.M. to drag one 18-pounder 250 yards through the ooze and slime. That was what Zillebeke was like!

On 4th August the 30th Division left the line, and the Divisional front was taken over and held by the 55th Infantry Brigade on the right and by the 54th Infantry Brigade on the left. The 18th Division was told off for another assault upon the German strong points in and about Glencorse Wood and Inverness Copse, positions of momentous value to the enemy for observation purposes. The 25th Division, which was to complete the capture of Westhoek Ridge begun by the 8th Division, also took part in the operation. The chosen day was 9th August, but once again the weather was against the British. A violent thunderstorm caused twenty-four hours' postponement.

Going up to take post on the shell-hole front line demanded a courage and endurance of its own, for the German artillery was keener than ever to deny ground to us. When the 7th Buffs went to relieve a battalion of the 30th Division on the night of 3rd August, 2nd Lieutenant A. C. L. Nicholson found himself in charge of his company, his company officer having been wounded. Rain was pouring down, it was pitch dark, and the enemy field-guns fired persistently. Nicholson, a small slight man, who to the end of the war showed himself possessed of a spirit greater than his strength of body—he gained two bars to his M.C. before the finish—took charge so satisfactorily that he led his men to their appointed position without one of them going astray. Then, when a patrol of his company had twice failed, owing to enfilading fire, to reach a deserted enemy machine-gun emplacement and sniping-post about a hundred yards in front of the Buffs' sector, Nicholson himself crawled out and found the post; the Buffs were able to prevent the Germans reoccupying a strong point from which things could have been made dangerous for the whole battalion.

The Queens had just had a draft when they went up with the West Kents and took over the old line at Sanctuary Wood. For the newcomers it was a frightful apprenticeship to active service. Nothing went smoothly: it was a pouring wet night; there were casualties on the way, "C" and "D" Companies losing their leaders in Captain Clapperton (wounded) and Captain Shearen (killed); the trenches had been shelled or swilled away; and, according to our reading of the map, which differed materially from the 30th Division's reading, an adjustment of some hundreds of yards was needed to put the line where it was by the official chart. And this had to be done in the dark, with the artillery on both sides shelling hard.

At first the West Kents made their headquarters in a shell-hole at the back of Stirling Castle, a ruin that concealed a wonderful pill-box. The Queens some days later used the pill-box itself. It conferred on its tenants not merely safety but comfort. There was a kitchen with two double beds, there were easy-chairs and a settee, and the walls and roof were so strong that 4·2's bounced off like peppercorns. Also, as it was shown on all the maps, it was easy to find. The shell-hole position was not. So vague was it, that the

from machine - guns, and having lost practically all their officers they had to be content with small progress. The Boche still held Inverness Copse and the country between it and Glencorse Wood In spite of this, the Bedfordshires dug in and sent men to link up with the Fusiliers. While touch was maintained in this way, the Bedfordshires holding Glencorse Wood were forming a very nasty salient, and were subject all day to fire from their right flank, from pill-boxes manned by determined machine-gunners and snipers. Many casualties were suffered.

"In the late afternoon it was apparent that the Boche was preparing a determined attack from Polygon Wood. But the Bedfordshires had not been idle, and had thoroughly consolidated their position and received supplies of ammunition and machine-guns. Also our artillery was warned, and when the Boche started to deliver his counter-attack he was met with a deluge of fire from both infantry and artillery, causing shocking casualties. Needless to say our line was intact at the end. That night the Bedfordshires were relieved."

The official record shows that the Bedfords held on to their final objective for more than four hours. Three companies did what they could to establish posts where the state of the ground made any continuous line impossible. At 9.17 A.M. Captain Driver reported that two companies on his right flank were badly bent back. By midday the Bedfords had adopted Jargon Trench, about halfway between their starting-point and their final objective, as their main line. Three posts on their left flank kept touch with the 74th Infantry Brigade of the 25th Division.

There were strong counter-attacks from Nonne Boschen Wood. All were withstood. At dusk the enemy tried again under cover of a smoke barrage. It was to no purpose. He had a reception from our artillery and riflemen that sent him back to cover.

Captain Driver's exploits that day were rewarded with the Military Cross. His reconnaissances were invaluable, and though fired at repeatedly, he continued to visit his posts.

It is related that as he lay on the ground after being hit by a sniper, Driver heard Captain Kingston

of "C" Company, the Bedfords, dictating a report of
his death to the sergeant-major. Driver had been
shot through the jaw. The bullet had pierced his
tongue, and he could not speak, but he managed to
turn over and write on a piece of paper, "I'm not
dead, blast you, give me a bandage."

He and the message reporting his death arrived
simultaneously at the dressing-station. Even when
weak from loss of blood he wrote a full account of the
situation.

The day brought deserved honours to many Bedfordshire officers and men. Captain J. A. Colley was
awarded a bar to his M.C. for the way in which he
rallied the right wing; Sergeant Peck gained the
D.C.M. and Corporal Fitzgerald the M.M. for putting
enemy machine-guns out of action. Peck bombed a
whole team. Corporal Spring, going to the German
side of the ridge, maintained visual signalling under
fire. Another Glencorse M.C. went to Captain Vlasto,
the Bedfords' Medical Officer, who worked ceaselessly
in the firing line during a gas and smoke cloud.
He attended to over 300 cases. As many as 250
wounded were collected by Captain Vlasto's orderly,
Corporal Ernest Jones. Four times in succession the
corporal carried in men under heavy fire. Some of
the wounded took refuge temporarily in a tank to
which Jones made several journeys. During a heavy
burst of artillery fire, one man's arm was almost
severed. Corporal Jones held the artery until the
wound could be dressed.

The 11th Royal Fusiliers, as has been already seen,
were early in difficulties. Portions of the two attacking companies reached the objective, but a gap of
300 yards divided the battalion from the Bedfords
farther north. The right reached Fitzclarence Farm,
but could not get in touch with the 55th Brigade.
By 6 A.M. all the Fusiliers' officers had fallen.

Preceded by parties bombing up Jargon Trench
and other trenches between the two woods, the Ger-

mans launched a counter-attack from Inverness Copse. Their machine-guns forced the Fusiliers back, and, under orders from the 54th Brigade, the battalion took a line on the ridge in front of Clapham Junction. The idea was that they should join up with the 55th Brigade then consolidating Green Jacket Ride. Reinforced by a company of the 12th Middlesex Regiment, the Fusiliers held this line until relieved.

"The barrage opened at dawn," writes a Fusiliers' officer, "and the men got away very well. They got into Glencorse Wood, and, on the open ground, some of 'D' Company, including Captain Gray, got right up to Fitzclarence Farm. Unfortunately the battalion on our right did not get on at all. Our men were consequently caught by a heavy enfilade machine-gun fire, and soon afterwards the Boche came out from Inverness Copse in force and got almost in rear of our support company.

"Casualties had been very heavy, especially amongst officers. In 'B' Company, Captain Fuller was shot through the head while trying with his Lewis gun sergeant, Sergeant Franklin, to rush a machine-gun in a concrete emplacement. Horton, his second in command, was hit by a bullet through the chest shortly after leaving the strong point. Calthorpe had been killed. In 'D' Company, Gray was last seen lying in a shell-hole close to Fitzclarence Farm, shot through both knees and using his revolver over the top of the shell-hole. Watt, commanding 'C' Company, was twice wounded, but continued fighting until wounded again, this time mortally.

"In 'A' Company, Stovell, another plucky lad, was killed by a bomb. Sergeant Bott, who had got the D.C.M. at Thiépval, and was, on this occasion, commanding a platoon, was killed on the edge of Glencorse Wood. Captain Hoare of 'A' Company was the last surviving officer, and he was shortly afterwards sniped through the head from the direction of Glencorse Wood.

"By this time the Fusiliers were withdrawing from their advanced posts, and a line was established 200 yards east of Clapham Junction.

"At this stage things were critical. We had very few men left to man all this line, and there were no troops in reserve behind us nearer than Sanctuary Wood. The Fusiliers had no company officer left, and only one company sergeant-major—Burch of 'C' Company. However, Lewis guns, and later, machine-guns, were placed to cover the gap on our right.    Pearcy, the signalling officer, came up from Headquarters, which was in Menin Tunnel, with all available men—servants, runners, and pioneers,—and a company of the Middlesex Regiment came up from Sanctuary Wood and went into the line just north of the Menin Road.    Two platoons of the Northamptonshire Regiment, who were there to garrison certain strong points which were to have been established forward, were also on the ridge, and Captain (now Lieut.-Colonel) E. C. T. Minet of the 54th Machine-Gun Company, and Captain Shepherd of the 6th Northamptonshires, took charge and organised the line."

It was dogged and disjointed fighting.    Fierce conflicts raged round little fortresses, high and dry like so many islands in a sea of marsh and mud.    Besieged and besiegers constantly changed places.    As one leader fell, another arose to take his place.    In many cases the mantle of the officer descended upon a corporal.    Nor were the qualities of adaptability and readiness for responsibility that were the salt of the New Army lacking on this hard-testing occasion.

Five of the Fusiliers' N.C.O.'s won D.C.M.'s by their skill in shepherding officerless companies and rallying waverers to new and amazing resistance to the weight of the outnumbering Germans.

Sergeant Ernest Wilson's D.C.M.: When all the company officers had become casualties, he collected his men, garrisoned a very important strong point, and beat off repeated counter-attacks.    Later, when surrounded and overwhelmed by great numbers, he and his garrison were driven from their positions, but he rallied his men, attached them to another unit, and helped to recapture the position.

Sergeant Henry Berry's D.C.M.: When all his officers had become casualties, he took charge of his company.    Although wounded, he organised the defence of the line and successfully destroyed repeated enemy counter-attacks.    When the troops on his left were dislodged temporarily from their positions during the night, he organised and led part of the counter-attack which regained the position.

Sergeant (Acting Company Sergeant-Major) Burch's D.C.M.: When all the company officers had become casualties, he took

charge of his company, rallied the men at a critical moment,
and then organised the line, garrisoning a strong point of
vital importance. By careful judgment in placing Lewis
guns he destroyed German infantry who were trying to form
for attack. During the night he and his garrison beat off a
very determined counter-attack.

Corporal H. Hallett and Corporal T. Wright also won
D.C.M.'s by skilful handling of their men when officers had
become casualties.

By such men and such measures was our imperilled
right wing saved. There was a private named Adams
—not William, but Tom—who earned merited fame on
this occasion. He was a stretcher-bearer. Time and
again he carried wounded men from the thickest part
of the barrage to the aid post. Contemptuous of
danger, he still went forward when some of the
infantry were dropping back. His example encouraged the waverers; he even posted little groups of
stragglers in the line. For his tireless and heroic
exertions, he was awarded the D.C.M. Another
private who distinguished himself was Arthur Jakes,
M.M., who, cut off and surrounded by the enemy,
played the part of sniper. When darkness fell, he
crawled across the German lines and rejoined his
battalion.

Lieutenant Pearcy's part was recognised by a bar
to the M.C. gained at Boom Ravine. Colonel Minet
received the D.S.O. At the moment of the Colonel's
intervention, recounted in the personal narrative already quoted, the Brigade was outflanked. The
Colonel, one of the characters of the Division, assumed
command of all the troops in the vicinity and built
up a defensive flank. "Throughout the day," says the
'Gazette,' "he was in the front line passing from gun
to gun, controlling the fire and encouraging all ranks."

With a nominally minor mission, the Northamptonshire Regiment found itself bearing a large share of
the burden of the day. A company under Captain
Grace followed up the Fusiliers so impetuously that

40 German prisoners were secured, the majority being caught in their dug-outs on the south edge of Glencorse Wood. From this point some of the "moppers-up" went ahead with the attacking force. Lance-Corporal J. F. Norris took his Lewis-gun team to the aid of some men who were held up by two enemy machine-guns. These obstacles the corporal and his comrades speedily reduced, putting both guns out of action. Just afterwards one of our airmen flew down over another German machine-gun post and fired Tracer bullets at it. Without being effective himself, the airman disclosed to Corporal Norris a desirable target and the service was not wasted. This gun was also silenced. Yet another German crew went down before two of our Lewis gunners in the most inexplicable way. It was a case of two against nine. The two privates—F. L. Smith and F. Farrer—rushed the position. Farrer killed a couple of Germans while Smith engaged the gun. Then Smith himself plunged into the group, which seemed petrified by the suddenness of the onslaught. He killed one German and wounded another. The remaining five surrendered. D.C.M.'s went to Smith and Farrer as well as to Corporal Norris.

Carrying was no picnic in this area. Thirty per cent of a 12th Middlesex Company engaged in bringing up small-arms ammunition from Zillebeke to the front line got knocked out. But 80,000 rounds were delivered.

A count of the 18th Division's casualties from 31st July to 10th August showed 244 killed, 1,106 wounded, and 176 missing. A count of prisoners taken during the same period showed 59. For the time being everything favoured the Germans' new and elastic system of defence. There was a blend of blunders, and the conditions were appalling. Long afterwards, officers who went over this ground expressed surprise that the Germans should ever have been dislodged from their "pill-box" strongholds.

P

It was in no very encouraging circumstances that the 53rd Brigade were called into the line. The troops scrambled up towards Stirling Castle over the slippery shell-churned surface in the dark, amid persistent shelling, with the rain falling. It was difficult for the guides to tell one spot from another, and the 10th Essex, who were relieving the Queens, owed much to the 55th Brigade-Major, Captain Runge, who, when he found the guides at a loss, led the Essex up himself.

Barely had the 8th Norfolks relieved the Fusiliers and the Bedfords at 4.15 A.M. on the 11th ere the enemy penetrated our line and carried a strong point. The Norfolks had come up from Canal Reserve Camp and had been on their legs nearly twelve hours. They were dog-tired. The reverse stung them into fresh feats of endurance. Without any barrage, they pressed forward, and by 6 o'clock, under Captain Morgan's leadership, had retaken the post, and rescued several of their comrades who were in the enemy's hands, and two of our machine-guns with them. This pill-box at J.14 A.25 wore a familiar look. It was the one that had held up the 53rd Brigade on 31st July.

The better to hold what the 54th Brigade had taken—namely, the edge of the wood—it was hoped to improve our position in this quarter by an attack next morning. The orders were issued at 10.15 A.M. on the 11th to the 8th Norfolks, 10th Essex, and 6th Berkshire Regiments. Later, on account of the Norfolks' losses in the sudden Boche raid, the 8th Suffolks were substituted in the orders. But they did not come. All that night officers of the Essex and Berks Regiments were asking where were the Suffolks? Zero hour arrived—4.25 A.M. The barrage opened. The morning was perfect, the light just right; but the Suffolks were not on their starting-off line, and the attack had to be cancelled.

The contretemps came about in this way: At

5 P.M. on 11th August, when the Suffolks should have
begun their move up to join the Essex and Berkshires,
the Boche put down a tremendous "area strafe,"
using every form of shell, upon Zillebeke and round
about Dormy House and Ritz Street Trench.  It
lasted until 7 P.M., and to avoid casualties Colonel
Hill postponed the departure of his battalion until
then.  When they did start, and got to the edge of
Sanctuary Wood, an enemy aeroplane signalled a
target in the wood.  The German gunners answered
the signal with workmanlike promptitude, and this
compelled the Suffolks to bear towards Hooge.  They
missed the guides who were to have conducted them
to the assembly place.  Night came on and they
struck the Menin Road at a place where it was
unrecognisable as a road, and in the darkness crossed
it without knowing that they had done so.  All the
wires at 53rd Brigade Headquarters at Dormy House
had gone in the Boche's two-hours' intensive shelling,
so that Colonel Clay of the Berkshires and Colonel
Frizell of the 10th Essex were without news of the
Suffolks' change of plans.  They were kept in an
unenviable state of suspense.  Captain Banks of the
10th Essex was dodging in and out of the Norfolks'
"pill-box" headquarters all night seeking news of the
missing Suffolks.  Soon after zero hour the Suffolks
found themselves.  But it was too late; the attack
had been cancelled.

The Divisional Artillery on the side of Zillebeke
Lake and in the neighbourhood of Ritz Street Trench
got a full share of the enemy's 5 P.M. to 7 P.M. "area
strafe" on 11th August.  There were many casualties, and another tragic loss in the death of Major
L. I. C. Paul, who had commanded "D" Battery,
82nd Brigade R.F.A., since that fine officer Major
W. F. Armstrong had lost an eye trying to rescue
several men of his battery buried by a big shell just
after the battle of Cherisy on 3rd May.

Major Paul was another Regular Artillery officer,

a sound soldier, good-looking, bright in manner, amazingly dapper, extremely popular. At 4.30 P.M. he had attended a Battery Commanders' conference to discuss the 53rd Brigade's attack of the morrow, held in the dug-out in Ritz Street occupied by Colonel Seagram and Colonel Thorp. The Boche began his two-hours' intensive shelling just as the conference ended, but all the Battery Commanders, Paul among them, decided to leave what shelter the dug-out offered and to get back to their batteries.

About 6.15 P.M. a young subaltern of Major Paul's battery—Lieutenant V. B. Jones, a very capable horseman, who earlier in the year had won the Divisional Artillery jumping competition—was seen wandering along the Ritz Street Trench, his arm hanging limp, his jacket half off. He called out through the din of the shelling that Major Paul had been hit by a shell while taking him to the dressing-station the other side of Zillebeke. Colonel Thorp told his orderly officer, Lieutenant G. H. F. Nichols, to call for a stretcher and some volunteers, and with the Colonel and Lieutenant Nichols carrying the stretcher, and their servants, Gunners Searle and Woodgate, and one of the signallers, Corporal White, in attendance, the party set off, guided by Lieutenant Jones, to find Major Paul. They went 300 yards towards Zillebeke, across a stretch of land that was being pelted with Boche shells. Near the collection of derelict tanks knocked out in the 31st July battle, the party started to search for Major Paul. Nichols was hit immediately, but Colonel Thorp and the others found Paul lying unconscious near one of the tanks. Colonel Thorp did famous work that evening. Twice under the tremendous shelling he went through to Zillebeke, first to find Captain Batt, the 83rd Brigade doctor, and then to bring up stretcher-bearers, another badly-wounded gunner having been picked up near the tanks. The Colonel seemed to bear a charmed life that day. Major Paul was got

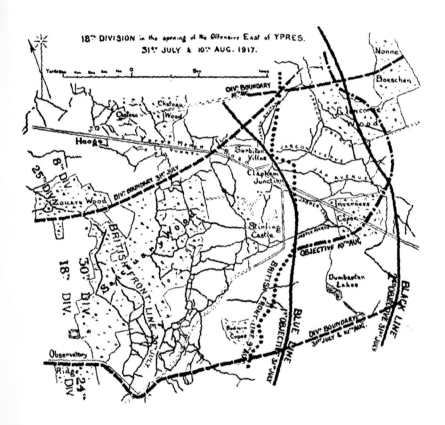

18TH DIVISION in the opening of the Offensive East of YPRES.
31ST JULY & 10TH AUG. 1917.

away safely, but he died the next morning from stomach wounds.

Upon the men of Captain Banks' company of the 10th Essex, up beyond the Menin Road, devolved—according to the orders for 12th August—the duty of taking a "pill-box" in front of Inverness Copse. In charge of two platoons chosen for the assault was Lieutenant Compton, a big, hefty, very earnest young officer. Just before the move up the line, Compton had heard that the 24th Division, in which his brother served, was close by, and he walked over to see him. He learned that his brother had been killed the day before the 24th Division went out of the line.

On his return he told Captain Banks of his loss, and said he wanted to lead the attack against the "pill-box." He kept saying he was dead keen to do this. Captain Banks felt that he ought not to accept the offer, but circumstances compelled that he should do so. Owing to sickness and other causes no other officer was available for the task.

At 4.5 A.M., when he heard that the attack was not to take place, Captain Banks sent a double runner to Lieutenant Compton, who was lying out in front, telling him to bring in his men before daylight. A runner came back and said he had given the order.

But, as was learnt afterwards, in spite of the countermand, Lieutenant Compton called for volunteers and attacked the pill-box. Most of his men went with him. The barrage, which it had been impossible to stop, descended on a line beyond the pill-box. The Germans quickly discovered that there was no general attack. Compton was killed and his party cut to pieces.

Another Essex loss on 11th August was the son of Mr Will Thorne, the Labour leader. A married man of about thirty years of age and of splendid physique, he was an efficient bomber. He was with a party that went through Zouave Wood on to the Menin Road. They were near the Berks' headquarters

when a dozen shells burst about them.  The men
dropped into trenches in the pitch darkness.  When
the survivors were collected by Captain "Bill" Skeat
of the 10th Essex, Thorne could not be found.  Five
of his party lay dead in the trench in which they had
sought shelter, but there was no trace of Thorne's
body.  Nor did inquiries, extended to the German
camps and hospitals, throw any light upon what
always has been a mystery.

On 13th August the 53rd Infantry Brigade was
placed under the orders of the 56th Division.  With
a view to a further attack, the 7th Bedfords were
attached to the 53rd Brigade; the 12th Middlesex
and 1/4 London Regiment also came under General
Higginson.  On the 15th, the Germans counter-
attacked from Polygon Wood.  For at least two
hours there was no artillery fire, and the infantry
fought it out with rifle and bayonet.  The Berks
and Norfolks displayed remarkable resilience and took
heavy toll with the bayonet, four men claiming ten
victims each.  Gas was discharged from projectors
into Inverness Copse; and on the 16th the fresh
attack by the Bedfords and 1/4 London Regiment
was launched, but without success.  The Bedfords
tried again at the north-west corner of Inverness
Copse, but they were too weak to make headway
against the German machine-guns.  The 53rd Brigade
was relieved on the night of the 17/18th August.

From the Glencorse area the 53rd Brigade went to
Rubrouck, the 54th and 55th to the Buysschere and
Wormhoudt areas.  There, worn-out men became fit
again, thanks to the cheering influences of recreation,
baths, and the entertainment offered by that cheerful
troupe the "Vin Blongs."

During this period of rest, the Corps Commander,
General Hunter Weston, inspected many units of the
division, and especially praised those that favoured
the prohibited "shorts."  He also revealed his interest
in culinary and sanitary arrangements.

# CHAPTER XV.

## THE TRIUMPH AT POELCAPPELLE.

*A model 53rd Brigade operation in which General Higginson bluffed the Germans—The dummy figures—A victory in the mud—Norfolks capture the Brewery in the opening dash, a clean piece of work —10th Essex advance another 1,000 yards and seize Meunier House against determined opposition—The pill-box adventure of Sergeant Dupree.*

THE 53rd Brigade's victory at Poelcappelle on 22nd October 1917 came after bitter and repeated disappointments, like a beam of light in a dark place. It was one of the few solid gains won by the British Army in that year's appallingly costly campaign, and has especial distinction because, like Thiépval and Albert (1918), it is included in the sixty-one important operations officially described as "Battles" by the War Committee on Nomenclature.

The final capture of the cluster of tree-stumps, pill-boxes, and bits of brick that stuck sufficiently far out of the mud to be recognised as Poelcappelle, and also of Meunier House and Tracas Farm, was effected by a brilliant operation in which General Higginson bluffed and outmanœuvred the Germans. A Chinese attack to the south of the village, where dummy figures on poles drew the enemy fire, masked a move in which the weight was thrown to the north, and two battalions of the 53rd Brigade, the 8th Norfolks and the 10th Essex, won strongholds whose conquest had defied all previous attempts.

The triumph was won against terribly adverse

conditions.  Nothing seemed consecutive in this region save the casualty lists; nothing continuous save the rain.  A few yards were as hard to win here as a mile on some portions of the front.  It seemed, indeed, as though at Poelcappelle nobody could do anything right.  One brigade after another went up and knocked its head against a brick wall and retired hurt.  The 53rd Brigade's plan broke away from convention.  According to convention, assaults had to be delivered to the south, and artifice could not be expected to succeed in a sector that was so completely overlooked.  General Higginson reasoned differently.  He considered a little spice of dissimulation well worth trying.  And he was abundantly justified.  It was not worth while at the time to interest the German Staff by mentioning the ruse in the published accounts of the affair.  But the plan was circulated at once throughout the British Army, for reference as a model effort.  The war correspondents also were allowed to lift the veil far enough to reveal the names of the successful battalions, an unusual favour for a plain English Division like the 18th.  For that was a period of glorious anonymity.  English units that dared and did mighty things were compendiously called " English Troops," or " English County Regiments," or something equally vague.

The situation when the 18th Division went up to Poelcappelle early in October was heart-breakingly difficult.  By an assault on a seven miles' front between the Menin road and the Ypres - Staden railway, the British line by 4th October had been carried to the west end of the village.  During the next week it wobbled about, the Germans trying local counter-attacks, and our men hanging on to exposed positions by the skin of their teeth.  In the middle of the month it ran roughly north to south through the middle of the village, passing through the church, which had enough stones left one upon another to be a conspicuous object amid the cluster

the slime from getting above his knees. He was well
served by a runner, Private Boarer, a cheerful and
imperturbable fellow whose good spirits were an asset
to the battalion. Boarer made six journeys under
fire to battalion headquarters in daylight. When
not acting as a messenger he went to an aid post for
stretchers. Four badly wounded men owed their
rescue to his efforts, and Boarer's Military Medal was
one of the most popular awards ever made in the 7th
Buffs. Mark Tapleys were needed in the battalion
at that time. The companies had been much upset
by an air-raid disaster that preceded the Poelcappelle
enterprise. A low-flying enemy plane dropped six
bombs on their camp, and caused 90 casualties, 30 of
them fatal.

Like the Buffs, the East Surreys were severely
punished when they tried to tackle the German
machine-gun nests. That the assaulting companies
were held together was due in large measure to two
officers—Captain C. G. M. Place, who won the D.S.O.,
and Lieutenant Dawson. Though wounded, Captain
Place continued to organise fresh attacks, and his
injury was not dressed until hours afterwards. The
Berkshires lost Colonel Longhurst killed. Their
adjutant, Rochfort, lost an arm, but carried on for
a couple of hours afterwards. Nothing could affect
the moral of the Berkshire men. One man of "C"
Company staggered down laden with two Lewis-gun
drums as trophies. He had been told he might dump
them, but he refused, fearing that the Berks might
not be credited with them. So fagged out was
another private that he dropped plump on the duck-
board and fell fast asleep while Captain Hudson was
talking to him.

The 55th Brigade attack had failed, but Poelcappelle
was to be won.

While the 53rd Brigade prepared for the next
assault the Divisional Artillery—shelled at every
hour, and living night and day in cold filth and

conditions. Nothing seemed consecutive in this region save the casualty lists; nothing continuous save the rain. A few yards were as hard to win here as a mile on some portions of the front. It seemed, indeed, as though at Poelcappelle nobody could do anything right. One brigade after another went up and knocked its head against a brick wall and retired hurt. The 53rd Brigade's plan broke away from convention. According to convention, assaults had to be delivered to the south, and artifice could not be expected to succeed in a sector that was so completely overlooked. General Higginson reasoned differently. He considered a little spice of dissimulation well worth trying. And he was abundantly justified. It was not worth while at the time to interest the German Staff by mentioning the ruse in the published accounts of the affair. But the plan was circulated at once throughout the British Army, for reference as a model effort. The war correspondents also were allowed to lift the veil far enough to reveal the names of the successful battalions, an unusual favour for a plain English Division like the 18th. For that was a period of glorious anonymity. English units that dared and did mighty things were compendiously called "English Troops," or "English County Regiments," or something equally vague.

The situation when the 18th Division went up to Poelcappelle early in October was heart-breakingly difficult. By an assault on a seven miles' front between the Menin road and the Ypres - Staden railway, the British line by 4th October had been carried to the west end of the village. During the next week it wobbled about, the Germans trying local counter-attacks, and our men hanging on to exposed positions by the skin of their teeth. In the middle of the month it ran roughly north to south through the middle of the village, passing through the church, which had enough stones left one upon another to be a conspicuous object amid the cluster of rubbish-heaps once the homes or shops of the long-evicted and far-scattered inhabitants.

Poelcappelle showed up on the drab mournful landscape even after three years of war's ruthlessness. But its one-time girdle of pleasant farms had been blotted out. Their names survived to distinguish grassless pastures that now grew nothing but machine-guns.

The main approach to Poelcappelle, the Langemarck road, was more than hard to find. Intelligence officers trying to trace it turned geologists and sought in shell-holes for fragments of the road-metal as the best clue to its direction. To cross the oozy wilderness one followed the tortuous tracks of semi-submerged duckboards. There were five miles of them to the front line. One Berks officer declared that he walked 500 miles over duckboards during the Poelcappelle period. Though up and down lines were laid the congestion of traffic was chronic, the interruptions by shell-fire incessant. The thin threads of communication were being broken and mended at all hours. Front trenches meant a zig-zag of scattered shell craters. A particularly large hole protected by a hurdle might be a battalion headquarters, a lesser hole might hold the leader of a company. The difficulty of conveying orders or of allotting objectives in such circumstances needs no emphasis, yet seldom did it receive sufficient allowance in high places.

Strictly speaking, the campaigning season was over. In a tongue of water-logged territory hemmed in by the enemy on two sides and dominated by the concentrated German artillery, the British Army groped and floundered. Passchendaele was the goal still some five miles off. Westroosebeke Ridge just ahead was a necessary step towards it. A pause before Poelcappelle involved quite plainly only two alternatives: wintering in an impossible swamp, or a withdrawal and the abandonment of the dear-bought gains of weeks. But the 18th Division was now a unit in the army of General Plumer, who made no traceable mistake throughout the war. More heartening still, we belonged to Maxse's 18th Corps. And General Maxse trusted the Division he had brought out to France. So much our brigades learned before their rehearsals at Poperinghe were finished. General Maxse saw them practising the then unfamiliar "leap-frogging" attacks. Telling the officers something of his intentions, he observed: "I have arranged a very nice battle for you gentlemen, with lots of Huns to kill." It was the old familiar Maxse, and the Division rejoiced that it was so.

A few days later the 55th Brigade led the way over the much-barraged Steenbecque crossing during the night of 10th October. It was pitch dark, and gaps were a good deal easier to find than guides. Nominally the 55th relieved the 32nd Brigade that night, but as the 32nd units were mixed up, much of the taking over was guesswork.

On 11th October it rained all day. A low-flying hostile aeroplane spent the morning hovering over us. During the day it was decided to alter the jumping-off line, and during the night the barrage "lifts." On the 12th the "nice" battle—an attack to secure Poelcappelle and Meunier House—began anything but nicely. Leap-frogging was the method, but no method on the 12th could conquer the mud. Every step required a great physical effort, every man was drenched to the skin. Many men stuck in the mud and were too exhausted to reach the lining-up tape. Most of our 18-pounders sank, lowering the muzzles and shortening the range.

Our barrage opened at 5.20 A.M. Within a minute the Boche replied with all his force. As soon as his machine-gunners located an occupied shell-hole, they aimed about a yard in front of it, and bullets singed through the mud of the lip, and wounded men in the crater. The 55th Brigade went over in snake forma-

tion, Surreys and Buffs on the right and West Kents
on the left. The German barrage was much heavier
on the south side of the village, and our right wing
could make little headway. The chief obstacle was
the Brewery. The withering fire from this stronghold and from Helles House made the streets of the
village beyond a certain point impassable. The situation round Requette Farm, to the north, remained
obscure till the afternoon, owing to so many runners
being killed. At noon the Germans launched a
counter - attack towards the west of the village.
Beaten back, they tried again two or three times
during the afternoon. A gap between the Suffolks,
who were in support, and the right of the 4th
Division in front, tempted the enemy twice. The
first move was observed about noon by Lieutenant
Jordan and Sergeant Eaves. The Sergeant was killed
almost at once, but fortunately, at a time when many
weapons were useless, Lieutenant Jordan found two
still effective Lewis guns, and from a small sap distributed a large enough dose of discouragement to
make the Germans go back. The second attempt
of the Germans came about 5.30. A bombing party
worked stealthily along a hedgerow, but lost heavily
without making any impression.

Night, which brought another deluge, found us
little further advanced than in the morning. Save for
the assistance it gave to the troops on the flanks, the
attack was a dismal fizzle. Soaked to the skin and
shelterless, the men remained in the mud fatigued and
famished. There were no arrivals of rations till next
day, and some companies went two days without food.
One man in the Suffolks died of exposure, and over
twenty others were evacuated suffering from exhaustion. Most of them had to have their socks cut from
off their feet. The ration issues were made at a roadside dump near three derelict tanks. A track round
the tanks was laid by the Sussex Pioneers, but the first
limber that came along slipped over the side and

blocked the traffic. The infantry carried two water-bottles apiece, or they would have gone thirsty as well as hungry.

Darkness and chaos on the duckboards compelled supply columns to work by daylight. To ease the burden of the distressed horses, the Yukon pack was tried for ammunition. The Yukon pack—a frame of wood and canvas—would hold about 120 lbs. We owed this contrivance to the Canadians, who had used it at Vimy Ridge. It was a success on the Somme, where a foothold was possible. Flanders was a different story. There the pack proved too heavy : it was a millstone that dragged the beasts of burden down into the mire, and it was abandoned.

The mud clogged everything, even shells and rifles. The 53rd Trench Mortar Battery could not fire after 11 A.M. on the 12th because the ammunition was too wet and dirty. Some of the machine-guns were withdrawn for the same reason. "The conditions were the worst we ever experienced," says an officer of the 7th Queens. "We seemed to be simply waiting for death." Heavy toll was taken of the R.A.M.C., though the Germans respected the Red Cross and doctors went into No Man's Land without being fired upon. But out of 44 doctors, 14 became casualties at Poelcappelle ; 7 were killed ; within a fortnight 150 other ranks of the R.A.M.C. were put out of action.

The Suffolks' casualties on the 12th numbered 227. The Buffs went back to Boesinghe counting only 100 of all ranks. "D" Company advancing against Gloucester Farm was practically wiped out by machine-gun fire after going 150 yards.

The Buffs' officers who survived, among whom Major Nicholson, Captain Hayfield, and Lieutenant Tupper especially distinguished themselves, organised posts in shell-holes with such fragments of platoons as they could collect. Major Nicholson at one of these points had to raise himself repeatedly to keep the slime from getting above his knees. He was well served by a runner, Private Boarer, a cheerful and imperturbable fellow whose good spirits were an asset to the battalion. Boarer made six journeys under fire to battalion headquarters in daylight. When not acting as a messenger he went to an aid post for stretchers. Four badly wounded men owed their rescue to his efforts, and Boarer's Military Medal was one of the most popular awards ever made in the 7th Buffs. Mark Tapleys were needed in the battalion at that time. The companies had been much upset by an air-raid disaster that preceded the Poelcappelle enterprise. A low-flying enemy plane dropped six bombs on their camp, and caused 90 casualties, 30 of them fatal.

Like the Buffs, the East Surreys were severely punished when they tried to tackle the German machine-gun nests. That the assaulting companies were held together was due in large measure to two officers—Captain C. G. M. Place, who won the D.S.O., and Lieutenant Dawson. Though wounded, Captain Place continued to organise fresh attacks, and his injury was not dressed until hours afterwards. The Berkshires lost Colonel Longhurst killed. Their adjutant, Rochfort, lost an arm, but carried on for a couple of hours afterwards. Nothing could affect the moral of the Berkshire men. One man of " C " Company staggered down laden with two Lewis-gun drums as trophies. He had been told he might dump them, but he refused, fearing that the Berks might not be credited with them. So fagged out was another private that he dropped plump on the duck-board and fell fast asleep while Captain Hudson was talking to him.

The 55th Brigade attack had failed, but Poelcappelle was to be won.

While the 53rd Brigade prepared for the next assault the Divisional Artillery—shelled at every hour, and living night and day in cold filth and slime—pounded away at the enemy. The artillery casualties continued to be appallingly heavy. In the 82nd Brigade, of the older officers only Colonel Thorp, Major D. J. Fraser, Captain F. J. Rice, Major Wilfred Dennes, and gallant old House, the adjutant, remained. That splendidly athletic soldier, Major J. F. P. Thorburn, of A/82, who took his cold "tub" in the open, even on the shell-swept shores of Zillebeke Lake, had been so sorely wounded that only his exceptional physique enabled him to survive; Major P. G. M. Elles, C/82, was also so badly hit that he never came out again; Major J. P. Wheeler, another Regular officer, who had succeeded to the command of D/82, was killed by a shell at the guns; so was his captain, S. A. Rodney - Ricketts, a South African Rhodes Scholar, a fine athlete and a natural soldier. Lieutenant R. D. M'Donald, of B/82, who was trained at the "shop," coming back from leave was rushed forward to take charge of a battery that had lost all its officers, and was killed within an hour of his arrival. In the 83rd Brigade Major L. J. Samuels, who commanded B/83, met his death at the battery position. Colonel Seagram at Poelcappelle was left with only Major A. A. A. Paterson, Major Keyes, Major M'Pherson, Major R. K. Hewer, Captain C. H. Atkinson, Captain T. A. Jones, and his adjutant, Captain Cruickshank, out of the accomplished band of officers who came with him into Belgium. Truly Flanders 1917 was the "Gunners' Hell!"

Two of the batteries dwelt in pill-boxes, 12 feet by 6 feet, where men not on the guns baled out water, to prevent kits and maps from floating away. The Steenbecque position — almost virgin sward up to 11th October—was in a dreadful plight. The natural dip favouring some sort of cover was packed with guns. Supply animals after leaving the road had to traverse a slippery morass for the last 150 yards, and the most sure-footed mules were brought to grief. When a duckboard tilted up and spurted foul water,

the stench was sickening. The men of C/83, Major
Paterson's Battery, were between the devil and the
deeps on the Poelcappelle road. Their position at St
Julien was marked by a couple of trees about 800
yards from the front line. When shells came hurt-
ling round that target, there was no chance of escape
save by plunging into the pools that lay to right and
left. During a ten weeks' sojourn in this place the
battery fired 30,000 shells. It lost 12 men killed
and 17 wounded, and drivers had to be called up to
man the guns. It was the rule to keep 1,500 rounds
per gun in each position, and not infrequently
800 rounds had to be fired in a night. It was the
gunners' mission to break the spirit of the enemy.
There was no rest for gunners at Poelcappelle. There
were batteries that had no N.C.O. left at the waggon lines. C/82 could boast only a corporal and two
bombardiers at the guns. It was C/82's business one
day to advance from Kitchener's Wood to the cross-
roads called Winnipeg. The approach was littered
with derelict vehicles and dead horses. Fifteen
stranded waggons were passed within 300 yards.
The 18-pounders were dragged forward, but got bogged
500 yards from their appointed destination. There
were no proper platforms for the guns, but by super-
human heaving the detachments hauled them round
40 degrees, and they were fired that way from the
side of the road.

Towards 20th October the artillery duel became
more and more intense. On the 17th the Germans
put down a 15-minute barrage every hour from 4 A.M.
till dawn. The Middlesex Regiment recognised this
as a special welcome to themselves. They had a long,
troubled march up to the line, and Lieutenant Ander-
son, an American doctor who was making his début
on the western front, was called upon to attend to 96
casualties on the way.

The now famous dash of the Essex and Norfolks
was reserved for the 22nd. Zero hour was 5.25 A.M.,

and followed 48 hours' unremitting shelling. With
their ranks thinned, the two battalions reached a
headquarters on the Langemarck road some few
hundred yards west of the church, and close to the
ruins of the first house in Poelcappelle. Here an old
pill-box was converted into a combined office, mess,
telephone exchange, and casualty clearing station.

No one who saw that headquarters is likely ever
to forget it. Just before the battle there were fifty
or sixty people in the tiny room, including two colonels
and their staffs. The place was more like a shambles
than a living-room: officers dealing with codes and
messages had to step over the wounded lying at
their feet. Shells were dropping all round. One
man was killed as he stood in the entrance.

It was thought wise to lay the forming-up tapes
before darkness set in on the night of the 21st. They
were studded with aluminium discs to prevent them
being lost in the mud. The Boche was sending over
a lot of heavy stuff when the platoons crept to their
allotted "leaping-off" places, and the men were told
to dig in for protection. One could not dig far without reaching water—two or three feet at most. Yet
the digging-in proved a valuable precaution. Had
the men been lying out in the ordinary way they
must have been killed like flies. As ill-luck would
have it, a farm behind the Essex men blazed up and
silhouetted them, making them a wonderful target.
Everywhere could be heard the popping of gas
shells.

The Norfolks went over first, and the Essex companies made ready to follow with "C" on the right,
"A" in the centre, and "B" on the left. "D" lay
low some distance away to the south, where the
dummy figures were worked with ostentatious energy
to take the enemy's attention off the march upon the
Brewery. That stronghold had to be seized first, and
—joyous inspiriting news!—it was not long before
the Norfolks sent back word that it had yielded.

Q

It was a clean piece of work, and not much "mopping-up" was left for the Essex men as they moved forward to the new line One shell-hole post held out in front of Captain "Bill" Skeat's left platoon, and Lieutenant Freeman who engaged it was wounded. Sergeant-Major Hammond then took command and forced the German garrison to surrender. Eleven survived to be taken prisoner. "B" Company then clambered over the ruins of the village and went through the Norfolks, who cheered them lustily.

The 10th Essex jumped forward at 7.30 A.M., Captain Skeat's well-recognised voice penetrating the din of the shelling as he bellowed out instructions such as "Come up that man on the left," more often than not calling on individual men by name. The 53rd Brigade, to all appearances, had flung itself upon an island that was marooned by overwhelming gun-fire. But these East Anglian troops never looked back. They swarmed through the village and tackled the remaining objectives. Noble's Farm fell to "B" Company. They found it a mere pile of bricks, with six broken pill-boxes in the midst of the wreckage. Our 12-inch guns had scored many hard hits on this position. Of one pill-box there was left a piece of concrete no bigger than a man's hand. Plugging ahead in front of his platoon, his rifle on his shoulder and a big stick in his hand, Sergeant-Major Hammond was wounded on the final objective. It had been his greatest day in the battalion, and such a finish was for him an unhappy anti-climax. "A" and "C" Companies of the Essex combined against Meunier House and captured it against determined opposition. On rather higher ground this place had been guarded by thickets of machine-guns, and the advance represented 1,000 yards beyond the Brewery. The success was signalled by sending up lights. A few fireworks were justified. To advance a thousand yards in that

awful mud was a test of endurance apart from facing
Boche shelling and machine-gun fire.

The 10th Essex objectives had all been reached
when "D" Company put a finger into the pie and
pulled out another plum.    In front of the line lay
Tracas Farm, on a contour not shown on our maps.
Tracas Farm was going to overlook us if we stopped
where we were.    The question was, were we bound
to stop?    Major Banks asked that of himself, and
answered in the negative.    Volunteers to reconnoitre
the farm under an artillery barrage were sought.
Corporal Bowley and a couple of men responded.
They carried out their mission unhurt, and returned
with the tidings that the Germans had gone.    Major
Banks telephoned to the artillery to lift the barrage,
and "D" Company occupied the farm.

There was indeed one conflict in connection with
the seizing of Tracas Farm ; it was on somewhat
bizarre lines.    It arose through a venturesome inspection of a pill-box in No Man's Land by Regimental
Sergeant-Major Bishalk and Sergeant Dupree.    On
their own initiative they went forward for a prowl.
They took no weapons—except a Very Lights pistol
that Dupree had in his pocket.    They looked for
Germans, and found them, twenty of them and an
officer, in the pill-box.

What happened only became known after the
Armistice.    Dupree, in a statement made after his
release from Germany, says that when he and Bishalk
went round the corner of the pill-box they came upon
two Germans and a machine-gun.    The Germans put
up their hands, and Dupree yelled for Bishalk to hold
up the other door.    Hearing the shouts a number of
Germans came out.    Dupree blazed away with his
Very Lights pistol, and, dashing at the machine-gun,
pushed it into the water.    He finished up by setting
about the Germans with his fists.    They would not
fire for fear of hitting their own comrades, but finally

one of the Germans struck Dupree on the head with
a rifle, and when he came to he was a prisoner. He
saw no more of Bishalk. The German officer asked
him if the 10th Essex were going to attack the pill-
box. Dupree replied " Yes," and the officer remarked,
" If they do we shall go back."

At the German Headquarters Dupree was asked
the names of his colonel and of his brigadier. He said
he did not know. " Well, we can tell you," said a
German intelligence officer, and gave the names. He
gave them correctly, except that he described General
Higginson as General Higgins.

The afternoon of the 22nd was quiet, but about
5 P.M. there was a demonstration by the enemy to
the rear of Noble's Farm. About 200 Germans
showed themselves on a road that led to the farm. A
half-moon of deepish water lay between them and the
Essex company posted there. The Essex men bided
their time till the Germans were well within range.
Then a couple of Lewis gunners leapt on to the top
of a pill-box and opened fire. One of the pair—
Corporal Tebbitt—jammed his gun in his eagerness.
Nursing it as the fight went on, he kept his perch,
took the gun to pieces, treated the parts with vase-
line, reassembled them, and resumed firing. It was
a wonderful example of calmness and efficiency. The
German attack stopped 70 yards short.

During the night German stretcher-bearers were
heard spluttering about in the water collecting their
wounded. The Germans who lay close up to the
Essex outposts in advanced shell-holes kept well
under cover; a free use of rifle-bombs caused even the
bolder spirits to be chary of showing their heads very
often.

On the following night the triumphant Essex and
Norfolks were relieved by the Middlesex Regiment
and the Fusiliers, and they tramped back to hear the
whole Division—and General Maxse—singing their
praise.

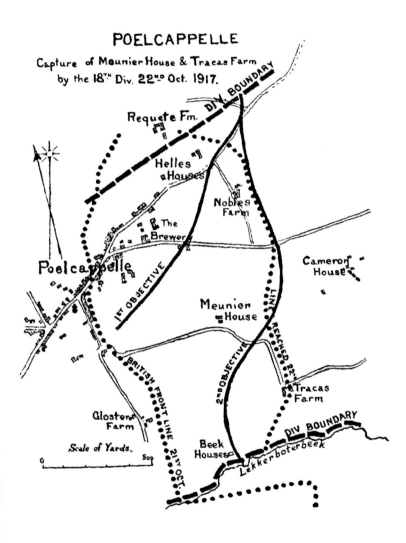

POELCAPPELLE

Capture of Meunier House & Tracas Farm
by the 18TH Div. 22ND Oct. 1917.

DIV. BOUNDARY

Requete Fm.

Helles Houses

Nobles Farm

The Brewer

Poelcappelle

Cameron House

1ST OBJECTIVE

Meunier House

LINE REACHED 22ND

BRITISH FRONT LINE 21ST OCT.

2ND OBJECTIVE

Tracas Farm

Gloster Farm

DIV BOUNDARY

Scale of Yards.

Beek Houses

Lekkerboterbeek

0          500

On 22nd October Brigadier-General C. Cunliffe-Owen, completely exhausted by the heavy fighting in endless quagmires, retired from the command of the 54th Brigade. He was succeded by Brigadier-General L. de V. Sadleir Jackson, who joined the 18th from the 58th Division.

# CHAPTER XVI.

## HOUTHULST FOREST.

*A winter of mud and misery—How pedicuria cured trench feet—The 2,500 yards wire—The burning of Elverdinghe chateau—Hubert Podmore accidentally killed.*

THE November that saw the Canadians reach Passchendaele, and ended with the flow and ebb of the first Cambrai, found the 18th Division holding fast at Houthulst Forest north of Ypres—crouching in icy mud, drenched with pitiless rain, shelled day and night. The acme of filthy hideousness, a Calvary of misery, and none could foresee the end !

There was nothing sylvan about Houthulst, whatever imagination may have conjured up from the name. It was a flat, low-lying 600 acres of broken stumps and wreckage, a swamp with many a deep and treacherous hole to trap the unwary walker and let him in up to the neck. There are stories that the Germans, in as much draggled misery as ourselves, came at times to pull out with ropes men of ours who had got engulfed in the slime. It was mud that stank : when the rain ceased the nostrils had to accept a faded musty smell that hung in the air five miles behind the line—a smell that told of desolation and decay, of gas shells, of dead men.

Trenches were impossible. The men in the line garrisoned a few shell-holes, protected here and there with breastworks that were constantly becoming submerged ; company and battalion headquarters were in old pill-boxes, where the concrete was cracked and no longer water-tight; the line was reached by duck-board tracks from brigade headquarters 6,000 or 7,000 yards in rear. It was inadvisable to attempt to cross the intervening area in the daytime, and it was a difficult adventure in the darkness because the nightly shell-fire constantly introduced new pitfalls. Frequently a man reaching a place where the track ended abruptly in a hole would grope round and lose his direction. Finding and following the duckboards again, he might discover that he was back at the place whence he had started. No one who has not essayed a journey over duckboards in a mid-winter mist can realise how easy it is to move in a circle and lose oneself. A short-sighted doctor in the Bedfords was always relieved in the daytime on this account. Once when he completed his duty at night, he wandered round the loop in Hunter Street for two or three hours.

At first it was customary for battalions to spend four days in the line and four days out—at the well-named Dirty Bucket Camp. Put in other words, it meant that men were four days wet through and four days dry. Experience showed that the reliefs were not sufficiently frequent, and casualties from trench feet rose until they averaged 100 per battalion. This brought about the institution of pedicuria establishments. The results were remarkable. In a very short time trench feet disappeared. After the spell of shell-hole duty had been cut down to 24 hours, there were only three cases.

The pedicuria system provided that a man should march up in his boots, change into dry socks and waders; then, after a tour of 24 hours, undergo pedicuria treatment at platoon headquarters, change into dry socks and waders when "in support," and finally march down in his boots. Sometimes feet were so badly swollen that the men could not get their boots on, and had to march up and back in waders. And if one fell into a shell-hole in waders, it was very difficult to climb out without assistance, and even then all equipment had to be pulled off first.

The state of the ground rendered it impossible to manœuvre infantry in any numbers.  For weeks there was nothing to report, though neither British nor Boche was idle.  Once, in November, the Germans essayed to capture a part of the French line adjoining ours, and incidentally one of our Lewis-gun posts.  The field-greys advanced across the open in two lines.  Before reaching their objective they stuck fast in the mud, and a Bedford gun-team taking them in enfilade, made short work of their chance of becoming dangerous.  The lesson was learnt.  The enemy fell back on less venturesome measures, and did what he could to worry us with snipers and machine-guns.  Had he realised how thin was the force that held this sector, he might have displayed more enterprise notwithstanding the wet.  Though our patrols were pretty active, we were actually holding the whole Divisional front in January with one brigade—the 55th.  Moreover, it was a sadly depleted 55th.  Several companies were down to 50 men.  The Lewis-gun teams hardly averaged a trained man apiece.  The 7th West Kents on one occasion could not relieve the 7th Buffs because they mustered only 170 rifles.  To meet the difficulty the Buffs lent the West Kents a newly-arrived draft of 30 reinforcements.

A census of the 8th East Surreys taken after Houthulst disclosed that only 108 of the original battalion remained, and these included transport men. Of the actual fighting men only about 6 per company were left.

Among the improvements introduced to the Houthulst Forest position during our tenure of it was a camouflage screen of rabbit wire stuffed with canvas. There were 1,500 yards of it, and other people coveted it exceedingly, notably the 19th Corps.  During two moonlight nights at the end of November 600 infantrymen carried up the canvas in rolls.  On the first night one party was shelled while crossing the Steenbecque and suffered 7 casualties, and on the following night there were 7 casualties at exactly the same spot. The screen was erected in places within 70 yards of the enemy, and for a day or two the Germans did not discover it. Afterwards they shelled continuously; but parties were able to walk on a road 300 to 400 yards behind the screen. The front was also wired for a distance approximately of 2,500 yards. Dumps were organised by Captain Davies of the 79th Company, Royal Engineers, and, with the assistance of the 55th Brigade, carrying parties were formed to the number of 2,500. The wiring was done by trained men of the Middlesex and Bedfordshire Regiments on a particularly black night. Next night it was completed by the Northamptons and the Fusiliers. While some of this work was being done, General Lee and Colonel Symons, the C.R.E., passed a party of Fusiliers who were in a shell - hole. Addressing them, the General said cheerfully: " Why don't you get out and try to drain the place." Two minutes later the General and Colonel Symons had to drop full length in the mud to avoid a salvo of German shells.

Looking round for ways of strengthening the 54th Brigade position, General Sadleir-Jackson was caught once in a "strafe" between Egypt House and Ajax House, whereupon a certain Sergeant Lancaster exclaimed: "Let me take charge; we don't want any dead Brigadiers round our pill-box." And he pushed the General inside. Lancaster, who had been a showman at the White City, was something of a comic character, and the joy of his own particular unit.

The burning of Elverdinghe Chateau, the Divisional Headquarters, was a memorable incident of this period. It occurred on the night of 13th January 1918. A Primus stove caused the outbreak. Troops stood up in the front line to watch the spectacle. Many documents were destroyed, and Colonel Cutbill and the

LIEUT.-COLONEL H. PODMORE, D.S.O.

Headquarters Staff were driven to seek shelter in huts and dug-outs vacated for them by a field company. Some days later the Staff had another experience. The river overflowed, and they were flooded out. Captain Chell woke up to find his bed an island, and despatch-boxes and a table floating round him.

It was while the Division was holding Houthulst Forest that the 6th Northants had one of the losses they felt most in the war. Hubert Podmore was killed by an accidental explosion of ammunition on 31st December. One says the 6th Northants, because Podmore's name will always be associated with that battalion, although he died as Lieut.-Colonel Podmore commanding the 12th Middlesex. He had been wounded for the second time in August, and returned to the front in December. He had only been in command of the 12th Middlesex eight days. Podmore's name had become known to most officers and men of the Division. As a Rugby colleague wrote of him : "There was a noble simplicity about him, a complete absence of egotism, which made his very strength seem like some form of gentleness." He was only 30 years of age when he was killed. Rugby School, where he was scholar and master, has rightly honoured him. His portrait, in oils, hangs in the Temple Speech-room ; and Doctor David, the headmaster, has said of Podmore : "He was brave and strong, and faced work and trouble serenely without fussing or fear. He took up burdens, his own and other people's, cheerfully. He grudged no labour which could help."

The Royal Fusiliers also sustained a grievous loss at Houthulst Forest in Captain O. C. Whiteman. Captain Whiteman had become Adjutant when Captain Cumberlege was appointed Brigade-Major. He had been with the battalion from its first arrival in France, and was highly popular. He was killed by a shell while going in advance of the battalion up Hunter Street.

Towards the close of the month of January news came of the new brigade organisation of three battalions, and the consequent disbandment of certain units. On 3rd February the 6th Royal Berks were disbanded at Portsmouth Camp, Proven, and supplied reinforcements to the 1st, 2nd, and 5th Battalions.

Their place in the 53rd Brigade was taken by the 8th Berks. There were sore hearts among the men of the 6th who had fought with the 18th Division since its early days. The 12th Middlesex, the 8th Norfolks, and the 8th Suffolks also had to go ; while later, after the Villers-Bretonneux fighting, the 7th Bedfords, the junior service battalion of that regiment, were replaced in the 54th Brigade by the 2nd Battalion. In this case, however, it was little more than a change of numerals. That gallant and capable young commander, Lieut.-Colonel A. E. Percival, D.S.O., M.C., who had commanded the 7th, now led the 2nd. The surviving officers and men of the 2nd Battalion came to join the 18th Division, one might say, like a draft. The blend proved a happy and successful one, and Colonel Percival's men accomplished notable things in the last year of the war.

# CHAPTER XVII.

## THE GERMAN ATTACK, MARCH 1918.

"In the grapple against the 18th German Army, the 18th Division was to our southern front, what our 18th Corps was face to face with St Quentin. It resembled a well-built groyne thrust into a high tide."—*From 'The Fifth Army in March 1918,'* by W. SHAW SPARROW.

*On 21st March, with a 9,000 yards' front, 18th Division kept its battle zone intact—The system of defence for the expected attack—Four German Divisions against us—Col. John Crosthwaite's famous last message—Magnificent work by the Divisional Artillery—Gunner Stone's V.C.—The death of Major Wilfred Dennes—Col. Ransome and 7th Buffs H.Q. hold out till 1 A.M.—The strategical withdrawal over the Crozat canal.*

ON that ever-to-be-remembered date, Thursday, 21st March 1918, when Ludendorff's armies began the mightiest, most overpowering assault in military history, the 18th Division was the centre Division of Lieut.-General Sir R. H. K. Butler's III. Corps, the Corps of General Gough's Fifth Army that lay next the French. The historians and the apologists of the politicians and of the Higher Command have not yet decided who should be blamed for allowing this part of the British line to be so undermanned while 200,000 troops remained "guarding the coasts" in England. There is, however, the definite fact that the Fifth Army front was 42 miles wide, and that at the beginning of the cyclonic battle, General Gough had only eleven Infantry Divisions in line, one foot Division in support, and Cavalry equalling approximately another Infantry Division, to oppose forty-three German Divisions, while the Third Army along a front 26¾ miles wide had seventeen Infantry Divisions against twenty - four German Infantry Divisions.   Also there is proof from Lord Haig's despatches that the Fifth Army did not withdraw from the Somme in the Peronne sector until the Third Army was some six miles behind its left. These are the larger issues.

As for the 18th Division's share in opposing the German storm flood, let it first be stated that on 21st March the Division defended a front of the great length of 9,000 yards against four German Divisions; that at the end of the day its battle zone was intact and a number of strongholds in the forward area were holding out; that up to 25th March it had 32 officers killed, 64 wounded, and 110 missing, and among the ranks 299 killed, 1,309 wounded, and 2,649 missing; and that three Victoria Crosses were among the honours won by the Division during that tremendous time.

About the middle of February, the Division, battered and worn, and with many new faces in it after its seven months in the Salient, bade a glad good-bye to the dismal, comfortless Houthulst Forest sector in Belgium, and moved to the vicinity of Noyon.   Early in March it was settled upon a grassy, restful-looking piece of front that stretched from a point just north of Travecy to Alaincourt.   The 58th Division, the British Division nearest the French, was on our right, and the 14th Division on our left.

The great length of the 18th Division's front was, to some extent, discounted by the fact that throughout most of it we were separated from the Germans—who were entrenched in their Hindenburg Line—by the canalised river Oise, which, flowing through a broad marshy plain, formed an obstacle to the advance of large bodies of troops.   For the rest, our positions were well sited on high ground, embracing some of the old defences of La Fère, although the systematic destruction by the Germans of all cover during their March 1917 retreat gave them better observation over our front than we had of theirs, and rendered the concealment of our defences, batteries, and movements a matter of difficulty. Also the reduction of British Divisions had robbed the 18th of three battalions: the 8th Norfolks and the 8th Suffolks had been withdrawn from the 53rd Brigade, and the 12th Middlesex—who became an entrenching battalion— from the 54th. The 7th Royal West Kents were transferred from the 55th to the 53rd Brigade. The total strength of the Division was now not more than 12,000 men.

The German offensive was known to be imminent, and General Gough expected it to come on the Fifth Army sector with the immediate object of capturing Noyon, thrusting down to Compiègne, and manœuvring into action all the enemy's spare strength from La Fère to Rheims. General Lee's every effort was bent, therefore, towards strengthening the defence of his exceptionally long line.

Three defensive belts known as the Forward Zone, the Battle Zone, and the Rear Zone—three terms which explain themselves, although some of the men could not understand why the Forward Zone was not the Battle Zone—were established. No attempt was made to construct a continuous trench system, both the means and the time at our disposal being inadequate; but each zone was designed to consist of a number of defended localities so sited as to afford mutual support. Both the Forward and the Battle Zones were covered by the cross-fire of machine-guns organised in depth and supplemented by Lewis guns. A considerable amount of work had been done on the first two zones by the French, who had occupied the sector up to the time of the extension of the British Front, but a great deal still remained to be completed; and up to this date practically no work had been done on the Rear Zone. The responsibility for the

construction and maintenance of defences in the Forward and Battle Zones rested on the Divisions holding
the line; so all our energies were devoted, in the
short time that was left, to improving the wire,
infantry posts, and machine-gun emplacements of these
two zones, and to the construction of a switch line
from Vendeuil to Ly Fontaine. A switch line from
Ly Fontaine in front of Gibercourt and Montescourt,
known as the Camisole switch, was also under construction.

The Divisional Artillery was also organised in depth.
Each of the eight batteries had one section forward
for the defence of the Forward Zone and two sections
at the back for the defence of the Battle Zone, or
*vice versa.* There were also a few detached guns for
sniping and for special tasks. In order to deceive the
enemy the positions of the forward guns were constantly changed. It was owing to this that the gun
positions in general escaped the worst of the Boche
bombardment on 21st March. The gunners also had
the new experience of circling their battery positions
with barbed wire, and of receiving instruction in Lewis
gun manipulation, all for defensive purposes.

Meanwhile the weather during the early March
days was magnificent. The country up to Fort
Vendeuil showed hardly a shell-hole. Birds were
singing their spring songs. The first wild flowers
were peeping out. The earth of the fields smelled
sweet and clean. There was one curious sight: white
tendrils of fluff—the output, apparently, of myriads
of spinning spiders — spread clinging threads over
telephone wires and tree-tops and across miles of
growing fields.

It was delightful to be here after the din, the
danger, and the stinking devastation of Flanders. The
Germans gave no sign. Almost up to the day of
attack an inferior Division—the 13th Landwehr—
continued to hold the line facing us.

Then came the moment. On 20th March a significant thing happened. Prisoners from several different regiments were taken in a raid by General Maxse's 18th Corps on a narrow front near St Quentin. Little doubt now that the assaulting troops were in position, and that only a few hours remained before the grand attack, which for a fortnight had been discussed, expected, and joked about. The " Prepare for Attack" warning was issued at 3 P.M. on the 20th, and every unit of the Division awaited the great to-morrow.

On the early morning of 21st March the dispositions of the Division were as follows :—

The 18th Division was the centre of the III. Corps, with the 58th Division on its right and the 14th Division on the left. The 18th Divisional sector was divided into two Brigade sectors, and the dispositions were as follows :—

*Left Sector.*—53rd Infantry Brigade (Brigadier - General Higginson) holding the left Brigade sector, with the 8th Royal Berkshires (Lieut.-Colonel Dewing) manning the left sub-sector Forward Zone, and the 7th Royal West Kents (Lieut.-Colonel Crosthwaite) holding the right sub-sector Forward Zone. The 10th Essex (Major Tween) were defending the Battle Zone.

*Right Sector.*—55th Infantry Brigade (Brigadier-General Wood) with the 7th Buffs (Lieut.-Colonel Ransome) in the Forward Zone and the 7th Queens (Lieut.-Colonel Bushell) in the Battle Zone, while the 8th East Surreys (Lieut.-Colonel Irwin) were in Divisional reserve concentrated in Haute Tombelle Camp. The 54th Infantry Brigade was in Corps reserve concentrated in the Caillouel-Rouez area.

*Machine-guns*—Machine-guns of the 18th Machine-Gun Battalion were disposed in depth so as to cover the Forward and Battle Zones, except eight guns attached to 54th Brigade.

*Artillery.*—The 83rd Brigade (Lieut.-Colonel Seagram) was covering the 53rd Infantry Brigade sector. The 82nd Brigade (Lieut.-Colonel Austin Thorp) was covering the 55th Infantry Brigade sector.

*Heavy Artillery.*—Heavy Artillery, 51st R.G.A., consisting of three 6-inch howitzer batteries, one 9·2-inch howitzer battery, and one 60-pounder battery, was also covering our front.

*Heavy Trench Mortars.* — Two 6 - inch Newton Trench

R

Mortars were in position covering the eastern and northern approaches to Fort Vendeuil. Two 6-inch Newtons covered the valleys running north-east and south-east from Guingette Farm. Two 6-inch Newtons were covering the approaches to Ly Fontaine from the east and the north.

*Royal Engineers.*—The 79th Field Company R.E., with attached infantry platoons, less one section, garrisoned the strong points, " Darrell," " Dauntless," and " Dashwood," in the Battle Zone. The 80th Field Company R.E. concentrated at Mennesis. The 92nd Field Company R.E.—one section with two infantry platoons—formed part of the garrison of Fort Vendeuil. Two sections and one platoon formed garrisons of strong points on the edge of Bois de Quenet and Verger. One section took up position on bridges over the Crozat Canal, ready to destroy them should the necessity arise.

*8th Royal Sussex Pioneers.*—Formed garrisons for the defended localities, " Durham," " Dinky," and " Country," in the Battle Zone.

The Forward Zone held by the 7th Buffs in the Vendeuil sector was typical of the other Forward Zones occupied by battalions of the Division. To begin with, the frontage was some 5,500 yards in extent, a very extended front for two companies disposed in depth to occupy. The system of defence adopted was that of platoons disposed in depth, occupying portions of the old French trenches, or located in the ruins of Vendeuil village. In rear of these two companies was a support company disposed across the whole battalion front, and a reserve company, of which one and a half platoons also held defended localities. This left two and a half platoons as battalion reserve, available either for local counter-attack, or for occupying part of the Vendeuil-Ly Fontaine switch.

Fort Vendeuil, an obsolete fort, was garrisoned by a mixed detachment under Captain H. Fine, 7th Buffs. The garrison consisted of one platoon, 7th Buffs, two R.E. infantry platoons (7th Queens and 7th Buffs), some R.E., and one (or two) machine-guns. In each company area a " keep " was established and stocked with reserve S.A.A., rations and water.

The Boche bombardment began at 4.40 A.M., a bombardment that swelled into a deep roar along the whole front. The 18th Divisional area back to the Crozat Canal was drenched in gas, and as the German artillery programme developed, it became clear that for the first two hours their gunners were searching for our guns; next, their object was to bombard our infantry positions with gas and high explosives; afterwards hundreds of mortars assisted in a culminating crescendo of shelling that acted as escort to the advancing German infantry and continued to ravage our positions and road approaches. Our own outnumbered guns replied spiritedly, and at 5.12 A.M. our troops manned the "Battle Stations."

Almost immediately the telephone lines to General Higginson's headquarters, and to the 53rd Brigade battalions and the 83rd Brigade R.F.A. batteries, were cut by hostile shell-fire. Also, though the day had dawned fine and warm, a clinging mist hung over everything, and it was impossible to see more than twenty yards.

At 9 A.M. came definite news that the Germans had crossed the Oise. It came from the neighbouring 58th Division, who reported that their Forward Zone had been penetrated and that one of their battalion headquarters, between La Fère and Fargniers, was surrounded. Shortly afterwards, General Wood, of the 55th Brigade, reported that about 50 Germans had occupied Lock Post, west of Mayot, on the extreme right of his sector; and at 11 A.M., when communication was at last re-established with the 53rd Brigade, they were found to be without news of the West Kents or of the Berkshires, though up to that time no attack had been made on their Battle Zone.

At midday, Colonel Tom Seagram, commanding the 83rd Brigade R.F.A., got word through that Major R.H. Farren, B/83, reported that Germans had come through the mist and had enveloped all the 83rd Brigade's

forward gun positions; while, shortly after, Colonel
John Crosthwaite, commanding the West Kents, reported by runner that his battalion headquarters at
"Durham" was surrounded, but that they were
"fighting it out there." He asked that a barrage
should be put down on the St Quentin-La Fère
road, to cover that side of his position, and this was
arranged. But at about 1 P.M. Colonel Crosthwaite's
last message was received at General Higginson's
headquarters. It ran: "Holding out 12.30 P.M.
Boches all around within 50 yards except rear. Can
only see 40 yards, so it is difficult to kill the blighters.
(Signed J. D. CROSTHWAITE)." Handsome John
Crosthwaite was a gallant and inspiring leader. He
and those left with him who remained alive were
captured by the enemy.

The Germans were forcing the attack with overpowering numbers. They showed courage and initiative; and in the mist, which lasted until noon, Colonel
Minet's specially arranged machine-gun cross-fire
proved of no avail.

At 1.20 P.M. more bad news came from the 53rd
Brigade. The Berks headquarters at Guingette Farm
and the high ground at Cerizy had been lost, and
detachments of the enemy were nearing the Battle
Zone. Half an hour later survivors made it clear
that all the Brigade's forward positions had been
captured and the garrisons either killed or made
prisoner. At that time the Brigade's Battle Zone
was still intact, but large parties of the enemy were
massing on the spur by Moulin Farm and opposite
the Vendeuil-Ly Fontaine switch. Attacks were
shortly afterwards made at those points and beaten
off by rifle and artillery fire, and an assault on
Caponne Farm was also repulsed by a company of
the 10th Essex.

Out of a rifle strength of 884 only 182 men of the
8th Berks were left from this fighting. In the general
reduction of battalions, the 6th Berks, the 18th

Division's original battalion of the Royal Berkshire Regiment, had been merged into the 8th Berks who came from the 1st Division, with Lieut.-Colonel R. E. Dewing, Royal Engineers, in command. That well-known officer, Major Douglas Tossetti, M.C., who had joined the 8th Berks from the H.A.C., was one of the first to be killed. The Germans came in swarms through the mist to surround the forward posts, and when they were known to be enveloping the battalion headquarters at Guingette Farm near the St Quentin-La Fère road, cooks, tailors, shoemakers, and Brigade clerks were rushed up to assist Colonel Dewing to fight his way back to General Higginson's headquarters. Lieutenant S. A. G. Harvey, the Headquarters Works Officer, came out of his dug-out in Guingette Farm and met a German officer face to face. He and the Boche officer fired their revolvers simultaneously. Both were killed on the spot. Not one of the Berkshires who killed a Boche at close quarters escaped death. The enemy were too numerous. Colonel Dewing had many narrow escapes before he and the remnants of the party got back to Brigade Headquarters. Lance-Corporal Ernest Harry Noyes was in command of three Lewis guns situated in isolated positions in the neighbourhood of Ly Fontaine. Superintending the firing of these guns, he moved from position to position regardless of German machine-gun and rifle fire, and his three guns checked the enemy for a considerable time. When all his men had become casualties, he operated one Lewis gun himself and continued to fire it until ordered to withdraw by his commanding officer. Another Berkshire N.C.O. who fought very bravely in the neighbourhood of Ly Fontaine was Sergeant William John Spokes. A bombing party under two officers was ordered to clear Seine Alley communication trench, so as to cover the withdrawal of the battalion headquarters' party and the survivors of the battalion. The officers became casualties, and Sergeant Spokes, left alone, continued to bomb down the trench. Unable to progress single-handed against the on-coming Germans, he returned, and on his own initiative organised another party and led them down the trench, and they bombed with such effect that the trench was cleared and the survivors of the battalion were enabled to withdraw in orderly fashion. The Signalling Sergeant of the West Kents, Sergeant Frederick Hubble, made heroic efforts to maintain communication between Colonel Crosthwaite and his forward companies. When the Germans' preliminary bombardment had smashed all the telephone lines, Hubble went forward through the enemy barrage, two thousand yards to the front line, and laid down new wires. He got completely surrounded by the advancing Germans, but contrived to get back to our lines.

Perhaps the grandest work of all on this fateful March morning was done by the Divisional gunners. Never before had they had opportunity to fire over open sights, to be in visible touch with the Divisional infantry, and to support them by mowing down the German hordes who assailed our thin-kept line. It was undoubtedly the 83rd Brigade gunners who enabled the 53rd Infantry Brigade to end the day with its Battle Zone intact on 21st March.

With Major A. A. A. Paterson at Divisional Artillery Headquarters, Captain Leslie M‘G. Haybittel, who previously had served with the Divisional Artillery Trench Mortars, was in command of "C" Battery, 83rd Brigade. His battery was in action in three section positions south-east and south of Benay. At 11.15 A.M. the German shelling increased in violence, and our infantry coming through the most forward section of C/83, reported that the enemy were on top of them. Captain Haybittel ordered the breech-blocks to be removed from the two 18-pounders, and told the detachments to withdraw to the next section of guns 400 yards in rear. Scarcely was the order given when the Germans came out of the mist.

All the party got back except 2nd Lieutenant Patterson and three gunners. Haybittel shot one of the Germans who was marching Lieutenant Patterson away. While the two guns in the second position were being trained on the enemy, more Germans, coming from the direction of Lambay Wood, appeared on the left flank; so the breech-blocks were again removed and the detachments withdrawn to a sunken road between Benay and Hinacourt. This position was held for an hour with rifles and a machine-gun. Meanwhile communication to the two 18-pounders of C/83's rear section was opened, and they fired hard and with great effect on masses of the enemy in front of Lambay Wood. At about 12.45 P.M. the telephone line was cut, and looking back Captain Haybittel saw that Germans were trying to cut him off from his rear guns, so he fell back 50 yards to a position from which he could protect the right flank of the K.R.R.'s of the 14th Division, who were now just west of Benay. The retirement was under heavy machine-gun fire, and two of C/83's men were killed, leaving only six rifles and no machine-gun.

Haybittel was now determined to get into touch again with his two rear guns; so, leaving one of his subalterns—Lieutenant Harold J. Raban, who earlier, wearing his gas mask, had fought two of the forward guns for three hours—to guard the flank of the K.R.R.'s, he went back and directed the fire of his two remaining 18-pounders with such effect that two enemy machine-guns were silenced and many Germans were killed; Raban's party retired unharmed, and the K.R.R.'s were enabled to form a strong point under Captain Haybittel near the two rear guns.

And here, triumphant, they remained, though they were shelled by an 18-pounder that had been captured from the 83rd Brigade, though the Germans brought up more machine-guns and snipers, and several times tried to rush them. And all the time the battery's two 18-pounders fired merrily.

D/83, which had two sections of 4·5 howitzers east
of Ly Fontaine and one section north of Ly Fontaine
close to Colonel Seagram's headquarters, also did
telling work. The rear section was so heavily shelled
in the preliminary bombardment that Major A. D.
M'Pherson, M.C., and all the detachments became
casualties. Colonel Seagram turned out his headquarter staff with rifles to defend these howitzers,
while reinforcements were sent for from the waggon
lines, and 2nd Lieutenant Lyle Fullam Ellis was
instructed to come back from one of the forward
sections to take charge of the rear position.

Ellis proved to be another artillery officer who
showed unwavering determination and the finest qualities of leadership. He had to go through a German
barrage to reach the guns he was sent to command.
He arrived there at 11 A.M. and proceeded to clear
the gun-pits ; and at noon, the reinforcements having
arrived just in time—since the Germans were now
advancing over the ridge—D/83's howitzers opened
fire again at 500 yards' range. The enemy continued
to come on, and the range was reduced to 250 yards,—
the gunners had indeed to crouch to avoid splinters
from their own shells. The enemy swept the position
with machine-gun bullets, but Ellis and his men
never stopped firing and did not allow the Boche to
get any closer. Seeing a German battery coming into
action 1,500 yards away, Ellis turned his guns on to it
with most inspiring effect. The horses bolted and the
German battery failed to fire a single shot all day.

Further forward, Major Keyes of A/83 was so
severely wounded that he could not be moved. He
was captured when the Germans rushed the position,
and died in captivity ; but another section of B/83
was kept going by 2nd Lieutenant Harold Hughes, an
officer forty-one years of age who had been a schoolmaster before the war, and whose health was never of
the best. Hughes remained in action until 10 P.M.
and got his guns safely over the canal. Indeed his

were the only guns of the 83rd Brigade that got away at the end of the day.

Meanwhile the situation on the 55th Brigade front developed more slowly. By thrusting forward large numbers of troops the enemy had stove in the defences of the 14th Division on the north and of the 58th Division on the south. There had been so far no big frontal attack on the 5,500 yards of line held by the 7th Buffs. But by noon bodies of Germans, unperceived in the fog, had come from north and south, and had got in rear of the company headquarters in "Cardiff," which was behind the 55th Brigade's front line. Also they had worked round behind "Commander," close to the village of Vendeuil. Both these strongholds were subsequently surrounded, and Vendeuil was occupied. In "Cork," south-west of Vendeuil, the reserve company of the Buffs had come into contact with parties of the enemy between them and Fort Vendeuil, and another Boche party attacking from the south-west had been driven into Ronquenet Wood.

As with the 53rd Brigade and the 83rd Brigade, R.F.A., every company, every battery, every section even, had its own history that day. It was all largely individual fighting. The line was so thinly held, it had to be so. The enemy had made surprise rushes through the mist. Corporal Waters, who with six men held the left forward post of the 7th Buffs, heard the opening bombardment, but it did not look as if the Boche attack was on his sector. The next thing he remembers was a large body of Germans on top of his position. Before the Germans could remove these seven Buffs to the rear they bolted in the fog and made their way back to their company, which they found retiring through Vendeuil. There was also the cook of "D" company of the Buffs. He was taken prisoner. He offered his German captors some bacon to let him go. They made him eat some of it, and then started clawing it hungrily. So the cook made a dash and got clear. These minor incidents indicate how diffuse and bewildering was the fighting on this part of the 18th Divisional front.

About 12.30 P.M., before the mist had cleared, a hundred Germans, with three machine-guns, came suddenly out of Ronquenet Wood and pounced upon the forward guns of " C " Battery, 82nd Brigade. Captain R. D. Hodgson, who was commanding the battery in the absence of Major F. J. Rice, was shot, and only one subaltern, Lieutenant R. G. Sharp, and three men escaped death or capture. The forward guns of A/82 and B/82, alongside the Remigny-Vendeuil road and in view of Fort Vendeuil, were firing hard ; close by, Lieut.-Colonel A. L. Ransome of the Buffs and his headquarters party in the quarry " Dublin " remained ready for all eventualities.

At 2 P.M. the mist cleared and it became possible to grasp the general situation. On our left, the Germans were now in Essigny, Benay, and Lambay Wood, having completely penetrated the Battle Zone of the 14th Division. On our own Divisional front the Forward Zone had been pierced, but several of its strong points, notably " Durham," " Fort Vendeuil," " Cork," " Country," and " Cardiff," were still holding out. A very heavy bombardment, assisted by low-flying aeroplanes, was again being directed on the Battle Zone of the 53rd Brigade, and an 18-pounder, which had been installed near Moulin Farm for anti-tank defence, had been captured and turned on to the Brigade Headquarters. The East Surreys, Divisional reserve, had been ordered to move forward at 12.30 P.M. to an assembly position immediately west of Remigny, between the Crozat Canal and the battle line, there to await orders as to their future action.

Up to 3.30 P.M. the situation appeared unchanged, except for enemy attempts to capture positions still holding out in the Forward Zone. A large body of Germans tried to storm Fort Vendeuil ; but Captain Harry Fine of the 7th Buffs and his garrison kept them out with rifle and machine-gun fire, and the 18-pounders of A/82 and B/82, fired over open sights, exerted such telling effect that the assault crumpled up. Further attempts were made on the 7th Buffs' headquarters at "Dublin." These, too, were beaten off by Colonel Ransome's confident and energetic garrison, which was made up of runners, signallers, cooks, water-cart men, and a few stragglers. Captain C. K. Black, the Adjutant, and Lieutenant G. J. Howcroft, the Intelligence Officer, showed any amount of resource in organising the defence of this quarry headquarters. One of the signallers, Private A. C. Coleman, had been out four hours, exposed to gas shelling and machine-guns, trying to restore communication with Fort Vendeuil. The Boche shelling had broken Coleman's wires in over 40 places.

But at 3.30 P.M. a critical situation arose on the 18th Division's flanks. Colonel Minet, commanding the 18th Battalion Machine-Gun Corps, reported that the Germans had taken Hinacourt on the Division's northern boundary; at the same time the 58th Division reported that heavy fighting was in progress in the eastern outskirts of Fargniers. To meet this double threat, orders were sent to the 8th East Surreys to man the Gibercourt-Ly Fontaine switch line, so as to prevent further penetration on that side, while two regiments of the 4th Dismounted Cavalry Brigade, who had been placed at General Lee's disposal, were sent down to reinforce the right of General Wood's Battle Zone, and, if necessary, to form a defensive flank facing south. An hour later the East Surreys reported that one of their companies had reinforced the Battle Zone south of Ly Fontaine, so as to guard its junction with the Vendeuil switch; while their remaining two companies were moving up to the Camisole switch. A counter-attack to be made by the 7th Queens, to re-establish the 55th Brigade's Forward Zone, was also organised, but subsequent developments caused it to be abandoned.

On the 53rd Brigade front, the West Kents and the Berks had by now been wiped out, but the 10th Essex were holding on to Caponne Farm and Moulin Farm, while the guns still in the possession of Captain Haybittel of C/83 and Lieutenant Ellis of D/83 continued, though machine-guns and snipers were brought up to riddle the two batteries, to do great execution among the Germans each time they tried to break into the 53rd Brigade's Battle Zone.

One gunner of C/83, Charles Edwin Stone, M.M., earned undying fame during this exciting period. Stone had started the day by working at his gun for six hours under gas and shell fire. When Captain Haybittel ordered the retirement to the sunken road between Benay and Hinacourt, Stone, with a rifle, lay out in the open, under machine-gun fire, about a hundred yards from the enemy. Calmly and effectively he shot down the Germans who rushed forward to capture the position. When the withdrawal to the two rear guns was made, Stone did even more daring and gallant work. He took up a position on the right flank of the two guns and, entirely unsupported, held the enemy at bay, though again and again they tried to outflank Captain Haybittel's party. Some of them managed at last to break through. Gunner Stone, regardless of the machine-gun fire, charged at these Germans and, single-handed, killed them one by one. His fiery valour undoubtedly saved the flank of the position.

At 8 p.m., when only one of the two guns was in action, jamming badly too, and Captain Haybittel realised that final withdrawal was necessary, Gunner Stone was one of a party of six, under Lieutenant M. N. S. Jackson, that went out to cover the retirement. The six gunners did more than that. They captured an enemy machine-gun and its team of four, who in the gathering dusk had got round to the rear of Captain Haybittel's position. Gunner Stone chased one German a hundred yards before he caught him.

For his magnificent example and the effectiveness of his work in keeping the enemy back, Gunner Stone was awarded the highest honour a soldier can attain —the Victoria Cross.

Captain Haybittel finally evacuated the position at 9 P.M. when both his 18-pounders were out of action. But 1,900 rounds had been fired by these two guns, and the stubborn resistance and alert leadership shown by Haybittel in this most critical stage of the retreat was full value for the D.S.O. awarded him.

The gallant 2nd Lieutenant Ellis of D/83 also gained the D.S.O. He kept his remaining 4·5 howitzer in action until 6 P.M., when his ammunition gave out; and it was not until he received a written order from Colonel Dewing, O.C. of the Berks, that he retired, taking with him the breech-blocks and dial sights of his 4·5 howitzers.

At 5 P.M. the enemy made his heaviest attack of the day on the 55th Brigade front. Fort Vendeuil came under a shower of shells. Then about 800 Germans in dense formation swarmed over the ridge, and came towards the 7th Buffs' headquarters.

The forward guns of "A" Battery and "B" Battery, 82nd Brigade, had all day engaged succeeding parties of the enemy in front of the wire of the Ly Fontaine-Vendeuil switch line, about 300 yards from A/82's position, and had taken heavy toll of the Germans. At 3.40 P.M. Major Wilfred Dennes, commanding A/82, sent off the following message to 82nd Brigade Headquarters in the quarry near Liez :—

" I have fired 2,200 rounds and have only 200 rounds left. My S.A.A. (Small Arms Ammunition) for Lewis guns and rifles is also running short. Can more ammunition be sent, please ?

"The enemy has got through the wire in front of the battery, and is now on two sides of us. If the infantry can assist we can hold out until dark, when I will retire to rear position."

Major Dennes's note reached Colonel Thorp at

4.30 P.M.   Colonel Thorp telephoned immediately to Captain Runge, General Wood's Brigade-Major, and the reply to Major Dennes ran :—

"Hold on; you are doing splendidly.   Counter-attacks are being organised.   Teams with limbers to withdraw your guns to rear position by 8 P.M. are being sent for."

But the counter-attack which was to be made by the 7th Queens did not take place.   The enemy's big assault at 5 P.M. did.   The day ended tragically for A/82.

After the despatch of the message to Colonel Thorp, parties of Germans got through the barbed wire and worked up close to Major Dennes's position.   Rifles and Lewis guns were used by A/82's gunners, and Colonel Ransome's garrison at "Dublin" joined in. But the Germans got nearer and nearer to the guns of A/82.   Major Dennes was shot in the head by a sniper and killed.   A solicitor before the war, Major Dennes had been with the 82nd Brigade since it was formed. He was a man of very high ideals.   He hated war. It was against all his beliefs and principles.   But no one felt more strongly than he that it was his duty to fight in this war.   2nd Lieutenant R. G. M. Jones took command, and tried to send a message to the nearest infantry post saying he would hold out to the last if the infantry could assist him ; but the runner lost his way.

Five hundred yards behind, south of the Remigny-Vendeuil road, the forward section of B/82, commanded by 2nd Lieutenant A. E. Bishop, well seconded by 2nd Lieutenant J. H. Lightbody, was still supplied with ammunition.   But parties of the enemy were closing round this battery as well.

When at 5 P.M. the 800 Germans surged towards the Buffs' headquarters and towards the two batteries, A/82 and B/82 both fired at point - blank range. Dozens of Germans were slaughtered.   All at once

A/82 ceased firing. Their ammunition had run out. For ten minutes no firing at all came from the battery. Then suddenly about 100 Germans sprang up from the grass, rushed forward and bombed the gun-pits. One of the first to be killed was a bombardier who, during the last two hours, had used a Lewis gun most skilfully and gallantly. A German, a left-hander, crept behind this bombardier and hurled a bomb when he was not looking that way. The surviving gunners of A/82 were marched off into captivity.

And then a most exhilarating thing happened. As soon as the survivors of A/82 had been taken away, Lieutenant Bishop, who had watched everything through his glasses, turned the guns of B/82 on to A/82's old position. A hundred rounds at "gun-fire" were loosed off. The Germans who had settled in the gun-pits skeltered away. Many of them were killed. B/82 fired until 6 P.M. 800 rounds at close range. They nobly avenged their comrades of A/82.

At 6 P.M. Fort Vendeuil was again heavily shelled. No lamp-flash signals from the Fort to Colonel Ransome's headquarters were noted after this, and the next heard of Captain Fine of the Buffs was that he was a prisoner in Germany. 2nd Lieutenant J. I. Dutton, of "C" Battery, 82nd Brigade, who had been acting as Artillery F.O.O., was killed in the Fort. After this, enemy shelling and machine-gun fire on the Divisional front died down. A notable fact, showing how isolated was some of the fighting on this part of the line, was that one 18-pounder of C/82 and a 4·5 howitzer of D/82, in action south of Fort Vendeuil, about 2,000 yards in front of Major Dennes's ill-fated battery, fired until 5.45 P.M. Sergeant Batchelor, who was in charge of the 4·5 howitzer, tried vainly at 4.30 P.M. to get into touch with the Divisional Infantry. He returned to the two guns, and the two detachments dispersed some Germans who threatened them with rifles. At 5.45 P.M. the two detachments came away, first in business-like style blowing up the howitzer

and removing the breech mechanism and dial sight of
the 18-pounder.

The attack on the neighbouring 14th and 58th
Divisions was still being strongly pressed, and on the
south it was clear that the Battle Zone of the left
Brigade of the 58th Division was almost entirely lost,
as the Germans had entered Quessy and Fargniers.
On our left also, the Battle Zone of the 14th Division
had been lost. Consequently, while the 18th Division's
Battle Zone remained intact, the situation to right and
left involved a withdrawal. General Lee explained
to III. Corps his arrangement for a counter-attack,
but at 6 P.M. instructions were received that retirement to a line behind the Crozat Canal was to take
place as soon as darkness permitted. The certainty
that the 18th Division could have stood firm is proved
by the fact that at dusk, following orders from the III.
Corps, the 54th Brigade occupied the Camisole switch
between Montescourt and Ly Fontaine. By this
time the critical situation, already described, on the
Division's flanks had developed ; so no sooner had the
Brigade settled down to consolidate their positions than
orders came to form a rearguard covering the retirement of the whole Division across the Crozat Canal.

First, what was left of the Divisional Artillery was
withdrawn to positions immediately in rear of the
Canal so as to cover the retirement of the Infantry
and protect the canal crossings. Of the Infantry, the
garrisons of the Forward Zone whom it was still
possible to reach were then withdrawn. The garrisons
of "Dublin" (7th Buffs' headquarters), "Cork," and
"Country" got away. Fort Vendeuil's garrison could
not be reached. After dark Colonel Ransome sent
out patrols to try and get touch with the reserve
company of the Buffs and with the Fort. The Boche,
however, was found to be holding all approaches.
About 11 P.M. an officer's patrol of the 7th Queens
arrived at Colonel Ransome's headquarters. The
officer reported that all troops had to be west of the

Crozat Canal before dawn. Colonel Ransome asked for written orders; the officer had none, but he insisted that he had instructions to escort the Buffs' headquarters by the only clear route to Liez. Colonel Ransome waited while his Adjutant, Captain Black, bicycled to Remigny to obtain information. Captain Black returned and said he had telephoned to Liez and the orders were correct—all troops to be west of the Crozat Canal by dawn. Patrols were sent out again to try and reach Fort Vendeuil and the reserve company, but without success. So having destroyed all papers that could not be removed, and leaving behind—reluctantly—a quantity of whisky, port, and beer, the Buffs' headquarters party set out for Liez about 1 A.M.; eventually they reached Liez at 2 A.M. Eight 18-pounders and five 4·5 howitzers belonging to the 82nd Brigade were got safely across the Crozat Canal. The two 18-pounders of the rear section of B/83 were the only guns of the 83rd Brigade saved. Ammunition was got up, and the guns fired all through the night. The enemy made no attempt to interfere with the retirement. It occupied the remainder of the night, but by 6 A.M. on 22nd March all our troops were safely across the canal. All through the night bombing aeroplanes flew over but did little damage, though the country for miles around was illuminated by burning aerodromes, camps, and supply dumps, which had been fired by our Engineers to prevent material from falling into the hands of the enemy.

So had passed the first day of this tremendous battle. It had seen the 18th Division's line withdrawn 2,000 yards. But our Battle Zone had remained intact throughout the day; the only two organised attacks on it, at Caponne Farm and Moulin Farm, had been repulsed. The rank and file felt that they were up against great odds, but they had fought stolidly, and it is a reasonable assumption that had the general situation and the state of affairs on our flanks per-

S

mitted, we could have carried out a counter-attack that would have regained the whole of our Forward Zone. The success of the Germans in penetrating our forward defences must be attributed largely to the thick mist which made observation impossible until the afternoon. They fought well, but they also chose their day well.

The attack on the 18th Division was, apparently, carried out by four enemy divisions. The 34th, 37th, 103rd, and 211th were identified, and in all, as many as eight enemy divisions were identified on the Corps front. The objectives of the Divisions were given by prisoners as follows :—

34th Division—Line Montescourt-Jussy.
37th Division—Line Hinacourt-Gibercourt.
103rd Division—Ly Fontaine-Remigny.
211th Division—Vendeuil and Liez.

Our artillery and machine-guns were also at a great disadvantage, observation being impossible during the most critical hours. Fire could not be brought to bear upon threatened points, and guns continued firing on S.O.S. lines long after penetration of our defences had taken place. When the mist lifted and the situation became clear, many targets were engaged at close range with good effect.

# CHAPTER XVIII.

## 22ND MARCH—THE FIGHT FOR THE CROZAT CANAL.

*Again superb weather, and again a curious mist—Canal bridges not
properly destroyed—Germans bring up trench mortars—North
amptonshires and Bedfordshires drive enemy back over Montagne
bridge—Canadian Cavalry come up to help—Enemy brings up
fresh Divisions.*

COOL counsels and a high and steadfast faith were
needed now. We knew nothing of what was taking
place farther north, whether the storm that had burst
upon the III. Corps and the Fifth Army generally
had also visited the rest of the British front. Rumours
came, but they were mixed. The most confirmed
optimist in our ranks realised that we were up against
the heaviest attack yet launched in the war. None
of us knew much more than that, and the immensity
of the German effort was better realised by casual
newspaper readers in England.

At half-past eleven on the night of 21st March the
58th Division reported that all their troops on their
left flank, the 173rd Brigade, were across the canal,
leaving the 18th Division's right flank exposed.
Reports were also received that Boche parties were
in the village of Tergnier. The Machine-gun Squadron,
4th Cavalry Brigade, was therefore ordered forward
to take up positions to cover Quessy and the canal
crossings. The enemy, however, did not press his
attacks here during the night, and at 8 A.M. on
Friday the 22nd the situation on the 18th Division's
front was approximately as follows :—

The 54th Brigade (General Sadleir-Jackson) held the line of the Canal from the east edge of Jussy to the north edge of Menessis, and were now under the orders of the 14th Division.

The 3rd Cavalry Brigade and the 12th Entrenching Battalion held the line of the Canal as far as the vicinity of Quessy, whence it was prolonged to the southern Divisional boundary by details and men left out of action by the 55th Brigade. The 3rd Cavalry Brigade and 12th Entrenching Battalion had been placed under the orders of the 18th Division the previous day and had taken up their positions that afternoon.

The crossings of the Crozat Canal (which joins the Somme and the Oise five miles east of Ham) were being guarded by detachments of the Reinforcement Training Camp.

The 55th Brigade (General Wood) and 4th Cavalry Brigade, after crossing the Canal, had taken up support positions as follows:—

7th Queens [In the valley to the north of Vouel]. 7th Buffs, 3rd Hussars, and Oxfordshire Hussars [In Frieres Wood near La Faisanderie (The Pheasantry)].

The 53rd Brigade (General Higginson) had their head-quarters overnight near Frières Faillouel, with the 8th Royal Berkshires and the 7th Royal West Kents in the vicinity, the 10th Essex farther south, and two companies of the 8th East Surreys in support. During the morning, however, this Brigade was withdrawn to Rouez and the East Surreys returned to the 55th Brigade.

As to Artillery, our front was covered by the surviving guns of the 18th Divisional Artillery, consisting of the 82nd and 83rd Brigades with eight 18-pounders and five 4·5 howitzers (82nd Brigade) and one section (the only surviving one) of the 83rd Brigade. These guns had come back from the Canal and were in action along a line behind the Bois Hallot.

In addition, the 3rd and 4th Brigades, R.H.A., had been placed at our disposal, and were in action respectively east of Rouez and at Frières Faillouel.

On the 22nd, two batteries (the 410th and 409th) of the 96th Brigade, R.F.A., were also sent to us and were attached to the 82nd Brigade, R.F.A., and the 5th Brigade, R.H.A., respectively, but these did not come into action till about dusk.

Heavy artillery were in action on the road from Faillouel to Jussy.

The Sussex Pioneers and Royal Engineers, in view of the nature of the fighting now taking place, were withdrawn into Divisional Reserve, Pioneers going to Villequier Aumont, and the three Field Companies of the Royal Engineers to Rouez Camp, where they were employed on the defences. The gallant Major G. Bremner, R.E., commanding the 80th Field Company, was killed here. He had done fine service in the war, and had won both the D.S.O. and the M.C.

Seventeen machine-guns, in addition to the eight attached to the 54th Brigade, were brought back and placed in likely defensive positions.

The weather on 22nd March was again superb, but again there was that curious mist. Soon after daylight, the Germans began their attack on the canal crossings. Field-guns and trench mortars opened heavily on the whole front, while 5·9's gave Faillouel and Rouez no rest. Then at 8.40 A.M. a piece of bad news came. The bridges over the canal between Jussy and Menessis had not been demolished, and were all passable by enemy infantry. It was said that old French charges were at fault. As a last hope the Bedfordshires tried to blow up the Montagne bridge with trench-mortar shells, but they did not succeed. The failure to destroy these bridges had an important effect on the subsequent fighting. Indeed it ultimately contributed largely to the loss of the canal line.

The canal makes a sharp bend north of Jussy, and machine-guns were able to enfilade the village; so that the 11th Royal Fusiliers on the left of our line found that movement could be made dangerous by a watchful enemy. At 9 A.M. the Germans brought up trench mortars and machine-guns and opened a hot fire all along the north bank of the canal between Jussy and Menessis, especially in front of the Montagne and Menessis bridges. Presently their infantry started to work up to the canal.

On our right the situation continued to be obscure, but reports came that Tergnier had been lost, which meant that the enemy had crossed the canal there.

General Wood therefore ordered the 4th Cavalry Brigade to reinforce his right and the southern bridge boundary. A counter-attack there was made by the 6th Dragoon Guards, but it was held up by machine-gun fire. At 6 P.M. a very heavy bombardment of the 54th Brigade's front proved to be the signal for a determined assault on the Jussy and Montagne bridges, both of which fell for a time into the enemy's hands.

But General Sadleir-Jackson was not the type of Brigade Commander to allow the Germans, strong in numbers though they were, to hold such positions without a desperate struggle. An hour later a dashing counter-attack by three companies of the Northampton-shires and one company of the Bedfordshires drove the enemy back across the Montagne bridge. Three machine-guns and several prisoners were captured and many Germans were killed, while the bridgehead was re-established with a machine-gun. In the counter-attack, the Northamptonshires lost 2nd Lieutenant Pointer (attached from the Middlesex Regiment) killed, while that excellent officer, Captain R. F. Fawkes, who had been with the 6th Northants from their origin, 2nd Lieutenant Woodland, and 2nd Lieutenant Jones, were wounded. Good leadership and ability to organise under intense artillery and machine-gun fire were shown by Captain H. C. Browning, Adjutant of the Bedfords. Things were so bad before the counter-attack sent the Germans back over the canal, that the enemy got to within 200 yards of the Bedfords' headquarters, and Colonel Percival and Captain Browning destroyed all the battalion maps and documents. The situation at Jussy was restored by the reserve squadron of the 16th Lancers. The two 18-pounders of B/83 north of Menessis were, at 6.30 P.M., so heavily shelled that Captain J. F. M'Donnell—the M'Donnell who played golf for Oxford—had to withdraw the detachments and bring away the breech-blocks. The 83rd Brigade was thus now without any guns at all.

At 8 P.M. General Sadleir-Jackson again reported that the canal bridges were still not destroyed, and that unless this were done the 54th Brigade could not hold its position against further heavy attacks. He himself made every effort to see that the work was done, but the original arrangements made for the demolition of the bridges had failed and adequate supplies of explosives were not on the spot. An hour later, half the Canadian Cavalry Brigade was placed at General Lee's disposal and was ordered to move up from Villequier Aumont to be in reserve to General Sadleir-Jackson in anticipation of further attacks on the canal next morning.

At 10 P.M. information was received that the 58th Division had passed under the command of the 6th French Army, and that the 125th French Division was moving up on our right to counter-attack and regain the line of the canal in the neighbourhood of Tergnier, an operation in which the 18th Division was asked to co-operate.

On the front of the gallant 12th Entrenching Battalion, which had come in to play the part of infantry, without Lewis guns or signalling gear, there was confused fighting throughout the night of the 22nd, and at one time this battalion reported that it had been forced back to the eastern edge of the Bois Hallot, but a spirited counter-attack restored the ground that had been lost.

The night brought no rest. The Germans were obviously putting in new and fresh divisions. The peril of the canal bridges and the report of the Boche penetration of Tergnier on the 58th Division's front boded ill for the morrow.

# CHAPTER XIX.

## TWO VICTORIA CROSSES WON IN THE WITHDRAWAL.

*General Sadleir-Jackson's last effort to hold the line of the canal—
54th Brigade in danger of being cut off—Lieutenant A. C. Herring,
of the 6th Northants, an ex-A.S.C. officer, holds the Montagne
bridge and wins the V.C.—What the Kaiser afterwards said to
Herring—7th Queens assist the French in a counter-attack to
regain the canal crossing at Tergnier—French only have 35 rounds
per man—Colonel Bushell leads both French and English and wins
the Victoria Cross—Buffs' and Queens' stern fight in the orchard—
Troops now fifty-four hours without sleep—Germans' superiority in
machine-gun fire—The withdrawal from Faillouel—Major A. S.
Tween's gallant death—The final French counter-attack.*

THE enemy did not wait for daylight. Before dawn
on 23rd March heavy attacks were resumed on the
18th Division, on the 14th, and on the left Brigade of
the 58th. The night of the 22nd had been radiant,
a silvery moon and a star-spangled sky; but next
morning, for the third day in succession, a puzzling
mist prevailed. Again the enemy brought up fresh
troops through the little valleys that led to the canal;
and again the fog concealed them from our not
numerous but ever-watchful gunners. Then at midday, as if it had been rolled up by orders of the
German staff, the mist suddenly lifted, and low-flying
Boche aeroplanes came coolly over and took stock of
our thin line of defence.

23rd March saw some of the bitterest fighting of
the Great Retreat: it showed clearer than ever that
the Germans were in mighty force; that our un-
reinforced battalions were by now skeleton battalions,

and that our men, though still disciplined and purposeful, had become wearied unto death.

About 9 A.M., 54th Brigade patrols pushed out into the fog and found that the enemy was over the canal at Jussy and closing in on the 11th Royal Fusiliers' left flank. A counter-attack, carried out by a weak platoon of the Fusiliers, 30 Royal Scots Greys, and 60 of the Reinforcement Training Camp, drove the Germans back into Jussy. But almost immediately it was reported that the 9th Scottish Rifles had been forced to retire to the level-crossing half a mile south of Jussy; so a detachment of Northumberland Hussars, who had just reported to the 54th Brigade as reinforcements, were sent up with Hotchkiss guns to aid in covering the Fusiliers' left flank. At about 11 A.M. the Bedfordshire Regiment sent news that Germans had got across the canal and were in the cemetery at Menessis. Four machine-guns of the Canadian Mounted Brigade, who also had come up, were placed in the line, and, fired at close range, did deadly work. But the German numbers were now having effect, and by 11.45 A.M. Colonel Percival of the Bedfords reported that touch on his right was lost and that strong bodies of the enemy were advancing from Menessis. The 9th Scottish Rifles had been compelled to retire still farther from Jussy, and Germans were beginning to march down the Jussy-Faillouel road.

General Sadleir-Jackson made a last valiant effort to hold the line of the canal. Two hundred Canadian Dragoons had come up. A hundred of them were ordered to prolong the left flank of the Fusiliers, so as to throw the 54th Brigade's left flank astride the Jussy-Faillouel road. The remaining hundred were rushed up to prolong the right of the Bedfords. But by 12.15 A.M. Germans had advanced as far as the Bois de Frières in rear of the Fusiliers. The whole Brigade was in danger of being cut off. It was clear that nothing now could stop the enemy from crossing the canal. Reluctantly, General Sadleir-Jackson gave the order to retire to the Tombelle Ridge.

The 11th Royal Fusiliers had had a very bad time. As one of their officers put it :—

"The fog had been thicker than the London pea-soup variety, and parties of Germans trickled in on both flanks and cut off our men who were in the advanced positions. In this way we suffered a number of casualties, including Lieutenant Simmons and Lieutenant Knott, who were killed, and several other officers who were wounded.

"Lieutenant Knott had killed four Boches with his revolver, and, having exhausted his ammunition, was clubbing another when he was killed. . . . A fresh line of defence was formed 200 yards behind the canal, but matters were in a confused state. The forward companies did not receive the order to retire, and the enemy subjected us to terrible machine-gun fire. At 2 P.M. the position became untenable, and an attempt was made to withdraw by those in a position to get away; the rest had to surrender.

"The few who escaped withdrew behind the railway line, about 600 yards farther west, where another stand was made with the help of Battalion Headquarters' details; but again we were outflanked. The Colonel only just escaped in the first withdrawal."

Captain Brookling of the Fusiliers held his company position on the canal line for fourteen hours against repeated attempts of the enemy to cross. He was badly wounded, but continued to encourage his men, and his leadership had much to do with preventing the piercing of the 54th Brigade front at the junction of the Fusiliers with the Bedfords. Private H. Jordan, a signaller, was called upon with others to surrender when the Fusiliers were being withdrawn. His answer was to organise a number of men, and the Germans were driven back at the point of the bayonet. Jordan was wounded, but his bravery enabled the company to retire in orderly fashion. He was awarded the D.C.M. So was Sergeant W. Brisby, M.M., whose accurate rifle fire caused the withdrawal of an enemy machine-gun team. When at last some men of Brisby's company were forced to surrender, Brisby rallied the rest; then he rejoined a remnant of the Fusiliers who were making a last stand under heavy fire. Brisby was wounded, but he escaped capture.

And greatest stand of all on this part of the front was that of Lieutenant Alfred Cecil Herring, of the 6th Northants, at the Montagne bridge. Herring and his men occupied a post that became isolated. He did not receive the orders to retire. When, after fierce fighting, the Germans crossed the bridge, the party were surrounded. But they counter-attacked with such dash that the post was recaptured and twenty prisoners and six machine-guns were taken. And here Herring stayed, beating off all attacks. It was an amazing effort, that stayed the German advance over the canal at this point for eleven hours.

Herring and his men were captured in the end, but he won the Victoria Cross. With other officers he was presented to the Kaiser at St Quentin. The Emperor said they had put up a very fine fight, and he shook hands with Herring. Herring says that Hindenburg was there as well, but did not speak to the captured Englishmen. Herring was an accountant by profession. The previous stages of the war he had spent with the Army Service Corps. 23rd March was, in fact, his first time in the fighting line.

Lieut.-Colonel B. J. Walker and his Sussex Pioneers had come up at 11.30 A.M. to support the right of the 54th Brigade. The remainder of the Canadian Cavalry Brigade also joined in, while the 7th Cavalry Brigade took up positions along the eastern edge of Frières Wood. At 1 P.M. a regiment of the 1st French Cavalry Division passed through Ugny on their way to relieve our hard-pressed troops.

The experiences of the 55th Brigade form a separate part of the story of this memorable 23rd March. In the early hours it was known that the 125th French

Regiment was to make a counter-attack to regain the crossing of the Crozat Canal at Tergnier which had been lost by the 58th Division.

In a small wooden hut on the eastern side of the Bois de Frières, General Wood held a conference, at which Lieut. - Colonel Ransome of the 7th Buffs, Lieut.-Colonel Christopher Bushell of the 7th Queens, and Lieut. - Colonel E. C. T. Minet of the 18th Machine-Gun Corps, were present. It was arranged that two companies of the Queens should assist the French.

About 6 A.M. the French infantry arrived. They had marched far and fast, but every officer and man of the 55th Brigade was impressed and comforted by their appearance. Their uniforms were smart and new, they looked more matured than our men, their air was one of activity and confidence.

But the counter - attack which was launched immediately they arrived failed badly. The Frenchmen did not know the ground, the mist made observation impossible, and there was the crowning and most unlooked-for disadvantage that they had come up with no more rifle ammunition than thirty-five rounds per man.

The fog was so thick that some of the Queens also lost their way going to the attack. A gallant runner, Private C. W. Ponsford, found one wandering platoon and led it straight to its position, enabling it to be up in time to join in the attack. The Queens, like the West Kents and the East Surreys, always had brave and resourceful runners.

Though the attack failed, the Queens did not fail, and glorious gallantry and leadership that gained him the Victoria Cross was shown by Colonel Bushell.

He took charge of the left of the French as well as of his own two companies, and led them to the assault under fierce and sustained machine-gun fire. He was struck by a bullet in the head, but again and again he rallied the troops, walking up and down in front of

LIEUT.-COLONEL C. BUSHELL, V.C., D.S.O., M.C.

them, encouraging them to fresh efforts. Although little progress could be made, Colonel Bushell's up- lifting bravery kept the line firm. Not until he had assured himself that his positions were intact did he go back to Rouez to report to General Wood. Even then, when his head had been bandaged, no one could prevent him from returning to command his battalion as it retired in front of Faillouel. He showed himself very excited—the effect of the wound —but he still kept urging on his men. He carried on until he fainted from exhaustion. Then Major Tortise, his second-in-command, and Colonel Ransome of the Buffs persuaded him to go back. He fainted again and had to be carried out of action. Colonel Bushell was a barrister in civil life. He became an earnest and accomplished military leader. He had spent November and December 1917 with the French as a Liaison Officer, and returned to the Queens to take command when the Division went south from Flanders.

About 10 A.M., when the French had entirely run out of ammunition, the Germans poured forward to the attack. The Queens had to fall back, but they retired in orderly fashion. It was indeed a retirement carried out according to the manuals, with proper covering-fire and companies falling back by sections. The field-guns of the 82nd Brigade, sited south of Hallot Wood and east of Frières-Faillouel, fired per- sistently, and in the end over open sights; but, as the 54th Brigade on the left had found, the German numbers were overwhelming and the withdrawal had to be.

Up to 9 A.M. there had been no infantry action on the East Surreys' front, and at 10.15 A.M. Major Wightman reported to General Wood that his bat- talion were still in their positions. An attack, how- ever, must have developed shortly after he left the line. The details of the fighting which ensued on this front are very obscure, but from the evidence collected it is possible to piece together some sort of a narrative. The enemy first attacked and drove back the French troops on our right, who were handicapped, as already stated, by shortness of ammunition. The East Surreys and the 12th Entrenching Battalion were then heavily attacked and pushed back through the Bois Hallot, whose western edge the enemy reached about 1 P.M. Subsequently these troops were pressed back still farther into Frières Wood, and at 4 P.M. were on the line of the Noureuil-Frières-Faillouel road, where they put up a stubborn defence. The fighting was very confused. The woods were so thick there was a field of view of only 50 yards. The 7th Queens and 7th Buffs, with oddments of other troops, held out a long time in front of the village of Rouez, and, both on our side as well as on that of the enemy, the fight for fire superiority was prolonged and stubborn.

At 11 A.M. the remnants of the Buffs were withdrawn by Colonel Ransome to an orchard south of Frières Wood, where, in some old trenches and gun-pits, two lines were organised by the Colonel and by Major Tortise. And here the remainder of the Buffs and Queens made another stand for the rest of the day. Ten Vickers and Hotchkiss guns were collected, and there is no doubt that the stubborn resistance of these detachments held up strong enemy attacks intended, in conjunction with the attack from the north, to cut off the troops in the wood.

At 1 P.M. the 80th and 92nd Field Companies were moved from Divisional Reserve into positions in front of the northern portion of Noureuil and along the Noureuil-Frières-Faillouel road, where they were in touch on the right with the French, with elements of the 173rd Brigade of the 58th Division, and also with details of the Bedfordshires. They too held their ground against repeated attacks all the afternoon. At 6 P.M. Nos. 3 and 4 sections of the 80th Field Company, under Lieutenant C. E. J. Richardson, even carried out a little counter-attack of their own, and continued their advance until they were nearly surrounded.

The situation of the Division as a whole was, at 3 P.M., a very difficult one. The enemy had been attacking heavily since before dawn, the pressure being greatest on our flanks. For fifty-four hours our troops had been engaged without any pause for sleep or reorganisation, and they were greatly exhausted. In most units, especially in those that had been fighting in Frières Wood, considerable disorganisation existed, and the losses in all ranks had been very heavy. To add to the anxiety, conflicting and disquieting reports on the general progress of the enemy came continually to hand. In the light of subsequent knowledge it seems that many of these reports originated because French uniforms were mistaken in the mist for the Boche "field-grey" by troops unaccustomed to working with the French. On our right and left the situation continued to be obscure. Neither from the 14th Division nor from the 58th could definite information be obtained beyond the fact that they had been heavily attacked.

Worst outlook of all! By 3 P.M. all the 18th Division's reserves had been committed to the fight; consequently early relief was imperative.

At 4 P.M. General Sadleir-Jackson, whose 54th Brigade had taken up a line on the ridge south of Faillouel, and had also received welcome reinforcements in the shape of two hundred of the Canadian Mounted Brigade (Fort Garry Horse and Lord Strathcona's Horse), realised that a further withdrawal was inevitable. The Boche had shelled and seized the hill north-west of Faillouel, from the 14th Division. He had definitely established a superiority in machine-gun fire, and was bringing up more machine-guns and trench mortars. His artillery fire went on all the time and was very deadly. The position of our troops north of Faillouel became untenable. So they too fell back fighting, through Faillouel. Fresh German troops, brought in lorries, arrived there as our men went out. The hostile shelling and machine-gun fire continued, and at last the 54th Brigade, covered by a rearguard of two squadrons of the Canadian Brigade, was withdrawn through a prepared line to Villequier Aumont.

One piquant incident of this confused and difficult time concerned General Sadleir-Jackson and Captain W. H. Baddeley, of the Sussex Pioneers. Captain Baddeley's company was told off to hold Frières-Faillouel. The orders for the retirement did not reach Baddeley. The Bedfords and Northants fell back through the Sussex Pioneers, and it was clear that the Boche was coming on fast. Still Captain Baddeley's orders were to stay, and he remained in a sunken road. One of the Pioneers came in and reported that an officer with curled-up moustaches, a tin hat, and a short leather jacket, had asked what his battalion was. When the man told him, the officer had said, " You had better be getting back." A few minutes afterwards Captain Baddeley saw some one looking at him over the top of the sunken road, and a very military voice called out, "You had better be getting back, young man." Now Baddeley had only just returned from leave. He had never seen General Sadleir-Jackson, who had come to the 54th Brigade not long before the Division came south from Houlthurst Forest. What Baddeley did observe was a fine set of curled-up moustaches and a short jacket of unusual cut. He asked the officer who he was, and at the same time drew his revolver. "That's all right, young man," said the officer, grasping him by the shoulder, "I'm General Sadleir-Jackson," and Baddeley was at last convinced. Baddeley, who finished the 1918 campaign with a D.S.O. and a bar to his M.C., became second in command to Colonel Irwin of the East Surreys. After the Armistice he returned to Keble College, Oxford, to resume preparation for the Church.

The afternoon experiences of the 53rd and 55th Brigades were equally severe. At 3 P.M. the 10th Essex, who were in front of Rouez Wood, with the battalion headquarters in a shell-hole, found Germans swooping down upon them. Touch was lost on the flanks, and though a stout fight was put up, the enemy came on in such numbers that Major A. S. Tween and his men were steadily forced back. Major Tween had done inspiring work since the early hours of 21st March; he looked worn and tired. Suddenly he realised that not only were the Germans driving the leading troops back; they were also securing important high ground. Grabbing his revolver, Tween said abruptly, "We have to attack that hill quickly before the Boche gets there," and calling on his headquarters men he dashed forward. He only got a few yards. A bullet hit him in the stomach. He was taken away on a sheet of corrugated iron, suffering great pain and begging his men to shoot him. He died that night in Chauny. One of the best officers of the Division was most lamentably lost, but poor Tween's last act proved to be as valuable as it was courageous. His men went on to win the high ground and to check the enemy's advance at a most critical moment.

A composite battalion made up of remnants of the West Kents and the Berkshires fell back fighting. The guns of the 82nd Brigade, R.F.A., were withdrawn through Villequier Aumont by 4.30 P.M. The 55th Brigade still held on in front of Rouez.

Their only hope now was to stick it out till dark, and then retire. The Boche had manifestly won the long-sustained fight for fire superiority. The rattle of the machine-guns became ear-splitting in its intensity. At 6 P.M. French reinforcements assembling in Rouez Wood went through the Buffs and Queens and made a frontal counter-attack. Colonel Ransome says it was one of the most gallant efforts he ever witnessed.

T

"But," relates Colonel Ransome, "the outburst of German machine-gun fire that met it was almost sickening to hear. The French reached our front line and lay down. At 6.10 they got up and retired, and so did the whole of our front-line troops.

"I do not think our men could be blamed. They had been fighting since dawn on the 21st, and had fought hard all that day. Fortunately the Boche diminished his fire to follow up, and the crowd of French and British troops retiring through the wood did not suffer so heavily as I had anticipated.

"A line was formed about 500 yards inside Rouez Wood, and a small party was actually led *forward* from here by my Adjutant, Captain Black. This checked the Boche, who did not press us before dark, and we were able to collect, reorganise, and march back to Villequier Aumont.

"It was on this day that the 'battle surplus' of the 55th Brigade—the officers and men left out of action to replace casualties—were more or less wiped out. They had been hurriedly put into the line on the 22nd, and suffered severely about Vouel and Tergnier.

"As regards our march to Villequier Aumont, our party, composed of the 10th Essex and remnants of the 7th Queens and 7th Buffs, were guided by the major commanding the former battalion. He assured me he feared we were surrounded, but he knew the orders were to go back to the Villequier Aumont. We arrived there safely, and I met Brigadier-General Higginson, commanding 53rd Infantry Brigade, who told me my Brigade was to go back to Bethancourt, where Brigadier-General Wood already was. So picking up more stragglers, I marched on there and bivouacked.

"I borrowed our padre's camp-bed and went to sleep for a few hours. About 8 A.M. while I was having a bath—every one laughed at me for having a bath, but it made all the difference to me afterwards—General Wood came to see me and a conference took place."

The 53rd Brigade bivouacked for the night in Commenchon, and the 54th in Caillouel, leaving the front to be held by the three regiments of Cuirassiers of the 1st French Cavalry Division, along a line which may be approximately indicated as connecting Noureuil, Athiemort, and Caisnel. At 11 o'clock that night Divisional Headquarters were moved back to Caillouel.

Some idea of the fighting the Division had gone through will be gained from the fact that at the close of the day the 11th Royal Fusiliers could only muster 2 officers and 250 other ranks, while the Northamptonshires and Bedfordshires each numbered about 6 officers and 200 other ranks.

The only guns lost on the 23rd were those of the 410th Battery, which was absolutely smashed up by shell-fire. At the close of the fighting on the 23rd, however, only two complete machine-guns were left out of the original complement of 48. Six new guns were received at Ugny, and on the 24th eight were available to go into the line.

From noon 22nd March to noon 23rd March, 37 officers and 1,150 other ranks passed through the 18th Division's Casualty Clearing Station, which had been established at Les Hezettes, one mile north-east of Guivry. Of these, 12 officers and 420 other ranks belonged to the 18th Division. 21st March started badly for the advanced dressing-station at Remigny. The dug-out used as a dressing-room received two direct hits. At the same time two Ford ambulance cars, one motor cycle and a water-cart, were put out of action. However, at the end of the day it was estimated that the Divisional Field Ambulance had collected from 30 to 40 per cent of the casualties. On 22nd and 23rd March, when the Cavalry which had been in Corps Reserve and the French troops were thrown into the line, it was found that they had no medical organisation of their own, so that nearly all their wounded came to the Les Hezettes station, as did a large number of the 14th Division wounded.

Throughout the night of 22nd and 23rd March the stretcher-bearers worked with splendid steadiness. The longest and most dangerous " carry " was that running north of Faillouel towards the railway triangle.

At Les Hezettes on the 23rd the main road became congested with retiring transport, and at one time there were 70 stretcher and 300 walking cases awaiting evacuation westward by way of Babœuf. Four aeroplanes came over and machine-gunned them as they lay there.

# CHAPTER XX.

## 24TH AND 25TH MARCH—THE BATTLE OF BABŒUF.

*The whole Division in danger of being cut off—The traffic block at
Caillouel — Northamptonshires fired on by the French — 54th
Brigade's swift counter-attack at Babœuf to save French guns—
An amazing effort—270 Germans and 10 machine-guns captured—
18th Division safely over the Oise.*

To those who were in it, the outstanding feature of
the Fifth Army Retreat—compared to which the Mons
Retreat, with infinitely less shelling and machine-gun
fire, was a skirmish—was the equanimity of the rank
and file, and their conviction that we were falling
back for strategical purposes. That the British Army
as a whole was in danger of being smashed or of being
irrevocably out-manœuvred occupied no place in their
imaginings. In the 18th Division the favourite belief
remained that we were retreating with a definite aim ;
that against very heavy odds we were to carry on a
fighting retirement until Haig launched an attack
further north that would make the enemy regret
he had devoted so many divisions to exhausting the
Fifth Army. The Divisional infantry never lost their
keenness for personal contact with the oncoming foe,
and their trust in their own generals did not waver ;
that was why, when at Bethancourt and Caillouel on
24th March they had dug hard and well in readiness
to face the Germans from prepared positions, they
grumbled because orders came for a further falling
back. They complained that the trenches they had
sweated at under a hot sun were wasted. They did

not, of course, know then that von Hutier's forces had
made such swift advance on our left that the whole
Division was in danger of being cut off.

But by 9 A.M., with the French falling back rapidly
north of us and east of us, that catastrophe did menace.
The 18-pounders of the 82nd Brigade, R.F.A., were in
action at the Rue de Caumont until 9.30 A.M. The
82nd Brigade was the last unit of the Division to withdraw. The French General had informed Brigadier-
General Evans that he hoped to relieve the 18th
Divisional artillery by 9 A.M. But no relief came.
Soon after 10 A.M., acting under fresh orders, Colonel
Thorp's Brigade was again in action west of Bethancourt, firing a protective barrage while the 55th
Brigade joined the 53rd and 54th Brigades in preparing a wired defence line along the Caillouel Ridge,
2 miles farther back.

The valley between Bethancourt and Caillouel was
full of troops, guns, and transport, French as well as
British, all moving to the rear. It was an unforgettable spectacle. The centre of Bethancourt—whose
civilian inhabitants had been sent to the rear the
night before—was crammed with troops and military
impedimenta ; the straight road that led down into
the valley, across the stream, and up again to Caillouel,
was just a ribbon of blue and khaki : waggons, lorries,
and camp kitchens, all moving slowly back—at times,
oh, so slowly ! Once, the whole cortège was at a
standstill for over an hour. Caillouel was blocked with
traffic, and Colonel Walker of the Sussex Pioneers,
Captain R. A. Chell, the 55th Brigade's Staff Captain,
and that sound golfer, Lieutenant D. H. Fish, General
Evans's Reconnaissance Officer, showed themselves as
cool and resourceful sorting it out as London police-
men on point duty might have done.

By noon the three Infantry Brigades were in position covering Caillouel, with the 55th Brigade in the
centre, the 54th on the left, the 53rd on the right,
and the 12th Entrenching Battalion covering the

Bethancourt-Caillouel road. The Sussex Pioneers took up a support line running through Crepigny, one company prolonging the left of the 54th Brigade to gain touch with the French (9th Cuirassiers) about Beaugies. Battalions had been paraded and, as far as possible, reorganised; "battle surplus" had been picked up at Caillouel and used as reinforcements; and a few stragglers had come in. In these ways, the 11th Royal Fusiliers, for example, became once more a battalion, though containing only 8 officers and about 180 other ranks, including transport and other details.

There were slight patrol encounters during the day, and the artillery engaged some enemy targets with effect. The Germans were slowly and surely coming on. During the afternoon they worked up through Commenchon, Bethancourt, and Rue de Vignes. Later, Caillouel began to be heavily shelled, and at 6.15 P.M. a strong enemy attack, covered by heavy machine-gun fire, succeeded in driving the French out of Guivry. Beaugies was still held by our allies, but, after dark, officer patrols sent out to ascertain the exact position on our left, reported on their return that the Germans were in the north edge of the village, and that the French were withdrawing in the direction of Maucourt. At 10 P.M. the fall of Beaugies was definite and the situation on our left became critical, as the enemy were now only a short march from the Apilly-Grandru-Maucourt road. Once there, they would be in a position to envelop the whole of our line. This menace was communicated to III. Corps, together with General Lee's suggestion that the whole line should be brought back to the Crepigny Ridge. Corps ordered the withdrawal to be carried out during the night. General Evans arranged that the 82nd Brigade, R.F.A., Colonel Thorp's Brigade, who had now fought four days and nights without any chance of rest, should be relieved by the 83rd Brigade, Colonel Seagram's Brigade, who had not been in action since their splendid support of the 53rd Infantry Brigade on 21st March.

By 3 A.M. on the 25th the new line was occupied and touch gained with the 9th Cuirassiers in the Bois d'Autrecourt. An hour later the Division was placed under the command of the 1st French Cavalry Corps. During the remaining dark hours of the morning heavy firing was heard on our left, and at dawn General Sadleir-Jackson, with his liaison officer, Lieutenant Lee of the Fusiliers, and two mounted men, rode off to see how things were looking at Maucourt.

From the woods on the high ground overlooking that village he perceived German columns, with bugles all a-blowing, marching along the road to Quesny. A little later, Captain Cumberlege, the 54th's Brigade-Major, and an officer patrol on the Grandru spur, saw columns of German troops and transport marching along the valley to the north, headed by a band in full blast. So far as these latter columns were concerned, a couple of machine-guns were speedily got into position, and, opening unexpectedly, put the transport—and the band—to flight.

The general situation, however, was more menacing than ever. By 7 A.M. it became evident that the enemy's design was to turn the Bois d'Autrecourt from the north; were he successful, it would mean the enveloping of the whole of the British and French forces on this part of the front. It was clear that he was advancing in force. General Lee immediately issued to all brigades instructions that, in the event of a further retirement, the ultimate line to be taken by the Division would be Mont de Behericourt-Babœuf-Apilly; and at 8.30 A.M. the retirement began in conjunction with the 9th Cuirassiers, the 11th Royal Fusiliers acting as the covering force on the left flank, where the threat was especially dangerous.

For troops who were more or less in contact with the enemy all the time, it was a matter of difficulty to regulate this withdrawal through the many woods and villages, and for a while the whole line was in a state of confusion, especially on the right, where by 11 A.M. troops of the 53rd Brigade and French troops were withdrawing through Montescourt in some disorder. But these men were rallied and a position was established between Montescourt and Babœuf. The general line, however, was far from complete. The 53rd Brigade had no troops on their right, the 54th Brigade were out of touch with the French on their left and with the 55th in the centre. The Germans were still advancing with the intention not only of turning the woods but of cutting off our escape across the Oise river. Our retirement, always under heavy machine-gun and artillery fire, had to be resumed to the Behericourt position already alluded to, and this position was reached about 12.30 P.M.

The 54th Brigade's retirement, with the enemy apparently gathering in speed and in numbers each quarter of an hour, was in truth full of incident. The Northamptons were being withdrawn in artillery formation, and the leading platoon had just got over a crest when suddenly it came under hot machine-gun fire from the ridge to which it would retire next. It was French troops firing by mistake. The French were disinclined to admit responsibility until a tin of bully beef was produced from a Northants officer's haversack with one of their bullets in it. Then they apologised handsomely.

The Fusiliers and the Bedfords did a withdrawal from Grandru to Behericourt to a peppering accompaniment from Boche field-guns and machine-guns, and one very rapid march through the woods had to be done in single file. But not a man fell out, and not a single rifle was thrown away.

To extricate the Fusiliers, the Bedfordshires were first withdrawn by platoons to the Mont de Behericourt. Then the Fusiliers, under continuous machine-

gun fire, were got back, also by platoons ; everything
was done in contained orderly fashion, and finally
junction was made on the left with the Northamptonshires and with some French cavalry who had been
rushed up, and the situation was saved. The Brigade
was not cut off from the crossing over the Oise, but
it had been a near thing.

At 1 P.M. the enemy opened a very heavy fire with
a large number of light machine-guns on the 53rd
Brigade's sector, and the whole of the 289th French
Regiment fell back.  At the same time German troops
were seen advancing in thick lines, with the intention
of attacking our right and forcing a way to Apilly.
An hour later this attack had developed, and once
again retirement was the word.  Once again was it a
case of falling back and digging in.  Not, however,
without administering punishment to the enemy.
Four armoured cars of the 2nd Groupe de Mitrail-
leuses Automobiles du 1re Corps de Cavalerie happened to be on the spot.  Again and again they went
forward under heavy fire and inflicted severe losses
on the enemy.  These cars also covered the retirement
of the 53rd Brigade and continued to do so much
execution that the enemy's advance at this point was
checked.  Owing to the situation created on its right
by the withdrawal of the 289th French Regiment, the
55th Brigade had also been compelled to go back to
the west of Babœuf, where new positions were established with the idea of preventing the enemy from
getting down to what had now become the vitally
important river crossing at Varesnes.

It was at this stage of the day's fighting that Major
J. Wightman of the East Surreys again showed himself a great natural leader.  He supervised the taking
forward of Lewis gun teams to positions from which
they could rake the advancing enemy.  He remained
with them and directed their fire from an exposed
position ; and numbers of Germans were killed.  When
the East Surreys were forced to retire, he took com-

mand of the exposed right flank and controlled the retirement of alternative companies with covering fire. To do so he had to walk up and down under intense enemy machine-gun fire. He brought the battalion back in perfect order and with very few casualties.

The Queens, having no Lewis gun ammunition, massed themselves four deep on a hill to secure concentrated fire.

The 18th Division's three brigades were now ready to cross the Oise. But by this time the compact unharmed village of Babœuf was in German hands. Worse, there was a 2,000 yards' gap between the French troops on the high ground north of Behericourt and the 53rd Brigade on the railway line to the south of Babœuf. Several French batteries of 75's were in this long gap firing towards Babœuf, with no infantry in front of them. The French Infantry Commander explained the situation to Brigadier-General Sadleir-Jackson.

Sadleir-Jackson, ever quick thinking, resolved upon the bold step of an immediate counter-attack—a swift move that would mean seizing the village of Babœuf and the high ground north of it, delay the German progress, and rescue the imperilled French guns.

This operation—the battle of Babœuf—was really an amazing thing, one of the memorable incidents of the Retreat. The officers and men who carried it through were now in their fifth successive day of continuous hard fighting. All were thoroughly spent. That at such a moment they should possess the spirit and the strength suddenly to turn upon the triumphant enemy, stop him and inflict a reverse upon him, was something at which to wonder. But they did it! The 11th Royal Fusiliers and the 7th Bedfords, now less than half their normal strength, were faced about, and shortly after 5 P.M. were deployed for the attack. The front extended from the Babœuf-Chauny main road on our right to the southern edge of the woods above Babœuf. The Royal Fusiliers were on the right, the Bedfordshires on the left. The Northamptonshires were kept in reserve.

Within half an hour of the decision the attack, led in person by General Sadleir-Jackson, was launched without any artillery preparation.

In the sudden excitement of the change from retreat to assault, fatigue and hardship seemed to be forgotten. The men went forward with a sort of fierce enthusiasm. Babœuf was held by machine-guns, but the Fusiliers and the Bedfords pressed on with surprisingly few casualties. Perhaps the defending Germans thought that something bigger lay behind this assault that was carried out by a tired, hard-fought brigade, shrunk almost to the dimensions of a battalion. At any rate they did not withstand the dash of Sadleir-Jackson's men. Germans were killed in the streets and cellars of Babœuf. The Fusiliers met with some resistance when they "mopped up" the south side of the village, but two companies of the Northamptonshires, moved forward to assist them, made their success secure. There was house-to-house fighting, and machine-gun bullets swept the principal streets. One bizarre spectacle was that of a calf wandering up the main street in front of our advancing forces. Bullets sang over and around the animal. None touched it. By 6 P.M. the village was cleared of Germans, and the 54th Brigade was digging trenches in the meadows on the German side of the village. Touch had been regained with the threatened French batteries, ten enemy machine-guns and 270 Germans had been captured. It was a very complete little success.

As night came on, Germans were seen digging-in about 800 yards from Babœuf, and later shells began to descend in the village. But the object of the 54th Brigade's counter-attack having been gained, there was no intention of holding on to Babœuf. During the night our cavalry and infantry, with that of the First

French Cavalry Division, withdrew across the Oise to bivouac in Pontoise, and in Varesnes, town of old-fashioned plaster houses, squat green doors, and a Mairie with railed double steps. The civilians had been evacuated the day before.

The establishment of a line south of the river brought to an end the retreat on the Noyon-Chauny sector of the front. On 26th March the Division, less the Divisional Artillery Headquarters and the 83rd Brigade, R.F.A., who remained with the French until the 30th, was withdrawn for a very brief rest and for refitting in the Nampcel area; and on 27th March it was placed in reserve to the 58th Division, which still held its line in the Barisis sector. On 28th March orders were received to rejoin the Fifth British Army near Amiens, and the infantry were moved by omnibus during the night, the transport following by road. The 8th East Surreys, it might be added, were rather proud of the fact that they had saved their drums, but the silver bugles, presented to them by the Stock Exchange before they left England, fell into the hands of the enemy.

# CHAPTER XXI.

## THE DEFENCE OF AMIENS.

"Even the 14th and the 18th were brought up to the Amiens front after their grapple against Hutier, so pitiless in its consequences was the tragical need of more men. Will civilised nations in time of war ever impose a fitting punishment on those statesmen who fail to supply enough troops?"—*From* 'The Fifth Army in March 1918,' by W. SHAW SPARROW.

*The " Back to the Wall " period—The two German attacks of 4th April —14th Division, Australians, and 7th Buffs forced back—A deadly counter-attack by the 8th Berkshires—Colonel Dewing killed leading it—Major Wightman of the East Surreys also killed—An example of the German method of pressing home an initial success—The Frenchwoman found by the 7th Queens.*

LIKE Ypres, Messines, Thiépval, and Cambrai, Villers-Bretonneux is one of the place-names that spring sharply to the memory of any one who was in the war. The battered, physically exhausted, but still unbroken Fifth Army had been driven by the end of March back to the neighbourhood of Amiens. Amiens, the cathedral city on the main railway route between Calais and Paris, was the prize for which the German High Command sought desperately in the closing stages of the tremendous assault that had as its ultimate object the forcing asunder of the British and French Armies. Villers-Bretonneux, the one-time snug green village on the long straight road that runs from Peronne to Amiens, was the key to Amiens—a high sighting-place that gave observation over Amiens itself and over the valley of the Somme. Villers-Bretonneux had to be held at all costs. Further strategical retirement could not be thought of, and the 18th was one of the spent, skeleton divisions that formed the last guard and kept the enemy out. From 30th March to 24th April, when the Boche made his final attempt to sweep through to Amiens, the 18th held on, sticking to it against odds, and like the good boxer who accepts punishment without losing his form, fighting back. After the Armistice, when Lord Rawlinson accorded the highest of praise to the 18th, General Lee said that he was never so proud of the Division as during the Villers-Bretonneux period. The Division that can carry out counter-attacks after resisting heavy attacks from numerically superior forces must, he remarked, be a good Division. That is what the 18th did at Villers-Bretonneux, while still woefully under strength, before its fresh recruits, most of them raw youths, could be imbued with the corporate spirit of the Division. It was a more grim, more anxious time than the Great Retreat : for days at a stretch no sleep, no rest, no food but iron rations ; the worst terrors of mustard gas, continuous losses, and hard deadly fighting by day and by night.

At the time of the 18th Division's arrival in the Amiens area, the advance of Von der Marwitz's Second German Army had been checked on the general line running from south to north by Demuin, Aubercourt, Marcelcave, Warfussee, Sailly, Albert, and Beaumont Hamel. The portion of the front between Marcelcave and the river Luce was held by elements of four Divisions, the 66th, 61st, 39th, and 50th, all of which, like the 18th, had been in action since 21st March, had suffered grievous casualties, and were now very exhausted. Their immediate relief was imperative, especially as the enemy was expected to make further and early attacks in this sector. In addition to the Divisions just mentioned, there were also present in this sector portions of the gallant and well-advertised "Carey's Force" and the 9th Australian Brigade.

The immediate business of the 18th Division was

the relief of the wearied troops between the Marcelcave-Cachy road and the river Luce. Our own men, as may be guessed, were in little better case. They had come out of the line in the early hours of 26th March, had marched a distance of eight miles that day to Nampcel, marched again the following day to new billets, and now, after one day's rest, had undertaken another journey lasting twenty-four hours to this new area. All the battalions were still extremely weak both in officers and experienced N.C.O.'s.

The 53rd and 55th Brigades were the first to appear. They had been conveyed through a night of torrential rain by French lorries. Most of these lorries were driven by men who had been on the move for a week at a stretch, and they could hardly keep sufficiently awake to avoid collisions with trees and other roadside obstacles. The village of Boves, which still contains the ruins of the chateau in which Henri IV. once sojourned with the fair Gabrielle d'Estrees, was the "debussing point," about 5 miles south-east of Amiens. There was no time for reorganisation, and at noon on 30th March came orders that the Division was, that night, to relieve all the troops in the line between the river Luce and the Marcelcave-Cachy road. By daybreak on 31st March the 53rd and 55th Brigades were in the line, and the whole southern half of the III. Corps front between the Villers-Bretonneux road and the river Luce was under the command of the G.O.C. 18th Division—an arrangement which brought the 9th Australian Brigade, who held the northern portion of the sector, under General Lee. The 54th Brigade arrived the same day and were sent up to Gentelles.

The Division faced the enemy in the following order: the 55th Brigade in the centre; the 53rd Brigade on the right; and the 9th Australian Brigade on the left; while the 54th Brigade occupied the high ground between Hangard village, held by the French, and Hangard Wood, held by the 53rd Brigade. In general, the ground was flat, affording little cover.

Hangard Wood, shaped like a butterfly, consisted of short undergrowth, and lay for the most part in a hollow. The chief tactical features of the sector were two spurs situate north and west respectively of the village of Domart-sur-La-Luce, the high ground of the Villers-Bretonneux plateau, and the Gentelles-Cachy plateau.

Like the high ground on which Villers-Bretonneux stood, the Gentelles-Cachy plateau gave observation over Amiens. It also dominated the valley of the Avre. Its loss would render untenable all positions east of the Avre; while a withdrawal to the west bank would uncover the great city on the south. Of equal importance, though it was not included in our sector, was the retention of the line of the river Luce, for an advance of the enemy in this direction would outflank Villers-Bretonneux and the Gentelles-Cachy plateau. Lastly, the possession by us of the village of Hangard was necessary to block the advance of the enemy up the valley of the Luce.

Small wonder then that General Lee issued orders that all positions were to be "held to the last." If lost, they were to be retaken immediately by counter-attacks. "Every yard of ground" was to be fought.

Our front line was merely slits and organised shell-holes connected in places to form a rough trench system, but with no wire in front! A reserve line, following the general line Berteaucourt - Gentelles, through the Bois l'Abbé to the Villers-Bretonneux road, was being dug. Little of it had been completed, and there were no other defences sufficiently advanced to form any obstacle worth mentioning. The weather remained atrociously wet, and nothing in the nature of hot food or drink could be got up to the line till after nightfall. The Boche gunners shelled intermittently. On the 30th a shell broke into the dug-out that was General Lee's advanced headquarters, and Colonel Wallace Wright, V.C., his G.S.O.1, was blown down the steps and lost his hat. On the other hand, although Brigadier-General Wood made his headquarters in a large farm close to the "Monument," on the road leading south from Villers-Bretonneux, and the buildings were in full view from the German positions at Marcelcave, the enemy never shelled the place before 4th April. It was a thoroughly comfortable house, and General Wood slept upstairs in a spacious bedroom every night.

The cellars of Villers-Bretonneux were well stocked —a military danger; an edict went forth for the destruction of their contents, and the gutters flowed with good wines. The destruction was not completed immediately, for the day after the order General Lee, accompanied by Major Hopwood, his G.S.O.2, and Major Porter, A.D.C., were returning from a visit to General Wood, when they came across a party of Australians heavily laden with sacks on their backs. The General, guessing what the sacks contained, attacked them with a thick oak stick, and caused cascades of red and white wines to flow freely down the Australians' backs. His action was resented, and a difficult situation was saved by the timely arrival of Australian officers.

The Germans went in for "direct action" on the afternoon of 31st March with a heavy thrust on our right against the 20th and 8th Divisions who lay between Hangard and Moreuil. They secured some valuable observation ground east of Rifle Wood, and also obtained a footing in the village of Hangard.

This high ground was not recovered; and as on 2nd April Germans were seen digging-in on the ridge north of Aubercourt, a ridge that would be invaluable to us for early information of a Boche advance up the valley of the Luce, General Lee planned to seize this high ground and advance our line.

Accordingly an attack was arranged to be delivered by one company of the Bedfordshires on the left and one company of the Royal Fusiliers on the right. After forming up among the trees in the river valley

—which here runs practically east and west—the two
companies were to advance in a north-easterly direction
from the valley of the Luce, east of Hangard, and
capture a German trench on the spur west of Aubercourt. On reaching this objective, a white Very light
was to be fired ; and when they saw this signal, the 7th
Royal West Kents were to advance into line with the
Bedfords and the Fusiliers.

The attack was first timed for 6.45 P.M., but it
happened to be an unusually bright evening, so the
hour of assault was put back to 7 P.M. Even then the
enemy got in the first blow. The assaulting companies
moved out of Gentelles in the dim dusk by half
platoons, but as they were endeavouring to " trickle "
into the forming-up places, enemy observers caught
sight of them, and realised what was in preparation.
Exactly a minute before 7 o'clock a tremendous
barrage was put down on our front line. The
Fusiliers were fired on from front and rear and from
the right flank, and had all their Lewis guns knocked
out ; and during the ensuing quarter of an hour the
shelling and the machine-gun firing increased to such
intensity that messages were sent back that the two
companies would be unable to advance without reinforcements. By this time, in fact, the Royal
Fusiliers had lost two officers and forty other ranks,
while the Bedfordshires' losses had been still heavier
—four officers and sixty other ranks. To make
matters worse, the West Kents, mistaking a German
white light for the prearranged signal, advanced
to their objective, only to march straight into a
similar machine-gun hail. It became only too clear
that the Germans were holding this particular piece
of ground in strength, and that a larger operation,
involving a simultaneous advance south of the Luce
across the important point east of Rifle Wood, would
be necessary to capture and hold the wanted positions.
The costly and frustrated attempt was therefore
abandoned.

2nd April also produced a queer inexplicable incident that officers of the 7th Queens and 55th Brigade
Headquarters still discuss, because the swift passage
of events in that bewildering, rough-and-tumble time
prevented them from learning the denouement.

A Frenchwoman, about twenty-seven years of age,
hatless, dressed like a peasant, passed the Queens'
headquarters, walking towards our front line. No
civilian was supposed to be within miles of such a spot,
and Major Tortise sent an orderly-room clerk to bring
her in. The woman said excitedly that she came from
Villers-Bretonneux, and for four days had tried to
get to Marcelcave where her mother lay ill. Major
Tortise told her the Germans were at Marcelcave, and
entrusted her to the orderly-room clerk, telling him to
take her back to General Wood's headquarters for
examination.

On the way, this unexpected visitor to the front
said over and over again in broken English that she
must go to find her mother. She asked how far the
British line extended. Then, says the orderly-room
clerk, "a couple of whizz-bangs came over *and we both
flopped.*" At the 55th Brigade headquarters, Captain
Runge, examining a pass the woman produced, found
that it was four days old, and that it was signed by
an interpreter. She admitted that she had been
to Amiens during the four days. Captain Runge's
solution was to give the Queens' clerk a chit and to
instruct him to take his charge to Divisional Headquarters at Boves. As they neared Cachy the woman
tried to get away and the clerk had to grasp her by
the arm. They arrived at Cachy while the village
was being shelled. A house had received a direct hit,
and 40 Australians, killed and wounded, were being
taken out ; so the woman was placed in a cellar for
protection. After that she was got on the road to
Boves. She broke away again and tried to tell her
story to some French civilians, but they refused to
listen, and said she must be a spy. Intelligence

officers examined her and found 700 francs on her, but no papers. The interpreter who signed her pass could not be traced. She was sent further to the rear, and the 7th Queens, at any rate, never heard what happened to her.

3rd April brought heavy shelling along the whole front, and upon Villers-Bretonneux, Cachy, and the Bois l'Abbé in particular. At 4 P.M. a very violent barrage came down upon the 53rd and 55th Brigade sectors. A sharp attack followed, the line buckled, and the impulse to retire spread down to the area of the 54th Brigade. But General Sadleir-Jackson, on horseback and under fire, galloped up and down the line, cursing fluently; and the rot that threatened was stopped. As a 54th Brigade officer who was there puts it : " The men were met by an infuriated figure. Aghast at the awful language, they stopped. It was the General. It was safer in the line, and they returned." In the bombardment that accompanied this attack, the enemy obtained a direct hit on a moving motor ambulance between Villers-Bretonneux and Bois l'Abbé, and the driver and both the wounded men were killed. This was the only known case in Colonel Pritchard-Taylor's experience of a moving Ford ambulance car being put out of action.

It rained in torrents that night, and the men up in front were soaked to the skin. Captain Wattenbach, adjutant of the 11th Royal Fusiliers, describing how the Fusiliers, who were in Divisional Reserve, moved up at dusk to the north of Hangard Wood, where our line was very weak, says :—

"The battalion formed up just north of Gentelles, and all officers in possession of compasses took careful bearings. We launched out into artillery formation over very thick plough. The men were wet through, and sank well over the ankles in mud; it was getting darker every moment, and it was very cold. There were no stars to guide the way, and maintaining touch with companies, platoons, and sections was no easy matter.

" We carefully counted the roads we crossed, and on nearing the wood, which was on our right, several Boche Very lights went up. Runners were constantly coming in from the front (goodness only knows how they found their way, as we were continually on the move). On the right there was no touch, and we came to the conclusion that we had to fill a gap in the line. For all we knew there were no British troops for miles. With great difficulty, and after consultation over soaked maps with an electric torch under a waterproof sheet, we eventually constructed a line on paper, and endeavoured to conform to it on the ground, with a fair amount of success.

" Major Gwynn was sent back by Colonel Sulman to explain the situation, and point out the necessity for another battalion at least to help fill the gap with us. The Essex Regiment arrived just as we were consolidating our new line, and things were more or less straightened out.

" We were then informed that we should have to side-slip past one battalion, and take up the line of the road with our left resting on the Monument (on the Aubercourt-Villers-Bretonneux road). It became purely a question of time, as dawn was breaking in a drizzly mist, and the battalion began to trudge wearily towards Villers-Bretonneux to take up the new line. This we did, and the battalion got into its new position, and the Essex Regiment came up on the right just as dawn broke."

A heavy mist lay over all that well-wooded country when dawn broke on 4th April, and it was under cover of drizzle and fog that at 5.30 A.M. the Germans loosed off along the whole Corps front a violent bombardment that proved to be the preliminary to a twelve hours' assault, in which six, and possibly seven, German Divisions tried to break through. But once again steadfastness and determined leadership kept them off.

After an hour and a half of intense shelling, in which many trench mortars took part, the enemy came forward in dense masses. He selected as his first point of assault the front of the 35th Australian Battalion, and of the 55th Brigade (7th Buffs and the left of the 7th West Kents). But our own artillery barrage came down right in the middle of the thick masses of German infantry, and cut great gaps in their formations. They still came on, but only to meet the maximum fire-power of all the infantry units in the line. Their casualties were tremendous. They got to within three hundred yards of our line, but no farther; and at that point the attack withered away.

On the 18th Division's left the Boche had more success. The 8th Rifle Brigade (14th Division) were driven back, and the enemy, entering their trenches and working down them, attacked the 35th Australian Battalion on our left flank, and compelled them to fall back, fighting and well covered by their machine-guns, to the support lines. The 7th Buffs on the right of the Australians had to do likewise; but the 7th West Kents, still farther to the right, stood firm and beat off the assault on their part of the front.

When battles go well and according to programme, the General who has planned things need do little more than stand by. His task ends at zero hour. But when disaster threatens, or plans go awry, generalship counts. To meet the situation caused by the yielding of ground on our left, General Lee ordered the two reserve battalions of the 9th Australian Brigade to take up positions that covered Villers-Bretonneux on the east, south-east, and north-east. The Brigadier of the 9th Australian Brigade also ordered three companies of the 33rd Australian Battalion to move up to the support of the left flank. One company of the 7th Queens was sent by General Wood of the 55th Brigade to hold the line of the railway south of Villers-Bretonneux, and two other companies were ordered to be ready to counter-attack in case of a further withdrawal. Earlier in the morning, General Lee had sent the 6th Londons, who had come as reinforcements, to help General Wood, and they were in position by 8 A.M.

For a while the fighting died down. But the Germans were preparing their next attempt. At the

moment the general situation was as follows : The
14th Division on our left had fallen back behind the
Bois de Vaire and along the Villers - Bretonneux-
Hamel road; but our own left line had now been
firmly established, and was in touch with the 1st
Dragoon Guards, who had moved up in support of
the 14th Division. On our right, an attack on the
141st French Regiment had been completely repulsed.

The second attempt to break through our line was
launched at 4.30 P.M. Preceded by a hurricane
bombardment from artillery of all calibres and from
trench mortars, large infantry formations advanced
against the French in Hangard, and against the
Northamptonshires and the East Surreys.

This attack had some success at the beginning.
The French were driven out of Hangard Cemetery
and out of the copse to the north of it ; the Northamptonshires were forced back to the line of the Cachy-
Hangard road, and the East Surreys, with only three
officers and 80 men left, also gave ground. Pressing
his advance through the wood a little farther north,
the enemy then threatened to cut off the Royal West
Kents, who were holding a line in front of the south-
east corner of this wood ; thus menaced, the West
Kents fell back to the eastern edge of Hangard
Wood.

But General Higginson's 53rd Brigade was ready
and waiting. A swift and deadly counter-attack was
launched by the 8th Royal Berkshires. Lieut.-
Colonel Dewing, who had had such a strenuous time
on 21st March, was killed leading it ; but the coolness
and dash shown checked the German advance at this
point.

Colonel Dewing had established his headquarters,
east of Gentelles, behind a mangel bank—a "pie" as
they call it in Yorkshire,—a solid-looking bastion,
although on this day rifle and machine-gun bullets
poured through it. The advancing Germans were
200 yards from the mangel bank when Colonel Dew-

ing called upon the Berkshires for their effort.  Rifle
and Lewis gun fire rolled over scores of Germans;
the enemy were stopped, and the Berkshires were
going forward with the bayonet when Colonel Dewing
was shot through the leg.  Captain R. Holland was
shot down and killed going to his assistance.  Captain
H. le G. Sarchet, son of the Chaplain-General,
was also shot, as was Lieutenant E. Wallis, the
Berkshires' signalling officer.  Then Private Bailey,
Colonel Dewing's servant, got to him, picked him
up, and started to carry him to a dressing-station.
But Bailey's gallantry did not save Colonel Dewing's
life.  He had got a hundred yards the other side of
the mangel bank, when a stray bullet went through
the Colonel's mouth.  Bailey was hit himself, but was
saved by a bully-beef tin in his haversack.

The Berkshires "did their bit" in this counter-
attack, but they were nearly wiped out.  The battalion that night could only muster 58 men.

Another grievous loss to the East Surreys and to
the whole Division was sustained during the enemy's
second attack.  That fine young officer, Major Wightman, was mortally wounded.  Wightman had much
about him that was extraordinary.  He was only
twenty-four years of age, and before the war was a
junior schoolmaster.  He had a passion for thoroughness.  When the war broke out he enlisted in
the Irish Guards — his way of learning soldiering
thoroughly.  In 1915 he was commissioned, and by
December came to the 8th East Surreys as bombing
and scouting officer.  On 1st July 1916 he showed
such bravery carrying messages under fire that he
was recommended for the Victoria Cross,—and got
nothing.  Then he was given command of a company,
and won his M.C. in Schwaben Redoubt.  Later,
when Colonel Irwin was wounded, he commanded
the battalion for three months.  Wightman was a
magnificent athlete, good at all games.  He could
also be described as a natural soldier.  He was ab-

solutely courageous, but never reckless. He seemed
instinctively to know exactly the right thing to do at
precisely the right moment. News of his D.S.O.
award came after he had been killed.

Major Wightman's servant and runner, Private
F. Newman, showed heroic devotion. When Wightman was hit, and lay out in an exposed position,
Newman made several attempts, with other men who
were near, to get him away. After three of his
companions had been knocked out by close-range
machine-gun fire, Newman stayed with Major Wightman till dark, and then got him safely away to a
dressing-station. Major Wightman died in Picquigny
Casualty Station on 9th April.

It was now five o'clock, and the general situation
was highly critical. The rapid advance of the enemy
had brought back the Buffs — Captain Black, the
adjutant, could only muster 50 men next morning—
and the East Surreys, whose rifles and Lewis guns
had got clogged with mud, and both battalions were
in some confusion; although, to show how well some
of the Lewis gunners fought, it may be noted that
Corporal Waters of the Buffs fired 2,000 rounds
through his Lewis gun without a stoppage of any
kind, and one of his achievements was to put out of
action a German trench mortar, 600 yards distant
from his gun. But the Germans had reached the
road leading to Villers-Bretonneux from the south,
the "Monument" road. Our whole line was in a
state of flux. At any moment the enemy might
set about outflanking Villers-Bretonneux from the
south. Counter-attack was the only policy, so a
vigorous effort by the 36th Australian Battalion,
assisted by two companies of the 7th Queens led by
General Wood himself, was made south of the Villers-
Bretonneux-Marcelcave railway. It was met with
heavy machine-gun fire from the chateau that stood
by the roadside, from haystacks, and from every scrap

of cover that the Boche could find, but it succeeded in establishing a new and better line, and incidentally it brought with it the capture of four of the enemy machine-guns.

This lightened the situation, but not sufficiently, and at 7.20 P.M. a 54th Brigade counter-attack was launched in conjunction with an assault by the French, who had been driven out of Hangard. As a result, we were able to advance to a line just short of the sunken road running north from Hangard village to Hangard Wood. The 6th Northamptonshires, finely led by Colonel Turner, had 1,500 yards of country to cross, and they lost several men from shell-fire early in the advance. Midway to their objective was a straw stack that had caught fire, and, silhouetted against this light, the oncoming figures made a ready target for the German machine-guns.

When the Northants got to within fifty yards of the sunken road, the enemy's rifles and machine-guns united in a murderous hail of fire; and at this moment a heavy shell exploded just in front of them, wounded Colonel Turner, and killed Major Stewart and 2nd Lieutenant Cuzens. "No one who took part in this counter-attack," says a Northants officer, "will forget how Colonel Turner led the remnants of his battalion forward, himself at the head, urging them on, and finally, when wounded, sitting up and encouraging his men." By this counter-attack the original line was re-established, and when the Northants had dug in, the French sent the welcome news that they had driven the enemy out of Hangard Cemetery.

But even now the day's fighting was not ended. A brilliant little operation took place a couple of hours later. At 10 P.M. it was realised that our line in the vicinity of the railway passed through very low-lying ground. Accordingly, the 34th Australian

Battalion was ordered to move forward and retake the support line, from which the 35th Australian Battalion had fallen back in the morning. This difficult operation, carried out on an intensely dark night, over sodden ground and in the face of very strong opposition, was brilliantly carried through, although the Australian casualties were heavy. By dawn the line had been consolidated. From about 2 A.M. the fighting on this part of the front died down.

It had been a day of very great anxieties and of supreme exhaustion, but the outcome of the bitter fighting was that the enemy had everywhere been prevented from attaining his objectives. Our own losses had been severe, but his were heavier still. The 9th Australian Brigade gave 4,000 Germans killed as a careful estimate on their front alone. Nine German officers and 250 other ranks were taken prisoner by the 18th Division. The prisoners belonged to three Divisions, the 9th Bavarian Reserve Division, the Guards Ersatz Division, and the 19th Division. It is highly probable that fresh Divisions were close at hand ready to exploit the expected successes, but all that the Germans achieved was the penetration of our line here and there to a maximum depth of 1,000 yards.

The operations of the enemy on 4th April 1918 furnished a good example of the German tactics of pressing the attack wherever a point of weakness was found. Thus their initial success against the 8th Rifle Brigade was exploited by further assaults at this point, combined with an immediate flank attack upon the 35th Australian Battalion. Again, when the big attack in the morning failed, it was not renewed against the same sectors; in the afternoon different parts of the line were assailed in the hope of finding a weak spot.

But the great thing was that General Lee still

had his troops in ordered formation, and that Villers-Bretonneux still marked the extreme westernmost limit of the German advance. Other testing days were to come, but the 18th Division had breathing-space to lick its wounds; its determination to hold on burned more fiercely than ever.

# CHAPTER XXII.

## THE STRUGGLE FOR VILLERS-BRETONNEUX.

*The 10th Essex and the French retake Hangard on 12th April—24th April the climax of all the German attempts to get through to Amiens—Enemy's first use of Tanks—Many untried lads of 19 now in the Divisional Infantry—" B " Battery, 83rd Brigade, deals with a Boche Tank at 100 yards' range—54th Brigade's 10 p.m. attack assists Australians to retake Villers-Bretonneux—230 West Kents lost within an hour—The D.S.O. exploit of 2nd Lieutenant Tysoe of the Bedfords—General Barker's first meeting with the 10th Essex.*

AFTER the fierce encounters of 4th April, the bigger histories give small mention to the Villers-Bretonneux fighting until the Germans' great culminating—and unsuccessful—effort of 24th April. But 12th April is of vivid interest to the 18th Division, for on that day the enemy, making his third bid for the village of Hangard, captured it; and the 10th Essex and the 7th West Kents, joining in with the French, made counter-attacks that again brought us possession of this much-harried village.

The 18th Division's crippled infantry battalions had been withdrawn to Boves and Gentelles, except that the 7th Royal West Kents and the 10th Essex took turns in occupying counter-attack positions. The counter-attack of the French and the Royal West Kents was launched at 10.15 A.M., and had the village of Hangard and the copse north of it as objectives. To show the amount of fighting the West Kents had gone through since 21st March, one has only to mention that on 12th April " B " Company, under

Captain A. V. Macdonald, M.C., contained all the survivors of the old original 7th Battalion. The French failed to reach Hangard, but they and the West Kents held on to the western edge of the copse, which, because of its position, was the key to the village. Some of the houses on the western edge of Hangard also fell into our hands, and the chateau was still held by the French. It was obvious, however, that a fresh and bigger effort was necessary ; and at 7.20 that evening a spirited attack by the 10th Essex, with the French alongside, proved brilliantly successful.

Among the 10th Essex, 12th April is known as Byerley's Day—Captain A. M. Byerley, one of the few original officers of the battalion who came through the war. Colonel Frizell had come back from leave, but he, Captain " Bill " Skeat of the stentorian voice, and Captain Hardaker were gassed in the battalion's cubby-hole headquarters, while rare old Forbes, the Adjutant, had been wounded by a rifle-shot while looking through his binoculars earlier on. During the afternoon, Colonel Frizell held a forming-up rehearsal, a practice that proved exceedingly useful when the actual attack began. He also gave the 10th Essex one of his celebrated addresses. The forming-up line was below a crest north of Domart, and the feature of the forming-up was that the French waited to see the Essex coming over the hill before they started themselves. The Essex being bang up to time, the attack began with British and French splendidly in line. A heavy German barrage of 4·2's and 5·9's was put down, but our men moved through it with exemplary steadiness, and in just over an hour the report came through that Hangard had been captured, that a German officer and 120 other ranks had been taken, and that large numbers of German dead were found in the village and in the copse north of it. The whole operation was a well-conducted little triumph, and the prisoners taken confirmed the belief that the enemy losses in the morning fighting had been very heavy indeed. Arthur Byerley received the congratulations of the Corps Commander next day, and is supposed immediately to have ordered a new jacket with a larger chest measurement!

On 24th April came the climax of the Boche attempts to get through to Amiens. His artillery preparation had commenced exactly a week before— St George's Day was supposed to be The Day—and during that period Yellow Cross gas was poured not only into Villers-Bretonneux, but into Little Cachy and the Bois l'Abbé. At dawn on the 24th the bombardment was heard loudly enough in Amiens —now denuded of its civilian population—to suggest that something very big was pending, and, sure enough, by 7 A.M. four German divisions began their onslaught.

The Germans meant to go all out on this 24th April. They used tanks for the first time. Their machine-gunners showed splendid fearlessness in the attack, their trench mortars went right through to the front, and their infantry came on with the courage of desperation. Not only did they force British and Australian troops out of Villers-Bretonneux by mass attacks ; the advance penetrated as far as the Cachy switch line, north of Gentelles, while farther south, the oncoming hordes established themselves in the Bois d'Aquenne. General Rawlinson, whose 4th Army Headquarter Staff, since 28th March, had taken over the work of the 5th Army Headquarters, realised the fatefulness of the moment. He resolved at all costs to retake Villers-Bretonneux and the positions that commanded it. So far the world has heard little save what the Australians did on that memorable 24th April. But there were other troops who fought and won that day—and among them were the 53rd and 54th Brigades of the 18th Division.

Since 12th April General Lee had been busy superintending the training and reorganising of battalions, and the incorporating of the new drafts that had been rushed out from England. Colonel Hickson, wounded at Cherisy in 1917, had rejoined the 7th West Kents, so had Major A. E. Phillips and Captain Waddington; and with strong drafts of third-line Yeomanry and Kent Cyclists who had undergone a lot of training on the East Coast, the battalion was made up to a ration strength of 700. The 8th Royal Berks had received goodly drafts of rustic Berkshire boys and Birmingham lads; excellent soldiers they made, although there were now in the battalion 350 untried youngsters under the age of 19. Sixty per cent of the 7th Queens, who for the moment were attached to the 53rd Brigade, were also boys under 19 who had never fired a round a week before. The spirit of them shines out in the example of a lad who, on 25th April, was wounded three times, but refused to go back. "No fear," he said, "I might get shot if I do. I'll stop where I am." There was also the small man of the 6th Northamptonshires, whom Captain Ashley, the Northants medical officer, met bringing back some prisoners. "How many prisoners have you?" asked Captain Ashley. "Twenty-one when I started, sir, but one of them handed in his ticket on the way down," replied the lad in brisk well-disciplined tones.

In the earlier part of the day the Germans held on tenaciously to the ground they had gained. Our first counter-attacks made no headway against their heavy artillery and machine-gun fire.

The batteries of the 83rd Brigade, R.F.A., who had been in position north of Villers-Bretonneux since the 22nd, were, with the scratch team known as "Shepherd's Force"—two companies of the 6th Northants, and units from other Divisions, under Major Shepherd of the 6th Northants—the first Divisional troops to come under fire on the 24th. "Shepherd's Force" held the line in front of Cachy, which village, owing to continuous bombardment, had become a mere heap of road-mending material.

x

Both "Shepherd's Force" and "B" Battery, 83rd
Brigade, made speedy acquaintance with the German
tanks. When the Boche infantry broke through,
one of the tanks came on until it was on top of the
barbed wire put up by Major Shepherd, and there it
stuck. The German infantry was driven off, and
"Shepherd's Force" brought in the tank as a trophy.
Later, when more Germans advanced to the assault,
and it looked as if "Shepherd's Force" would shortly
be struck off the strength of the British Army, several
of the new British light, fast tanks came out of the
Bois l'Abbé and went full steam ahead to meet the
enemy. These "Whippets" dashed to and fro among
the Germans, shooting and crushing them down. They
saved the situation, and to the 6th Northants' delight,
it was observed that the Tank Commander was none
other than Major T. R. Price, once Adjutant of the
6th Northants—the Price who won the D.S.O. at
Boom Ravine. Unfortunately Price was not able to
stay and receive the congratulations of his former
regimental comrades. Boche machine-gun bullets
found a way through the door of his tank; he was
wounded, and suffered severely.

The meeting of "B" Battery, 83rd Brigade, with
the German tanks was even more dramatic. The battery had 600 rounds per 18-pounder, and two forward
guns, under 2nd Lieutenant Butler, were placed behind the railway bank overlooking the Bois l'Abbé
and Villers-Bretonneux. Night firing was carried on.
Then at 3.45 A.M. the German barrage descended.
The officers' dug-out mess was blown in, and one
shell smashed the gunners' rum jar, which devastating
news was diplomatically kept from the men. Then
one of the two forward guns was knocked out, and
the horses came up under heavy shelling and took
it away.

"At 7 A.M.," says Lieutenant Butler, "machine-gun bullets
began to come, and we could see the 8th Division infantry
coming back in line. Wounded passed us and told us that

the enemy was in Villers-Bretonneux.   Then we saw the first of the tanks coming along the valley; there were five about 2,000 yards away, and they were followed by small batches of German infantry.

"My remaining gun engaged these, and the Boche infantry scattered like rabbits.   Four of the tanks disappeared in the direction of Bois l'Abbé, and one turned into a dip in the valley and was lost to view.

"After reporting to Lieut.-Colonel Hill of the East Lancs, who asked me to protect the withdrawal of his infantry, I ran my gun up on to the railway bank itself, where I could get better observation.   The 8th Division infantry then retired, leaving my gun as the 'front line,' and at this moment, about 9.45 A.M., a Boche tank suddenly appeared about 200 yards from the railway bank.

"I had my gun slewed round.   The tank still came on. Then when it was about 100 yards away, our first round was fired.   It fell short.   The second round—percussion shrapnel —burst right on top of the tank.   There was a large cloud of smoke, and the tank turned round and went into the dip again, just as our third round burst under its tail."

Lieutenant Butler then sent for his gun team, and while waiting for the horses, made the gun detachments and some of the infantry line the railway bank. As the gun was being driven away, a driver was killed by a rifle-shot.   Butler got up, took the driver's place, and brought his gun back to safety.   This gun had fired continuously for seven hours.   1,100 rounds were fired.

Twenty minutes after Butler had reached his retiring position, B/83 received the urgent message from Brigade: "Your ammunition return due at 8 A.M. not yet received.   Please hasten."   Fighting or no fighting, the machinery of war still had to be.

The night before the Boche attack of 24th April there had been a big farewell dinner at the 53rd Brigade Headquarters at St Fuscien, in honour of Brigadier-General Higginson's promotion to the command of the 12th Division.   General Lee had attended the function, and the party broke up at midnight.   At 3 A.M. windows in Boves were shaken by the thunder of bombardment, the morning mist was pierced by gun-flashes all along the front, and above our straggled lines was heard the whirr of German reconnoitring planes.

Roused by Captain James, V.C., the 53rd Brigade's new Brigade - Major, the 8th Berkshires, the 10th Essex, and the 7th West Kents turned out from comfortable billets and marched forward to where the struggle against the oncoming Boche rocked and swayed. The 10th Essex had a draft of eight new officers who had arrived the evening before. A brief spell of war's glories theirs! Within three days there remained only one of them who was not wounded or killed! It was in this phase of the defence of Amiens that J. C. Parke, the famous lawn-tennis player, came to the 10th Essex. He partnered Captain Peter Nunn at the head of "B" Company and soon fitted in. It was at this period also that Captain Runge proceeded to the 58th Division, and was succeeded as Brigade-Major to the 55th Brigade by that energetic, clear-thinking officer, Captain R. A. Chell.

Touch with the 8th Division was established. Then the news spread that the real task of the 18th was to be done that night, when the 54th Brigade would assist the Australians to recapture Villers-Bretonneux. The 7th West Kents were transferred from the 53rd Brigade for this memorable effort; and Colonel Hickson, riding forward with General Higginson to General Sadleir-Jackson's headquarters—a slit dug-out shielded by a mangel pile near a spinney north of Gentelles—learnt that the 54th Brigade was to attack between Cachy and Hangard Wood, Bedfords on the left, West Kents on the right, Northants in support linking up with the Australians' right. The Q.V. Rifles of the 58th Division were to advance on the right of the West Kents.

It was an attack in the dark, launched at 10 P.M. There was little definite information about the objective to be reached, except that it was 2,000 yards ahead, and General Higginson attached Captain James, the Brigade-Major, who by now knew the ground well, to assist Colonel Hickson. The artillery barrage was especially arranged—also because of the darkness. It opened 1,000 yards in front of the line from which the Bedfords and West Kents moved off, and they had half an hour in which to reach it. Then it jumped another 1,000 yards, and between 10.30 P.M. and 11 P.M. our troops had to move towards this line of falling shells. There was the extra difficulty that when the German reply barrage descended, it did not prove easy to distinguish which was their barrage and which was ours.

The Australians had the advantage of a definite line and discernible objectives; and fighting with that combination of dash, skill and individual resource which made them so singularly formidable, they won back the village of Villers - Bretonneux. The 7th Bedfords on the Australians' right twice had their dug-out headquarters—it was an aid post as well—blown out by German shells before they moved off. When they did start they came under machine-gun fire almost at once; but, pushing on, they reached a belt of our own wire—ground which the enemy had captured in the morning—and, trickling through, they dealt with a number of Germans in slits and shell-holes, many of whom gave themselves up. Then, in the darkness, now and again weirdly lit up by German star-shells, the Bedfords moved steadily on, until they rushed what they took to be their final objective and dug themselves in.

By this time only two Bedfords' officers were left, 2nd Lieutenant W. Tysoe and 2nd Lieutenant E. J. Scott, and they decided to halve the battalion front. 2nd Lieutenant Tysoe on the left had got in touch with the Australians, but 2nd Lieutenant Scott could find nothing but Germans. So he borrowed a platoon from the helpful Australians, and, sending out a patrol to his right, found that the enemy had begun to work

round behind the battalion. And there was another
danger! Ammunition was running out! And here
Private G. A. Hughes of the Bedfords did a gallant
and handy piece of work. One of our old ammunition
dumps was believed to be about 150 yards in front of
the line now occupied by his company. Hughes went
out, found the dump, then took out a carrying party
and brought back five boxes of the badly-needed
ammunition. The Boche shelling continued. It was
still dark; and the whole situation between Villers-
Bretonneux and the Bois Hangard remained disquiet-
ingly vague and threatening.

The 7th Royal West Kents to the right of the
Bedfords had also come quickly under heavy fire.
The enemy held forward shell-hole posts which had
entirely escaped our artillery barrage. 230 of the
West Kents were lost within an hour. "B" Company,
on the left, reached their objective, or got as near it
as they could identify in the pitch darkness, but
they had to send back Captain Lovatt wounded.
"A" Company reached the Villers-Bretonneux-
Domart road in the early hours of the morning. But
the West Kents were in touch neither with the
Bedfords on their left nor with the Q.V. Rifles of
the 58th Division on their right; and though it had
been reported that the Q.V. Rifles had got into Bois
Hangard, machine-gun bullets were fired at the
West Kents from that direction as day began to
break. Just after midnight a 58th Division dressing-
station in the north-east corner of Gentelles Wood
was blown in, and the medical officer and a number
of wounded were killed. During the night 80 stretcher
and 250 walking cases were dealt with by the 54th
Brigade Field Ambulance.

In the morning, Colonel Hickson found that with
only 160 rifles he was holding an 800 yards' front.
2nd Lieutenant Scott of the Bedfords had been
wounded and taken prisoner, and 2nd Lieutenant
Tysoe was alone and in command of the whole situation

on that part of the front.   But all that day the West
Kents and the Bedfords held the ground they had
won back, and when they were relieved by the famous
French Moroccan Division, they found their way back
towards Boves knowing they had done real work for
England.

Lieutenant Tysoe made Company Sergeant-Major
O. H. Kirby his second in command, and he divided
the remnants of the Bedfords into thirties, just
wherever they happened to be, with N.C.O.'s as
platoon commanders.   He sent back two runners
to report the position to battalion headquarters.
Nothing further was heard of these two men.   Two
more runners were sent.   In half an hour one of them,
Private A. G. Bailey, came back.   His tin hat and his
equipment were gone, but he described his experiences
with lucidity.   He and his companion had been attacked
by a Boche patrol, he said, and his companion had
been wounded.   He himself fired and hit three of the
enemy, and in the confusion slipped away.   His story
made it clear that the battalion was surrounded.
Moreover, the Australians reported to Lieutenant
Tysoe that their left flank was now in the air.   Long
minutes of doubt and uncertainty went by.   Soon
parties of Germans could be seen moving about in the
copse that surrounded the youthful Tysoe and his
little force.

But Tysoe and his troops, who averaged 19 years
of age, remained "full of heart."   When, at about
8 A.M., two Germans bearing a white flag approached,
the Bedfords took it that they had come in to announce
a surrender.

It was not so.   The chief visitor, a German sergeant-
major who spoke excellent English, told Lieutenant
Tysoe that he had come to demand that the Bedfords
should surrender to avoid further bloodshed.   The
German commander had instructed him to say that
the Bedfords were surrounded by two Divisions, and
would be blown out of the ground if they did not

yield. The sergeant-major added confidentially that he was to get the Iron Cross, First Class, if he could persuade the Bedfords to give in. Tysoe's reply was a refusal, but the Boche sergeant-major badly wanted an Iron Cross, and it was agreed that if he and the private who accompanied him liked to be blindfolded, they should be taken back to battalion headquarters to proffer their request there. So off they went under the escort of Company Sergeant-Major Burles and his batman. Of the escort, nothing was heard for some days, when it was learned that they had been wounded and taken back through another Division's area. The German emissaries were found wandering about our lines still blindfolded.

Another flag-party was seen coming across an hour or so later, but Lieutenant Tysoe refused to have anything to do with these visitors, and they turned back.

Tysoe then crept from shell-hole to shell-hole until he could speak to the nearest Australians, and he agreed with them to hang on. About noon an Australian Brigade attacked and captured the Bois l'Abbé and restored the situation on the left flank; but at 1 P.M. the German artillery shelled the Bedfords very heavily,—perhaps it was a following-up of the threat communicated by the German sergeant-major. Lieutenant Tysoe, crawling from shell-hole to shell-hole, organising his defence for the infantry attack which seemed imminent, fell into a slit on top of a German who was reading a document. Tysoe was first with his revolver. The Boche surrendered and was sent back to the Bedfords' headquarters.

The shelling and machine-gun fire continued, and towards dusk groups of Germans could be seen forming for an attack. They launched it just as darkness descended, and got through a gap in the wire on the right of Lieutenant Tysoe's force. But Tysoe ended the day victorious. He counter-attacked at once;

the youngsters who followed him used the bayonet
freely, and the enemy were driven off.

About midnight a message reached Lieutenant
Tysoe that the French were coming to relieve him ;
and at 4 A.M., reporting that the French were already
formed up behind for an attack, the Australians moved
off. So Tysoe and his men passed through the French
and went back to a deserved rest. Tysoe was awarded
the D.S.O., and the official account said with great
truth : " The fine example of gallantry and leadership
by this young officer was entirely instrumental in
holding the ground gained, with many young soldiers
who were in action for the first time."

But Amiens was not yet safe. The situation was
too haphazard for the Germans to be allowed to settle
on the line they occupied. Hangard Wood was still
in their possession. So the 10th Essex and the 7th
Queens were called upon to join in when the Moroccans,
among them the celebrated Foreign Legion, went
forward in their high-spirited way to the assault that
began at 5.15 A.M. on 26th April.

General Barker, General Higginson's successor as
Commander of the 53rd Brigade, came up to the front
for this attack. In a cramped headquarters in an old
practice trench, with a rough hurdle roofing so low
that it was impossible to sit upright, General Barker
had his first meeting with Colonel T. M. Banks and
the company commanders of the 10th Essex ; and
fealty was sworn over a cup of lukewarm cocoa. The
new General, who stood 6 feet 4, had started the war
as a captain in the Lincolnshire Regiment, and
was one of the youngest brigadiers in the army.
But it was not long before the 53rd Brigade got
to know him and to swear by him. His tirelessness,
his pride in his brigade, his dash, his very youth
proved to be great assets, particularly in the swift-
moving warfare of the Hundred Days. And he found
a rare brigade - major in gentle-voiced Captain H.
James, V.C., whose polite imperturbability could, on

occasion, flash out into steely forcefulness, electric in its effect.  On this grey misty morning of 26th April, James, in his determination to see that the 10th Essex and the 7th Queens were in their right forming-up positions, rode out on horseback in front of the assembled troops almost up to the German posts.

The taking of Hangard Wood, the hardest task of the day, had been left by the French to the two English battalions.  No sooner did their khaki lines show through the mist than up rose the Boche, and our men fell thick and fast.  But the Essex and Queens plodded on through the dense undergrowth ; the raw boys revealed steadiness and pluck.  Half Hangard Wood was taken and hung on to, and two days later the French completed the victory by a tank assault.  Amiens was never in serious danger afterwards.  Colonel Banks has written a peculiarly vivid personal narrative which well illustrates the nature of the fighting.

"Went over with the third wave, and had nearly reached the wood border, when ping! went something through my boot, and a sting in the big toe announced a gold stripe. Hit number one!

"Could see then that we were in for a rough passage, so pushed forward through the undergrowth to see things straight in the forward lines.  Bullets fairly zipping round, and vicious cracklings from all sides from Boche concealed in the brushwood.  Found that we were properly held up in one corner ; and the French suddenly started a rearward move-ment, which was spreading panic-like to our men ; but managed to stem this, and we held the ground gained. Nothing for it but to dig in here, so got the men busy, when bang! another bullet through the fringe of my sleeve, grazing my wrist, and killing a Frenchman behind.

"About this time my first runner became a casualty, so I went back to headquarters for reports and control, and got another one.  He, poor fellow, had a short life, for while I was trying to push through the wood to see whether any of our fellows had reached the further side, the Hun laid a trap for us which did him in.  We had got forward with a small

party, until we saw some figures beckoning us some fifty
yards ahead.  Thinking they were some of the leading
companies, I went on, until suddenly suspicions flashed over
me.  Got glasses out to see.  They were Boche!  Opened fire
on them at once, but the cunning blighters had a machine-gun
close up on our flank, and they let drive simultaneously.
Poor Church, a faithful friend of olden days, was killed at my
side by a shot through the head, and another rapid tear in
my sleeve announced a third hit.

"Remainder of that day and night was spent with reorganisation and consolidation.  Our worst plight was for officers.
Only four remained.  We were promised relief that night,
but it never came, so had to hang on till the following one.
Two hours of continuous strafing on the night of the 26th.
Only shell slits saved us from disintegration.  Relief came in
the shape of the French battalion Patriache at 2 A.M. on
28th April, and with a few more years on our lives we
stumbled through the darkness to the welcome of a sweet
couch on a grassy sward within a copse."

The Essex nearly lost J. C. Parke in this, his virgin
fight with the 10th.  He went out through hordes of
machine-guns to learn the situation, and he got caught,
with his runner wounded, in a shell-hole, within close
range of a vicious gun.  Parke got back and brought
his runner with him.  When Colonel Banks got down
to have his wounded toe attended to by Captain
Battin (U.S.A.) in a quarry aid post, the tension of
the time had so exhausted him that he fainted away
amongst the wounded waiting huddled together in the
candle-light.

The 7th Queens faced and overcame the same
difficulties as the 10th Essex.  When casualties from
machine-guns and snipers were so heavy that men
were beginning to waver, 2nd Lieutenant K. A. H.
Hassell collected the remnants of his own platoons
and of other units, including the French, and dug in
on a line that stood fast until relief came on the 27th.
2nd Lieutenant H. P. Clarke, finding himself the only
officer left on a 500 yards' sector, took command, and
as his party still suffered losses from rifle and machine-

gun fire, he led his men forward and cleared that part of the wood. He was hit in the head; but after having his wounds dressed, he returned to the front line and carried on the whole of the next day until the French relieved him. Lieutenant G. C. Evans not only made a reconnaissance that proved invaluable for securing the safety of the Queens, he also guided a party forward and wired the wood in front of the battalion's position. The whole story of 26th and 27th April well illustrates the general temper with which, at this most momentous period, all ranks obeyed Lord Haig's injunction to stick it out "with backs to the wall." Captain James, the 53rd's Brigade-Major, won his V.C. in Gallipoli, but in communicative moments he says he learned more soldiering in the Villers-Bretonneux fighting and in the sternest moments of the Hundred Days than in all his previous experience.

One episode remains. On the night of the 24th, when the West Kents went forward to help in the recapture of Villlers-Bretonneux, a youthful private, Private W. Megors, was in the first wave. He and a companion went right ahead and had to crouch in a shell-slit. Morning broke. Megors' companion reloaded his rifle, looked up, and was immediately shot through the head. Megors crawled further ahead, through the wire; he was so far forward that he was in advance of the West Kents' snipers and could hear the Germans talking. He lay in a shell-hole all through 25th April. It struck him that if he went back his own comrades might mistake him for a Boche and fire at him. He lay there until the French Foreign Legion swept forward for their attack on the morning of the 26th. When first he saw them their long coats made him think they must be Germans, and he wondered if in the night he had turned himself around. "I wanted to see one of them wounded and taken away," he explained, "so that I

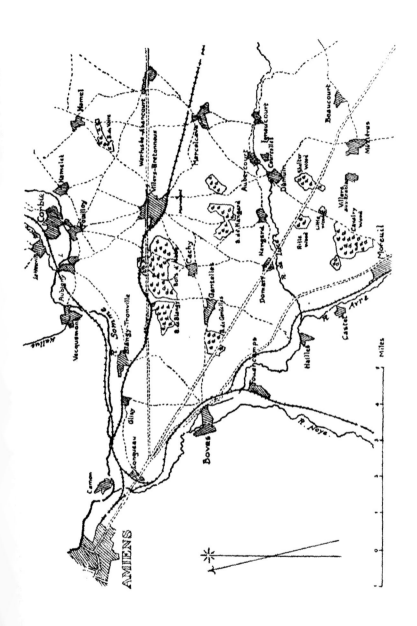

should know which way to go back to company head-quarters."

Colonel Hickson asked Megors what he thought of the Foreign Legion in attack. "What I noticed," says Megors, "was a Frenchman marching through the bullets, blowing a trumpet—as if he was enjoyin' himself."

During May, June, and July the Division held the line opposite Albert. There was much patrol work and a few minor raids, and the 54th Brigade in particular made a serious effort to oust the Germans from the defences at the north-west corner of Albert, known as the "hairpin" system. Generally speaking, British and Boche were testing each other's strength, preparing for the great battles that were to set the world ablaze later in the year. Troops of two American Divisions, the 29th and the 33rd, were sent to the 18th for training in front-line warfare. Colonel Wallace Wright left to become B.G.G.S. of the XVII. Corps, and Lieut.-Colonel Guy Blewitt took over the duties of G.S.O.1.

[The author is indebted to Captain P. A. B. Ashmead-Bartlett, M.C., G.S.O.3, for the large map of the Retreat from the Oise, and for the official narrative of the Retreat and the Defence of Amiens.]

# CHAPTER XXIII.

### 8TH AUGUST—THE BATTLE OF MORLANCOURT RIDGE.

*The secrecy of the 8th August attack—A historic race meeting—Astounding procession of ammunition—The German attack on 6th August—18th Division formed the protective flank for the Fourth Army attack—The death of Lieut.-Colonel Bushell, V.C.—The advance of the 10th Essex—A German battery captured—The mist and our wandering tanks—Germans heavy fire on the Berks—The Essex retirement, only fifteen survivors—Gressaire Wood not taken, but the Division had fulfilled its main task—Lieut.-Colonel Pritchard-Taylor, Lieut.-Colonel Banks, and the Americans.*

WHEN in the first days of August the Division took up a line astride the Bray-Corbie Road south-west of Morlancourt, the secret that the now historic attack east of Amiens was to be launched on 8th August was still in extraordinarily safe keeping.

During the fortnight's rest in the fir and gorse-clad stretch of country round Picquigny in the latter half of July, whispers had trickled through of an approaching British push in Flanders : tanks were known to be concentrating at St Pol, casualty clearing stations were being erected, Canadian troops were getting into line on the Kemmel front. We of the 18th Division did not know then that this was part of a giant plan to mislead the Boche as to Marshal Foch's real intentions, and perhaps to keep the secret from us as well. When on 19th July the newspapers burst forth into the heartening story of Foch's masterly counter-attack near Soissons, we did not realise that this marked the final passing of the initiative from the Boche to the Allies. True, it told that the German offensive was now definitely scotched, but it still seemed to be the *rôle* of the French and British to hold tight until the Americans could come in in force after the turn of the year.

Had we but known, how much keener would have been our speculations upon the apparently casual assembly at the 18th Divisional Race Meeting near Cavillon on 25th July of Sir Douglas Haig, of a well-known French staff-officer, and of Sir Henry Rawlinson, Commander of the 4th Army, which was to see more days of battle and gain more ground than any other Army during the HUNDRED DAYS OF VICTORY. It is known now that two days before that race-meeting upon the rolling uplands near Cavillon there had been a conference, at which Marshal Foch had asked that the British, French, and American Armies should prepare plans for local offensives to be taken in hand as soon as possible. Sir Douglas Haig, in his Victory Despatch of 21st December, states that he came to the conclusion that of the tasks assigned to the British forces, the disengagement of Amiens and the freeing of the Paris-Amiens Railway, by an attack on the Albert-Montdidier front, should take precedence as being the most important, and the most likely to give large results; he also wrote that on 28th July the French First Army, under the command of General Debeney, was placed by Marshal Foch under his orders for this attack; so that a place in serious history can really be claimed for that cheerful race-meeting to which Sir Douglas came without any official warning, where he walked about practically unattended, taking a more than keen interest in the racing, which many will remember for the spectacle of one race—"The Other Ranks"—in which were 60 odd starters, and not so many tumbles as one might have expected. At any rate it is certain that it provided a meeting-place for Haig and Rawlinson, at a moment when the most far-reaching decisions were being made. The only

hint of big things to come during the succeeding days
was when the Divisional Horse Show was suddenly
put forward a couple of days. General Lee was away
on leave, but a cryptic message brought him back a
day or two earlier than was expected, and by 1st
August the Division had marched along the Albert-
Amiens road through Heilly, of 1916 tea - shop
memories, and settled into its appointed area.

The rest, the fine weather, and the reunions of the
fortnight out of the line had wrought a change in the
spirit of the Division. The bitter bewilderments of
the March retreat, the deadly anxiousness of the
stubborn defensive fighting in Villers-Bretonneux,
the Bois Hangard and the village of the same name,
had been put behind ; so had the nervous apprehen-
sion of the watching and waiting in the Albert sector
in May and June, when large reinforcements of
untried lads, and of home troops who had never
heard a shot fired, had to be blooded. The sports,
the football contests, the meetings with men of other
battalions, had meant a strengthening of *esprit de
corps*. The newcomers had learnt more of the traditions and past achievements of the Division. There
was a new note of buoyancy, confidence, and expectation. The training of the 27th and 33rd American
Divisions by attachment to battalions in the line also
had a psychological effect, and the knowledge that
many more Americans were arriving added greatly to
the moral of our men.

Never had the Division participated in a battle
which was kept so secret. The general plan was
communicated to brigade and battalion commanders
on 3rd August, and it was emphasised that only
certain officers should be informed ; no other officers,
N.C.O.'s, or men were to be allowed to learn the
date and scope of the operation. In this respect
the artillery had a particularly difficult task. By
the night of 7th August 600 rounds per 18-
pdr., and 500 rounds per 4·5 howitzer, had been

conveyed to the positions from which the batteries would open fire on the morning of 8th August. As these positions were in view of the enemy, there was no preliminary digging of gun-pits, no earth was allowed to be upturned; reconnaissance had to be reduced to a minimum; the guns themselves were not to be moved up until the night of the 7th. Also the thousands of rounds of ammunition had to be taken up under cover of darkness, and sorted and stacked, and hidden beneath hedges, under banks, among the uncut cornfields. The roads through Mericourt and Heilly on the night of 3rd August offered an unforgettable spectacle; hour after hour, through blinding torrents of rain, there moved an unending stream of ammunition waggons. For three nights these astounding processions continued. But in spite of them—in spite even of the Boche surprise attack of 6th August—the great secret did not leak out.

On a still night the creaking of the wheels of ammunition waggons can be heard a mile away. So still further to deceive the enemy, wheel tyres were lapped with rope, leather washers muffled the play of wheels, along parts of the Bray-Corbie road straw was laid, as in towns it is laid outside houses where the seriously ill are lying. The tanks, which also are noisy movers, were not brought into the area until the very eve of the battle.

Preparations for the attack were practically complete; General Lee and his staff were satisfied that nothing which should be done had been left undone. The sharp bursts of fire that on three mornings the enemy had put down on our front line, suggested that he was apprehensive and nervy; confidence that the Division was about to give a notably good account of itself grew stronger and stronger. Then suddenly on 6th August came perturbation, if not dismay. The Boche made a swift violent attack, and penetrated a thousand yards behind the line which the Division held astride the Bray-Corbie road.

The Boche assault came at a peculiarly awkward
moment, during an incompleted side-stepping relief.
On the day of battle the 58th Division was to range
itself alongside the 18th Division north of the Somme;
but in furtherance of the policy of keeping dormant
the suspicions of the enemy, this change was not to
be made until dawn on 6th August. So on the
night of 5th August the 54th Brigade were to hand
over to the 58th Division the part of the line from
the Somme northwards that had been held by the
2nd Bedfords. The 2nd Bedfords in their turn were
to side-step north, and take over the ground held by
the East Surreys, as far as the Bray-Corbie road.
The Bedfords were remaining in the line in order to
preserve quite fresh the 11th Royal Fusiliers and the
6th Northants, who were to be the 54th Brigade
storming battalions in the actual battle. The 55th
Brigade, Brigadier-General E. A. Wood, for whom
the 7th Buffs held the line still farther north, were
keeping the 7th Queens clear of all fighting until
the day, as it was this battalion's part to form a defensive flank on the left of the Division, and thus on
the extreme left of the Fourth Army.

It was not an ideal line to hold. There were
numerous winding and puzzling trenches, captured
from the Boche by the Australians in the raiding
fights in which the Australian was such a master; but
they were only knee-deep—the Australians had not
allowed the Boche to do more digging than that—
and the heavy rains since the 18th Division relieved
the Australians had churned them into sticky messes
reminiscent of Regina Trench, Flanders, and Schwaben
Redoubt. The night of the 5th was dark, and there
was to be no moon; it was obvious that the 58th
Division should take over as early as possible. At
first it was arranged that the 8th Londons, of the
58th Division, who were going into the line, should
meet the Bedfords' guides at 8.15 P.M., but the appointed time was put back, and it was 10 P.M., and

pitch dark, when the relief of the Bedfords actually began. The incoming troops of the 8th Londons were very tired, and by 3.30 A.M. on the 6th the C.O. 2nd Bedfords, realising that he could not relieve the East Surreys as arranged, sent word that he would carry out the relief by daylight.

But by 4.20 A.M. the 8th Londons were still coming up, while Major Baddeley of the East Surreys had as yet seen only a few runners from the Bedfords. It was at this moment that German guns of all calibres burst forth into a fierce bombardment of the Divisional front; long-range shells that played havoc in the Somme Valley as far west as Vaux-sur-Somme, and in the Ancre Valley as far as Heilly, showed that the German effort was on a big scale. Ten minutes later the German infantry came over, moving forward on a two-mile front. Wet and tired, in an unsettled state because the relief had not worked according to programme, outnumbered by four battalions of the German 27th Division, a storm Division which had been out of the line practising intensive training for upwards of three months, our men were flung back ; and by 5 A.M. the Boche had got as far as the quarry along the Bray-Corbie road, north of Cemetery Copse, which Royal Engineers had been preparing as a battle headquarters for Brigadier-General Sadleir-Jackson.

Recovering from the first shock, our troops retaliated upon the Boche, and within half an hour the 2nd Bedfords had cleared him out of the quarry and taken a number of prisoners ; while by 9.45 A.M. further attacks by East Surreys, and by the 6th Northants, who had been immediately pushed forward by Colonel Turner to fill the gap between the Bedfords and the East Surreys, resulted in the retaking of half the ground that had been lost.

But the moment was an exceedingly anxious one. The Boche had swept over ground dotted everywhere with ammunition which was to be used on 8th August. He had taken prisoners. It seemed certain now that

he must know something of our plans for 8th August.
All through that day there was hard trench fighting;
reports as to the line the Division occupied varied
from hour to hour.  It was inevitable that there must
be a change of plan, and of the times fixed for the
attack on the 8th.  General Lee decided that the
main consideration now was to fix upon and secure a
forming-up line for the attacking battalions on the
8th; so, to ensure the Burke Line as an assembly
trench, he ordered General Sadleir-Jackson to attack
at dawn on 7th August, and to recapture the Cummins-
Cloncurry Trenches, which were situated well to the
east of Burke Line.  A stray shell wounded Major J.
C. Willis, the young, very able, and zealous commander
of the Divisional Signal Company.  To the great grief
of all who knew him, he died the following day in
Vignacourt hospital.

Meanwhile preparations for the big offensive of
8th August went on smoothly, and with an added
note of determination.

Had the Bedfords got to the quarry alongside the
Bray-Corbie road a few minutes earlier, they might
have been in time to rescue the party of sappers who
had looked up from the shaft they were building for
General Sadleir-Jackson to find Germans standing at
the top.  Their officer, Lieutenant Mackay, groped
for a rifle, and was immediately wounded by one of the
two bombs which the German raiders threw down
the shaft, after which the party was marched off as
prisoners.  One of them, Corporal W. A. Gregor of
the 80th Field Company, describes with pointed detail
his subsequent escape.  The party were taken to a
Boche headquarters near Suzanne, later to Caudry,
on the other side of the Hindenburg Line, where
they were kept six weeks, and then to Le Quesnoy.

"After four days in Le Quesnoy," he says, "we
were marched to the station and bundled into some
cattle-trucks (forty-five men in each truck), and we
stayed in the trucks for thirty-two hours before the

train moved. While in the train we were given two meals per day. I was on very friendly terms with a C.S.M. in the D.L.I., and on the morning of our second day in the train I told him I was fed-up, and intended making a move. The train moved off at eight that night, and it was rather dark, and I saw my opportunity, and took it. Every one had got down for the night, and as I made for the ventilator I stood on any one and anything. The result was 'language'; but I reached the ventilator and squeezed through, and dropped on to the line. I heard another fall, and after keeping still for a few minutes went to see who it was, and found it was a corporal of the 1/21 London Regiment who had been in the same truck as myself, and who had followed me out. We agreed to make for the lines together, and we travelled all that night as hard as we could (this was the night of 5th October).

"Just before daybreak we came across an old trench and the beginning of a shaft — there were eight frames fixed—so we decided to spend the day there. We did, and I never spent a worse day in all my life ; until darkness came we dared not move.

"During the day I had determined to use the road and risk being spoken to, so I put a few stones in my pocket in case of accidents. On the second night we got along fine, risked everything, and passed through the heart of two villages, one of which was rather large, full of M.T. and soldiers, and just before daybreak we came to another village that was under our own shell-fire. After making quite certain which were the Boche billets, we filled a 'rabbits' hutch' with straw, got inside, and made ourselves as comfortable as possible between the straw. We slept well that day, and after dusk went round two or three gardens and got some turnips to keep us going and to eat during the following day.

"We got going again, and thought it best to keep to the fields now,—what an experience ! After going some distance we came to a large dump, and made up our minds to go straight through it, as we might run up against a sentry if we tried to walk round it; so we crawled along and eventually got through, the time seeming like hours, or rather days.

"Our next job was to make our way across the fields and to watch for and keep clear of the guns—this we did with a lot of luck. We had travelled some distance, and the Very lights seemed to be only about eight kilos away when we struck a canal and could not see any signs of a bridge, so we walked along the tow-path in the direction of the line, and had gone about 500 yards when our progress was pulled up with a jerk, for some one spoke, and looking round I saw it was a Boche sentry.

"Well, I know very little German, so I merely said 'Ja,' as if I were annoyed, and we hurried on.

"I cannot imagine the thought of the sentry, as he never attempted to stop us; and as we saw a bridge in front of us we kept going and got across.

"We now came to the most trying part of our journey: we were nearing the line and never knew what we might walk into, but we seemed to be blessed with luck, for we passed two parties from the front and lay low in the grass until they had passed. The lights were now much nearer, and we had to keep still when they were fired, and when they went out, walk forward almost double so as to make as small a target as possible in case we were spotted. Quite suddenly we heard a cough in front of us, and dropped flat, crawling forward to see what and who it was. We found a sunken road, manned by two sentries about fifty yards apart, so we got between them, crawled down one bank, across the road, and up on the other side (more sweat). After crawling for about sixty yards among thistles, &c., we thought we'd try to walk again. Almost immediately two rifles cracked, and we dropped and then crawled along as quickly as we could.

"Our next job was to find our own posts; the lights from the Boche had told us that we were actually in No Man's Land. I determined to go slowly now, as I did not want to be shot by our own men, and just as day was breaking we made for a small copse from which we could observe without being observed, and when we reached it we saw one of our posts about 200 yards to our right front. The Boche line was about 800 yards to our rear, so we kept on crawling until we got within hailing distance. We then let the men in the post know who we were, and finished the journey at the double on the morning of 4th October. We were given drink and food, and then sent farther back."

The counter-attack on 7th August served its purpose, although it was not thoroughly successful. One company of the Bedfords and one company of the Northants gained the objective on the right, so did the company of the East Surreys on the extreme left; but the enemy maintained a wedge in the left centre of our line opposite the Royal Fusiliers, and though hard fighting went on till 6 P.M., during which time the Fusiliers threw over one hundred boxes of bombs, and the 54th and 55th Trench Mortar Companies kept the Boche on the stretch with Stokes mortars, he was not dislodged. However, sufficient ground was retaken to ensure the position of the required forming-up line; thirty prisoners and a number of machine-guns were captured, while the enemy, besides suffering heavy casualties, also found himself burked in the making of a fresh strong attack.

There was one unfortunate result of the severity of the fighting. It unfitted the 54th Brigade for a share in the battle of 8th August; their place had to be taken at short notice by the 36th Brigade (Brigadier-General C. S. Owen, C.M.G.) of the 12th Division, who were, of course, unfamiliar with the ground over which the advance was to be made.

The air that night was moist and heavy. The

Boche gunners were not slow to observe this, and from 9 P.M. onwards gas-shelled the Bray-Corbie road, and the road through Treux and east of Mericourt-l'Abbé, along which the batteries were moving up, greatly hampering them. In the early morning, too, the battery positions were plied with enemy H.E. Several horses were killed while bringing the guns up, an officer of "A" Battery, 82nd Brigade R.F.A., Lieutenant Leadbetter, died from wounds in this preliminary work, while the 83rd Brigade R.F.A. had 5 officers and 79 men badly gassed in the opening stages of the fight. The 11th Royal Fusiliers had their American Medical Officer, Lieutenant J. F. Baldwin, killed during the assembly. Uncertainty was in the air, and zero hour was awaited with the feeling that a stiff task lay ahead. The thought running through all minds was : How much has the Boche learned of our plans ?

At 4.20 A.M., 8th August, the guns supporting the attack of General Rawlinson's Fourth Army burst forth into a tornado of flame and sound upon an eleven-mile front, from just south of the Amiens-Roye road to the southern edge of the ruined village of Morlancourt, which lay 1,000 yards from the extreme left of the 18th Divisional front. To the 18th Division was apportioned the vital task of securing the high ground along the Bray-Corbie ridge, thus forming a protective flank for the main Fourth Army attack. If this ridge could not be obtained and held the advance south of the Somme would be imperilled.

A heavy, grey, ground mist, something like that which cloaked the operations of the Boche infantry on 21st March, lay over the battle area. Maybe on this occasion it bewildered the enemy, but it was also the chief reason why our tanks failed to turn up in time ; this, combined with the disturbance of our plan, caused by the Boche attack of 6th August, was the reason why the day was not so fruitful for the 18th Division as had been hoped. Six tanks had been allotted to accompany the 7th Queens when they moved to the attack. It was their mission to seize the ground north of the Bray-Corbie road, to preserve the Division's left flank. Meantime the 7th Royal Sussex and the 9th Royal Fusiliers, who were taking the place of the 54th Brigade, advanced due east. Considering that they knew nothing at all of the front on which they were operating, and had come in at such short notice, the 12th Division Infantry did more than well. They retook the ground lost on the 6th and cleared the old British trenches. But, in spite of losing over 20 officers and some 500 men, they did not reach the first objective, the road running between Morlancourt and Malard Wood, a task which was completed by the 10th Essex when they leap-frogged the 36th Brigade.

The earliest feature of the battle was the almost complete silencing of the enemy's long-range guns. Hardly a shell fell in our back areas. Our own field batteries suffered casualties from shell-firing in the opening quarter of an hour, but subsequently the Boche gunners became more or less passive.

When the 10th Essex advanced, they found stiff work before them in the road that constituted the first objective. The Boche machine-guns were well placed, and the men of the 27th German Division, men of spirit and magnificent physique, fought unyieldingly. It cost the Essex the best part of 200 men, but they conquered, and in the fog went forward to the final objective, leaving the 36th Brigade to follow up and consolidate the road which had been the opening objective.

The 7th Queens were undergoing a bad time. They came upon machine-gun nests within a short distance of their start-off line, and they missed the tanks again when they ran up against enemy machine-guns in Cloncurry Trench, which was part of the line the Division had lost on 6th August. By 7 A.M. it was plain that the Queens were a long way from their objective, and their C.O., Lieut.-Colonel Christopher

Bushell, not long recovered from the wounds that had accompanied his glorious winning of the Victoria Cross on 23rd March, went forward from Battalion Headquarters to cope with the situation. His presence inspired his men to a supreme effort. Cloncurry Trench was carried by bomb and bayonet, and when the mist cleared, with the tanks now lurching into sight, it looked as if all difficulties would be overridden. Colonel Bushell had encouraged the men with news that the attack was going well on other parts of the front. He had directed one tank, and was crossing the open grass-lands to point the way to a second tank. A sniper's bullet sang out, and the Colonel fell, shot through the neck. His runner, Private A. E. Morris, a gallant soldier whose knowledge of the country was instinctive, who earlier in the day had led the advance platoons to their assaulting positions, and had been at Colonel Bushell's elbow when he first came to clear up the situation, rushed across the open to where the Colonel lay. Though the ground across which he carried the Colonel was swept by hostile machine-gun fire, he brought him in. But it was a heroism that counted for nothing. Colonel Bushell had been fatally wounded.

Colonel Bushell had sacrificed his life, but his inspiring leadership had saved the situation. Greatly cast down though they were, the Queens did not forget his exhortations. They stuck to their task, in spite of harassing Boche attacks from Morlancourt. When about noon the 9th Fusiliers of the 12th Division rushed a machine-gun pocket of the enemy who were holding out near the Bray-Corbie road, and captured an officer, thirty men, and three machine-guns, the pressure on the Queens was released, and they held on for the rest of the day.

Colonel Bushell was the very finest type of the officer who had been a civilian before the war. He had seen General Lee just before going forward to join his men; the General told him he had a difficult and hazardous task; but he was full of the highest courage.

In a beautiful and wonderful letter which Mrs Bushell wrote to General Lee after hearing of her husband's death, she said:—

> "My husband wrote the night before the attack that it was going to be a 'magnificent show,' and indeed I think it was. In spite of all the unspeakable pain and loss, I am simply filled with pride and thankfulness for all he was and for his inspiration, which can never die. It is the end he would have asked for, I know—to lead his beloved men against heavy odds to victory.
>
> "I am so proud of the Division he belonged to, and knew to be unrivalled. Please accept my sympathy for you in the loss of a gallant officer—one among so many."

Meanwhile the 10th Essex, leaving the 36th Brigade in possession of the first objective, forged ahead. It was a weird sort of advance; the grey fog still clung to the ground. Lieut.-Colonel T. M. Banks, Major Forbes, and the eighty men left, after their losses in the road between Morlancourt and Malard Wood, seemed as they crossed the open fields to be cut off from the rest of the world. They were not in touch with the West Kents on their left; they had encountered no Boche. Hugging the Bray-Corbie road, they threaded their way, guided by the machine-gun fire on either side. When they had advanced 1,000 yards they halted. Boche machine-guns could now be heard firing directly behind them. Colonel Banks deliberated within himself; and then allowed his line of conduct to be guided by the maxim " when in doubt, kill Boche." He gave orders for the march through the mist to be continued.

The 10th Essex had advanced 2,500 yards; there was still no communication with West Kents nor

Berks. All at once the mist lifted, and Colonel Banks
and his men found themselves within a few hundred
yards of the northern continuation of Gressaire Wood.
What was more enlivening still, they were on top
of two Boche 4-gun batteries, one a whizz-bang, the
other a 4·2 battery. The Boche gunners were taking
an easy; they believed our attack to be merely a
local raid on their front trenches. They were men
of fine stature, much bigger than the youths who
composed the remnants of Colonel Banks's force. But
they were too knocked off their balance to put up
any resistance; the surprise was complete. Soon the
Essex men were receiving souvenirs, mostly revolvers
and field-glasses; and Colonel Banks, having few men
to spare, sent his prisoners back in charge of a
wounded man. As the party started off, Colonel
Banks called out a final order; the prisoners, startled
and afraid, thought that the Colonel had decided that
it would be a wise solution to shoot them. The
Boche mind has faith in the efficacy of gifts—and,
in their distress, those of the prisoners who had
nothing else to offer pulled off their boots, and with
ingratiating gestures laid them at the Colonel's feet.
The Colonel, like a good opportunist, appreciated that
a bootless Boche would find it difficult to run away;
so he accepted the boots, and sent off the prisoners
in their stocking feet.

With time now to study landmarks, the Colonel was
satisfied that he was on his final objective. What
puzzled him most was the extraordinary solitariness
of the neighbourhood. Not a soul was in sight; larks
were singing overhead. The 10th Essex seemed to
be beyond the zone of battle. The two Boche
batteries were so well camouflaged that they had not
shown on the aeroplane photographs.

Colonel Banks felt that if the Berks came along as
undisturbed as he had done, and touch could be obtained with the West Kents, the day would end in
triumph for the Division. He sent back news that he

was on his final objective, set his men to dig in, and waited. It was now 7.20 A.M. Half an hour later he received word that Captain A. V. Macdonald, of the West Kents, in spite of the difficulties caused by the Queens hold-up, had come along the Bray-Corbie road as far as the brickyard. Two tanks, arriving near the Bray-Corbie road three hours after zero, had put terror into the Boche, and had helped the West Kents to take prisoners. Captain Macdonald, tall, athletic, possessed of a spirit that was at its highest in actual battle—he was destined to do more good work before the HUNDRED DAYS were completed—had achieved a real success in linking up with the 10th Essex, but his force was now a very weak one.

Suddenly through his glasses Colonel Banks observed a couple of Boche guns in Gressaire Wood, and realised that the Berks were not yet in possession. Before long he was to discover that a Boche reserve battalion was in the wood, and that his own right flank was bare. Still, here he was with his second in command, Major Forbes, and his eighty men. He again reported the situation to Brigade Headquarters, and awaited developments. There was still an extraordinary calm on this part of the front. Occasionally our heavies dropped shells just beyond where the Essex were digging in, and into the wood beyond. The major commanding the guns taken by the Essex had his quarters in a dug-out in the wood, and knew nothing of their capture. He had spent a peaceful morning, believing that the British attack was a purely local one, and he thought that it had now died away. But a message from the German headquarters farther back informed him that things were much more serious, and that his guns must maintain their fire. He came unsuspectingly out of the wood into the sunshine, walking easily, a big hairy fellow, flicking the heads of the standing corn with his cane and smoking a cigarette. His first inkling that he was now without a battery came when he found a

dozen rifles levelled at him; his calmness did not
entirely leave him, but he became almost obsequious
in his politeness to Colonel Banks. "I am your
prisoner, sir," he said with some show of anxiety.
Without delay he was sent back a prisoner, but his
300 yards' walk to where his battery had been altered
the situation for the 10th Essex. Boche observers in
Gressaire Wood saw what had happened, and from
500 yards' range a field-gun opened fire on Colonel
Banks and his party.

The position of the 10th Essex was now a serious
one. Germans from Morlancourt were counter-attacking the West Kents, who, with a greatly reduced
force, were lined on their portion of the 2,500 yards'
flank. Enemy firing was going on behind the Essex.
On the right, the young lads of the Berks, who in the
fog had at first taken direction from the corn and
grass trampled down by the advancing 36th Brigade,
had come along at good speed, but without the expected tanks. Of the twenty tanks allotted to co-
operate with the 53rd Brigade, 6 had been put out of
action before reaching the original front line, and none
of them arrived on the first objective in time to move
off with the Berks and Essex. One tank did indeed
reach the southern edge of Gressaire Wood; but by
the time the fog lifted, when they might have been
of real assistance, most of the tanks had run short of
petrol. Colonel N. B. Hudson experienced more and
more difficulty in shepherding his troops in the mist,
but he continued to move ahead—when without warning he found himself within fifteen yards of half a dozen
Boche machine-guns. He dashed forward, but from
ten yards' distance was hit in five places—on the legs
and in the body—and underwent more than a miracu-
lous escape. The ground hereabouts was criss-crossed
with roads and trenches. Somehow he scrambled
back behind a bank and was attended by his men.
When the fog lifted it was certain that the Berks had
reached the western edge of Gressaire Wood. But

the enemy had discovered them, and a tremendous fire opened from machine-guns, and from a field-gun a thousand yards away. Colonel Hudson was got away by his orderly, and the Berks remained forty minutes before—having had six officers and eighty-two men wounded and twenty-one men killed—they withdrew at 9 A.M. to the line of the first objective. While being assisted down, Colonel Hudson came suddenly behind thirty Boche in a trench, gazing towards our original front line; but he escaped capture by flinging himself down among the standing corn and working a painful way round them.

By this time Colonel Banks had learned that he could hope for no further assistance. At 9 A.M. he was counter-attacked from Gressaire Wood. It was a bitter thought that he would have to give ground when complete success seemed to be so near, but his right was being encircled, and more counter-attacks were being delivered upon the West Kents on his left rear. He had remained three hours on his final objective, but there was nothing for it now but to withdraw and establish touch with the companion battalions. He did what damage he could to the breech-blocks of the Boche guns. Then, marching steadily, with Boche machine-guns closing in on both flanks, the eighty men of the 10th Essex began their 2,000 yards' march back. It was touch and go at one stage; a bottle-neck of about 300 yards had to be straggled through under a withering machine-gun fire. When they reached the line of the first objective, and at last found themselves in touch with the Berks and West Kents, the 10th Essex had dwindled to a party of fifteen, and Major Forbes had been wounded.

The Essex casualties numbered 290 that day, against the 166 of the Berks, and the 192 of the West Kents. The Queens, with 256 casualties, were the second severest sufferers in the Division.

It was on this line that the fighting for the day ended. The enemy inaugurated a counter-attack on

the left at about 6.30 P.M., but our Divisional Artillery
and machine-gun observers were too alert for them,
and the effort was crushed by artillery, machine, and
Lewis gun fire, before it could gather strength. The
line was held that night by the 55th Brigade on the
left and the 36th Brigade on the right, to whom were
attached the 7th West Kents under Major Philipps.
The 53rd Brigade were withdrawn into Divisional
Reserve.

The Division had failed in its endeavour to capture
Gressaire Wood, but in spite of the heavy losses and
the disappointments of the day, it had fulfilled its
main task—that of denying to the enemy the high
ground along the Bray-Corbie road, thus protecting
the Fourth Army forces south of the Somme, which had
advanced between six and seven miles. By nightfall
the enemy was blowing up dumps in all directions,
while his transport and limbers were streaming eastwards. 13,000 prisoners and over 300 guns had been
taken by the Fourth Army, while farther south the
French Army, attacking on a four-mile front, enjoyed
a haul of 3,350 prisoners. On the first day of the
HUNDRED DAYS advance the Paris-Amiens Railway
had been disengaged and the way opened to three
months' unbroken Victory.

On the evening of 9th August, the 12th Division
attacked through the 18th Division, and, with the
33rd American Division, gained a line east of Chipilly-
Morlancourt and Dernancourt.

The really fascinating war history would reveal the
play of mind and character in certain moments of
stress and need for decision. A case in point ! On
10th August, Lieut. - Colonel Pritchard - Taylor,
R.A.M.C., of the 54th Field Ambulance, was upon the
Bray-Corbie ridge, making sure that the British
wounded on 8th August had all been picked up and
got away. He found himself among the infantry of
the American 33rd Division, who now held the line.
From the foremost American shell-slits the ground

sloped up a mile away to a scrub-covered rise that
looked down upon the Bray valley. A great inactivity
had settled upon the front. In particular, the scrub-
covered rise seemed a haven of solitude and quiet.
The Americans were not certain whether Boche were
there or not.

Now Colonel Pritchard-Taylor, R.A.M.C., pos-
sesses certain qualities that would be in accord
with the best attributes of a first-class battalion
commander. He is forceful, quick in action, fearless,
and has an understanding of country. It struck him
that the scrubby ridge must be valuable for observation purposes. He made known his thoughts to an
American company commander. Being an unwilling
non-combatant he could do no more.

But there was nothing to prevent his galloping
back to where Brig.-General Barker had his headquarters, the quarry that was in Boche possession for
half an hour on 6th August; and it was natural that
he should narrate what he had seen. "I believe the
Boche is a couple of thousand yards from the present
front line," he observed.

General Barker's mind works very quickly. In
five minutes Lieut.-Colonel T. M. Banks—who, after
the wearing excitement of 8th August, was staying
at Brigade Headquarters while his battalion was being
brought up to strength—had set out to look into the
situation. And what more to be expected than that
Colonel Pritchard-Taylor should accompany him!
"I was supposed to be taking a rest," says Colonel
Banks. "Instead I plunged into ten minutes of the
keenest emotionalism. The American company commanders were very willing to accept suggestions. I
told them that I knew the country, and offered to
conduct a patrol party up the ridge. It seemed
pretty clear that the Boche believed us to be already
in possession there. We went gingerly at first, taking cover and making little darts forward. Finally
we reached the cross-roads at the top, and saw our

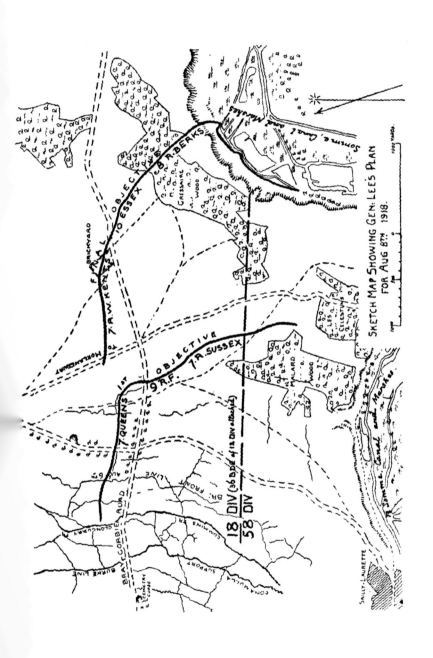

SKETCH MAP SHOWING GEN: LEE'S PLAN FOR AUG 8TH 1918.

first Boche—at the foot of the slope on the other side. There was just one thing to do. We—or rather the Americans—must dig in and make sure of that crest before the Boche could realise we were not there already."

And undoubtedly it was Colonel Pritchard-Taylor, R.A.M.C., who was observed hastening back to the American lines, the very moment that Colonel Banks said it was imperative that a couple of Lewis guns should be brought to the cross-roads. Colonel Taylor has his own methods of suasion; be that as it may, the American Lewis guns and their teams came towards the crest at the double.

"At the end it was a race between the Boche and the Americans," says Colonel Banks. "I got rather qualmish at one point. I lay there watching, and then noticed several parties of Boche creeping up through the undergrowth. We had a dozen rifles amongst us, and it was our policy to fire as heavily as we could, so as to deceive the Boche as to our real strength. But they kept getting closer, and eventually brought a machine-gun into action. The last five minutes became quite anxious ones. If the Boche had rushed the final fifty yards he would have carried the hill - top. His caution saved us. When the American Lewis gunners did arrive they performed very stoutly, and even drove off a German field-gun. When I came away they were digging-in and receiving reinforcements. I felt very glad that it was all over.

"I ought to add that we had come so far forward that our own heavies dropped shells behind us; it became very necessary to inform them of the fact. You will not be surprised to learn that Pritchard-Taylor carried out this life-saving mission. He passed the news through a field-battery telephone, and then went back to resume his due and proper work."

# CHAPTER XXIV.

## THE CAPTURE OF ALBERT, 1918.

*Resumption of the Fourth Army attack on 22nd August—54th Brigade get across the Ancre before zero hour—A daring impromptu that saved many lives — German battalion headquarters captured — Captain Doake of the Bedfords on Shamrock Hill—The East Surreys in Albert—General Sadleir-Jackson wounded.*

A PAUSE for rest and preparation followed the varying fortunes of the early days of August 1918. Then came for the 18th Division the dramatic events of 22nd August. The attack of the British Third Army to the north preceded that of the British Fourth Army and the French First Army on the front between Albert and Montdidier by forty-eight hours. When the offensive was resumed on the Fourth Army front on 22nd August the 18th Division was holding the line in the Albert sector on a two-brigade front. The 12th Division was on the right of the 18th, with the 38th Division of the V. Corps of the Third Army on the left. The enemy was holding the line of the Ancre in strength, with Albert as a bridgehead. The general *rôle* assigned to the 18th Division was that of covering the flank of the main attack of the Fourth Army by taking Albert and the high ground east of the town.

The 54th Brigade held the more southerly part of the Divisional line extending from the Ancre about 500 yards east of Dernancourt along the railway to the southern outskirts of Albert ; the 6th Northamptons lay on the right, and the 11th Royal Fusiliers

on the left, while the 2nd Bedfords were in reserve.
The 55th Brigade—8th East Surreys on the right,
7th Queens on the left, and 7th Buffs in reserve—
carried the line northwards through the western outskirts of the town as far as the Ancre floods between
Albert and Aveluy. The western outskirts of Albert
had been evacuated by the enemy a fortnight before,
but the greater portion of the town was still in his
hands and was formidably held.

The attack of the 18th Division was to develop
from south to north. One company of the 6th
Northants, aided by four tanks, was to advance at zero
hour along the Dernancourt-Meaulte road and gain
a footing on the rise east of Vivier Mill simultaneously with the advance of a battalion of the 12th
Division, aided by tanks, to the capture of Meaulte.
While this was going on a heavy barrage was to
be placed along the Divisional front east of the
Ancre until zero plus 30, when that part of it south
of Albert would move east to allow the remaining
companies of the 6th Northants and the 11th Royal
Fusiliers to force a passage of the stream north of
Vivier Mill and make the line of the Western Albert-
Meaulte road while that road was being patrolled by
tanks.

The ruins of Albert—as every one who visited the
town during the war will recall—were honeycombed
with cellars which offered admirable facilities for
defence; and they were cunningly and thoroughly
manned and equipped. Our fighting patrols had
learned that on the numerous occasions on which they
had endeavoured to penetrate the town; and it was
to be demonstrated once more—happily for the last
time—in the obstinate resistance offered on 22nd
August.

Farther south the crossing of the river was quite
likely to prove another hard task, for the Boche
had destroyed all the bridges, so that the operation involved the carrying up of bridging material

to enable infantry and horse transport to get across a stream 14 feet wide and 6 feet deep, with wet and marshy ground on either bank, heavily cut up by shell-fire, and the enemy waiting in some strength in the neighbourhood of the Albert-Meaulte road.

The objective of the 54th Infantry Brigade was Shamrock Hill and the spur running down to the eastern exit of Meaulte. To the 55th Brigade was allotted the task of capturing the town of Albert, and this operation was divided into three distinct phases.

> *First Phase.*—Zero to zero plus 60 minutes, when the whole of the town east of the Ancre was submitted to a heavy bombardment. During this period the 8th East Surreys were to work their way to the Ancre, "mopping-up" such parties of the enemy as were west of the river.
>
> *Second Phase.*—A heavy bombardment of certain strong points at the eastern edge of the town, from zero plus 60 minutes to zero plus 120 minutes, during which time the 8th East Surreys were to clear the town east of the Ancre and west of these strong points.
>
> *Third Phase.*—At zero plus 120 minutes the bombardment was to lift clear of the town, to allow the 8th East Surreys to complete the capture of the remaining enemy strong points in it.

The next task of the 55th Infantry Brigade was to gain touch with the left of the 54th Infantry Brigade, and to form a flank from there to the floods north of Albert; this was assigned to the 7th Buffs. It was impossible to foresee at what hour this forward movement would become possible, and as it was expected that by that hour Shamrock Hill would be in the hands of the 54th Brigade, General Lee decided that the movement should be carried out without cover from a creeping barrage. Four brigades of artillery, the 235th and 236th Brigades of the 47th Divisional Artillery, and the

108th and 175th Army Field Artillery Brigades, and two companies of the 50th Battalion Machine-Gun Corps, in addition to the 18th Division's own Machine-Gun battalion under Lieut.-Colonel E. C. T. Minet, were available for the operation.

A brilliant impromptu on the evening of 21st August simplified the next morning's task of the 54th Brigade. Patrols succeeded in getting across the river Ancre, and in establishing themselves on the Albert - Meaulte road south of Albert and north of Vivier Mill. A number of light trestle-bridges, constructed by the Divisional Engineers, were then carried to the river and dropped across; and though enemy machine-guns raked the river-front continuously, and spite of the fact that the night was a cloudless one of bright moonlight, bodies of the Fusiliers and Northants got over the river. At one point three German machine-guns were firing so persistently that it seemed impossible to bridge the stream, but Private E. G. Hughes, of the Royal Fusiliers, jumped into the water, seized an end of the bridge, and swam and waded until he had placed it in position on the opposite bank. Sergeant C. Robinson of the Northamptonshires performed almost an exactly similar feat. By 2 A.M. so many of our men had crossed that the ground to be swept by our artillery and machine-guns in the opening phase of the barrage programme was already in our possession, and sudden orders had to be issued to meet the altered conditions. It had become certain also that the difficult and possibly very costly operation of forcing the Ancre against severe enemy opposition was now unnecessary. By zero hour, 4.45 A.M., sixteen foot-bridges were across the Ancre, and three companies of the 6th Northants, and the whole of the 11th Royal Fusiliers, were formed up on the other side of the Ancre, with the Albert - Meaulte road as their starting line. And here, when the guns burst forth, they waited one hour, the time

which had been allowed for the passage of the river.
During this time the remaining company of the
Northants fought its way forward in the face of
heavy opposition, and captured many prisoners and
machine-guns on the way.

This having been accomplished, the attack went
forward with tanks, under cover of a creeping
barrage which played havoc among the enemy's
carefully-sited machine-guns, disposed in pairs and
in depth along the whole front.  Eighty were captured by the 54th Brigade, and many more were
destroyed by shell-fire.  By 8 A.M. the Northamptonshires on the 54th Brigade front had practically
gained their objective for the day, while the Fusiliers, after overcoming strong opposition from the
direction of Albert, Bellevue Farm, and Tara Hill,
were holding a line about 500 yards east of the
farm.  Among the captures in the early stage of
the proceedings on the 54th front was a complete
German battalion headquarters.  In the dug-out
was found one of our own men, who had been
taken prisoner while on patrol a few hours earlier.
He now had the pleasure of escorting the German
battalion commander to the cages.

There was no pause.  Orders were now received
from General Lee that on the final objective being
reached, strong fighting patrols should be pushed
forward, and the ground thus reconnoitred made
good by companies following in close support.  This
was duly acted upon by the Bedfordshires and
Northamptonshires; and in the meantime the 8th
Royal Berkshires (temporarily placed under the
command of Brigadier-General Sadleir-Jackson,
G.O.C. 54th Brigade) were also moved across the
Ancre to support the further advance.  Meanwhile
the Fusiliers, who had been plugging away in the
centre, found this left flank held up by enemy
machine-guns, principally from a strong point on
the summit of Shamrock Hill, an elevation directly

east of Albert, and overlooking the level land south of the town. As a result they had to dig in. During the afternoon, however, a company of the 2nd Bedfords, ably led by Captain R. L. V. Doake, passed through the Fusiliers, captured the hill point, silenced its gunners, and enabled the Fusiliers to proceed.

In the meantime, on the 55th Brigade front, the capture of Albert had been proceeding according to plan, and by 9.10 A.M. the 8th East Surreys—to whom the task of storming and clearing the town had been entrusted — had finished their job, after nearly four and a half hours' determined fighting, much of it in the town itself.

Albert was ours again; but it was a tragically un-familiar Albert in which the men found themselves in the glare of that day's hot August sun. Streets, once picturesque and lively with the *va-et-vient* of British military life, had become mere paths littered with rub-bish, lined with stumps of walls and wrecks of buildings, and undermined in every direction with land-mines and charges. The cathedral, from which the golden image of the Virgin and her Babe had hung for so long, was there yet, and its vast nave still dominated the town, but it had become a mere huge forbidding shell of red brick. In front of it lay a wrecked Boche 'plane, and here and farther on, near the Singer factory, dead British patrols; and everywhere were German dead. One felt that the only fit setting for such a scene was absolute stillness—the silence of the grave. But beyond the town the noise of battle still went on. And inside the ruins one could hear and see Colonel Symons's sappers at work rendering harmless the land-mines left by the enemy under every road and bridge; 136 land-mines and charges they removed that day, and they did the work so thoroughly that not a single accident occurred. The Boche had done his best and bravest; but it was difficult not to feel, as one looked around the

hideous wreckage of what once had been a pleasant,
stately little town, that he had found a fitting tomb.
The battle progressed rapidly. The attack had
attained its object. The Bedfords were on Shamrock Hill by 10 A.M.; the East Surreys had "mopped-
up" Albert; the 6th Northants, on the right, were
in touch with the 36th Infantry Brigade of the
12th Division; and, on the left, the 7th Buffs,
debouching from Albert, joined near Black Wood
with the 2nd Bedfords, who were in support of the
11th Royal Fusiliers. The Buffs, who after the
8th August fighting had received two large drafts
—chiefly coalminers and munition workers, all men
of fine fighting quality — were also better provided
with company commanders than they had been for
a long time. Captains Stronge, Nicholas, and Whitmarsh were all experienced officers who *commanded*
their companies at all times, whether in or out of
the line; and, with so many new young officers and
men in the battalion, their qualities of leadership
counted for much. When the Buffs debouched from
Albert without a barrage, and advanced over open
ground, enemy machine-guns on Tara Hill met them
with a merciless fire, and the leading companies
lost heavily—especially " C " Company, whose company commander, Lieutenant Barber, a very excellent officer, was wounded. Captain Whitmarsh was
most conspicuous in this advance. He rallied his
men, and by skilful tactics methodically moved forward to Black Wood, and, in spite of heavy shelling
and machine-gun fire, held that valuable point until
dark. But his company lost all its other officers, and
suffered over 60 per cent in casualties.

The end of a long and significant day's fighting
found the line stretching from the railway, just
north of Meaulte as far as the Ancre floods between
Albert and Aveluy, with a generous and safe curve
in the right direction — the east. Many hundreds
of prisoners had fallen to our share: the Northamp-

tonshires had taken 670, and the East Surreys 110 in Albert. General Lee and all concerned could look back upon a satisfactory Divisional contribution to the opening stages of the great battle of Bapaume, which was to keep the Allies victoriously busy for the next nine days.

During the attack, Brigadier - General Sadleir-Jackson, G.O.C. of the 54th Brigade, having gone forward to secure a better control of the situation, was wounded in the knee by a bullet from a machine-gun firing over the crest towards Bellevue Farm. General Jackson was actually trying to get some Lewis gunners on to this gun when he was hit. He managed to walk back a considerable part of the way, but had to give in at last; and this piece of hard fortune kept him away from the Brigade until after the Armistice. The command was taken over by Lieut.-Colonel A. E. Percival of the Bedford-shires, who held it until the taking of the La Boisselle craters on the 24th. It was afterwards held by Brigadier-General J. A. Tyler and by Brigadier-General O. C. Borrett.

Shortly after the Armistice, General Sadleir-Jackson was able to rejoin his Brigade.

On the 22nd General Lee received various messages of congratulation. The commander of the III. Corps wired as follows :—

" I wish to thank and congratulate you and all ranks of your Division on the excellent work done to-day. . . . In spite of the great heat, and in the face of considerable opposition, the troops have gained a notable advance of territory and have inflicted heavy loss on the enemy."

And through III. Corps commander came also the following :—

" Army Commander wires as follows. . . .

Please convey to 18th and 12th Divisions my congratulations and best thanks for their success to-day. . . . The passage of the Ancre and capture of Albert and the high ground to the east was a difficult operation, and was well planned and very well carried out."

# CHAPTER XXV.

## THE TAKING OF USNA AND TARA HILLS.

*An example of the success that can attend surprise—A night advance by the 55th Brigade—Meaulte a dust-heap—The creeping up of the tanks—J. C. Parke, the lawn-tennis player, in command of the 10th Essex—How the 8th Royal Berks took the La Boisselle crater— Brilliant work by Captain G. W. H. Nicolson, Captain D. V. Sutherst, and 2nd Lieutenant N. H. G. Blackburn—Lord Haig's reference.*

FROM Ypres down to Reims the whole line was now ablaze, and the share of the 18th Division in the work of the next few days, if perhaps less spectacular than the operations of the 22nd, was to be no less arduous, and, from the tactical point of view, no less interesting.

Albert was in our hands, but the enemy's strong position overlooking the town from the east, the elevations to which some Hibernian had given the names of Usna Hill and Tara Hill, and the high ground west of Bécourt Wood, were still manned by the Boche, and if our hold of the town was to be secure, these positions had also to be captured. Accordingly an attack was ordered to be made on them at dawn on 23rd August.

As events turned out, this battle proved to be an example of the success that can attend upon surprise.

By way of preliminary, it was arranged that during the night, 22nd - 23rd August, the 55th Infantry Brigade, helped by a heavy preparatory bombardment, should advance and make good the small northerly part of the objective line which they had been unable to reach during the day. The 53rd Infantry Brigade—less the 8th Royal Berks, but with the 7th Queens attached—were then to attack at dawn in conjunction with the 113th Infantry Brigade of the 38th Division. Six tanks were to assist. Meanwhile, farther south, the 54th Infantry Brigade were to keep up a constant and harassing pressure on the enemy. Such was the programme for the 23rd August.

The first part of the operation—the 55th Brigade's preparatory part—was flawlessly carried out. A night advance is a good test of the stuff troops are made of. It is so easy to miss the way and to "imagine things" —and it was indeed easy enough, amid the dreary remains of civilisation left by the Boche in this part of the battlefield, to stumble into a shell-pit, and hard enough to spot enemy machine-gunners lurking behind the bricks of ruined houses or the timbers of deserted stables. But the 55th Brigade went forward sturdily, and by 2.20 A.M. had duly corrected their line and reached their objective.

Meanwhile, the half-dozen tanks crept in the dark from the village of Meaulte along the eastern bank of the Ancre—a stupendous piece of work—and by 3 A.M. were ready to help in the main event of the morning, the attack on the three mentioned positions. Poor little Meaulte! Some of the divisional troops had been billeted there in 1915 and had found it a pleasant place. It was now a dust-heap. "Not a soul in the streets, not a single house habitable, even for troops. Of the mill that had been the 82nd Brigade R.F.A. Headquarters three years before, one tiny fragment of red brick wall was left. The bridge in front had been scattered to the winds, and such deep shell-craters pitted the ground and received the running water that the very river-bed had dried up."

The difficulties of making the attack a surprise one were added to because it was found that even the assembly was not possible until 2.20 A.M., while the approach to the assembly area of the 113th Infantry Brigade of the 38th Division had to be made through Albert, and then due north along the eastern edge of the floods, through which it was necessary in places to wade waist-high. Also, when at last the real struggle began, the attack upon Usna and Tara Hill had to be a frontal one, made by troops who had the floods only a very short distance behind them.

But there was no doubting the success of the operation once it was launched. At 4.45 A.M. the artillery pealed forth the usual tremendous overture, and with cheers and a rush the fight for the high ground began.

The Boche infantry upon the slopes resisted stoutly, but the men of General Barker's Brigade could not be held. Captain C. F. Bland, a Territorial belonging to the 8th Essex, but attached to the 10th Battalion, was one of the officers who did dashing and decisive work. (The 10th Essex, by the way, were commanded at this time by Major J. C. Parke, the celebrated lawn-tennis player, while for this fight Major Warr was in command of the 8th Royal Berks during the absence in hospital of Lieut.-Colonel Hudson.) With the assistance of one N.C.O., Captain Bland rushed one after the other three machine-guns that were checking the advance of the battalion and inflicting many casualties, and he himself killed no fewer than five German machine-gunners. When he reached the objective near Bécourt Wood he established his own and other companies in depth against heavy shell and machine-gun fire, and all through he handled his men with coolness and resource. There was also Lieutenant Coles of the 7th Queens, who, when the objective on Tara Hill was reached, found himself the senior officer of the Queens. Practically single-handed, he pushed on with the work of consolidation; and his determination and leadership were the more outstanding, because his men, besides

being extremely fatigued, were most of them new
recruits, and only three young officers and very few
N.C.O.'s were left to help him. The tanks did their
part nobly, rolling over many machine-gun nests and
forcing the occupants to surrender.

By 6 A.M. Usna and Tara Hill and the high ground
west of the wood were in our possession, with the
satisfactory addition of one gun captured and 350
prisoners taken.

Meanwhile the 54th Brigade, farther south, had
duly kept the pot a-boiling. The Northamptonshires
and the Bedfordshires, as instructed, had maintained
a constant pressure on the enemy, and, by a series of
rushes, had advanced their line by a thousand yards.
The rout of the Germans was complete, and the rest
of the day was spent in consolidation and in preparation for the next move forward, which was timed for
the unusual hour of 1 o'clock next morning.

In that next day's programme the 38th Division
was to capture Ovillers and La Boisselle, places already
stamped with the hall-mark of British valour in the
Somme fighting of 1916. The 53rd Brigade (the 55th,
minus the 7th Queens, were now withdrawn into
Divisional Reserve west of Albert) were to work in co-
operation; and the 12th and 58th Divisions were also
to continue their advance on our right.

The 24th of August 1918 ought always to be remembered in 18th Divisional history for the magnificent bit of individualism by which the 8th Royal
Berks drove the Germans out of the notorious La
Boisselle crater, which at 8 P.M., in spite of bitter and
incessant fighting, still held out. The 53rd Brigade
was the only infantry brigade of the 18th Division
engaged in the day's attack. The main offensive
was that of the 38th Division on Ovillers and La
Boisselle.

The 53rd Brigade's task was to capture Chapes
Spur due east of Tara Hill, and thence to form a
defensive flank along the trench system immediately

north of Bécourt Wood. The 8th Royal Berks, who had reverted to the brigade on the previous day, and two companies of the 7th Royal West Kents, were detailed respectively for these two tasks. The attack was launched according to time-table, and in a short time practically the whole of the objective was gained, with the exception that the Berks had been held up by the strong force of the enemy in the La Boisselle crater, which was in the 38th Division's area.

In the early morning and during the day, patrols of the 53rd Brigade also occupied the Boche trench system east of Sausage Valley, while farther south they pushed through the stumps and holes called Bécourt Wood, and establishing themselves on the eastern edge of the northern portion of that plantation, gained touch with the 54th Brigade (of which Brigadier-General J. A. Tyler had that day taken over the command). The 54th Brigade's line now ran along the western edge of the southern portion of the wood.

All day, however, the big La Boisselle crater, the one on the left-hand side of the road to Bapaume, strongly manned and cunningly planted with machine-guns, was holding out—and, holding up the Royal Berks. This was the crater blown up in 1916, a deep hole about seventy yards across at the top, the biggest thing of the kind on the British front.

Captain Guy William Holmes Nicolson made intrepid efforts to force the strong body of Germans from their fastnesses in the craters. In spite of withering machine-gun and rifle fire he worked his company close up to the craters, and held his ground throughout the day, walking about, encouraging his men, and continuously reorganising his position, although he was in full view of enemy snipers. There was an N.C.O., too, Lance-Sergeant George William Hutchins, who did devoted work in the earlier attack. Suddenly encountering a German machine-gun, he, without hesitation, rushed the enemy gunners at the point of the bayonet. Later Hutchins

took out a patrol to secure touch with the neighbouring battalion. He did really distinguished work
throughout the day, and was severely wounded in the
evening attack on the craters.

With the attack held up so long, water was urgently
required at the outpost positions. Another N.C.O.,
Lance-Corporal Albert Walter Underwood, voluntered
to take it. He got through four times, though he
had to pass through heavy rifle and machine-gun
fire; his bravery enabled his comrades to hold out at
a very critical time in the day's fighting. And when
Battalion Headquarters were entirely without news of
the left company of the Berks, Private Albert Edward
James, a headquarter's runner, went out, worked his
way across ground swept by the fire of German
marksmen in the craters, found the left company, and
brought back the dispositions to Battalion Headquarters. This was yet another instance of fearlessness and devotion to duty which proved of real
assistance in enabling the operation of the day to be
carried on.

The day wore on. The Berks had suffered severely,
but the Boche still held on to the La Boisselle craters.
Something had to be done. At eight o'clock that
evening—the hour at which most of the plays in
London were beginning—an attack was organised by
the O.C. 8th Royal Berks, Major Warr, and brilliantly carried out by Captain G. W. H. Nicolson,
Captain D. V. Sutherst, M.C., 53rd Trench Mortar
Battery, and a force of sixty men. Trench mortars
were brought up, but there was no artillery barrage.
The operation was completely successful, and resulted
in the capture of the crater and of 250 prisoners.

An officer who also did splendidly in this admirably
organised exploit was 2nd Lieutenant N. H. G. Blackburn, of the Royal Berks. First he and his platoon
bombed an enemy machine-gun team that was cleverly
placed in the big crater; then he put a second team
out of action with his revolver; altogether twelve

German machine-gun posts were dealt with. After
the subduing of the machine-gun nests Captain Nicolson advanced his outposts 300 yards and captured
more prisoners.

2nd Lieutenant Blackburn (he was afterwards
killed at Le Cateau before his M.C. reached him)
and his servant had had a queer serio-comic adventure before the dashing attack of the evening. They
were approaching an old trench when Blackburn
noticed a Boche head ten yards away. Up went a
couple of Boche hands, followed by other German
heads and hands. "Surrender!" called out Blackburn, and up shot more heads. But Blackburn's only
weapon was his revolver, and his servant was the only
other person with him; and at last the Germans in
their turn began to shout, "*You* surrender!" A
parley began as to which side should lay down its
weapons, the two or the twenty. The dispute developed into a cursing match carried on with spirit in
both languages. When the Boches began to level
their rifles, Blackburn and his servant, like sensible
men, took to their heels. Blackburn tripped over a
wire into a shell-hole, and the enemy shots passed
over him, but he had to lie there a long time before
he could wriggle away.

By the night of 24th August it was clear that the
enemy were in a thoroughly disorganised condition.
Such counter-attacks as they had made were measures
of despair carried out in order to stem our advance
at critical points. Their troops were hurried up and
put in piecemeal without any general plan. The
machine-gun defence had been good, but the comparatively slight casualties suffered on the whole of
the III. Corps front made it clear that an artillery
barrage was not always a necessary preliminary to
the advance of troops making a proper use of their
weapons, and that in the conditions of open warfare
then prevailing the infantry could rely chiefly on their
own efforts to exploit any success gained.

General Lee decided, as soon as the situation should
permit, to reconstitute the line on a one - brigade
front, the leading brigade assuming the duties of an
advanced-guard, while the two other brigades were
organised in depth behind, the first for the defence
of the main line of resistance, the second to rest
before going forward to pass through the advanced-
guard brigade, itself to take up those duties.  Pending
the reconstitution, one troop of 22nd Corps cavalry
was attached to each of the two brigades in the line.

Lord Haig in his " Victory Despatch " referred to
the main operation of 24th August in the following
words :—

> "At 4.45 A.M. . . . the 18th Division and the
> right brigade of the 38th Division of the III.
> and V. Corps recommenced their attacks about
> Albert, and by a well-executed operation entail-
> ing hard fighting at different points captured the
> high ground east of the town known as Tara and
> Usna Hills."

Five days were still to elapse before ruined Bapaume
was to be re-entered ; and we now approach the grim
fighting which again, as in 1916, was to leave the
name of Trones Wood a memory of imperishable
tragedy and glory for the 18th Division.

Throughout the Hundred Days of victory in which
the 18th Division played so prominent a part, Major-
General Lee's unerring appreciation of the situation
and rapid conception of a plan, bold, and at the same
time tactically faultless, was the bedrock of the
Division's success.

The capture of Usna and Tara Hills was the first
of a series of coups effected by the 18th and 38th
Divisions in co-operation.   The next was to come on
1st September : the capture of Morval (38th Division)
and the Combles Valley (18th), and on the same
evening of Sailly-Saillisel (38th and 18th).

To the leaders of these two Divisions and their

mutual confidence in each other were these singular
successes largely due. Major-General Thomas Astley
Cubitt, commanding the 38th Division, though differ-
ing vastly in many attributes from General Lee,
possessed similar military qualities. Both were gifted
with imagination ; both had minds of their own ; both
were quick to make a plan and to see that it was
carried through. They were, in fact, what so many
in a similar position were not, complete commanders.

As a Brigadier in the 19th Division, it was General
Cubitt and General Cubitt alone who took command
of Kemmel Hill before it was handed over to the
French, and later lost to the Boche. He simply took
charge of the mêlée of troops with their four brigadiers,
and dealt with each succeeding crisis; and crises
occurred hourly. When later he took command of
the 38th (Welsh) Division—and it was sorely tried
and in need of men—General Cubitt wrote to Mr
Lloyd George for more Welshmen. A strong draft
turned up—whether the result of the letter or not
General Cubitt does not know. His own description
of the success of the appeal—and, as usual, most of his
words were unfit for print—was, "the little beggar
hadn't the decency to answer my letter ; but he sent
me the men."

# CHAPTER XXVI.

## TO AND THROUGH TRONES WOOD, AUGUST 1918.

*General Lee's attack based on assumption that 38th Division had Longueval and Delville Wood in safekeeping—Incorrect information —Berkshires with flank exposed met by heavy enfilading machine-gun fire—Forced out of wood by fresh battalion of Prussian Guards—Lieut.-Colonel Banks's evening attack—Valuable work by the gunners—A swift victory—The 18th Division monument in Trones Wood.*

AUGUST 25 saw more fighting in this region of hill and wood and river valley, and a steady continuance of the advance. At 2.30 A.M. the Division again attacked, with the 54th Infantry Brigade on the right and the 55th (which during the night had relieved the 53rd in the line east of Bécourt) on the left. The 54th were represented by the 6th Northamptonshires and the 2nd Bedfords, each on a two-company front; the 55th contained the 7th Buffs and the 8th East Surreys, with the 7th Queens (who had now passed back into this Brigade) in reserve.

The early business of the day was to secure as much ground as possible without becoming too heavily engaged, and in fulfilment of this part of the plan Bécourt Wood was soon cleared, Fricourt retaken, and the enemy generally put on the run. Between dawn and 10 A.M. a line had been reached running due north-south from the Contalmaison Road down to the east corner of Fricourt Wood.

Then came the order for a general advance. For this purpose the 55th Brigade was to function as an advanced-guard to the Division, and to assist him in his duties as advance-guard commander, Brigadier-General E. A. Wood was granted cavalry and cyclists as follows : one troop Otago Mounted Rifles and one company 22nd Corps Cyclists. General Wood was also given two brigades of the Royal Field Artillery, an R.E. company, and two machine-gun companies.

Here and there the enemy defended his holdings with energy. Our attack on the old German system of trenches west of Montauban, including the Pommiers Redoubt, where the 54th Brigade did so gallantly in 1916, was contested with particular obstinacy. Our advance, however, went steadily, and by 4 P.M. the day's struggle had brought our line forward till it stretched from the western part of Mametz Wood down to the eastern vicinity of Bunny Wood. One company of the redoubtable East Surreys had forged ahead, and meeting no opposition had penetrated Mametz Wood to its eastern edge. There they remained, apparently in the air, but, as it happened, safe enough until the advance next day brought the remainder of the Division into line with them.

The pressure on the weakening resistance of the enemy was continued. But the men who held the high ground at Montauban still had fight in them, and it was because of the skill and magnificent energy and leadership of Captain A. J. Whitmarsh of the 7th Buffs that the village was finally seized. Captain Whitmarsh was in command of a composite company made up of two companies that had lost heavily at Albert on the 22nd. He had only one officer and two sergeants with him. In face of heavy shelling and machine-gun fire, he pushed on, and by clever handling of his forces, although both his flanks were exposed, he had worked a way into the village from the west by 5 P.M. and captured 50 prisoners, his company strength then being about 60. The 11th Royal Fusiliers also penetrated the position from the south-west, and altogether 60 prisoners were taken, and the remainder of

the garrison killed and their machine-guns captured.
The prisoners complained that the flanking fire of
Colonel Minet's machine-guns from Marlborough Wood
had cut off their only chance of retreat. When hearing
this complaint, an officer of the Buffs said "Sorry!"
Not one of the Germans smiled.

The fine offensive spirit shown by the young and
inexperienced soldiers under his command was almost
entirely due to Captain Whitmarsh's personality, and
the D.S.O. which afterwards came to him was a most
popular one.

In the evening between 9 and 10 o'clock the 7th
Queens, as vanguard of the 55th Brigade, reached
the western edge of Bernafay Wood. Finding it
held in considerable strength, they took up an outpost line just east of Montauban, and in so doing
made a way for the 53rd Brigade to pass through
to the assault next day on Bernafay and Trones
Woods under an organised artillery and machine-gun
barrage.

We now come to Tuesday, 27th August, a date
which stands out as one of the tragical splendid days
in the history of the Division during those final
months — a day marked by prolonged and bitter
struggle, destined to be crowned with complete success in the capture of Trones Wood.

When orders were issued to the 53rd Brigade to
assume the duty of advance-guard and capture the
wood, it was known that the ground on the right was
held by the enemy, but assurances had been received
that Longueval and Delville Wood, on our left, were
safe in the hands of the 38th Division; and General
Lee's plan of attack was based upon this supposition.
The attack was, in fact, to take the form of a turning
movement from the north, where our left flank was
considered secure. The artillery were to fire a
barrage 1,000 yards in front of the starting-off line.
The barrage was to wait for the infantry, who had
been told that they would not come under hostile fire

for the first 600 yards. The infantry units to be employed in the attack were the 8th Royal Berks on the left and the 7th Royal West Kents on the right. The scheme was, first, to drive forward a wedge on the northern divisional boundary, and then to strike southward through Bernafay and Trones Woods and so secure the full objective.

The artillery barrage, for the attack of the Berkshires on the left, opened at 4.55 A.M., and halted for a quarter of an hour on the opening line to allow the assaulting troops to get close up. It was discovered that the enemy had a few posts in front of this line, but when the assault was delivered they melted away. But as the Berkshires and West Kents advanced, there came the discovery that the ground reported to be in occupation by the British was not so held. Instead of the 38th Division being in possession of Longueval, they had been temporarily driven out of it, and the Boche was strongly planted there "all gay and chirpy." Consequently, while our attack on the right progressed very favourably and prisoners and machine-guns were captured, our left was met with a sudden and murderous fire from enemy machine-guns. While our right pushed on and our centre also moved forward, though it suffered heavily, our left was disastrously hung up. Indeed, only 20 men of the Berkshires reached the final objective in this attack.

Once again there were exhilarating examples of cool and spirited leadership by young officers. When the Royal Berks found that they had come under an enfilading machine-gun fire, Captain Malcolm Wykes, M.C., an officer possessed of strong character, great alertness, and a rare fund of humour, realised that the battalion might waver. Repeatedly he went from one part of the field to another, and gave guidance in the maintenance of direction. When two companies were held up by machine-guns, he led forward a party that put the guns out of action, and in tackling a German who had shot one of the Berks officers, he was himself slightly wounded. Captain G. W. H. Nicolson, who three days before had so distinguished himself at La Boisselle, led his company through the machine-gun fire, and himself assaulted an enemy strong point and captured its garrison. In spite of the severe losses, he led the remnants of the company on to the final objective, and here, with men falling all round him, under the Germans' exceedingly accurate enfilading fire, he held on until the arrival of strong enemy reinforcements compelled him to withdraw. Again, in spite of the severest hostile machine-gun fire, he reorganised his men, and maintained the battalion line, although losses through the exposure of the flank were heavy and continuous.

The Berks could, at any rate, claim to be in the northern portion of the wood, while the southern part, which was higher and commanded the northern end, was also penetrated; so that, although the cost had been grave, the objectives had been reached.

But a sudden enemy counter-attack on our weakened left flank forced us out of the northern part, and it was only too clear that further difficulties were in store.

It was now 7 A.M. Two companies of the 10th Essex were hurried forward, with orders that one of them should be at the disposal of Lieut.-Colonel T. M. Banks, now commanding the 8th Berks, for reinforcement purposes, while the other should be kept in reserve for any counter-attacking that might become possible. Our artillery was still very busy. S.O.S. calls were numerous, and our batteries—themselves often under violent enemy fire—had to be turned on to one spot after another as the infantry demanded special artillery assistance.

An hour later, came a very heavy counter-attack on the southern part of the wood by a battalion of Francis Joseph's Prussian Guards, which had been brought up overnight, fresh from reserve. This counter-

attack succeeded in driving the West Kents out of
what still remained to us of Trones Wood, and the
gallantry and fighting qualities of our men had for a
while to be content with establishing a line along the
eastern edge of the neighbouring Bernafay Wood.

An immediate counter-attack to recover the lost
ground was impracticable. The enemy was in strength.
Owing to the exposed state of both flanks the line held
by the 53rd Brigade was a very long one for the force
available. Units by this time had become much intermingled, owing to the frequently recurring need for
lending reserves of one battalion to meet the urgent
requirements of another.

Accordingly, Brigadier-General Barker, G.O.C. of
the 53rd Brigade, after visiting the line and conferring
with the officers commanding, made arrangements for
an early evening attack after a deliberate "preparation." From 6.30 P.M. to 7 P.M. a bombardment by
artillery of all calibres was to be directed upon the
southern portion of Trones Wood—the wood was now
strongly held by the battalion of Prussian Guards with
many machine-guns—and at 7 P.M. a force of two companies of all regiments in the brigade was to go to the
assault.

Now when the Berkshires on the left had been
driven from Trones Wood by the drive of the Prussian
Guards, they were in the dangerous position of having
to hold a frontage of about 1,000 yards with an
exposed flank of double that length overlooked everywhere by the enemy. Also Lieut.-Colonel Banks,
through his glasses, had noticed that the Germans were
manning one particular post with many machine-guns.

So when Brigadier-General Barker came up to see
for himself what was happening, he arranged that
Colonel Banks should be in command of the composite
force, and that special artillery assistance should be
asked for to deal with this bunch of enemy machine
guns. General Barker went himself to demand the
help of the heavy gunners.

The two 18-pounders that came forward from where
the divisional artillery had been shooting, on the
western edge of Mametz Wood, belonged to "B" Battery, 82nd Brigade R.F.A. Major D. J. Fraser, M.C.,
the battery commander, did a reconnaissance during
the afternoon and selected a position close to Montauban Quarry for the two guns, and about half an hour
before the time fixed for the infantry to attack, the
guns and their attendant waggons, divested of their
trench warfare impedimenta and camouflaged so that
the gunners might ride easily on the vehicles, trotted
along Caterpillar Valley, which at the time was being
well shelled by the Germans. One gun went into a
shell-hole and the traces broke under the strain. The
other gun kept on its way, and when this gun and its
waggon reached the selected position its team was
sent back for the gun that lay stranded. Lieutenant
Herbert Andrews of B/82 remained in charge of the
guns, while Lieutenant H. A. Clist went forward with
his linemen to observe and to direct the fire. Lieut.-
Colonel Banks wanted rapid fire upon the German
machine-guns, commencing about five minutes before
the zero hour. The two 18-pounders did exactly what
was wanted: they fired 200 rounds in the first ten
minutes. Four men were wounded at the guns. The
53rd Trench Mortar Battery came up stoutly in full
view of the enemy, and also assisted to make the
preliminary bombardment of the wood a most effective
one.

When at 8 P.M. two companies of the Essex and two
of the Berks crept towards the barrage, they got so
close to it that Lieut.-Colonel Banks was afraid they
were courting the penalties of foolhardiness. But
their very bravery proved their salvation. As the
Boche himself admitted, they were on him before he
had recovered from the barrage. The highest fighting
qualities were displayed. Great hefty Germans were
laid low by youngsters of the Berks and Essex, who
scarcely averaged 5 ft. 8 in. in height.

It was a swift victory. Many of the enemy were killed in hand-to-hand conflict; fifty German dead and over forty disabled machine-guns were afterwards counted ; three officers and seventy men were taken prisoners. It was, indeed, a model little show. After the capture of Trones Wood the line was consolidated and a comparatively quiet night was passed. The night before the attack the 8th Berks received a draft of eight officers who were scrambled into the operation. Two of them were killed, three were wounded, one was hit going back to " Battle Surplus," one fell sick going up the line, one fought and came through.

As Colonel Banks and his victorious party marched back and came through Caterpillar Valley, it seemed, says Colonel Banks, as if a sort of unholy calm had settled upon the scene. The night was one of brilliant starlight, and after the uproar, ferocity, and moral tension of the day's work the contrast was almost oppressive.

Congratulations rained down. The Corps Commander wired as follows to General Lee :—

" Heartiest congratulations on the conspicuous gallantry and tenacity displayed by the 53rd Brigade in the capture of Trones Wood. This exploit is in keeping with the fighting traditions of your Division, and reflects the highest credit on all concerned in its planning and execution."

The tree-stumps and shell-holes of Trones Wood may now be traversed by the least adventurous. No doubt leaves are there again and the birds sing. The 18th Division knew it chiefly as a place of ugliness and horror, blasted with fire, echoing with curses, reeking with pain and death. The Boche, too, dirty cur that he was, had fouled every hut, every dug-out, before he left. But the 18th also knew Trones as a place made sacred by much courage and great sacrifice, and in it to-day stands a monument upon which

18TH DIVISION MEMORIAL IN TRONES WOOD.

French and British eyes will long look reverently. The tablet is inscribed as follows :—

TO THE GLORY OF GOD

AND

IN IMPERISHABLE MEMORY

OF THE

OFFICERS, N.C.O.'S, AND MEN

OF THE 18TH DIVISION

WHO FELL FIGHTING FOR THE SACRED CAUSE

OF LIBERTY IN THE

SOMME BATTLES OF 1916 AND 1918.

---

THE GREATEST THING IN THE WORLD.

"This is my commandment, That ye love one another, as I have loved you.

"Greater love hath no man than this, that a man lay down his life for his friends."                                        —St John xv. 12.

# CHAPTER XXVII.

## THE CAPTURE OF COMBLES.

*1st September 1918, a great day for the 18th Division—General Lee conceives a masterly turning movement—The necessity for taking Morval Ridge—Excellent sniping by the Divisional Artillery— More fine work by the 8th East Surreys—Bitter fighting round Priez Farm—700 prisoners taken—Sergeant Cornwall's exhortation: "Fight like Queens!"—The 7 P.M. capture of Saillisel by the 7th West Kents—53rd Brigade take St Pierre Vaast Wood— Another example of General Lee's encircling method—Captain Hume's motor ride through St Pierre Vaast Wood—The Division's seventeen-mile advance.*

FIELD-MARSHAL LORD HAIG could not get everything into his "Victory Despatch," and all he was able to say of the four days' work between 28th August and 1st September was that on one of them, 29th August, "the 18th Division entered Combles." But, indeed, although the Bedfordshires were able to enter Combles on 29th August, the German defence rendered it impossible for them to pass right through the village on that day, and it was not until 1st September that we were in complete possession.

1st September was undoubtedly a day of glory for the Division : General Lee conceived and brought off a masterly turning movement ; the Division captured 700 prisoners ; our own losses were trifling, and there was most workmanlike co-operation between artillery and infantry in bringing off a bold and unusual coup.

During the night of 28th-29th August information was received that the 38th Division on our left would attack at 5.15 A.M. It was decided that there should be an artillery barrage on our front also, and that the 18th Divisional troops should accept every possible opportunity of pushing forward. At zero hour strong patrols were sent out by the Bedfordshires, and they advanced in the direction of the dreary waste of battered Nissen huts, gaping holes, and heaps of broken bricks still entered on the maps as the village of Guillemont. At 9 A.M. the Bedfordshires reported that they had reached the western edge of Leuze Wood, and were encountering opposition from machine-gun and rifle fire, that they had taken several prisoners, and that the enemy had been driven off the high ground west of Bouleaux Wood. By midday the Northamptonshires, farther south, had pushed forward from the ridge running from Falfemont Farm to Leuze Wood to attack the high ground south of Combles and east of Savernake Wood. At the same time a company of the Bedfordshires, debouching from behind the Northamptonshires, attempted an attack on Combles from the south-west. This attack was, however, only partially successful.

Combles is an extensive village and lies low, and it was under vigorous protection not only from the high ground to the south, but also from the German positions on Morval Ridge to the north, from which the 38th Division had failed to expel the enemy. Presently Combles also came under shell-fire from the Ridge; the Northamptonshires withdrew; and it became clear that until Morval Ridge, the highest ground in the neighbourhood, was cleared of the enemy, Combles would be untenable.

It also looked as if the Boche infantry were preparing to make a defensive stand along a line about a mile to the east of the village, running from Priez Farm in the south, through the hamlet of Fregicourt, up to Haie Wood; and the final result of an only partially successful day's fighting was that our men were north and south of Combles, but not in it, and that everywhere they were under very heavy enemy fire from the north.

After a night of bursts of artillery fire on enemy cross-roads and approaches, the infantry's day's work on the 30th began at 5.15 A.M. with an attempt by the 11th Fusiliers to turn the enemy's Priez Farm line from the south, and to advance eastward to Rancourt in conjunction with the 47th Division (who had relieved the 12th).

Owing to the thick mist of an autumnal morning, and also to the very heavy machine-gun fire from Priez Farm, the attack made scant progress. In and around the farm itself there was bitter fighting, and the Fusiliers succeeded in capturing part of it, but were unable to retain what they had taken. The enemy was, in fact, in strength here and showed great determination; and the close of another day's hard work found our line much the same as it had been the day before, except that on the south-east of Combles we had got as far as the ridge east of Alderlee Woods, and that, in the north, we held Combles railway station.

In all this hard wearying fighting the two brigades of Divisional artillery co-operated splendidly with the infantry. The open type of warfare was giving the gunners new opportunities for sniping. Eighteen-pounders were pushed up close behind the infantry and handled with skill and spirit. On 29th August, for example, 2nd Lieutenant James Steele of "A" Battery, 82nd Bde. R.F.A., took a sniping gun into an open position to the left of the road between Leuze Wood and Combles, within three hundred yards of the enemy. In four hours he fired 150 rounds, though after each burst of fire the Germans retaliated upon him with 15 c.m. and 77 m.m. guns. On the 30th and 31st Steele again moved forward with the 54th Brigade, and his single gun fired 500 rounds with open sights, inflicting many casualties.

On 31st August Captain W. A. Currie, who was in

command of A/82, pushed his battery forward, and in
spite of heavy casualties from enemy shelling, kept
his gun firing and knocked out several machine-guns
which were impeding the advance of our infantry.

Still, so long as the German observers possessed
the Morval Ridge, neither our Field Artillery nor our
infantry could make an effective advance; so it was
decided by Corps that a set-piece attack was necessary, and General Lee announced the plan for 1st
September as follows:—

On our left the 38th Division was to capture
Morval and Sailly-Saillisel farther east; on our right
the 47th Division was to take Rancourt and the
trench system to the east of it, and to reach the
south-east corner of the St Pierre Vaast Wood; while
the objective of the 18th Division was the capture of
the north-western portion of the wood and the formation of a line astride the road leading from Rancourt
to Sailly-Saillisel.

The line of the 54th Brigade was drawn back
slightly on the right in order that our barrage might
deal with Germans in shell-holes and trenches close to
our front.

To the 8th East Surreys was allotted the job of
pushing forward to St Pierre Vaast Wood; the 7th
Buffs were to follow them, then wheel to the left,
and at zero plus 200 (*i.e.*, 9.10 A.M.) attack northwards, preceded by an enfilade barrage spreading east
and west, and secure the remainder of the objective.
The 7th Queens were to " mop-up " the area north-east
of Combles that was not attacked frontally. The
whole of the ground opposite the centre and left of
the 54th Brigade was to be kept under heavy
howitzer and machine-gun fire, while by arrangement
with the 38th Division a smoke barrage was put up
along a line running south-east of Morval to cover the
bold—one might even say hazardous—manœuvre of
the 55th Brigade.

General Lee planned for these very complete dis-

positions to result not only in the elimination of the
Morval hindrance, but also to cut off those enemy
forces which threatened to attempt a defensive stand
from Morval to Fregicourt.

It was—especially considering the type of warfare
which had ruled since 1915—a daring strategical
manœuvre, which, without most careful pre-arrange-
ment and first-class handling of troops, must have
been doomed to failure. But General Lee knew his
men. Largely because of the magnificent fighting
qualities of the 8th East Surreys, who bore the brunt
of the fight, and were, as usual, finely handled by
Lieut.-Colonel Irwin, the turning movement succeeded
triumphantly. The 7th Buffs, moving north, their
leading company well led by Captain Stronge, cut off
the Germans immediately in front of Combles and in
the village of Fregicourt; and the 7th Queens, coming
brilliantly into the operation, collected the enemy so
encircled. The 2nd Bedfordshires, the 18th and 50th
Machine-Gun Battalions, and the 55th Brigade Light
Trench Mortar Battery, also co-operated; and altogether 700 prisoners were taken, including two
battalion commanders. All our objectives were gained
at a trifling cost.

The bitterness of the contest which the East
Surreys had to wage around Priez Farm, on the way
to Rancourt and St Pierre Vaast Wood beyond, was
afterwards testified by the number of dead in the
vicinity—the total number of Germans considerably
exceeding that of the East Surreys.

Captain F. J. Gaywood, at the head of his company,
took the farm in the first rush, the garrison of about
100 retiring. But when the other East Surrey companies had swept past the farm and were two miles
ahead, the Germans counter-attacked. They fought
hard to regain possession of the farm, but Captain
Gaywood, assisted by two other officers, not only held
the farm, but at last, after seven hours' fighting,
rounded up the enemy and compelled them to surrender

Priez Farm was actually in the 47th Division's area, and a hostile strong post near the farm, which held out, was heavily bombarded by a Trench Mortar Battery of the 47th Division. In the end the battery commander and one man went out and accepted the surrender of the 80 Germans who had occupied the post.

The East Surreys captured a Boche ambulance at Rancourt that day. Colonel Irwin saw it coming along driven by a German chauffeur, with an East Surrey sergeant on top; the Boche medical officer was also in attendance. The chauffeur spoke very good English. He said he was going back; but Colonel Irwin told him he was going back the other way—towards the British rear. The ambulance was filled with our wounded, and sent to the rear; and on the way, as Colonel Irwin puts it, "the 47th Division pinched it."

In the attack and clearing of Fregicourt, Sergeant Cornwall of the 7th Queens showed great coolness and bravery in leading his platoon. The enemy put down heavy trench mortar and machine-gun fire. Cornwall walked in front of his platoon, in full view of the enemy, firing as he walked, never once attempting to take cover, exhorting his men to "fight like Queens!" It was largely his splendid example to a platoon composed chiefly of a new draft that carried his little force forward, and resulted in the capture of trench mortars, machine-guns, and over two hundred prisoners.

A D.S.O. was won that day by Major S. Vickers of the Divisional Artillery, a Territorial officer who came to command "D" Battery, 82nd Brigade, after the March retreat. The Queens were held up by fierce machine-gun fire. Major Vickers and Lieutenant Gough, one of his subalterns, crawled out to within a hundred yards from the machine-gun nest—"I was afraid all the time the Major's white riding breeches would give us away," Gough said afterwards—and noted its exact locality. The 4·5 howitzers of D/82 then bombarded the machine-guns to such effect that 19 Germans who remained in the position surrendered to Major Vickers, who brought them in himself. And still the tale of the day's triumph was not complete. At 7 P.M. the 7th Royal West Kents (who had been placed at the disposal of the 55th Brigade for the purpose) attacked Saillisel in co-operation with an attack from the north by the 38th Division upon the ruined village of Sailly-Saillisel. In eighty minutes the West Kents gained their objective at slight cost, and took a further 33 prisoners. Great initiative and excellent leadership were shown in this evening operation by Captain A. V. Macdonald.

Combles was not a good place for water, and water for the horses as the advance progressed was becoming an exceedingly serious question. As usual, however, Colonel Symons's sappers kept pace with the advance. Before Fregicourt was actually in our possession the 80th Field Company had six windlass wells going in Combles. Within twenty-four hours twenty-one wells were in working order.

The completeness of the Division's success on 1st September may be gauged by the swift advance that followed during the next four days.

On the morning of 2nd September the 53rd Brigade, with the 8th Berkshires on the right and the 10th Essex on the left, secured the high ground in the northern portion of St Pierre Vaast Wood, gaining all its objectives with the solitary exception of that melancholy heap of broken bricks and shattered timbers that stood in a shell-blasted grove of poplars and was known as Government Farm. And by the afternoon of the next day Government Farm also had become ours.

On the morning of 2nd September the 7th Royal West Kent Regiment also advanced about 2,000 yards on the left, securing the 53rd Brigade left flank : and in the course of that day the who

of St Pierre Vaast Wood was cleared by the 8th
Royal Berkshires.   Three great glares in the sky that
night, behind the heights occupied by the enemy,
suggested that he was burning his dumps prior to a
further retirement; and, sure enough, when the 53rd
Brigade, supported by the Divisional Artillery's sniping 18-pounders pushed forward next day, little difficulty was experienced in occupying Vaux Wood—
from which German field-guns had been firing copi-
ously the day before—and in establishing a line on
the western bank of the Canal du Nord, though the
enemy were still in strength on the eastern bank.
On the 4th our patrols crossed the canal and also
went over the Tortille river, and occupied the spacious Riverside Wood to its east.

Our men were pretty well tired out by then, and
the Divisional Infantry was that night (4th-5th September) relieved by the 12th Division who continued
the advance towards the high Nurlu plateau.

The taking of St Pierre Vaast Wood was another
example of the methods adopted by General Lee
during the period, 22nd August to 5th September,
that marked the transition from trench to open warfare.   It was an instance of capturing an important
position by refusing it, by taking it in side and rear.
During the Somme fighting St Pierre Vaast Wood cost
thousands of French lives.   On this occasion the 10th
Essex and the 7th West Kents secured the dominating ground on the fringes of the wood, after which
the wood itself was cleared by two companies of the
Berks who suffered no casualties in the process.   All
the casualties that occurred in St Pierre Vaast Wood
came from hostile shelling when the wood was in our
hands.

On the farther side of the Canal du Nord the Berks
came upon an abandoned enemy motor-car.   General
Barker told his reconnaissance officer, Captain N.
Hume, afterwards G.S.O. III. to the Division, to fetch
it.   Hume, who had had a good deal to do with motor-

cars, found that the car was supplied with petrol; he cranked it up and actually drove it back to the 53rd Brigade Headquarters through St Pierre Vaast Wood —an extraordinary drive, since the wood was full of shell-holes and tumbled trees.

For a few days the 53rd Brigade Headquarters staff found the car most useful; but there was no paint available for covering up the German signs upon it. The military police eventually took charge of it.

The moving warfare in which the Division had been engaged since the capture of Albert made the question of communications for the supply of troops and weapons one of the greatest importance. The small front upon which the Division manœuvred made the possibility of more than one route extremely unlikely, and the destruction of roads, bridges, and water-points, carried out with method by the Germans in order to delay our advance, as well as the effects of shelling, both hostile and friendly, made the work of repair a stupendous one. This work was carried out untiringly by the 79th, 80th, and 92nd Field Companies, and the 8th Royal Sussex Pioneers, and their success may be judged from the fact that at no time did the advance of the infantry outstrip that of the repairers of communications. To the 180th Tunnelling Company, who were attached to the Division, fell the work of searching for enemy traps; the number of huts and dug-outs bearing the welcome inscription, "Examined by the 180th Company R.E.," was legion.

On 7th September General Lee received the following communication from Lieut.-General Godley, commanding the III. Corps:—

"I wish to congratulate and thank all ranks under your command for the very fine work which has been done by the Division since it went into the line practically a month ago. For the greater part of this month the Division has been fighting daily and incessantly, and has to its credit the crossing of the Ancre and the Canal du Nord and the making of bridges over them, the capture of Albert, Tara, and Usna

Hills, the craters at La Boisselle, Montauban, Bernafay, Trones and Leuze Woods, Combles, Fregicourt, Saillisel, St Pierre Vaast Wood, and Vaux Wood, and the whole of the country as far east as the Canal du Nord, a distance of seventeen miles. 2,464 prisoners and 321 guns and machine-guns have been captured by the Division during this period, and the fighting has been very heavy. You may well be proud of the valour and endurance which the Division has daily and incessantly displayed in order to enable it to add such a record to its already long list of notable achievements."

Our total casualties in the fortnight from 22nd August to 5th September were as follows :—

|  | Killed. | Wounded. | Missing. | Total. |
|---|---|---|---|---|
| Officers | 21 | 102 | 2 | 125 |
| Other ranks | 330 | 1,947 | 450 | 2,727 |

# CHAPTER XXVIII.

## THE FIGHTING AROUND RONSSOY.

*The Division's attack on the outposts of the Hindenburg Line—German machine-gun fire more murderous than at any period of the war—Turning movement of 18th September not successful—General Lee's fears—Lance-Corporal Lewis of the 6th Northamptonshires wins the Victoria Cross—Brigadier-General Wood captures 29 Germans single-handed—55th Brigade's 5 P.M. attack repulses the counter-attack of a fresh German Division—" Nibbling" hand-to-hand fighting continues—" X," " Y," and " Z" copses captured on 20th September.*

A FORTNIGHT passed with the Division at rest, but with the Fourth Army continuing its splendid thrust. It was the outposts of the Hindenburg Line that the 18th Division was next to attack, and there was ample evidence that this celebrated system of military engineering would be defended by the enemy with the utmost obstinacy; that to overrun it would call for bitter struggle and much sacrifice.

This conviction was fulfilled. From 18th September to 24th September the 18th Divisional troops—by this time a very great proportion of them youngsters, with no battalion at full strength—gained ground only by heavy hand-to-hand fighting against machine-gun fire that was more murderous than at any period of the war, and against the ceaseless efforts of the German artillery to defend the vital points of the Hindenburg Line. Our final victory has to be credited not so much to leadership as to the sublime persistency with which all units and all ranks carried through their share in these wearying, complicated operations.

The attacks began definitely on the 18th September. They were designed to be carried out in close collaboration with the 74th, the "broken spur" Division on our right, and the 12th Division on our left. By this time the Fourth Army had fought its way to the line Le Verguier, Templeux-le-Guerard, Ronssoy, Epehy, and Peizieres, and the sector allotted to the 18th and the co-operating Divisions included Templeux-le-Guerard, Ronssoy, and Epehy.

A highly important factor in the position was the basin lying inside the triangle formed by the three villages, St Emilie to the west, Ronssoy to the east, and Epehy to the north; and Generals Lee and Higginson proposed that in the initial assault this basin should be avoided, that the 18th Division should attack south of the spur running from Ronssoy to St Emilie, while the 12th Division should attack west of the spur running from St Emilie to Epehy. Both these attacks would be secure from the enemy defences within the basin, and being on narrow fronts, would have the great advantages of concentrated artillery barrages and flanking machine-gun protection. Our R.E. made most beautiful and realistic dummy tanks, and placed them in well-exposed positions as if entering the basin, but visibility was so bad that they never drew fire. The heavy labour expended was not entirely lost, as the "tanks" provided most excellent accommodation for a Divisional conference held in stormy weather on the 19th.

It was further arranged that after passing through the villages the attacking troops were to wheel inwards and roll up the enemy's main line of defence which ran along the ridge joining Ronssoy and Epehy.

For the performance of this stiff task the 7th West Kents were attached from the 53rd to the 54th Brigade, and the 10th Essex, designated "the counter-attack battalion," to the 55th. In view of the fact that the advance was to be made on a narrow front, special care was taken in working out the assembly places and in timing the approach marches.

On the night of 16th-17th September the 53rd Brigade, for the time being a one-battalion brigade (the 8th Royal Berks), took over the line, east of St Emilie, from which the Division was to operate, and received orders to carry out active patrols; and on the morning of the 17th September a daylight patrol of this battalion obtained a valuable identification by capturing four prisoners of the 2nd Guards Regiment, which had been in the line six days, and, until that moment, had not been identified by us.

In spite of the rainy and pitch-dark night all units reached the starting line at the appointed hour. When the attack—it was a battalion after battalion attack—began at 5.20 A.M. on 18th September, it was still raining and foggy, and all day the light was poor, while the sodden ground was bad for the tanks, more than one of which got "ditched" in sunken roads and on steep embankments.

But the 7th West Kents leading the attack, and in touch on their right with the 74th Division, got well away under the barrage, and, notwithstanding the late arrival of the tanks, reached their objective, the southern portion of Ronssoy, approximately to time. The tanks were 300 yards behind their appointed line when our artillery barrage opened. The enemy artillery barrage started well, but it got thinner and thinner as the West Kents worked their way forward. But throughout the day the German machine-gun fire was accurate and sustained.

The 2nd Bedfordshires, who followed and "leapfrogged" the West Kents, were aided in keeping direction in the misty light by the trampled grass over which the West Kents had passed. They came up with Colonel Hickson's men and helped them to clear the enemy out of a copse in the early stages of the attack, but had to face continuous fighting along the way to their objective across the Hussar

Road, south of Basse Boulogne. However, they succeeded in reaching and capturing it except on the
extreme left. The "mopping-up" of the southern
portion of Ronssoy, notwithstanding the hearty co-
operation of a couple of tanks, took some hours
to complete, and because of this, and of the difficult
nature of the ground, the 11th Royal Fusiliers and
6th Northamptonshires, who, acting in accordance
with the Divisional plan, were striking north behind
a new enfilade barrage put down to carry them
forward, got mixed up; and although they reached
their forming-up line up to time, they only did so
at the expense of a number of casualties. By this
time, too, it was clear that while the 74th Division
was going strong on the right, the 12th Division was
held up at Epehy; and with the fog lifting our men
were under observation from that village.

It was in this fighting that Captains G. E. Cornaby
and Hornfeck of the Fusiliers won their M.C.'s. The
attacking lines of three battalions had become generally mixed. Captain Cornaby, in spite of heavy
machine-gun fire, got his men reorganisd and led
them forward again. This enabled his company to
keep with the barrage and to gain practically the
whole of their objectives. Captain Hornfeck, in conjunction with Captain Cornaby, took his men ahead,
and although his right flank was exposed and heavy
machine-gun and point-blank artillery fire came from
that direction, he also succeeded in gaining his objective, besides capturing two field-guns and several
trench mortars. Later, Captain Cornaby becoming a
casualty, Captain Hornfeck took command in this
area, and drove off two counter-attacks.

Another Fusilier, Private Alfred Smith, when the
officer and all the N.C.O.'s of his platoon had become
casualties, led the platoon to the objective, on the way
putting out of action a German machine-gun whose
harassing fire had cut off one platoon from its company.

Here also should be mentioned the work of Corporal

J. Hurst, who already wore the M.M., and now won
the D.C.M. His keenness and good leadership accounted for five German officers and forty men being
captured. He also secured a signal station complete,
shooting the operator who was sending a message.

And, greatest achievement of all, that of Lance-
Corporal Allan Leonard ("Albert") Lewis, of the 6th
Northamptonshires, who won the Victoria Cross.

Lewis was in charge of a section which he had successfully kept together. He was on the right of the
line. The battalion advanced to attack Ronssoy, and
the east and west barrage opened. The Northamptonshires reached a point where the Boche machine-gun
fire was so intense that it was a practical impossibility
to get forward.

The barrage went on and the Northamptonshires
were held up; and this was where Lance-Corporal
Lewis's magnificent bravery changed the whole
situation.

Working with his section amongst the crumbled
ruins of the village, he noticed opposite him two
German machine-guns that were enfilading the Northamptonshires. On his own initiative he crawled
forward single-handed, with bombs, got within range,
and bombed the teams that manned the enemy's
guns. The Germans left their guns and ran out of
the emplacement.

Lewis then used his rifle with such effect that the
whole enemy party surrendered. Lewis had wounded
six of them; the remaining four were brought in
unwounded.

It was undoubtedly the putting out of action of
these two machines-guns that enabled the Northamptonshires to resume their advance. Lance-
Corporal Lewis did not live to know that he had been
awarded the greatest of all military honours. Three
days later he was killed by a stray shell.

To return to the wider aspects of the fighting. A
situation similar to that in which the 54th Brigade

found themselves now confronted the 55th Brigade, who were due to pass through the Bedfordshires at 8.30 A.M. All the battalions of the 55th Brigade, and particularly the East Surreys as the leading battalion, had become involved in the confused fighting.

General Lee had foreseen this. Before the attack he had represented to Corps that the programme did not allow enough either of time or space for the 55th Brigade to pass through. Corps, however, was unfortunately unable to co-ordinate a longer delay on account of the advance programme of the adjoining Divisions. The 55th Brigade, by stout work, gained ground, but they reached their appointed line too late to be able to follow the barrage, and General Wood decided to postpone further advance for a while. By 11 A.M. he had concentrated three of his battalions in trenches and sunken roads, and there they remained for six hours.

General Wood, who ended the war with three bars to his D.S.O., had a memorable day. He had arrived in Ronssoy in the middle of the fighting. His orderly was killed, but immediately afterwards he entered a German dug-out alone and brought out seven fully-armed prisoners. Later, again single-handed, he captured a further batch of as many as twenty-two Germans by the simple and cheerful expedient of pelting them in their dug-out with lumps of chalk and old boots. In both these adventures General Wood was not only unaccompanied but unarmed, stalking along monumentally, a big cigar between his teeth, the familiar lance used as an alpenstock in his grasp. General Wood's unconcerned calm in the hottest of the fighting, and the smooth readiness of his decisions, had much to do with the success of the 55th Brigade in the great counter-offensive of 1918.

Here, too, may be recorded the courage and resource which won the D.C.M. for Corporal W. J. Hall of the East Surreys. Owing to the failure of the troops in

front to take their objective, his platoon came under
sudden machine-gun fire at close range. Corporal
Hall went forward single-handed with a Lewis gun,
located the enemy machine-gun, and shot down the
team, thus allowing his platoon to go forward without
casualties.

Later he noted a large party of the enemy in the
sunken Hussar Road, with a machine-gun, which they
were using with deadly effect at point-black range.
He informed his platoon officer, Lieutenant Lovell,
and together they crept forward with four men,
and so dominated the enemy with a Lewis gun and
by sniping, that the Germans surrendered. Corporal
Hall and his platoon commander then captured almost
single-handed two howitzers, one machine-gun, and
about sixty prisoners.

By 11 A.M. the Northamptonshires, after stiff fighting, had cleared the northern portion of the Ronssoy
Road, and a footing had been gained in the village of
Basse Boulogne. The trench systems round Quid
Copse, some 500 yards short of the objective on the
left, had also been secured, but it was not until some
hours later that the whole of Basse Boulogne, in
which the enemy held numerous small posts, was
captured and "mopped up" with the assistance of
two tanks.

Epehy was still being defended obstinately against
the 12th Division by the Alpine Corps, and it was
only after heavy fighting that the Northamptonshires
were able to establish a line from Quid Post along
Ridge Reserve, where touch was gained with the
Fusiliers who, with the Bedfordshires, were also advancing on their right. At 3 P.M. the 55th Brigade
were to have attacked again, but General Wood
decided that the time had not yet come for an attack
to have chance of full success.

Under intense machine-gun fire the General carried out a personal reconnaissance, in the course of
which he received a wound in the throat. But he

made the necessary observations and decided to attack
at 5 P.M. ; he issued his orders and personally superintended the forming-up.

And at that hour—the whole of Ronssoy having at
last been cleared of the enemy—the 55th Brigade,
under a creeping barrage, resumed their advance towards the second objective, which included Lempire,
Yak, and Zebra Posts.

Even now success was not destined to be complete.
On the right it prospered, and part of the day's final
objective was reached, but progress on the left was
small. The enemy had hurried up fresh troops.

From a group of copses known respectively as " X,"
" Y," and " Z " to the north and east of Colleen Post,
his nests of machine-guns held our attack in enfilade,
and inflicted heavy casualties ; and by 7 P.M. it was
recognised that even the forward positions we had
gained were not tenable. So at 9 P.M. General Wood
ordered a withdrawal to the line of the sunken road
running south-east from Basse-Boulogne, and known
as the Bellecourt Road. The General superintended
the withdrawal personally, not returning to Brigade
Headquarters until he had ascertained to his satisfaction that his brigade was disposed in depth and
was ready for any defensive tactics the enemy might
impose upon it.

In looking back on this strenuous day of section,
platoon, and company actions, it is to be noted that
Ronssoy had been defended by the 1st Guard Grena-
dier Regiment (the Alexander Regiment) of the 2nd
Guards Division. They appear, however, to have
cherished no particular prejudice against surrender-
ing, either individually or in parties. Over 600 of
them, and of the 232nd Division, were taken in the
course of the day.

From prisoners captured in Lempire in the afternoon it was learned that the Boche had hurried up in
omnibuses the whole of the 121st Division, which had
started from Maretz, fourteen miles back, at 7 A.M.,

and that the 56th R.I.R. of that Division had deployed at Bony (near the canal, just inside the Hindenburg Line), and had attacked at 5 P.M. with the object of retaking Ronssoy and the old German front line to its west.

This accounted for much of the "liveliness" observed in the three copses, and also for the resistance which the 55th Brigade's five o'clock attack encountered. The brigade attack, as has been shown, failed to reach its objective; but as Sir Archibald Montgomery, in his 'Story of the Fourth Army,' specifically points out, it broke up the energetic counterattack of an entirely fresh German Division.

The day's work left us in possession of the whole of Ronssoy, of the greater part of Ridge Reserve, of Lempire and Colleen Posts and Shamrock Trench, and of some hundreds of prisoners. Next day General Rawlinson sent the following congratulatory message, dated 19th September:—

"Please convey to the Divisions of the III. Corps my warm thanks for their successful attacks yesterday, carried out against strong hostile opposition and in circumstances of considerable difficulty. The gallantry and determination of all ranks is worthy of high praise, and reflects great credit on the Divisions concerned."

It is to be noted that Major-General Sir Archibald Montgomery, in his 'Story of the Fourth Army in the Battles of the Hundred Days,' chapter xiii., comments upon General Lee's flank attacks at Trones Wood, 27th August, Fregicourt, 1st September, and Ronssoy, 18th September, and suggests that the latter was a tactical mistake, seeing that the remaining divisions were making a frontal attack on a wide front by time-table.

Certainly General Lee's fears, expressed to the III. Corps before the battle, the inability of the III. Corps to get the time-table altered, and the actual progress of the battle, confirming, as it did, General Lee' doubts, do tend to endorse the justice of this criticism. Sir Archibald Montgomery is right in attributing the initiation of this turning movement to General Lee. But he is not right when he infers that the turning movement became the plan of only one Division, the 18th, and not, as was the case, that of two Divisions—the 12th and 18th—of General Sir Richard Butler's III. Corps, which comprised the 12th, 18th, and 74th Divisions.

During the night 18th-19th September there was a great deal of Boche shelling, but when day dawned the effect of our infantry's work of the day before became manifest; for it was discovered that certain points, including May Copse, north of the Ridge, and the approaches to " X," " Y," and " Z " Copses, had been evacuated.

It was thought that " X," " Y," and " Z " Copses had also been evacuated, but when patrols of the Bedfordshires and the 55th Brigade approached them it was to be received with a machine-gun fire which showed that as yet these copses were by no means clear of the enemy. May Copse, however, was promptly occupied by the Northamptonshires. The village of Lempire had also been converted into a stronghold by the enemy, and was being held by the Prussian Guards. Altogether, it was clearer than ever that these outposts of the far-famed Hindenburg Line were going to be defended to the last.

At 11 A.M. the 53rd Brigade (minus the 10th Essex) attacked under a creeping barrage. Their object was to clear the northern portion of Lempire, establish themselves on a line facing east of the village through the Yak, Zebra, and Braeton Posts, and get at last into touch with the 12th Division.

Once more, however, our men met with very heavy machine-gun fire, not only from the village but also from the three copses. The Berkshires, in particular, suffered heavily. They had marched forward under cover of the contours of the ground, only to find themselves, as at Trones Wood, pushing a wedge into the Germans with their flanks exposed. Doleful Post and Egg Post on their right were as yet untaken, and a raking fire from these points tore the Berkshires right flank to pieces. But on their left they were screened by a high bank north of Lempire, and the company on that side went straight up the road, got through in a brisk and dashing manner, and caused the Germans to retire hurriedly. In fact, the Berkshires came along so quickly that they captured an unopened mail-bag. Protected by the high bank, they were able to work round from the left towards the "green" objective. By 1 P.M. they had reached it, and by 4 P.M. were in possession of the ground that subsequently was their starting-off place for the attack on The Knoll.

The whole of this particular operation was a good instance of initial failure redeemed by "pegging away."

Many a gallant deed was performed by individual Berkshires that day. Lance - Corporal James Cecil Masters, for example, in the face of heavy machine-gun fire, reorganised a bombing party, bombed up a trench towards the machine-guns, and finally reached the enemy post, and captured two machine-guns and nine prisoners.

Lance-Corporal Arthur James Rawlings, in charge of a company of stretcher-bearers, repeatedly went out into the open with his squad, bringing in wounded men under heavy shell-fire and close machine-gun fire. An officer lay out in front of our lines badly wounded, and three stretcher-bearers had been hit trying to bring him in. This gallant N.C.O. went forward, dressed the officer's wounds, and brought him safely back.

At 2 P.M. the West Kents delivered another attack in which they jumped forward to a line Lempire Post-Yak Post-St Patrick's Lane; but the 12th Division on our left was still fighting for its objectives, and we were not yet able to get into touch with them.

But our "nibbling" never stopped. During the night Zebra Post was finally captured and occupied, and by 7 A.M. on 20th September the three copses were also ours, "X" Copse falling to the 7th Queens and "Y" and "Z" to the 7th Buffs, while farther south and east the 8th East Surreys had penetrated and captured Quenchette Wood. Three hours later a heavy bombardment in conjunction with a counter-attack farther north led to our advanced posts being temporarily withdrawn, but a long day's fighting ended in their being re-established by dark. It was on the 20th that Major J. C. Parke, who had been commanding the 10th Essex, was wounded returning from a reconnaissance.

There was scarcely a moment during these days of 18th, 19th, and 20th September when our men were not facing a desperate and skilful enemy at close quarters, and amid every form of difficulty, showing a steadiness and courage that this record can do little more than barely indicate.

There was 2nd Lieutenant J. E. Chilvers of the Buffs, who won the M.C. on 18th September. After his company commander had been wounded he took command of the company and displayed great cool-ness and skill at a very trying time. He led parties to the enemy positions in "Z" Copse. He was wounded in the head during the advance, but carried on until he was able to withdraw the patrols. Later, when an enemy machine-gun was causing casualties, he crawled forward with a small party of men and dealt with the garrison. During the withdrawal he was again wounded, and it was not until he had com-pleted his task of reorganisation that he reported his wounds. The official record of his work concluded with the words, "His behaviour is all the more com-mendable as it was the first time this officer had been in action."

And the way in which on the night of the 19th Lieutenant Attaye of the West Kents bombed up St

Patrick's Avenue to the junction of Bird and Mule trenches, where the enemy had a bombing post, a post never afterwards lost and ultimately handed over to the 12th Division; the gallantry with which Lieut.-Colonel Irwin, of the East Surreys, won a second bar to his D.S.O., and his runner Ambrose the D.C.M., by taking 29 prisoners between them — these are further memories of those repellent but splendid days.

The obstinate resistance offered by the 2nd Guards, 232nd and 121st Divisions and Alpine Corps, from the very beginning of the battle on 18th September, showed the intention of the German Higher Command to hold Templeux-le-Grand, Ronssoy, and Epehy as bastions to the Hindenburg System at all costs.

But the abandonment of "X," "Y," and "Z" Copses on the 18th Division front on 20th September made it clear that there would be no further attempt to recapture these three villages, and that this final defence of the Hindenburg Outpost System would rest upon the important tactical features known as Guillemont Farm and The Knoll.

# CHAPTER XXIX.

## DUNCAN, DOLEFUL, AND EGG POSTS.

*Ceaseless, wearing, unspectacular fighting against trench redoubts that really led to the breaking of the Hindenburg Line—Infantry's endurance pushed to its utmost limit—The attack of 21st September—West Kents capture Sart Farm—The withering fire from The Knoll—Five out of seven tanks knocked out—10th Essex suffer heavy losses—A moonlight resumption of the attack—Northamptonshires capture Doleful Post—German counter-attack riddled by our artillery barrage—Bedfordshires secure Duncan Post—200 Germans killed—Fusiliers' hot pursuit of retreating enemy.*

IN the list of places in France which the 18th Division will always associate with fierce, testing, and costly fighting appear the names of those formidable trench redoubts, Duncan Post, Doleful Post, Egg Post, and Tombois Farm. They were "key" positions that led to the important localities Guillemont Farm and The Knoll, which, with Quennemont Farm, formed the final outer defences of the stretch of the Hindenburg Line that lay opposite the III. Corps front. The Knoll was the objective given to the 18th Division in the attack launched on 21st September along the whole front of the III. Corps.

For four full days the fight was waged against picked German troops, fresh troops that had been sent to hold on at all costs. The depleted battalions of the 18th Division—the average strength of companies was not more than seventy men at this time—went again and again to the attack. Their endurance had to be pushed to its utmost limit. Never were the infantry more exhausted. And they stuck it out.

At the finish, though they still faced the tremendous shelling and machine-gun fire with fortitude, there can be small doubt that sheer physical fatigue had made them lose some of their fire, that the zest for personal conflict was beginning to leave them. But their task was to wear down the enemy, and they accomplished that task.

It was this ceaseless, wearing, unspectacular fighting, this hotly-contested series of struggles for the possession of small lengths of trenches, that finally led to the triumphant breaking of the Hindenburg Line.

On 21st September the 74th Division was still on our right and the 12th on our left. On our part of the front the 53rd Brigade advanced on the left, and the 54th Brigade on the right. The main objective of the 53rd Brigade was The Knoll, a feature of great tactical importance, as it commanded the village and canal-crossing of Vendhuile, and gave a view of the whole of the section of the Hindenburg Line that faced our Divisional front. There was good reason to know the organised strength of The Knoll, for in the Somme battle of 1917 it had proved invincible. We also knew that in the desperate position in which the Germans were beginning to find themselves, The Knoll would now be more strongly defended than ever. Accordingly seven tanks of the 2nd Tank Battalion were allotted to the 53rd Brigade for their part of the job. Between Lempire and The Knoll lay another enemy position, Sart Farm, a little stronghold of trench mortars and machine-guns which this brigade had orders to capture. For the attack on The Knoll the 10th Essex were employed, for that on Sart Farm the 7th West Kents.

To the 54th Brigade was allotted another stiff task the capture of the enemy trenches between The Knoll and the much shelled, but still strongly held, Guillemont Farm. The farm itself, which the enemy had also fortified in great strength, was to be the main objective of the 231st Infantry Brigade of the 74th Division, assisted by four tanks. The 54th Brigade was to attack with two battalions, the Bedfordshires on the right and the 6th Northamptonshires on the left, with the 11th Royal Fusiliers in reserve. The attack was to be under a creeping barrage. The forming-up line was on the Bellicourt Road.

The attack was launched at 5.40 A.M., and it promptly became manifest that the Germans were fully aware of our intentions, for they replied immediately with a very heavy defensive barrage. However, we made a good start. The West Kents quickly captured Sart Farm, while some of the Bedfordshires reached Duncan Post, and the more distant Doleful Post, which lay half-way between the forming-up line and The Knoll, and was particularly valuable to the enemy, as it dominated much of the immediate neighbourhood. Both these posts were known to be strongly organised, and an early report that our men had not only reached Doleful Post, but were actually in possession of it, was subsequently disproved. Meanwhile the 74th Division had also started off well; but presently, swinging slightly to the right, they left a gap between themselves and the Bedfordshires in the neighbourhood of Pot Trench, and this was to cause difficulties.

While this was going on, a section of the 10th Essex, aided by their tanks, had made progress over the sodden, war-mangled ground, and had reached The Knoll Spur, just above Tombois Farm, only, however, to encounter once again the difficulties of 1917. An overwhelming machine-gun fire—Colonel Frizell, who was back again with his battalion, said it was the hottest machine-gun fire he ever encountered —immediately burst upon them, not only from the front, but also obliquely from Guillemont Farm Spur on the right and from Braeton Post and Lark Trench on the left. The 10th Essex were unable to take advantage of the ground which they and their tanks had won, and under the blast of hostile metal the attack withered away. Five of the seven tanks were knocked out, and such of their crews as were able to get back declared that so heavy had been the enemy machine-gun fire that they had found it impossible to fight their guns.

The other section of the Essex Regiment had succeeded in pushing forward to Egg Post, another well-fortified stronghold, but they were immediately counter-attacked in force and driven backward into Pomponious Lane and Fleeceall Lane.

Indeed the general position at 9 A.M. showed plainly how little real progress had been made. Some of the Bedfordshires were in the neighbourhood of Doleful and Duncan Posts in a precarious situation; and a company of the Northamptonshires had got farther ahead, and had succeeded in pushing right through to Island Traverse, near The Knoll, where, however, they found themselves with both flanks in the air—and they were compelled later in the day to withdraw.

It was a tragic business. Our casualties were very heavy indeed, and some of the wounded who had been shot down within a few yards of the German trenches could not be got at. Not for a moment, however, did the moral of our scattered forces waver. Nor, as it happened, was the anticipation of a heavy counter-attack fulfilled. The enemy confined himself to strengthening his defences, while we made plans for the renewal of the attack. In the evening the crippled 10th Essex, who had suffered 280 casualties, were relieved by the 8th Berkshires and withdrawn for a couple of days into Divisional Reserve.

That night, with moonlight to show the way, the attack was renewed by the 53rd and 54th Brigades.

Originally it had been intended that the 53rd Brigade should attack Egg and Fleeceall Posts independently; but when General Lee discovered that Doleful Post, instead of being in the hands of the Bedfordshires, was still in full possession of the Boche the plan was altered to include a simultaneous attack by the Northamptonshires on Doleful Post, and by the Fusiliers and Bedfordshires on Duncan Post, with a bombing attack by the Berkshires on Egg and Fleeceall Posts, the entire operation to be carried out under a creeping barrage.

At 12.15 the attack began. Once again success was incomplete. On the right the company of Fusiliers swung too far to the right, and, instead of capturing Duncan Post, seized Cat Post and parts of Dog Trench and Pot Lane, where, however, they established themselves after sending back twenty prisoners. On the left the bombing attacks on Egg and Fleeceall Posts met with serious resistance, and were driven back after heavy fighting, though we were able to establish posts in the neighbouring Pomponious and Fleeceall Lanes. In the centre the Northamptonshires' storming party, some thirty strong, led by 2nd Lieutenant R. Bland, did well, capturing Doleful Post and over forty prisoners at a total cost of three casualties. To this good result careful reconnaissance of the position by 2nd Lieutenant R. Bland largely contributed, and the official account of his work, for which he was awarded the M.C., is worth quoting :—

"He was in command of a storming party with orders to capture and consolidate a post held by the enemy. His skilful reconnaissance of the position enabled him to bring his party forward in extended order until each man was within jumping distance from the trench. At a given signal the whole party stormed the trench, captured the whole post and forty-eight prisoners, and killed about twenty of the enemy with a loss of three casualties, slightly wounded. The success was due to the personal courage of this officer, and to his skilful organisation and reconnaissance."

For the same operation an M.C. was also awarded to 2nd Lieutenant E. Marlow, who led his men to the trench which he was one of the first to enter. Here he promptly shot two of the enemy, causing confusion, and enabling the rest of the trench to be rushed.

There was now a marked element of unsafety in the general line that had been reached, for the enemy in Duncan Post and in Duncan Avenue lay between the Fusiliers and the Northamptonshires, separating them. Units, moreover, had once more become mixed; and early in the afternoon of 22nd September the Germans were seen dribbling forward in numbers over the ridge south of Tombois Farm, evidently with the idea of a counter-attack on Doleful Post.

At 3.45 P.M. this attack developed without an enemy barrage, and was participated in by a force amounting to about a battalion.

Up went the S.O.S., and down at once came our barrage; but in spite of this the Boche attack got to within fifty yards of our line. Then a blast of rifle and machine-gun fire stopped it. The enemy were unable either to progress or to return our fire. They had nothing left for it but to retire, and they had to go back through our artillery barrage. Few got back, and those lucky ones who were able to hide in shell-holes were taken prisoners in front of the post. The line held by the 54th Brigade was at once consolidated, the 80th Field Company Royal Engineers, under Captain Weir, and the Sussex Pioneers undertaking the task.

Meanwhile Major L. H. Keep, D.S.O., temporarily Commanding the 2nd Bedfordshires, had arranged an attack to clear the trenches about Duncan Post at 3 P.M. after a ten minutes' bombardment. The bombardment, as it happened, did not materialise, for the very good reason that the artillery were standing by for the expected attack on Doleful Post.

The attack was carried out by Lieutenant R. T. Oldfield and 2nd Lieutenant W. Pennington with a storming party of forty-four men; and it had the gratifying result of capturing the entire position with from 100 to 150 prisoners, who, owing to the size and situation of the victorious force, had to be handed over to the 74th Division, though subsequently they were reclaimed.

In this spirited operation about 200 Germans were killed, and in Duncan Post alone eighty dead were found, all shot at short range.  Thirty machine-guns were captured.  About a hundred of the enemy scuttled eastwards, hotly pursued by the Fusiliers, who impetuously drove them into our artillery's Doleful Post barrage.  Unfortunately, some of our own men were caught in this barrage.  At 5 P.M. the enemy counter-attacked Duncan and Doleful Posts.  The attack was shattered, and a day of very heavy fighting ended with our men in wearied but confident possession of some of the hardest-won ground in the history of the Division.

The enthusiastic excitement of the troops who took part in the literal annihilation of the enemy during the counter-attacks on 22nd September was unprecedented.

On separate occasions companies of Northamptonshires, as well as of the Fusiliers, left their trenches to pursue the defeated foe.  During one of the enemy counter-attacks on Doleful Post a stretcher-bearer of the Berkshires, Private Ernest John Pocock, ran up and down the parados of a trench throwing ammunition to its defending riflemen as the enemy drew nearer, and shouting, "Shoot, boys, shoot!" almost as though he were at a football match!

Egg Post was still holding out against us, and on 23rd and 24th September three further efforts were made to capture it, two by the West Kents in daylight, with Stokes mortars and machine-guns, and one by moonlight and without a barrage, by two companies of the 10th Essex who had now returned to the line.  Heavy machine-gun fire caused these attacks to fail, however.  Its situation enabled Egg Post to meet every attack with a heavy enfilading fire from

414      DUNCAN, DOLEFUL, AND EGG POSTS.

commanding positions, and it had to be left to others
to reduce.

On the night of 24th-25th September the Division
was given a very necessary relief, and went back to
Nurlu for a rest, while the 2nd American Corps took
over the line.

Of these days, from 21st September to 24th September, as of those around Ronssoy and Lempire, a
host of stories of individual gallantry can be told.

It was, for example, in the bitter fighting of 21st
September that Lance-Corporal Lewis of the Northamptonshires, who had won his V.C. only three
days before, met his death—a fine soldier to the
last.

The official account of the circumstances under which
he fell ran as follows : " During another attack this
N.C.O. displayed splendid power of command ; when
his company was caught in the enemy barrage he was
the first to rush them through it until they came
under heavy fire from enemy machine-guns, whereupon he immediately began to place them out in shell-
holes. While doing this he was killed."

Nor should Captain Maltby's leadership of a company of the West Kents in the attack on Egg Post
on 23rd September be forgotten. Egg Post, it is
said, was originally named "Ego" until a mistake on
the map made it "Egg," and so it remained. The
attack failed in its objective, but succeeded in capturing
another Boche post in the neighbourhood with a bag
of three machine-guns and a dozen prisoners. And
the dash and gallantry of Private George Thomas
Colbran of the West Kents in the fighting at Sart
Farm ! He attacked seven Germans in a strong point
which was hampering our advance. Four of them he
killed, the others became his prisoners. On the night
22nd-23rd September Lance-Corporal Charles Leslie
Waghorn, also of the West Kents, led three separate
bombing parties against a strongly-held enemy position, and in the last raid held off the enemy single

handed until his companions had made a block in the trench, enabling the position to be securely held.

One young Essex subaltern, Lieutenant Parrack, came through a terrible, an amazing experience. His leg was shattered by a bullet when he was within a few yards of the German parapet. He fell into a shell-hole. The Jaegers counter-attacked across the ground where he lay, and left him for dead when they withdrew to their own trenches. For three days he lay there, close to the enemy, while our own shells battered and pounded all round him. It was not until the Americans of the 27th Division attacked The Knoll that he was rescued and sent down to the rear. His leg had to be amputated, but his life was saved.

This chapter may well be concluded with the following message from General Rawlinson, dated 24th September 1918 :—

*From* FOURTH ARMY COMMANDER
*to* III. CORPS COMMANDER, 24.9.1918.

During the last twenty-four hours all Divisions of III. Corps have carried out very heavy but successful operations in which valuable progress has been made, particularly by the 18th and 58th Divisions.

On the right, enemy attacked quadrilateral between Duncan and Cat Posts, and were repulsed with heavy losses, leaving 200 prisoners and 20 machine-guns in our hands, over 100 dead being counted in our lines. About 4 P.M. and again at 6 P.M. enemy attacked 18th Division between Doleful and Duncan Posts, but were driven back, leaving 21 prisoners. Attack in each case was made by about one battalion. Not content with repulse of attacks, our troops took advantage of enemy confusion, rushed and captured Duncan Avenue, taking over 100 prisoners and consolidating trench. Stiff fighting also took place during night in Pomponious and Fleeceall Lanes, which were cleared of enemy and blocks established. The 12th Division gradually worked down to Braeton Post against strong opposition, and secured 20 prisoners with 30 machine-guns. At 10 P.M. the 58th Division, in conjunction with the 33rd Division, again attacked Lark Spur, possession of which they had been unable to retain after their attack of the 21st instant. All objectives as far as eastern end of Spur were successfully captured, including Dados Loop.

The 12th, 18th, and 58th Divisions have been fighting continuously since 6th August, while the 74th Division has had heavy fighting during the last three weeks. Although opposed to Alpine Corps and four of the finest German Divisions, two of which have reinforced the line within the last forty-eight hours, they have by determination and hard fighting gained ground which is of the greatest importance, and which captured German maps show to be part of the main Hindenburg defences, and were to be held at all costs.

That message gives a good idea of the fighting of a single day. The other days resembled it in its difficulties and were not inferior to it in results.

# CHAPTER XXX.

## THE BREAKING OF THE HINDENBURG LINE.

*Why the 18th Division's rest lasted only four days—General Rawlinson's special selection—A fateful decision : Americans decide to assault Guillemont Farm and The Knoll without a barrage—Colonel Blewitt sees German counter-attack developing up Macquincourt Valley—Americans terrible losses on 29th September—Inexperienced staff work—Bedfords, Fusiliers, and East Surreys in Vendhuile on the 30th—18th Division's 2,573 casualties from Ronssoy to Hindenburg Line—1,415 prisoners taken—General Butler's "Au revoir" message.*

THE Division's rest was very brief, only four days. General Rawlinson did not want to use the 25th, 50th, and 66th Divisions until the Hindenburg Line had been actually broken, when his plan was for these fresh, full-strength Divisions to sweep forward towards Le Cateau. That was why the worn, hard-tried 18th had to come up again from Combles, Maurepas, and Nurlu to join with the American 27th and 30th Divisions in the final piercing of the Hindenburg system.

It was General Lee's task to prepare the Division for the new call upon it. He addressed each brigade during the short recess, congratulated all ranks upon their splendid achievements, and told them that General Rawlinson had specially selected the 18th Division to remain in the Fourth Army, to take part in the historic operation now immediately pending. The General was well cheered, although the battalion and company commanders had been calculating upon a very necessary three-weeks' rest for refitting and

2 D

for incorporating the new recruits, mostly youngsters, into its badly-thinned ranks.

The main attack on the Hindenburg Line on the Fourth Army front was fixed for 29th September. The part assigned to the III. Corps was to cover the left flank of the main attack on our right, which was to be carried out by the Australian Corps and by the II. American Corps (27th and 28th Divisions) who were affiliated to the Australian Corps. The attack on the III. Corps front was to be carried out by the 18th and 12th Divisions, the rôle assigned to the 18th Division being—

(1) The protection of the left flank of the 27th American Division by gaining complete observation over Vendhuile and the St Quentin Canal, and by keeping constant pressure on the enemy in the vicinity.

(2) The "mopping-up" of Vendhuile and the preparation of a way through for the passage of Divisions of V. Corps at the first possible opportunity.

The first of these objectives was allotted to the 54th Brigade, the second to the 55th Brigade, plus a "liaison" force of the 54th Brigade detailed to work with the 107th American Infantry Regiment. Half a company of the 18th Battalion Machine-Gun Corps was allotted to each brigade for the operation.

The 53rd Brigade were to be in Corps reserve.

The plan of attack was as follows : the attack of 27th American Division was to be in two phases :—

(1) An attack to capture the Hindenburg Line south of the open canal.

(2) A second attack to cross the tunnel, capture Le Catelet and Gouy, and exploit success northwards towards the high ground east of Hargival Farm and Richmond Copse.

The "liaison" force organised by the 54th Brigade to accompany the 107th American Infantry Regiment was composed of two companies of the 2nd Bedford shires, "B" Company of the 18th Battalion Machine-Gun Corps, the 80th Field Company R.E., and a detachment of the 54th Brigade Signal Section. It was commanded by Major Patterson, 18th Battalion M.G.C., and its task was to accompany the American attack on the southern side of Macquincourt Valley, take up a position astride the canal, and prevent the enemy from destroying the bridges at Vendhuile. It was also to keep up signal communication between the 107th American Infantry Regiment and the 54th Brigade.

As soon as opportunity offered the Royal Engineers were to push into the village of Vendhuile to reconnoitre the bridges and report upon them. Three sections of the 80th Field Company R.E., with a company of the 2nd Bedfordshires as escort, were kept in reserve at the 54th Brigade headquarters in readiness for any work that might be necessary on the bridges.

The 55th Brigade were to be within one hour's march of The Knoll by 8 A.M., by which hour it was hoped the canal tunnel would be in American hands, and that American forces would be exploiting their successes in order to clear the enemy from the high ground north of Le Catelet.

As soon as the situation permitted General Lee proposed to issue orders to the 55th Infantry Brigade to march viâ Macquincourt Valley, form to the left, and advance on Vendhuile from the south, keeping to the west of the canal. If serious opposition was encountered they were not to become involved in a direct attack on the town, but were to bring pressure to bear on its defences from the spur north of Macquincourt Valley, and to take every advantage of the slackening of the enemy's resistance in order to push into the town west of the canal. The 79th and 92nd Field Companies R.E. and 8th Royal Sussex Regiment (Pioneers) were to be employed in repairing the bridges in Vendhuile and the roads leading to them, and a troop of the 1st Northumberland Hussars was placed at the disposal of the 18th Division for the operation in general.

Meanwhile we knew that the German 8th and 54th Divisions had relieved the Guards and 232nd Divisions, who lately had been opposing us on this front.

Such was the plan. It combined confidence and caution, but no experienced soldier regarded the prospect lightly. Before us lay the vastest and most powerfully organised defensive line the world has ever seen, constructed at leisure and strengthened by every resource which the science of military engineering had at its disposal—wired belts enfiladed by concrete machine-gun emplacements, dug-outs, an extensive network of light railways and signal communications, a complete system of electric light and power, and last, but by no means least, the St Quentin Canal, which on the southern part of our front ran through open country, and on the northern through the strong and protecting Bellicourt tunnel.

When to all this is added the formidable German consciousness that, save for the unfinished Masnieres-Beaurevoir line, they had no prepared defensive works behind, it was easy to imagine the stubbornness with which this mighty "last ditch" would be defended.

One weakness menaced it on our part of the front. A most valuable memorandum, captured in August at a German corps headquarters, contained a defence scheme complete in every detail of the Hindenburg Line between the Oise and Bellicourt, and in this memorandum it was admitted that certain points of observation in front of the line must be kept out of our hands.

Among these, on the 18th Division's part of the front, was the high ground about Quennemont Farm, Guillemont Farm, and our old enemy The Knoll.

On 27th September the American 27th Division attacked and were reported to have captured the

" Hindenburg " outpost line, including Guillemont
Farm and The Knoll.

This would have meant much had it been true.
By noon on 28th September, however, it was discovered that the American forces held little or none
of their objectives of the day before. They had,
indeed, rushed forward impetuously through mist,
shell-smoke, and enemy gas, but they had suffered
terrible losses from the very start by raking machine-
gun and anti-tank fire; and though they had gained
a footing on The Knoll, they had subsequently been
driven off part of it by a strong counter-attack.
Except for elements still holding out, their line at
midday on 28th September ran as the 18th Division
had handed it over to them—Fleeceall Post-Egg Post-
Doleful Post; and they made no serious attempt to
improve the position.

During the afternoon of 28th September it was
decided—

(1) That in view of the presence of American ele-
     ments on The Knoll, the barrage would fall
     *east* of The Knoll.

(2) That the attack of the 107th American Infantry
     Regiment should fight its way to the opening
     line of the barrage in time to go forward
     with it.

Now the course of the battle will be better understood if the importance of these decisions is realised,
*for they sealed the fate of the 27th American Divi-
sion.*

Lieut.-Colonel Guy Blewitt, G.S.O.1, of the 18th
Division, was present at a conference called by General
Ryan, who commanded the 27th American Division,
at the 54th American Brigade Headquarters in Ronssoy at about midday on 28th September.

The conference had to do with the action to be
taken consequent upon the discovery of the American
staff that they had not taken any of their objectives
on 27th September. As a result, the barrage arranged

for the attack of 29th September (sixteen hours later) would now come down about 1,000 yards ahead of where the American infantry would begin their advance. It had also to be borne in mind that a change of barrage at this late hour would probably necessitate a twenty-four-hours' postponement of the operation on the whole of the Fourth Army front.

Suffice it to say that the reason ascribed for the barrage being put east of The Knoll in decision (1) mentioned above was in all probability fallacious. Also the task allotted to the 107th American Infantry Regiment in decision (2) entailed for them *the stupendous task of capturing Guillemont Farm and The Knoll in the dark, without a barrage, in order to get to the starting line.*

True, they had tanks, but tanks could not operate in the dark.

Now the 54th Brigade of the 18th Division had been kept constantly informed of the situation, but it was impossible for General Lee to issue his final orders until after receipt of the decisions made at the Ronssoy conference. It was not until 9 P.M. that the 54th Brigade got their fresh instructions for the assault next day.

Bearing in mind the rôle at first allotted to the 18th Division, it was clearly useless for the Division to start protecting the left flank of the 27th American Division until the Americans had had time to advance and expose a flank. Moreover, if the 27th American Division was prepared to attack without a barrage, the 12th and 18th Divisions were not.

It was these considerations that decided General Lee and General Higginson of the 12th Division to form a plan, the salient points of which were—

The barrage on the whole front was to move forward at zero plus 4 minutes until zero plus 4 minutes, when that part of it on the 54th Brigade and 12th Division front would lift back to take the 54th Brigade and the 12th Division forward a

zero plus 44, while that part of it in front of the
Americans proceeded without interruption.  The
54th Brigade were to form up behind the left
of the 107th American Infantry Regiment and
diverge in a south-easterly direction.

At zero hour (5.40 A.M.) on 29th September, after a
terrific artillery bombardment, the attack began.

On the left the 11th Royal Fusiliers, having the
Tombois Road to guide them, kept direction without
difficulty in spite of the mist and smoke.  On the
right direction was not so well kept, and some of the
Northamptonshires followed the Americans in a swerve
to the south and were lost.

The troops of the 12th Division and the 11th
Royal Fusiliers, and also the left of the Northamptonshires, reached their objectives up to time, while the
right of the Northamptonshires, after heavy fighting,
eventually established a line approximately along
Knoll Switch.

Throughout the morning the enemy made several
counter-attacks against The Knoll.  They proved fruit-
less, but both at The Knoll and farther south all our
movements were hampered by rifle and machine-gun
fire from Guillemont Farm.

At 8.45 A.M. General Lee ordered the 55th Brigade
forward.   As, however, the enemy was still in
strength at Guillemont Farm, and the Americans
had been unable to drive him either from the Hindenburg Line immediately south-east of Vendhuile or
from the high ground to the east, the proposed advance down the Macquincourt Valley was, for the
time being, impracticable.

Accordingly about 10 A.M., after a reconnaissance
of the situation, the 55th Brigade commander, General
Wood, ordered his leading battalion, the 7th Queens,
to man the Doleful Post line; the 7th Buffs were
halted in the Fleeceall-Pomponious Lanes area; and
the 8th East Surreys remained in position immedi-
tely north of Lempire.

About this time the G.S.O.1, Colonel Guy Blewitt, seeing a counter-attack that was supported by a withering machine-gun fire from Guillemont Farm on to The Knoll developing up the Macquincourt Valley, discarded his horse for a rifle and set to work organising a defensive flank that faced south against the Guillemont Farm spur, which by now should have been in the possession of the unfortunate 27th American Division. At the same time Colonel Blewitt sent back to report to the 3rd Australian Division, who were to go through the Americans, the hazardous state of affairs.

Another officer who made strenuous efforts to cope with the puzzling changes in the situation was Captain (Acting Major) F. J. Rice, R.F.A. Under heavy shell-fire he took his battery C/82 into action in the neighbourhood of Little Priel Farm, west of Vendhuile, and then pushed forward with his telephone wire so as to render the closest support to the attacking infantry. Foiled in one direction by enemy machine-gun fire, he succeeded in another, and obtained observations that enabled the guns of his battery to lend valuable aid to the attack.

At 1.25 P.M. the 55th Brigade were ordered to send a battalion by way of The Knoll to attack the enemy in the Grub Lane neighbourhood from the north. The situation on The Knoll was, however, so obscure, and the enemy machine-gun and artillery fire so deadly, that the operation could not be begun. The probability of a heavy enemy counter-attack had also increased.

As darkness descended the 7th Buffs were ordered to hold the south flank of The Knoll—i.e., Cochrane Avenue-Lion Trench-Egg Post. About the same time the 18th Division's "liaison" force with the Americans was withdrawn. As so little had been achieved on this day of stern fighting, the second objective of the 18th Division's attack, the preparing of a way through

Vendhuile for the passage of the Divisions of V. Corps, was not proceeded with.

About 10 A.M. on 30th September, however, came indications that an important change had taken place in the entire situation. News came through of the magnificent success of the 46th Division the day before, a mile or two farther down the line. It was also discovered that the enemy had withdrawn from Guillemont Farm, and our patrols following up, had little difficulty in reaching the outskirts of Vendhuile Trench and Vendhuile Village.

It was clear that the Boche was no longer holding Vendhuile. He clung in strength, however, to "Putney," on the north side of the canal, and to the part of the Hindenburg Line in the neighbourhood. The 7th Buffs and the 8th East Surreys were accordingly ordered to enter Vendhuile from the south.

Their orders were not to fight for the Vendhuile bridges, but to establish an outpost line along the canal, to push patrols across, and to locate the enemy. All attempts to cross the canal were, however, frustrated by enemy snipers and machine-guns. The East Surreys had many casualties from gas that night; thirty-five were gassed in Vendhuile, and next morning, when they marched out, the hot sun brought out the gas in the men's clothing and numbers of them collapsed.

During the night September 30-October 1 the 53rd Brigade, who during the operations of the preceding two days had been held in Corps Reserve, in the valleys south-west of Epehy, and afterwards in St Patrick's Valley, reverted to the command of the 18th Division, and relieved a portion of the line held by the 37th Infantry Brigade of the 12th Division, north-west and west of Vendhuile. The 37th Brigade had also established outposts on the canal, but in consequence of the very heavy enemy fire had been unable to cross.

During the following day, 1st October, the Australians, who had relieved the 27th American Division, made progress up the Hindenburg Line from Bony, but junction with us on the canal was not effected. Touch was, however, established between them and the 55th Brigade in Macquincourt Valley—and there the 18th Division's share in these operations ended, and, for a while, its prolonged share in the desperate fighting.

On the night of 1st-2nd October all three brigades were relieved by the 149th Infantry Brigade of the 50th Division, and the 18th Division moved back by omnibus to the Montigny area, leaving the 18th Divisional Artillery behind to carry on their good work, attached to the 50th Division.

It will have been observed that the Americans gradually faded out of this account of the two days of fierce fighting.

The reason is not far to seek. To the 27th and 30th American Divisions had been allotted a decisive part. When the storming of the canal and tunnel defences had, as was hoped, been achieved, and the Hindenburg reserve, or Catelet-Nauroy line, had been forced, the two American Divisions were to swing north and south : to the north with a view to cutting off the enemy holding Vendhuile, thus facilitating the task of the III. Corps ; and to the south so as to gain touch with the bridgehead to be established by the IX. Corps at Bellenglise.

But in the stress and excitement of their first big battle, fought as it was in a dense mist, the "moppers-up" of the 30th Division went on instead of dealing with the Germans who had taken shelter during the initial advance. The result was, that not only were the Americans attacked from the rear, but the Australians who followed also encountered strong resistance. Six hundred Americans went through Vendhuile and were cut off in this way.

The 27th American Division found itself beset with difficulties from the outset. Half its tanks were put out of action early in the fighting, and, although some of the troops reached and broke through the tunnel defences, the main force of the attack had to be expended against Quennemont Farm and Guillemont Farm, which were still held by the enemy when the 3rd Australian Division arrived on the scene.

The men of the 27th American Division were magnificent, but their staffs were lacking in experience. Such things as assembly positions and forming-up lines were disregarded. Their " communications " were lamentable; so much so that brigade and Divisional headquarters had no means of learning what was happening except from that somewhat unreliable source—the aeroplane observer.

On the 30th, Captain R. A. Chell, brigade-major of the 55th Brigade, came upon fifty or sixty Americans sitting in a trench on The Knoll. They asked him what they should do, and he put them in the way of getting on with the war. They said to him, "Thank you very much, sir. You are the first officer who has taken any interest in us to-day," and off they moved to attack.

Another party that had lost its way was accounted for in a note left sticking up on a machine-gun post in Vendhuile by a German cavalry officer. The note ran: "Dear Tommy,—From this place I shot 60 American soldiers with my machine-gun; they came like sheeps."

The 27th American Division's losses cannot have been far short of 5,000, a thing that should never have happened at that period of the war. Undoubtedly the chief reason for such appalling losses was that Guillemont Farm and The Knoll were attacked without a supporting artillery barrage.

In the twelve days of fighting between Ronssoy and

the Hindenburg defences, the 18th Division suffered the following casualties :—

|            | Killed. | Wounded. | Missing. | Total. |
|------------|---------|----------|----------|--------|
| Officers   | 24      | 87       | 2        | 113    |
| Other ranks| 402     | 1,921    | 137      | 2,460  |
|            | 426     | 2,008    | 139      | 2,573  |

The Division took 1,415 prisoners, of whom 20 were officers. We also captured 4 heavy guns, 9 field-guns, 17 trench mortars, 122 machine-guns, and a number of anti-tank guns. On the last day of September the following *au revoir* message was received from Lieut.-General Sir R. H. K. Butler, commanding III. Corps :—

*From III. Corps Commander, 30-9-1918.*

It is with the greatest regret that I bid *au revoir* to the 18th Division. Throughout all the operations of the III. Corps since March 1918, the Division has not only fought with gallantry and determination, but also with the spirit of mutual co-operation and comradeship which ensure success.

I also wish to convey my personal thanks to General Lee, the staff, and all ranks of the 18th Division for the loyal support and for the manner in which they have always "played up." I trust that it may be my good fortune, at no distant date, to have the Division in my command again in further victorious operations."

With these hearty words ringing in its ears, the Division proceeded to the enjoyment of the *entr'acte* of rest and recreation which was to precede—though few guessed it even in those days of victory—the Last Phase of the Great War.

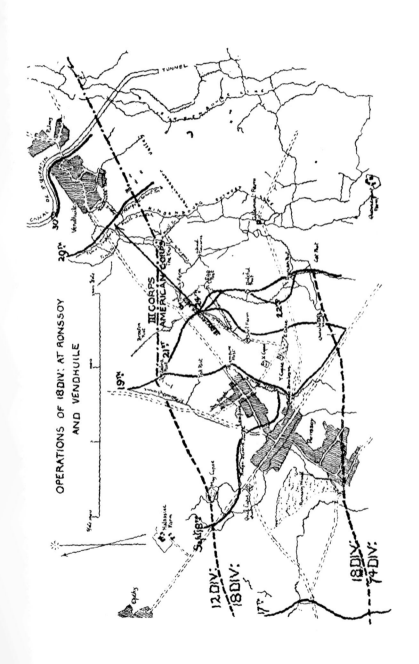

OPERATIONS OF 18 DIV: AT RONSSOY
AND VENDHUILE

## ORDER OF BATTLE.

### 18TH SEPTEMBER TO 30TH SEPTEMBER 1918.

Commander . . . Major-General R. P. Lee, C.B.
A.D.C. to Commander . Lieut. A. F. G. Everitt, General List.
A.D.C. to Commander . Captain N. Hanbury, Coldstream Guards.

### G. S. BRANCH.

G.S.O. 1 . . . . Lieut.-Colonel G. Blewitt, D.S.O., M.C., Oxf. and Bucks L.I.
G.S.O. 2 . . . . Major A. H. Hopwood, D.S.O., Lincolnshire Regt.
G.S.O. 3 . . . . Captain G. J. C. Welch, Royal Berkshire Regt.

### A. & Q. BRANCH.

A.A. & Q.M.G. . . . Lieut.-Colonel R. H. L. Cutbill, D.S.O., Army Service Corps.
D.A.A.G. . . . . Major A. H. B. Foster, D.S.O., Lancaster Regt.
D.A.Q.M.G. (Acting) . Major H. A. Philpott, M.C., R.A.

### ADMIN. SCOS. AND DEPTS.

A.D.M.S. . . . . Colonel J. Poe, D.S.O., R.A.M.C.
D.A.D.M.S. . . . Major A. J. Clark, M.C., R.A.M.C.
D.A.D.V.S. . . . Major L. M. Verney, D.S.O., A.V.C.
D.A.D.O.S. . . . Major C. A. Worssam, A.O.D.
D.A.P.M. . . . . Captain P. Cazenove, Herts Yeomanry.

### DIVISIONAL ARTILLERY.

Commander (Acting) . Lieut.-Colonel T. O. Seagram, D.S.O.
Brigade Major . . Major W. A. Stirling, D.S.O., M.C.
Staff Captain (Acting) . Lieut. H. E. Bullivant.
Reconnaissance Officer . Lieut. N. O. Hutton, M.C.
D.T.M.O. . . . . Captain R. K. Cannan.
82nd Brigade R.F.A. . Lieut.-Colonel A. Thorp, D.S.O. (under 12t' Division).
83rd Brigade R.F.A. . Lieut.-Colonel C. E. B. Dennis, D.S.O.
Div. Ammunition Column Lieut.-Colonel F. C. Johnston, D.S.O.
No. 1 Section, Signal Co. . Captain R. G. Browning.
290th Brigade R.F.A. (attached) Lieut.-Colonel Jones, D.S.O.
291st Brigade R.F.A. (attached) Lieut.-Colonel R. Longstaff, D.S.O.

110th Brigade R.F.A. (attached)    Lieut.-Colonel R. E. Milford, D.S.O.

44th Brigade R.F.A. (attached)    Lieut.-Colonel Bretwoode Robertson, D.S.O.

117th Brigade R.F.A. (attached)    Lieut.-Colonel W. Kinnear, D.S.O.

## DIVISIONAL ENGINEERS.

| | |
|---|---|
| Commander . . . | Lieut.-Colonel C. B. O. Symons, D.S.O. |
| Adjutant . . . . | Captain G. H. Kohl. |
| 79th Field Co. R.E. . | Major K. I. Gourlay, M.C. |
| 80th Field Co. R.E. . | Major G. Ledgard, M.C. |
| 92nd Field Co. R.E. . | Major E. D. Alexander, M.C. |
| 18th Div. Signal Co. . | Major N. S. Regnart, M.C. |

## 53RD INFANTRY BRIGADE.

| | |
|---|---|
| Commander . . . | Brigadier-General M. G. H. Barker, D.S.O. |
| Brigade Major . . | Captain H. James, V.C. |
| Staff Captain . . | Captain S. J. Price, M.C. |
| No. 2 Section, Signal Co. . | Lieut. J. L. Henderson. |
| 10th Essex Regt. . | Lieut.-Colonel C. W. Frizell, D.S.O., M.C. |
| 8th R. Berkshire Regt. | Lieut.-Colonel T. M. Banks, D.S.O., M.C. |
| 7th R. West Kent Regt. . | Lieut.-Colonel L. H. Hickson. |
| 53rd T.M. Battery . | Captain D. V. Sutherst, M.C. |

## 54TH INFANTRY BRIGADE.

| | |
|---|---|
| Commander . . . | Brigadier-General J. A. Tyler (18th/24th September). |
| Commander . . . | Lieut.-Colonel (Acting Brigadier-General) R. Turner, D.S.O. (25th/30th September). |
| Brigade Major . . | Captain the Hon. D. G. Fortescue. |
| Staff Captain . . | Captain L. W. Diggle, M.C. |
| No. 3 Section, Signal Co. . | Lieut. C. H. Webb, M.C. |
| 11th Royal Fusiliers . | Lieut.-Colonel K. D. H. Gwynn, D.S.O., M.C. |
| 2nd Bedford Regt. . | Major L. H. Keep, D.S.O., M.C. (18th/28th September). |
| do. | Lieut.-Colonel A. E. Percival, D.S.O., M.C. (29th/30th September). |
| 6th Northants Regt. . | Lieut.-Colonel R. Turner, D.S.O. |
| 54th T.M. Battery . | Captain P. J. Payton. |

## 55TH INFANTRY BRIGADE..

| | |
|---|---|
| Commander . . . | Brigadier-General E. A. Wood, D.S.O. |
| Brigade Major . . | Captain R. A. Chell, M.C. |
| Staff Captain . . | Captain R. W. Keown, M.C. |
| No. 4 Section, Signal Co. . | Lieut. L. W. Bird, M.C. |
| 7th Queens . . . | Lieut.-Colonel G. L. Harrison, D.S.O. |

| 7th Buffs . . . . | Lieut.-Colonel H. M. C. Curtis, D.S.O. |
| 8th E. Surrey Regt. . | Lieut.-Colonel A. P. B. Irwin, D.S.O. |
| 55th T.M. Battery . | Captain P. G. Heath, M.C. |

## M.G.C.

| 18th Battalion M.G. Corps | Major C. B. Hibbert, D.S.O. |

## PIONEERS.

| 8th Royal Sussex Regt. | Lieut.-Colonel B. J. Walker, D.S.O. |

## R.A.M.C.

| 54th Field Ambulance | Lieut.-Colonel G. Pritchard Taylor, D.S.O., M.C. |
| 55th Field Ambulance | Lieut..Colonel M. G. Winder, D.S.O. |
| 56th Field Ambulance | Lieut.-Colonel K. D. Murchison, D.S.O. |

## A.S.C.

| 18th Div. Train | Lieut.-Colonel R. R. B. Jackson, D.S.O. |
| 150th Company | Major Newall, Captain H. N. M'Call. |
| 151st Company . | Captain E. M. Ford, M.C. |
| 152nd Company | Captain E. M. West, M.C. |
| 153rd Company | Captain C. H. P. Lloyd. |

[*The author is indebted to Lieut.-Colonel Guy Blewitt for the outline plans of battles, for the large maps, and also for the official narrative of the Division's part in the Battle of the Hundred Days.*]

# CHAPTER XXXI.

## BOUSIES AND ONWARDS—18TH DIVISION CAPTURES 53 GUNS IN ONE DAY.

*The Hundred Days' Battle, the greatest the world has seen—Not a processional march—18th Division comes in again at Le Cateau, and thrusts Germans back 8,000 yards on 23rd October—The 7th West Kents' shattered breakfast—Germans start work with mobile trench mortars—Berkshires' 30 men killed within fifty yards of enemy field-guns—Fine leadership by Captain Hornfeck of the Fusiliers, Captain Whitmarsh of the 7th Buffs, and Colonel Thorp of the Divisional Artillery—The gallantry of Major H. H. Gardiner, R.F.A.*

THE phase of the war now entered upon was that covering the great battle of the Selle river and the Sambre river, in which, as Lord Haig said in his "Victory Despatch," the enemy's resistance was definitely broken, and the long conflict of more than four years came to a sudden and intensely dramatic end.

The advance of the British armies in France during the Hundred Days from August to November 1918 was not a sort of splendid processional march. It was a prolonged battle, the greatest the world has ever seen—a battle in which the enemy put up, for the most part, an obstinate resistance; in which he opposed to us nearly twice as many Divisions as those the British army put in the field, the exact proportions being 99 to 59.

The results were for all the world to see—187,000 prisoners in our hands, 2,850 captured guns, a routed enemy, the Armistice, and Victory. It was epic fighting that created new and splendid traditions; that

2 E

challenged the highest record of the British armies of the past, and will be an inspiration to the generations that come after.

A brief summary of the part which the 18th Division played in these tremendous concluding days may be conveyed by defining the country over which the Division fought. Our advance commenced at Le Cateau, which had been captured by the 66th Division on 18th October; and it proceeded in a north-easterly direction through Bousies, Robersart, Preux-aux-Bois, Hecq, the Forest of Mormal, and Sassegnies, as far as the Sambre river to a point just west of Leval.

This represented an advance of nearly fourteen miles in a country of abrupt slopes, small streams in the valleys, large tracts of woodlands, including the great Forest of Mormal and innumerable plots of pasture-land enclosed by high thick hedges. It was made against an enemy on the defensive, desperate, in fair strength, and still greatly skilled in military cunning.

Many of the German Army Orders captured in those days revealed the intention of the enemy to defend these places to the very last.

On 19th October the Division, the gaps in its numbers again filled, mainly by youngsters, received intimation that the general advance would be resumed at an early date. The Fourth Army, in conjunction with the Third, was to gain the western edge of the Forest of Mormal and objectives farther north. The task allotted to the Fourth Army was that of forming a defensive flank facing eastward to protect the major operation which would be carried out by the Third Army; and an important strategical operation in the programme of the Fourth Army was that of placing the vital railway junction of Leval—about thirty-five miles north-east of Le Cateau—under long-range fire.

The plan outlined by Sir Thomas Morland, commanding the XIII. Corps, was that the 18th Division should attack with the 25th Division on its right (in touch with the IX. Corps), and with the 33rd Division of the V. Corps, Third Army, on its left. The original intention was to attack on the early morning of 22nd October, but the date was altered to the 23rd.

General Lee decided to attack the first and second objectives with two brigades, the 53rd on the right and the 54th, minus the 6th Northamptonshire Regiment, on the left; while the other brigade, the 55th, with the 6th Northamptonshires attached, was to pass through to the capture of the third, fourth, and fifth objectives, all of which lay beyond Bousies.

Considerations of time and space led General Lee to decide that there was to be, on paper, no Divisional Reserve. As a matter of fact, the 6th Northamptonshires and 7th Buffs could always have been halted and placed in Divisional Reserve at any time during the attack of the 53rd and 54th Brigades, had that attack proved a failure. On the other hand, it was necessary to start all four battalions of the 55th Brigade without waiting for the attack of the leading brigades, so that they might be up to time for "leap-frogging" to their own attack on the more distant objectives. Also, bearing in mind the distance to be covered in the moonlight before forming up to attack at dawn, it was desirable to keep the 55th Brigade on a road as long as possible. And there were only two dependable roads across the Richemont river, the stream that ran about one mile to the north-east of Le Cateau—the Evillers Wood Farm Road on the right, which was in our area, but which the 25th Division wanted to use, and the main Montay-Forest Road, which was out of our area, but which the 33rd Division gave us permission to use providing we got clear of Montay within a couple of hours of the opening of the attack.

The 18th Division had relieved the 66th Division in the line on the night of 20th-21st October, an arrangement which allowed good time for reconnais-

sance.  During 21st October and 22nd October the
concentration of the Division in and around the town
of Le Cateau continued.

The tanks destined to fight with the 54th and 55th
Brigades crossed the Selle river by a crib bridge in
the 33rd Division's area, and lay peacefully camouflaged behind a spur north-west of the village of
Montay ; the Royal Engineers and the Sussex
Pioneers were, as usual, busy removing land-mines
and establishing the roads and bridges which had
been destroyed by the enemy in his flight.

Le Cateau, town of belfried towers and narrow
rambling streets, was still being shelled with devastating high explosives and with gas shells, particularly round and about the neighbourhood of the big
church.

There were still French civilians in the town.
They took things philosophically.  Every now and
then a Boche shell would blow a house across a street,
but these admirable men and women went on with
their day's routine, and, unless the shattered dwell-
ings happened to be their own, would appear each
morning and tidy the doorsteps as punctiliously as
though the war had passed by their town.

Colonel Hickson of the 7th Royal West Kents and
his Battalion Headquarters Staff tell a story of a
breakfast laid in the basement of a shop that they
had made Battalion Headquarters at 2 A.M. on the
morning of the battle.  There was a white table-
cloth, some good quality borrowed crockery, eggs and
bacon, and the first pot of marmalade that the expectant party had seen for weeks.  Just as all was
ready a German shell arrived.  It hurt nobody ; but
when the smoke and dust had cleared, the breakfast
had vanished.  Two hours later the same room saw
Colonel Hickson, revolver in hand, examining batches
of prisoners, with an officer inspecting their identity
discs by candlelight—a weird enough scene.  Scores
of houses in Le Cateau flew the French colours ; i

was vastly interesting to hear how the faithful citizens had kept the flags concealed during the four years' detested German occupation.

For the operations now impending, the following were attached to the Division :—

(a) "B" Squadron 1/1st Northumberland Hussars.
    "B" Squadron, less 1 troop, allotted to 55th Infantry Brigade, 1 troop allotted to 18th Division Headquarters.
(b) "A/C" Coy., 13th Cyclist Battalion.
    Allotted to 55th Infantry Brigade.
(c) 84th Army Brigade, R.F.A., who were originally 18th Divisional Artillery, but had become an Army R.F.A. Brigade at the end of 1916.
    65th Army Brigade, R.F.A.
    250th Brigade, R F.A. ⎫
    251st Brigade, R.F.A. ⎭ 50th Divisional Artillery.
    76th Brigade, R.G.A. (two 6-inch Howitzer Batteries, and two 60-pounder Batteries).
(d) 16 tanks, 10th Battalion Tank Corps.
    1 Section allotted to 53rd Infantry Brigade (2 tanks to co-operate with troops for first objective, 2 tanks for second objective).
    1 Section allotted to 54th Brigade (2 tanks to co-operate with troops for first objective, 2 tanks for second objective).
    2 Sections (8 tanks) allotted to the 55th Infantry Brigade.
    Also 6 supply tanks.
    1 wireless tank.
    1 cable-laying tank.
(e) 100th Battalion Machine-Gun Corps.
    To be employed in the initial barrage only.

The assembly was carried out in rain and under a clouded moon during the night of 22nd-23rd October.

The ground for forming-up was open, and presented no great difficulty to the two leading battalions of the 53rd Brigade, but owing to the close proximity of Le Cateau to the front line it was not easy to find a suitable place of assembly for the 8th Berkshires. Eventually a deep railway cutting east of the town was selected. It gave some shelter, although it more or less coincided with the enemy's barrage line.

"Zero hour" for the main attack of the Third Army was fixed at 2 A.M., and in order to bring the attack of the XIII. Corps level with the main attack, it was decided that the XIII. Corps should begin their assault forty minutes earlier. Accordingly, at 1.20 A.M. our advance began under a creeping barrage that went forward at the rate of twenty-five yards a minute.

By this time the rain had ceased, the sky was clear and the moon was up. The attack on the first three objectives was carried through with great dash, and was entirely successful, owing to a great extent to the excellence of our artillery and machine-gun barrage, and to the assistance given to the 54th and 55th Brigades in their advance by the close co-operation of the tanks. General Lee always said that tanks could only exert a successful influence when they were in full working touch with the infantry. They were so on this occasion.

The enemy replied promptly and heavily to our barrage, causing some casualties, but his infantry could not withstand ours, and no fewer than 700 prisoners, 53 guns, and large quantities of material were in our hands when the battle had been fought and decided.

The 53 guns captured in one day was a fresh record for the Division.

The 53rd Brigade on the right encountered difficulties. The crossing of the Richemont river was one of them.

On the aerial photographs this waterway looked a mere brook. Really it was a wide swamp. Deep railway cuttings also had to be negotiated, while direct hits and gas accounted for the inability of the four tanks allotted to the brigade to help in the attack. The enemy had also brought close up to his front line a number of trench mortars on wheels—another of his war novelties—and they did telling work defence. The gunners who fought them were admirable in their skill and fortitude. The battle provided a very real example of the value of mobile trench mortars used in open warfare.

It was in the crossing of the Richemont river that 2nd Lieutenant A. B. Cullerne of the West Kents was killed, and his company lost 30 men out of 65. Cullerne had won the M.C. in the fighting round Ronssoy; he fell in this battle before hearing of the distinction that had been awarded him. Still the West Kents made excellent progress, all their objectives were taken up to time; and the village of Corbeau, where Lieutenant Pegmar West, leading a small party, got 60 Germans out of the cellars at a cost of only one casualty, was assaulted and captured en route.

"B" Company of the West Kents, under Captain A. V. Macdonald, M.C., found itself isolated. There was no creeping 18-pounder barrage for the attack; 4·5-inch howitzers and machine-guns searched the ground and formed a standing barrage on the Richemont Mill and Copse. Advancing down the hill under cover of this fire, this isolated company, only 65 strong, attacked with such vigour that both Garde Mill—a small hamlet outside the Divisional area—and Garde Copse were captured. Many of the enemy were slain, and 75 were made prisoners at a cost of only 13 casualties.

Prior to the assault on Corbeau, daring and valuable patrol work was done by Private John Douglas Aitchison of the 7th West Kents. He located very accurately the enemy dispositions. He even crawled up to one German machine-gun and shot the crew. During the assault he led his men with skill and courage, and though severely wounded in the neck, carried on until the final objective was reached and the success of the operation was assured.

Sergeant Alfred Gregory also carried out some daring patrols on his own initiative, and in the actual attack he rushed and captured, single-handed, killing all the crew, an enemy machine-gun that had held-up the advance. When the final objective was reached, Sergeant Gregory's company was dangerously exposed on the right flank and right rear. So Gregory established two posts and proceeded to "mop up" a sunken road and the ground on his right flank, himself killing many of the enemy and capturing many prisoners.

On the left of the 53rd Brigade the 10th Essex also made good progress at first, but here again difficulty was experienced in crossing the Richemont river owing to enemy machine-gun fire from a mill on the east side of the river, near the battalion's left boundary. This was at last overcome by one platoon crossing the river north of the mill, and attacking and capturing it in rear. Further opposition was encountered on the high ground east of the river, and again from the practice trenches beyond, and the battalion, though it tried desperately, was brought temporarily to a standstill at a point about 300 yards short of the sunken road which was its final objective. The enemy was strongly entrenched in this sunken road. The right company of the 10th Essex forced its way slowly forward, and the right platoon of the company succeeded in reaching its objective, where it gained touch with the West Kents; but the machine-gun fire from the sunken road was too heavy to allow of a turning movement to assist the left company.

The Germans were resisting with spirit, but our men were outfighting them both in skill and in dash. At 2.20 a.m. the 8th Berkshires, detailed to "leap-frog" the West Kents and Essex on the first objective advanced from their assembling positions, keeping their right on the Evillers Wood Farm Road. Here again opposition was encountered in crossing the Richemont river from a machine-gun nest which had been missed by the 10th Essex, and the left company was delayed for a time; while on arrival in the vicinity of the first objective the battalion was held up o

the same line as the 10th Essex by the enemy
forces in the sunken road. The rushing up on their
left of troops of the 54th Brigade, who were pushing on to their final objective with tanks, enabled
a joint attack to be made by the Essex and Berkshires, and this drove the enemy out of his strong
position. It was found afterwards that the western
bank of the sunken road, which constituted the first
objective, was lined with machine-guns, and that
on the south of the ravine were two enemy field-
guns which had been fired to the last. In the fight
for them the Berkshires had lost thirty men, who lay
dead within fifty yards of the guns.

Owing to the stiff resistance at the river and the
sunken road, the Berkshires did not arrive at their
final objective till 8.30 A.M., when they got into touch
with the 25th Division on the right, and also with the
55th Brigade, whose East Surreys had captured Fayt
Farm from the north-west about an hour earlier.

The East Surreys had also had a trying time crossing the river, getting mixed up with the Scots of the
33rd Division. Receiving a message from Colonel
Curtis of the Buffs (Colonel Ransome was now a
Brigadier in the 57th Division), asking, "Why are
you not getting on?" they had replied, "We are
knee-deep in water, and Scotsmen." Another of the
day's jests was perpetrated by the West Kents at
the expense of the Berks. Finding a disused French
threshing-machine, they chalked upon it in large
letters the proudly familiar legend, "Captured by
the 8th Royal Berks."

To turn to the 54th Brigade, the 2nd Bedfordshires, accompanied by tanks, led the attack, and,
although troubled by machine-guns, advanced two
thousand yards to the vicinity of White Springs.

A certain amount of opposition had been encountered from three sunken roads immediately north-
east of Richemont Mill, but this had been overcome,
except for one enemy post which remained in action

after the Bedfordshires had passed over it, until it was dealt with by the 11th Royal Fusiliers. Many prisoners were captured on the way, and the enemy suffered casualties not only at the hands of the infantry, but also from our artillery. At White Springs, rather more than half-way to the first objective, the Bedfordshires had again to fight hard, and some of the companies reaching a road running directly across our front about 500 yards short of their objective, mistook it for the objective and halted. The 11th Royal Fusiliers passed through, however, and carrying on the advance captured 11 enemy guns.

One company of the Fusiliers, led by Captain W. Hornfeck, had an adventurous experience. At the beginning of the operation this company had to pass in single file under a railway bridge by Montay and across a narrow footbridge. The enemy had this point well marked, and they put down a heavy barrage upon it.

Seeing his men falter, Captain Hornfeck pushed forward to the bridge and remained there under hot artillery and machine-gun fire until the last man was across. Later, having moved through the Bedfordshires, this company passed though the northern outskirts of the village of Forest, and reached its objective north-east of Epinette. Here it found both its flanks in the air. Enemy fire came from all sides. The company was hung up for over two hours, and eventually withdrew behind a ridge, where it joined the other leading company, which had lost its way and was digging-in. The attack at this point came to a standstill until about 7.30 A.M., when the 7th Buffs of the 55th Brigade passed through the second objective according to programme, and went forward in front of Epinette.

Unluckily Captain Hornfeck had one foot practically cut off by a shell while forming up his company for the next day's attack. In spite of this he superintended the forming up under heavy artillery fire and again cheered his men on as they went forward. His leg was afterwards amputated.

Two officers of the 7th Buffs were awarded the M.C. for their work on this day.

Lieutenant L. C. Willis led his company with fine skill, and was instrumental in capturing a battery of enemy 77 mm. guns, together with a large number of machine-guns. As this was his first time in action, his coolness and daring earned genuine admiration. He rendered clear and concise reports of the situation, and was of great assistance to his commanding officer.

Captain A. J. Whitmarsh, D.S.O., now also won his M.C. When the leading company had lost its commander and had become disorganised, he took charge of it and of his own company, and led them forward under heavy fire. By his skill in handling his troops a battery of enemy guns was captured and the Buffs objective was gained.

The Divisional Artillery, with the 82nd Brigade R.F.A. as the advance-guard, followed hard behind the infantry as the attack developed. Colonel Austin Thorp did inspiring work in getting the guns of his brigade across the Richemont river at a time when the enemy was shelling heavily to prevent bridges being built. Some exceptionally fine driving was shown during the exciting period.

Farther back, near Le Cateau itself, the gunners of the other Divisional artillery brigade, the 83rd, stuck gallantly to their task, although the German artillery fire upon their positions was pitiless in its deadliness.

One exploit of the day was that of Major Henry Hamilton Gardiner, who was in command of "C" Battery, 83rd Brigade R.F.A., the battery for so long commanded by Major A. A. A. Paterson. Major Paterson was at this time acting as brigade-major to the C.R.A., General Seagram, Major W. A. Stirling being in England doing a staff course. When

Gardiner first came to the Divisional Artillery in 1915, it was as A.D.C. and Reconnaissance Officer to General Metcalfe. At his own request he went to a battery in 1917, serving under Major P. G. M. Elles of "C" Battery, 82nd Brigade, and then under Major F. J. Rice. He was badly wounded in the Flanders fighting of 1917, wounded again on Morlancourt Ridge on 8th August 1918, and had only just returned to duty and to command C/83 when the Division went through Le Cateau.

The German gunners found the battery positions of the 83d Brigade almost as soon as the battle started, and shelled them ceaselessly. Two officers of C/83 were wounded as they made their way to the gun-pits to direct the firing of the barrage. Major Gardiner then went up himself. He also was severely wounded in the leg, but he would not let his men carry him away: he remained seated in a shell-hole, watch in hand, controlling the "lifts" of the barrage by blowing a whistle.

He fainted three times, and twice blood from his wounds had to be emptied out of his boots. Two of the battery's guns were knocked out by direct hits, and all the time German shells and machine-gun fire sought for C/83's men and guns. But it was essential that every available gun should be fired in support of our advancing infantry. Major Gardiner controlled the barrage fired by C/83 to the end; and insisted on remaining at the control post until an officer from another battery came to relieve him.

Another battery of the 83rd Brigade that came under heavy fire was "A" Battery. Captain T. W. Berry, who was in command, sat up in the night working out the barrage. The house he had selected for shelter more than once received direct hits from enemy shells; the candle by which he worked was blown out. Soon after zero hour three of the four 18-pounders in use were silenced by German shelling but though partly gassed Captain Berry remained at the gun position, encouraging his men, and keeping the one remaining gun firing its hardest.

The task of the 55th Brigade, with the 6th Northamptonshires attached, had been to exploit the initial successes of the 53rd and 54th Brigades, capture the villages of Bousies and Robersart, and make good the general line of the Landrecies - Valenciennes Road. The leading battalions, with their tanks, followed the attacks of the 54th Brigade so closely that there was considerable risk of their becoming prematurely involved in the fighting. They were not, however, seriously engaged until at 7.20 A.M. they reached a general line about a thousand yards west of the second objective. It was here that the East Surreys captured Fayt Farm and the Buffs Epinette Farm, both formidable enemy strongholds. The protective barrage had "lifted" at 6.40 A.M., so that the 55th Brigade commenced its advance from the second objective forty minutes late. The fighting in which it found itself involved east of this objective was essentially "open fighting." The village of Bousies, which contained buildings of considerable strength, including one large factory, was surrounded and intersected by thickly hedged orchards. Among these hedges, as well as in barns and houses, the enemy had established posts and machine-gun nests. At 4 P.M. fighting was still going on in Bousies; troops of the flanking brigades were not up to the general line reached by the 55th Brigade, and it was clear that the 55th Brigade would be unable to get to the line of the fifth objective before nightfall. The troops on either flank did in the end succeed in getting almost abreast of the centre brigade, but it was decided that the attack should not be resumed until the next day.

The end of all this long and strenuous fighting on 23rd October saw the Division able to claim an advance of 8,000 yards, a notable accomplishment considering the broken ground, the darkness at the start, and the serious obstacle of the Richemont river. The whole of the scattered village of Bousies was by now cleared of the Boche, and 700 prisoners and 56 guns were in our possession. But the village of Robersart was still in the enemy's hands, and that was to be the next objective.

Two tanks were used in this battle to lay cables and to carry wireless equipment. Both gave valuable help. Captain D. G. Fortescue, brigade-major of the 54th Brigade, watched the capture of Fayt Farm and Epinette, and riding back to the cable tank, which was stationed near the practice trenches north-west of L'Eveque Wood, within a thousand yards of the fighting line, was able to report the situation direct to Divisional Headquarters.

This was only one example of a general excellence of communication which made the prompt transmission of accurate information possible throughout the day.

# CHAPTER XXXII.

## THE FIGHTING ROUND "MOUNT CARMEL."

*Hand-to-hand fighting in the orchards—Much depending on the platoon commanders—Lieutenant Hedges of the 6th Northants wins the Victoria Cross at Renuart Farm—The death of Colonel Austin Thorp.*

THE smooth working of the great military machine that for over four years had resisted the Allies' stoutest efforts was gone. For the first time in the war the Boche forces showed signs of demoralisation. But they still had in them a kick of the right kind. The fighting of 24th October was as bitter as that of the day before, and our progress was smaller. On 23rd October the Division had reached a line just east of Bousies. On 24th October we were to get as far as the tree-embowered village of Robersart, but not up to our full objective.

The weather was delightful; the country bore few of the scars of war, and looked beautiful in its autumn tints. Between Bousies and Robersart were many orchards with thick hedges. But the Boche did not concern himself with the fresh beauty of these hedges. He wired them. He also cut gaps that ran parallel with our line of advance, so that his look-out men could see easily on which side of a hedge our infantry were creeping forward to the attack. Success in the hand-to-hand fighting that went on at this stage of the war depended very much upon the platoon and section commanders.

The 4 A.M. attack of 24th October was carried out by the 54th Brigade on the left and the 55th on the right, under a creeping barrage that moved, like that of the previous morning, at a rate of 100 yards in four minutes. No tanks were available. The progress of the infantry, though steady, was slow and costly. Many machine-guns sited among the orchards gave a deal of trouble to the 54th Brigade, and within the first 700 yards of the advance the supporting battalions—the Fusiliers and the Bedfordshires—became involved in the fighting. At 6.20 A.M. the 6th Northamptonshires were counter-attacked, and near Bousies Wood Farm the Fusiliers were also counter-attacked. Both efforts were repulsed with loss.

A strongly-wired line across the west side of the ridge running north-west of Renuart Farm was passed by the Fusiliers, but the top of the ridge was swept by machine-guns, and the Fusiliers could get no farther; the Northamptonshires on the right were also held up by machine-guns in and around Renuart Farm; while others of these pests which had survived the advance of the 55th Brigade still further on the right, were now enfilading the front line of the 54th Brigade, and making movement in the rear of it very difficult. Because of these various hindrances the attack of the 54th Brigade came to a standstill pending further artillery preparation, which was arranged for with Division.

By 8.25 A.M. the 7th Queens of the 55th Brigade had pushed far enough through the trees and hedges to gain a footing in the western outskirts of Robersart. But the enemy made great play with machine guns from the bedroom windows of the scattered houses. The Queens continued to have casualties and by this time the holding-up of the 54th Brigade about Renuart Farm had caused the suspension of the whole advance; so Lieut.-Colonel R. Turner, commanding the 6th Northamptonshires, was ordered to extricate his three companies from Bousies Wood

Farm and to turn the enemy position about Renuart Farm from the north.

But in the meantime, one of the Northants companies held up in front of Renuart Farm had been exceedingly busy, and the officer who commanded it —Lieutenant F. W. Hedges of the Bedfordshires, attached to the 6th Northants—was responsible for an exploit so useful and so daring that it not only won for him the Victoria Cross, but, in conjunction with Colonel Turner's turning movement, enabled the whole line to resume its advance.

Hedges' company was on the right of the 54th Brigade front. It was held up by six machine-gun posts on a hill opposite. Hedges made up his mind to clear these posts. Armed with a revolver and carrying a cane, which he waved when he wanted his men to dash forward, Hedges crawled up the hill under cover of a hedge. A sergeant was with him. A Lewis-gun section followed some distance behind. Breaking cover, Hedges killed the first machine-gunner. Then he worked his way along the crest of the hill and dealt with three more machine-gun posts, taking the feed-blocks out of the guns and securing altogether fourteen prisoners. The Lewis-gun section came up to help. All the six Boche machine-guns were captured, and as suddenly it became clear that the three companies of the 6th Northamptonshires, who had been checked near Bousies Wood Farm, had by now worked round the enemy from the north, the German resistance collapsed. The 2nd Bedfordshires and the 55th Brigade swept forward to seize Renuart Farm, and by 6 P.M. two companies of the Queens and East Surreys—cyclist patrols were used on this occasion—had got as far as the church in Robersart. As the Germans retired the French inhabitants braved the shelling and came up out of cellars to welcome our men. There were smiles and excited shouts, and hot cakes and potatoes for the Queens and East Surreys that night.

2 F

Brigadier-General Wood had been indisposed since the opening of the battle, and on 24th October he became so ill that he had to be evacuated to England, and the command of the 55th Brigade was assumed by Lieut.-Colonel A. P. B. Irwin, who held it till the Armistice. A change of command also took place in the 54th Brigade, Lieut.-Colonel R. Turner of the 6th Northamptonshires deputising for Brigadier-General O. C. Borrett, who also had broken down in health. When General Borrett returned to France on 18th November he took command of the 55th Brigade.

25th October "passed quietly." So at least ran the official report. But all along the Divisional front active patrolling went on, and there were encounters with enemy machine-gunners and snipers, particularly in the neighbourhood of Robersart. At 1 P.M. the news was circulated that the Third Army, to the north of us, was continuing the attack next day, and that the 18th Division would advance and capture Mount Carmel in order to secure the Third Army's right flank. This attack was entrusted to the 53rd Brigade. The front on which the brigade was to operate covered some 2,500 yards, and the final objective was 1,200 yards distant. The country over which the advance was to be made was full of the difficulties with which the Division had lately become familiar. Not only was it intersected by closely-planted thorn hedges, but by streams. And here and there were houses known to be held by the enemy. Mount Carmel scarcely justified its title of "Mount." It was really no more than a cultivated field, slightly higher than those surrounding it, and owing to the enclosed nature of the country it afforded but little advantage for observation. However, it was deemed better that we should take it.

The night 25th/26th October was a black and rainy one. The attack began at 1 A.M., an hour selected as most suitable for the main operation on our left, that of the Third Army. But it was not the best for the 18th Division; the difficulty of traversing enclosed country was intensified by lack of light. Severe opposition was encountered by the 10th Essex and the 8th Berks as soon as they reached the Robersart - Englefontaine road—a long, straight-ruled Roman road of the type to be found in this part of France. When day dawned there was a thick mist, and although a lot of ground had been captured the progress of consolidation was greatly hindered by the bad visibility. Not until 8 A.M. did the mist drift away, and then the enemy opened so heavy an artillery and machine-gun fire that the left company of the Berkshires, aiming at Mount Carmel, was driven back to the sunken road immediately east of the Robersart-Englefontaine road. Here an important change was made in the day's programme. It was decided that this position, some 400 yards from the original objective the "Mount," gave a better and more defensible line than the one originally aimed at, so it was resolved to consolidate there. It was in large measure due to the personal exertions and the gallantry of Lieut.-Colonel "Nogi" Hudson of the Berkshires that the new line was firmly established. Colonel Hudson was hit—for the third time during the war—but fortunately not severely. Meanwhile the liaison company of the West Kents, attacking at the same moment as units of the 33rd Division, had pushed right through, and had reached the objective before any other troops. A few prisoners and some machine - guns were captured and a considerable number of the enemy were killed.

On 27th October the 55th Brigade advanced the line another 250 yards; but the enemy had strengthened his positions, and was showing plenty of fight, and during the next seven days harassing artillery and machine-gun fire became the settled programme.

The 18th Division went on preparing for what proved to be its final battle, that of 4th November.

It was during this happy, confident period, when we knew we had the enemy beaten, when men told one another gladly that the anxieties, the miseries, the dangers of the Great Adventure were soon to be thrust behind, that the Divisional artillery suffered one of its most saddening losses—the 18th Division rather,—for Lieut.-Colonel Austin Thorp, who was killed in Bousies on 30th October, was known, liked, respected, and admired in every unit of the Division. The higher authorities knew of his skill, and appreciated his zeal. His officers and men acted upon the simple unquestioning faith, that what the Colonel said or did was bound to be right. Colonel Thorp had commanded the 82nd Brigade, R.F.A., for two years and ten months. He was a Garrison gunner who showed himself a perfect Field Artillery commander.

Colonel Thorp was killed in the streets of Bousies after having visited the 53rd Brigade headquarters to confer with General Barker about artillery support for the attack of 4th November. He had also called to say farewell to Lieut.-Colonel H. P. Burnyeat, commanding the 65th Army Field Artillery Brigade, a horse gunner for whom many an artillery officer trained at Lark Hill has kindly memories. Colonel Burnyeat was going on leave. His leave warrant was in his pocket. He came out of his mess and walked with Colonel Thorp on the way to the farm house which was the 82nd Brigade headquarters. In their sudden, awful way three high-velocity shell came through the air. One of them must have hit direct. Both colonels were killed instantaneously. Of Colonel Burnyeat no trace of remains was found —nothing but the broken half of a signet-ring.

Colonel Thorp was buried in a beautifully-kept cemetery on a hill outside Le Cateau. The Division gave him a noble funeral, but his loss made a

LIEUT.-COLONEL AUSTIN THORP, C.M.G., D.S.O.

unforgettable difference to those who had served
under him.  His C.M.G., his Croix de Guerre, and
his Order of Leopold came after the funeral.  The
heart-breaking pity of it, that having come through
so long he should be killed twelve days before the
Armistice.

# CHAPTER XXXIII.

## THE ADVANCE THROUGH MORMAL FOREST.

*The last big concerted movement of the war—A rapid enveloping movement under elaborate artillery barrages—Aeroplanes to drown noise of tanks—Colonel Blewitt pushes a perambulator in Hecq—10th Essex sweep through a 200 yards gap and bring off a brilliant manœuvre—General Rawlinson's praise—54th Brigade's last day of war.*

IT was now the eve of the last big concerted movement of the war. On 29th October, orders were issued for a general offensive by the First, Third, and Fourth Armies on 3rd November, but the date was subsequently altered to 4th November, the day on which Austria-Hungary confessed herself beaten and signed an armistice. This course had already been followed by Bulgaria and Turkey, so that on 4th November Germany was facing the Allies alone.

General Morland, commanding the XIII. Corps decided that the attack of the XIII. Corps should be carried out on a three-Division front, as follows :—

*First Phase.*—The 25th Division, on the 18th Division' south, was to force the crossings of the Sambre-et-Oise Cana and operate on the southern bank, while the 50th and 18t Divisions, operating north of the Canal, were to attack on th south and north sides of their respective sectors and captu Preux-aux-Bois by an enveloping movement.

*Second Phase.*—The 66th Division, in Corps Reserve durir the first phase, was to pass through the 25th Division ar become the southern Division in the Corps. The 50 Division was to cross the Canal and operate on the southe bank.  The 18th Division was to continue to operate north of the Canal.

The 38th Division (V. Corps) was to be on the left of the 18th Division for the first phase, then the 33rd Division was to come in.  After the second phase, the 18th Division was to be "squeezed out" by the junction of the 50th and 33rd Divisions east of the Canal.

There is one most notable feature of these orders of Sir Thomas Morland.  For the first time the 18th Division was to carry out an enveloping manœuvre by order of a Corps.  All previous enveloping movements, for which the Division so justly had become noted, were initiated and carried through by General Lee in spite of, rather than by, order of the Corps in which the Division happened to be serving.

On 30th October, General Lee held a conference and explained the object of the operations, and the way in which he proposed carrying out the Division's share of them.

The starting-point was a line parallel with, and a little east of the Englefontaine-Robersart road; and the capture of a line beyond Hecq and just east of Preux-aux-Bois was assigned to one battalion, the 6th Northamptonshires, of the 54th Brigade, and one battalion, the 7th Royal West Kents, of the 53rd Brigade.

Another battalion of the 54th Brigade, the 2nd Bedfordshires, was to capture Preux-aux-Bois, attacking the village from the north, while the third battalion, the 11th Royal Fusiliers, was to hold the original front line and to assist in the attack on Preux, with one company operating on the right of the 2nd Bedfordshires.  The remaining two battalions of the 53rd Brigade, the 10th Essex and the 8th Berkshires, were to capture a line running through the western edge of the Forest of Mormal and called the "red" line.

The 55th Brigade—7th Queens, 7th Buffs, and 8th East Surreys—were to pass through the "red" line as soon as possible after its capture, and proceed through the Forest of Mormal to the capture of another line east of the straight road running from north to south on the east of the Forest, and called the "green" line.  It was decided that troops should move, where possible, along the edges of the uncut portions of the Forest, large patches of which had been felled by the Boche, and special arrangements were made to picket the sides. The importance of the capture of the Forest lay in its offering the short way to the Sambre valley and Maubeuge.

For these operations, the following troops were attached to the Division :—

(a) "B" Squadron, Northumberland Hussars (allotted to 55th Brigade less one troop allotted to 18th Divisional Headquarters).

(b) "A" Company, 13th Cyclist Battalion (allotted to 55th Brigade).

(c) 84th Army Brigade, R.F.A.
   65th Army Brigade, R.F.A.
   76th Army Brigade, R.G.A.

(d) 1 Company, 100th Battalion, Machine-Gun Corps (for initial barrage only).

(e) 10 Tanks of the 14th Battalion, Tank Corps, allotted as follows :—
   4 Tanks to the 54th Brigade.
   6 Tanks to the 53rd Brigade.
   Two of the latter taking part in clearing the eastern end of Preux-aux-Bois, before advancing with the 53rd Brigade.

(f) 1 Section, 17th Battalion, Armoured Cars.

The highly-elaborated task of the Artillery was as follows :—

*First Attack.*—A rolling barrage was to be put down by the 82nd, 83rd, and 84th Brigades, R.F.A., and a standing barrage by the 65th Army Brigade, R.F.A., to protect the right flank of the attack as far as the first protective barrage line, which was just beyond Preux-aux-Bois. Owing to the wooded nature of the country, 18-pounders formed rolling barrages over such portions of the country as were not covered by tall trees, while howitzers of all calibres searched through the high woods.

*Second Attack.*—The second attack consisted of an enfilade barrage to cover the attack on Preux-aux-Bois, and was to be carried out by the 82nd, 65th, and 84th Brigades, R.F.A., the 83rd Brigade, R.F.A., putting down a standing barrage to protect the left flank of this attack.

Two guns were put into forward positions in the open, do special tasks, one by the 65th Army Brigade, R.F.A., demolish a house infested with machine-guns in the northern outskirts of Preux, and the other by the 82nd Brigade, R.F.A., to be ready to engage any targets which might present themselves as the attack developed.

*Heavy Artillery.*—60-pounders searched in enfilade the routes and lanes through the Forest, while 6-inch howitzers put down a standing barrage on the west fringe of the wood, until such time as the rolling barrage overtook it, then lifted in conformity with the Field Artillery.

*Third Phase.*—The third phase consisted of a creeping barrage of 18-pounders and 4·5-inch howitzers of all four Field Artillery Brigades and the affiliated battery of 6-inch howitzers to the " red " line, the 18-pounders covering all open country, and the howitzers the wooded portions.

Thanks to good staff work, the assembly of the 53rd and 54th Brigades was carried out without hitch : low-flying aeroplanes—a piece of guile with which we were now becoming familiar—were employed to drown the noise made by the approaching tanks. " Zero " hour on November 4th was 6.15 A.M. ; this attack was a daylight one. The weather was clear and the visibility good. Twenty minutes later a thick fog came down. It did not clear until about 9 A.M., and our infantry turned it to account.

The 6th Northamptonshires and the 7th West Kents, under a notably accurate barrage, made rapid progress in their share of the enveloping of Preux-aux-Bois. The enemy's reply barrage came down within three minutes, but it was weak and did not cause many casualties. On the extreme right, however, among the hedgerows, German machine-guns enfiladed the Northamptonshires quite hotly. It was the skilful and courageous handling of his men by Captain R. B. Fawkes, who won the D.S.O. that day, that kept the advance moving, and by eight o'clock the Northants had reached the line north-east of Preux, besides capturing machine-guns and over a hundred prisoners. The West Kents also reached the line up to time, but they had had heavy fighting farther north in Hecq, where the Germans still held out. The cellars of Hecq could not be bombed, as the French civilians, who had waited so long to be released from the German yoke, were sheltering in them as well as the Boche. Afterwards, when the villagers took their courage in their hands and came up, they pointed out the cellars where the enemy were concealing themselves, and the customary measures were taken. The capture of Hecq was indeed rich in picturesque detail as well as in hard and prolonged fighting. In one farmhouse near the cross-roads were some old ladies and a family party. They were too scared to leave the farm until Colonel Guy Blewitt, the G.S.O.1, brought them out. To encourage them he put his steel helmet on the head of a small girl aged about three and wheeled the family perambulator. One old lady rushed up to the youthful Colonel Hudson of the Berks, kissed him, and hailed him as her saviour. But the chief "thrill" for the people of Hecq was their first sight of a Scot of the 50th Division in uniform. Careless of shells, all the women and children in the place crept from their lairs to stare and exclaim at the amiably grinning phenomenon.

Both through and beyond Hecq the infantry's task was a difficult one, and it was due to the admirable support of the tanks, as well as to the fighting spirit displayed by all ranks, that the operations here and farther south were so effectively carried out. One company of German infantry counter-attacked down the valley north-east of Preux, but they were driven off.

The second attack by the 54th Brigade, with Preux-aux-Bois as an early objective, got away well under another accurate enfilade barrage, but, after the first 500 yards, stiff opposition was encountered. A company of the Fusiliers, who had come in on the right of the Bedfordshires, was held up for a time by machine-gun fire from a house near the Robersar main road ; the two left companies of the Bedford

shires found themselves heavily engaged near the
cemetery and making but slow progress, and the
company of the Northamptonshires was again delayed by machine-gun fire from houses.  But the two
right companies of the Bedfordshires, with three awe-
inspiring tanks, fought their way into the village as
far as the church, the tall slender spire of which
soared above the trees of the surrounding woods, and
they gained touch with two companies of the 2nd
Munster Fusiliers, who had been sent by the 50th
Division to help from the south in the enveloping
attack on the village.  They then proceeded to "mop
up."  The tanks rendered most valuable aid.  One of
them, with three of its machine-guns out of action,
and its 6-pounder guns badly jammed by the enemy's
fire, found itself surrounded by Germans, who, pushing up the muzzles of the remaining machine-guns,
climbed on to the top of the tank and endeavoured to
throw bombs through the apertures.  The tank crew
stopped them with their revolvers at the psychological
moment, the Germans were driven off, and the tank
went on to complete its share in the "mopping-up"
of the village.

Captain R. L. V. Doake, M.C., of the Bedfords,
showed dashing and successful leadership in the actual
taking of Preux.  He got his own company forward
and helped the companies on either side of him.  He
was creeping through the orchards towards the
village, his batman with him, when through a hedge
not twenty yards away he saw four Germans and a
machine-gun.  Captain Doake and his batman opened
fire so rapidly and with such accuracy that it required only four rounds to bring all four Boche down.
Doake got his D.S.O. in this battle.  Another of
Colonel Percival's officers, Lieutenant Goben, found
himself face to face with a German who was half
hidden in a slit.  The Boche had a rifle, Goben a
revolver.  Four rounds were fired.  Goben was the
winner.

1,400 French inhabitants were freed from the Germans when Preux was taken, also several Alsatian soldiers who had been in hiding for a fortnight, waiting for the oncoming British. The eager, rejoicing civilians were ready with food and coffee for our men before all the Germans had been driven out of the village. When next morning Captain Doake took Colonel Blewitt to look at the four Germans he and his batman had shot, they were not the only sightseers. Small boys and girls of Preux were there removing the dead Germans' boots and socks for the use of their own families. It was significant of the abnormal state of mind to which direct association with war can bring human beings, that these small children laughed gaily as they engaged in the gruesome business.

The strenuous fighting around and inside Hecq and Preux delayed the advance of the two "leap-frogging" battalions, the 10th Essex and the 8th Berkshires, who had been detailed to continue the advance east of those villages. However, the two companies of the 8th Berkshires, who were operating on the northern edge of the wood, went through the 7th West Kents, picketed the ridges as ordered, and reached the first objective, the "red" line, about midday. And there under the admirable leadership of Lieutenant F. J Powell, D.C.M., M.M., they maintained their positions for three hours, although both flanks were in the air. Powell had only 36 men left when our troops on his flanks worked up level with him. The right company of the 11th Royal Fusiliers, by keeping constant pressure on the enemy, cleared the cross roads on the Robersart-Preux road, while a company of the same regiment, advancing from the north, and finely led by Lieutenant Hope, rolled up the enemy front at a point where machine-guns had proved very troublesome, capturing a number of these pests well as about a hundred prisoners.

The struggle in and around Preux-aux-Bois was still delaying the advance of the 10th Essex and the

two right companies of the Berkshires, and orders
were issued to them to work round the north of the
wood, then to move southward down the roads to
their proper frontages and push forward to their
objective.

But these fresh orders were cancelled because,
before they could be acted upon, that rare good Scot,
Forbes, now in command of the 10th Essex, brought
off a swift and brilliant manœuvre.  Reconnoitring
in the labyrinth of orchards and plantations that
reached to the edge of Preux, Forbes discovered an
opening, some two hundred yards wide, in the enemy's
line.   He determined to push the 10th Essex
through this gap.  He led them in person through
a gate within the German posts — the 10th Essex
have a photo of this gateway,—pushed on, formed
up the battalion behind the enemy's front line, and
advanced to the attack of the support lines and gun
positions while the German's forward posts were still
in action.   This surprise manœuvre had an immediate
effect.   The young lads of the 8th Berks operated in
the same way on the left of the 10th Essex ; the
advance completed the enveloping movement ; the
enemy's escape from Preux was rendered impossible ;
the 6th Northamptonshires were able to capture the
eastern edge of the village, and to resume their
advance.   The 55th Brigade (7th Queens), which had
followed in rear of the 10th Essex and 8th Berkshires,
assisted them to push forward to the "red" line,
which was reached at 2.30 P.M.

In all this rapid, strenuous fighting, the infantry
had been greatly helped by the tanks, artillery, and
machine-guns.   The forward 18-pounders were particularly well handled, and their effect on the enemy was
marked.   There were losses, however.  2nd Lieutenant
J. M'Nair Lamb, of C/82, was killed by machine-gun
fire while pushing forward with his gun along the
Preux-Robersart road.   The box-respirator worn on
his breast was found afterwards to be riddled with

bullets. Major A. A. Prentice, M.C., commanding A/82, going up the road under a hot fire to assist Lamb, was badly wounded in the hip. He crawled to the side of the road and lay alongside a wall, directing his men, until a rescuing party came.

The approach march of the 55th Brigade's battalions had been planned so as to allow them to begin their advance from the "red" line into and through the Forest of Mormal at 11.31 A.M. Owing to the holding-up of the two other brigades, the advance of the 55th could not start to scheduled time, and the 7th Buffs and 8th East Surreys remained in the vicinity of Petit Planty until about 12.30 P.M. When they were able to start they made up brilliantly for the delay, and, very well handled by Lieut.-Colonel Irwin, advanced at a rapid rate, greatly assisted in the fighting among the hedgerows by two armoured cars. The appearance of these formidable monsters along the muddy ways still further demoralised the Germans, and a number of them abandoned their machine-guns without firing a shot, and ran away as fast as their feet would carry them.

By 3.30 P.M. the "red" line was reached and the general advance began. The two armoured cars led the way and pushed along the Route de Preux through the heart of the Forest, putting to flight such pockets of the enemy as still lurked in the brigade's area. The East Surreys followed at a rare pace. At Carrefour l'Ermitage enemy machine-guns for a short time made it impossible for the line to be reached on the extreme right; but the East Surreys were irresistible, and at 7 P.M. held the "green" line, the day's last objective, as the outpost line, while the 7th Buffs and 7th Queens consolidated their positions on their objectives a little way behind.

Thus once more the 18th Division was "a day's march nearer home," and that night General Lee had the satisfaction of receiving the following message from

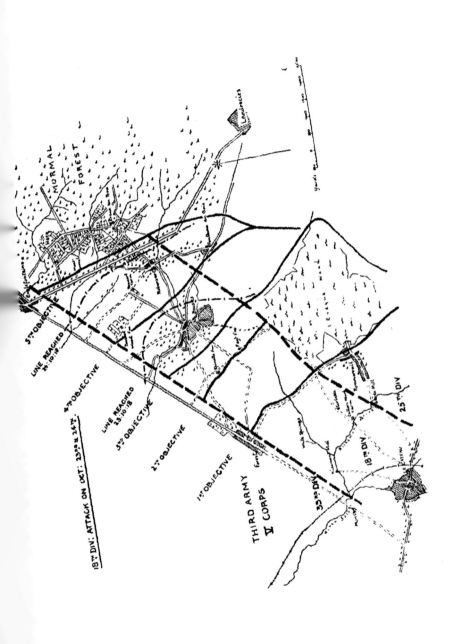

MORMAL FOREST

Landrecies

3RD OBJECTIVE

LINE REACHED 25.10.18

4TH OBJECTIVE

LINE REACHED 25.10.18

3RD OBJECTIVE

2ND OBJECTIVE

1ST OBJECTIVE

18TH DIV: ATTACK ON OCT: 23RD & 24TH

25TH DIV

18TH DIV

33RD DIV

THIRD ARMY
V CORPS

Yards

the Commander of the Fourth Army, Sir Henry (now Lord) Rawlinson :—

"FROM XIII. CORPS, 4/11/1918.

Message from Army Commander, begins—

*Please convey to 18th Division my congratulations on their success to-day in forcing their way through the Forêt de Mormal. The precision with which the various columns advanced through the forest shows the staff work and leadership were thoroughly good, whilst the gallantry and determination of the troops is deserving of high praise.*

(Signed)     RAWLINSON."

As has been shown, much of the progress through the great Forest, "this formidable obstacle," as Lord Haig called it in his Victory Despatch, had been swift and apparently fairly easy, thanks to the growing demoralisation of the enemy. Yet it has also been made clear that in the early part of the advance the fighting was stiff and the enemy resolute.

The night of November 4th-5th passed quietly. For the 54th Brigade it passed more quietly and more pleasantly than most nights during the preceding few years, for, after more than three years' close acquaintance with modern warfare, this brigade had now finished its job. The battalions went into billets that night among the cellars and broken houses of Preux. True, they had orders to be ready at half an hour's notice to take up the pursuit; but as a historian of the brigade has cheerfully written "the pursuit managed to do without us, . . . and on November 6th we moved back to rest at Le Cateau, where we were when news of the Armistice reached us."

Perhaps the last sight of the Great War vouchsafed to the 54th Brigade was the spectacle of a stout Frenchwoman of Preux chasing a big German down the street with a pitchfork in her hand.

# CHAPTER XXXIV.

## UNARM! THE LONG DAY'S TASK IS DONE.

*8th East Surreys the last battalion to be in action—Sassegnies, the last French village from which the 18th Division drove the Germans— Armistice Day: No frenzied rejoicings as in London and Paris— General Rawlinson's thanks "for the brilliant part which the Division has played"—General Lee's final address—No official homecoming to England, no cheering onlookers—The three Divisional Memorials and the Roll of Honour in Colchester Church.*

AT 6.30 A.M. on 5th November, in a drizzling rain, the advance was resumed—the 55th Brigade in the van, the Division's objective the line of the Sambre. On this and the following day, the 8th East Surreys, escorted by a troop of the Northumberland Hussars and a company of Cyclists, went steadily forward.

Of all the Divisions engaged in the Battle of the Hundred Days, only two, the 32nd and the 18th, began and ended the campaign in the Fourth Army. The 18th Division had more days of battle than any other Division in that tremendous and triumphant advance; the 55th was the last brigade, and the 8th East Surreys the last battalion of the Division, to do duty in the Great War.

It was a swift advance. Our men knew that this was the end. They had their tails up. The retreating Germans tried hard with well-served field-guns to delay our approach. They destroyed the bridges across the Sambre as we, at the end of March, had tried to destroy the crossings over the Oise. But they could not hold us. The clearings in the forest made

2 G

by the enemy for his pit-props, trench supports, and living huts simplified our advance, and there was short shrift for the isolated pockets of Germans concealed among the hedgerows and plantations who put up a fight.

Sassegnies, the last French village from which the 18th Division drove the Boche, was reached by 7.45 A.M., and touch was established with the two Divisions who were flanking us, the 33rd on the left and the 50th on the right. By 4 P.M. the East Surreys in front held the line of the railway south-east of Sassegnies, with patrols operating between the railway and the river; the 7th Buffs were in a position of close support; and the headquarters of both battalions were in Sassegnies itself, an undamaged village in which once again happy, released villagers crowded round to greet us. The remaining 55th Brigade battalion, the 7th Queens, with five machine-guns, held the main line of resistance, the Route Tourtenale, and had headquarters at Le Croisil Inn.

By dusk we had occupied the line of railway with patrols pushed forward to the line of the Sambre and at 8.40 P.M. came orders from the XIII. Corps that the 53rd and 54th Brigades were to withdraw to billets in back areas, that the 55th, holding Sassegnies were to keep in line with the 50th Division and V Corps till they gained touch next day, and that as soon as this happened the 55th Brigade also would withdraw.

Villages recovered, civilians released, the enemy infantry in flight, his artillery becoming disorganised great fires and explosions in the territory still occupied by the Germans—all told of victory, complete, satisfying, and so long waited for. And so we reach the Division's last day of the war. On 6th November with the rain still coming down hard, the two flanking Divisions, the 33rd and the 50th, continued the advance. The East Surreys sent out patrols to maintain touch and to report progress. All went well.

7.30 P.M. junction between the 33rd and 50th Divisions was completed on the railway east of Leval, and shortly afterwards the 55th Brigade received orders to withdraw according to the prearranged plan. The 18th Division had finished with the war.

Between 8 P.M. on 4th November and 1 P.M. on 5th November the brigade not only advanced 9,000 yards, but captured on the way 10 enemy field-guns and howitzers, as well as prisoners and much enemy material. During the fighting recorded in this and the three preceding chapters, the Division's casualties were :—

|  | Killed. | Wounded. | Missing. | Total. |
|---|---|---|---|---|
| Officers | 20 | 86 | 1 | 107 |
| Other ranks | 252 | 1,483 | 138 | 1,873 |

From the enemy during the same period we captured 25 officers (of whom 21 were unwounded) and 1,513 other ranks (1,421 unwounded), together with 15 heavy guns, 37 field-guns, 42 trench mortars, 297 machine-guns, 1 anti-tank gun and 1 anti-tank rifle. The bridging material of the Division was left at the disposal of the 50th Division for crossing the canal, and our Field Companies and Pioneers also remained to carry on repairs to roads and bridges on the XIII. Corps front. But, as a Division, our task was completed, our job was done.

The guns supporting Lord Rawlinson's advancing Divisions were still belching forth death and havoc upon the broken Germans as the troops of the 18th Division, very spent, but happy and thankful for their final release from the risks of war, marched out and settled in the villages round about Le Cateau. When 11 A.M. 11th November came, and bugle-blasts and trumpet-calls told that the Armistice had been signed, there were no frenzied rejoicings such as broke out in London and in Paris. It was a more solemn moment for the men out there. A quiet thankfulness was the first feeling. Then minds turned to comrades who were not there, who had not lived to see the triumphing of the cause for which they had laboured, which had bound them all, dead and living, together.

After the signing of the Armistice, General Lee received the following letter from the Commander of the Fourth Army, General Rawlinson. The letter and the reply epitomise the history of the Division:—

"H.Q. 4TH ARMY,
23rd *November* 1918.

" MY DEAR LEE,—I have not had time to come and see you, and therefore write these few lines to express to you, and to all ranks of the 18th Division, my warmest thanks for the splendid work that has been done by the Division, not only during these 100 days which have won the war, but from March 1918 onwards.

"The fine spirit of discipline and fighting energy which characterised the 18th Division throughout these operations has filled me with admiration, and I offer to all ranks my warmest thanks for their gallantry and skill in so many hard-fought battles.

"I specially call to mind the strenuous times before Gentelles and Cachy, the taking of Albert and Meaulte, the capture of Bernafay and Trones Woods, the forcing of the Tortille River, the battles around and beyond Ronssoy, and finally the attacks on Bousies, Hecq, and the Forêt de Mormal.

"It is indeed a record that every officer, N.C.O. and man, has a right to be proud of, and I very much regret that you are not marching to the frontier with the Fourth Army.

"The very best of luck to you all, and again a thousand thanks for the brilliant part which the Division has played in these battles of the Hundred Days.—Yours sincerely,

"(Sgd.)  H. RAWLINSON.

" Major-General R. P. LEE, C.B.,
Commanding 18th Division."

To this Major-General Lee sent the following reply :—

"25th *November* 1918.

"MY DEAR GENERAL,—All ranks of the 18th Division join in thanking you for your generous appreciation of the part they have played in the closing phase of the Great War.

"The Division has done much of its fighting in the Fourth Army, commencing with the Somme battles in 1916 an ending so gloriously in the 100 days of victory, and will ever be grateful to you for your counsel and leadership.

"Many of us still hope to rejoin your army in Rhineland.—Yours sincerely,

"(Sgd.)  R. P. LEE.

"General Sir H. S. RAWLINSON, Bart.,
    G.V.C.O., K.C.B., K.C.M.G.,
        Commanding Fourth Army."

The King and the Prince of Wales and a glittering staff came to see all units of the Division and to congratulate General Lee, and at the final review on 2nd December General Lee issued the following to the 11,000 or so officers and men who mustered on parade :—

## ORDER OF THE DAY

BY

MAJOR-GENERAL R. P. LEE, C.B., COMMANDING
18TH DIVISION.

"TO ALL RANKS,—I was more than pleased with the review of the Division to-day, and congratulate all ranks on the turn-out, and the admirable precision which marked all the parade manoeuvres. It was a reflection of their glorious deeds.

"The Division has taken part in most of the great battles from 'The Somme' in 1916 down to the Armistice—i.e., The Somme,' 'The Ancre' (both autumn and spring), Arras,' 'Flanders,' 'The Retreat from the Oise,' 'The Defence of Amiens,' and lastly, 'The 100 Days' Victory.'

"During these historical operations, the Division has proved itself equally strong both in attack and defence, and as earned a reputation second to none through the courage, resolution, and achievements of the officers, non-commissioned officers and men, that it is, and has been, my pride and privilege to command.

"I take this opportunity of again thanking you all for our unfailing loyalty, and of expressing my admiration for our gallantry and devotion to duty.

"(Sgd.)  RICHARD P. LEE,
            *Major-General Commanding*
                *18th Division.*"

The units forming Kitchener's New Armies were the first for disbandment, so the 18th Division did not take part in the march into Germany. From December to March all hands were employed clearing up the battlefields, a very necessary and at times dangerous undertaking. The 7th Buffs were singularly unlucky, having 10 men killed by the explosion of a live shell.

During this period there was earnest, but not perhaps very fruitful, effort to put into effect the War Office plan for preparing men who knew no trade to face the battle of life that would come when khaki was finally put aside; that human and sincere man and uplifting orator, Dr Alexander Irvine, gave the men some well-remembered addresses, full of hope and inspiration for the future; there was a cheerful final divisional race meeting near Serain, and another, held by the Divisional Artillery, at Reumont, when the snow was on the ground; and theatrical parties from London came to brighten the wintry monotony of those last days in France.

But England and home was now the thought that dominated. Demobilisation went on. General Lee went on leave in January, and was retained by the War Office to take over command at Tunbridge Wells and assist in the demobilisation. He was then appointed to General Rawlinson's Committee which was formed to apply the practical military lessons of the war to the reorganisation of the Corps of Royal Engineers. Officers and men in hundreds trickled back to their civil occupations, and it was a very thinned-out force that, on 19th March, heard read the last Order of the Day, issued by Brigadier General O. C. Borrett, who was commanding the Division and his own 55th Brigade as well. The historic notice was worded—

## SPECIAL ORDER

### BY

### BRIGADIER-GENERAL O. C. BORRETT, C.M.G., D.S.O., COMMANDING 18TH DIVISION.

"19*th March* 1919.

"To-day, 19th March 1919, the 18th Division, as such, ceases to exist. All cadres and men not yet demobilised or sent to the Army of Occupation will, from this date, be administered by Brigadier - General Commanding 55th Infantry Brigade.

"All correspondence will be addressed to 18th Divisional cadre.

"From midnight 19/20th all brigadiers and surplus staff officers will stand by and await orders. Acting brigade commanders will revert to their permanent appointments.

"Correspondence to and from units will be sent to the staff captains of their former respective brigades.

"Before the Division ceases to exist, the G.O.C. wishes to thank all officers, N.C.O.'s and men who have passed through the Division, for their loyal support under all circumstances.

"The Division, which came out on 25th July 1915, has taken part in most of the great battles from the Somme, 1916, down to the Armistice—*i.e.,* 'The Somme,' 'The Ancre' (both autumn and spring), 'Arras,' 'Flanders,' 'The Retreat from the Oise,' 'Defence of Amiens,' 'The Advance through Morlancourt,' 'The Ancre to Tortille,' 'Ronssoy,' 'Vendhuile,' Le Cateau,' 'Robersart,' 'Mormal Forest, to the Sambre River.'

"The Division has had many very marked successes, as evidenced by the following table of awards and honours gained by the Division :—

### STATEMENT OF HONOURS RECEIVED BY 18TH DIVISION FROM JULY 1915 TO NOVEMBER 1918.

| | | | | | |
|---|---|---|---|---|---|
| C. (5 officers) | . . . | 11 | Bar to D.S.O. (includes 5 second | | |
| C.B. | . . . . | 1 | bars) . . . . | . | 40 |
| B. . | . . . . | 4 | Major-General | . . | 1 |
| I.G. | . . . . | 11 | Brevet Colonels | . . | 9 |
| .E. | . . . . | 5 | Brevet Lieut.-Colonels | . | 14 |
| B.E. | . . . . | 1 | Brevet Majors . | . . | 13 |
| .O. | . . . . | 130 | Promoted Captain | . . | 5 |

| | | |
|---|---|---|
| M.C. . . . . . 630 | M.M. . . . . . 2570 | |
| Bar to M.C. (includes 8 second | Bar to M.M. (includes 30 | |
| bars) . . . . . 96 | second bars) . . . 204 | |
| D.C.M. . . . . . 477 | M.S.M. . . . . . 180 | |
| Bar to D.C.M. (includes 7 | Royal Humane Society's | |
| second bars) . . . 32 | Medal . . . . 1 | |

"The great fighting qualities and tenacity of purpose shown by all ranks of the Division has assisted considerably in the final victory of the Allied arms, and the Division will live as one to which we are all proud to have belonged.

"The 18th Divisional Office will close at Ligny at midnight 19/20th March 1919, and will not reopen.

"O. C. BORRETT,
*Brigadier-General Commanding*
*18th Division.*"

This list of Honours is incomplete. Many others were awarded in the Gazettes of 1st January 1919 and on the king's birthday. The 18th Division might, however, be excused from wondering if any other Division won as many as 11 Victoria Crosses in three years of active service in the Great War.

There was no official homecoming to England, not even to Colchester, where, in the anxious days of 1914, the 18th came formally into being; no spectator-lined streets, no radiant welcoming cheers, no solemn service of thanksgiving over the return of the last remnants of this typical English Division. The 10th Essex, who had had 1,103 killed out of 5,500 officers and men who passed through the battalion, broke up in Wiltshire, the 8th Sussex went to Shropshire to be disbanded, some of the Divisional Artillery heard the final "Dismiss" in Wales. Better in some ways that it should be like this, for the 18th was a Division that was born with the war, and died with the war. Its truest, most enduring associations were with the torn soil and the wrecked towns of Northern France. In due course, a Memorial and a full Roll of Honour will be placed in Colchester's Parish Church, but for the men who were Out There, the Division's real

memorials are the three to be put up in its honour upon
the battered nothingness that once was Thiépval, at
that place of shuddering horror, Clapham Junction
near the Menin Road, and among the splintered tree-
stumps of Trones Wood.   They tell of triumph and
tribulation, hardship and misgiving, perhaps of an
exaltation of soul that can be conceived only dimly
by those who did not belong to the Great Brotherhood
which fought in France.

The spirit of the Division lives on.   Every year, on
4th November, General Maxse, General Lee, and
other officers proud to have served with the 18th,
meet to dine and to talk again of events burnt into
the minds of all of them.   There is, too, a permanent
Memorial Committee that includes General Lee, Lieu-
tenant-Colonel B. J. Walker of the Sussex Pioneers,
Major A. E. Phillips of the West Kents, and Major
C. H. Atkinson of the Gunners, with Major A. F. G.
Everitt (Greycourt, Goring-on-Thames) as Honorary
Secretary.

When, in December 1918, during the dull days of
gathering up abandoned wire and derelict corrugated
iron, and carting away unused shells, the first orders
for demobilisation came through from England, there
was one man, a miner, who went to his Adjutant for
his final papers, and to say good-bye.   He was a
natural fighting man, and up in the line had been of
the keen resourceful type that warms the heart of
company commanders.   But, away from the atmos-
phere of battle, discipline irked him : more than once
he had come up for reprimand, and after the Armistice
he gloated openly over his prospect of speedy release
from the Army.

But when the moment of farewell came, and the
Adjutant shook him by the hand and wished him
good-luck on his return to civil life, this man showed
the depth of feeling that was in him.

"We've had times out here, sir," he said halt-
ingly, "good times, that we can never have again,

in no other kind of life. And," he added quickly, "there was no Division in France as good as ours." He gripped the Adjutant's hand hard, and his eyes were moist.

That was how more than one man felt when he bade farewell to the 18th Division. Here was a plain English Division that did its duty, took pride in being competent, groused sometimes at the calls made upon it, but forgot hardships and disappointments in the glowing moments of test.

The world may not have emerged nobler and better from the sacrifice and the suffering; but to most of those who actually fought, there remains the choice thought that in those days of imperishable memories in France, gain and advancement came not into the count when men put forth the best they could give in skill and willingness to secure the honourable triumph of the Cause they believed to be right.

## VICTORIA CROSSES WON BY OFFICERS AND MEN OF THE 18th DIVISION DURING THE WAR.

Sergeant WILLIAM E. BOULTER, 6th Northants. Trones Wood, 14th July 1916.

Private FRED J. EDWARDS, 12th Middlesex. Thiépval, 26th September 1916.

Private ROBERT RYDER, 12th Middlesex. Thiépval, 26th September 1916.

2nd Lieut. TOM E. ADLAM, 7th Bedfords. Thiépval, 27th September 1916.

Private CHRISTOPHER AUGUST COX, 7th Bedfords. Achiet-le-Grand, 15th-17th March 1917.

Capt. HAROLD ACKROYD, M.C., R.A.M.C., attached 6th Royal Berkshires. Menin Road, 31st July 1917.

Gunner CHARLES EDWIN STONE, M.M., C Battery, 83rd Brigade, R.F.A. 21st March 1918.

Lieut.-Colonel CHRISTOPHER BUSHELL, D.S.O., 7th Queens. Crozat Canal, 23rd March 1918.

2nd Lieut. ALFRED CECIL HERRING, R.A.S.C., attached 6th Northants. Montagne Bridge, 23rd March 1918.

Lance-Corporal A. L. LEWIS, 6th Northants. Ronssoy, 18th September 1918.

Lieut. FREDERICK WILLIAM HEDGES, Bedfordshire Regiment, attached 6th Northants. Bousies, 24th October 1918.

## THE CASUALTIES.

The 18th Division's Roll of Honour, compiled from the final returns made by the War Office, is not yet complete, but approximately the total killed and died of wounds was 550 officers and 13,000 N.C.O.'s and men.

The 7th Royal West Kents, the 6th Northants, and the 7th and 2nd Bedfords suffered the greatest number of casualties, each having over 1,200 killed and died of wounds. Then follow the 10th Essex, the 8th East Surreys, and the 7th Buffs, each battalion with over 1,100. The 7th Queens, the 11th Royal Fusiliers, and the 6th and 8th Royal Berks each lost over 1,000.

# INDEX.

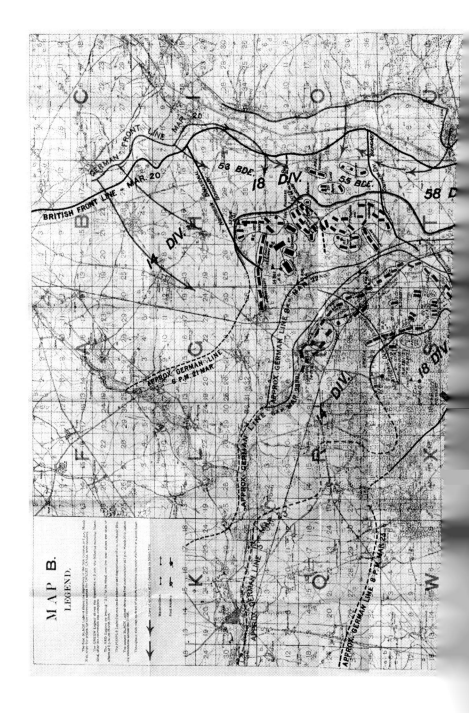

MAP B.

LEGEND.

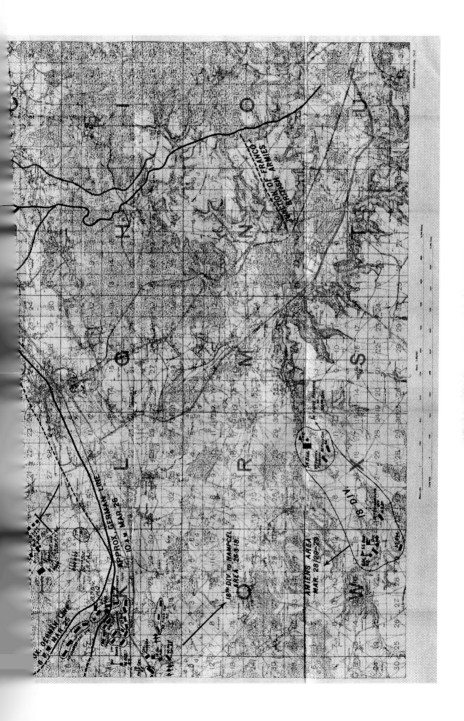

# TRACE "B 1"

*TO BE FITTED OVER MAP 'B'.*

35    3

5    X    6

5

5ᵀᴴ
B DE.
R.H.A.

18ᵀᴴ DIV.
H.Q.

82 ND B DE.
R.F.A.

3 RD B DE.
R.H.A.

53 RD B
H.Q.

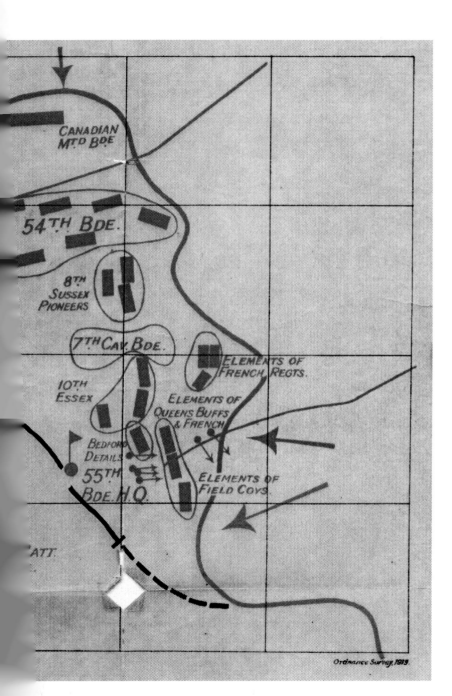

CANADIAN
MT.D B.DE.

54TH B.DE.

8TH
SUSSEX
PIONEERS

7TH CAV. B.DE.

ELEMENTS OF
FRENCH REGTS.

10TH
ESSEX

ELEMENTS OF
QUEENS BUFFS
& FRENCH

BEDFORD
DETAILS

55TH
B.DE. H.Q.

ELEMENTS OF
FIELD COYS.

ATT.

Ordnance Survey 1919.

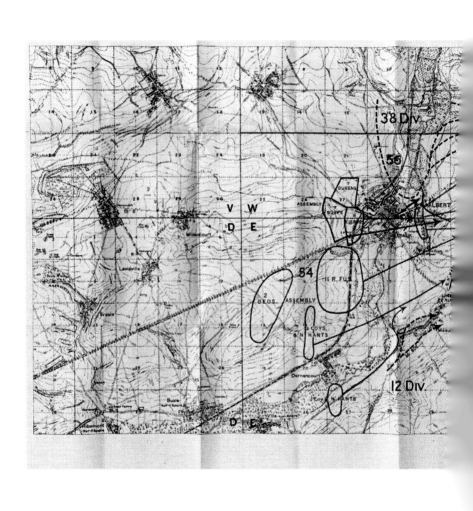

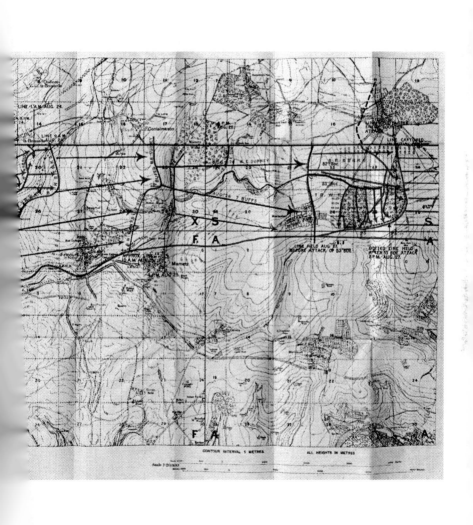

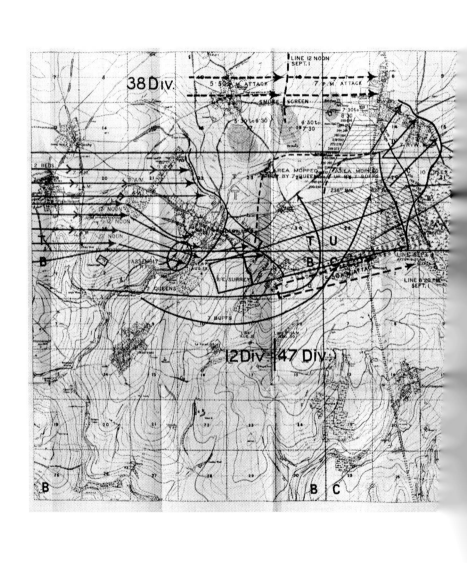

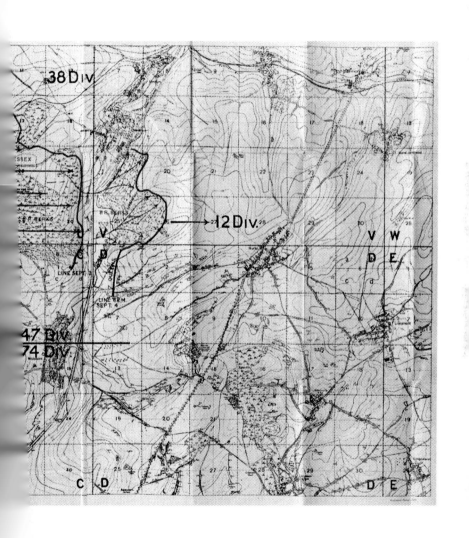

Lightning Source UK Ltd.
Milton Keynes UK
07 December 2009

147158UK00002B/13/A